GOLDEN RULES, ONE ROOM SCHOOLS
and MISSOURI MULES

POST OAK SPROUTS ALONG BELLY ACHE CREEK

by GRACE BACON FERRIER

Lahmeyer-Ferrier Press
California City, California
2001

Lahmeyer-Ferrier Publishing
10131 Rea Avenue
California City, CA 93505

Cover illustration courtesy of Amy Ferrier Truesdell

Manufactured in the United States of America

Library of Congress Control Number 2001116544

ISBN 0-9709062-1-8

*Golden Rules, One Room Schools
and Missouri Mules*

POST OAK SPROUTS
ALONG
BELLY ACHE CREEK

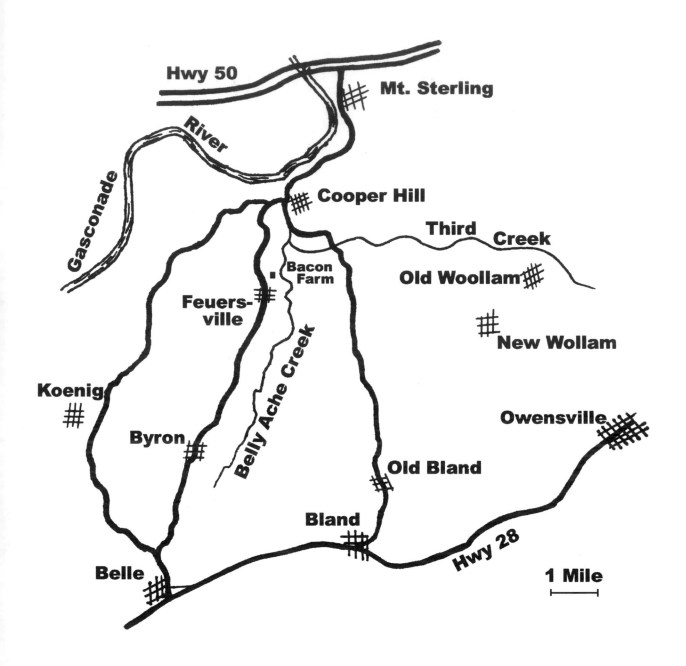

Region Around Belly Ache Creek

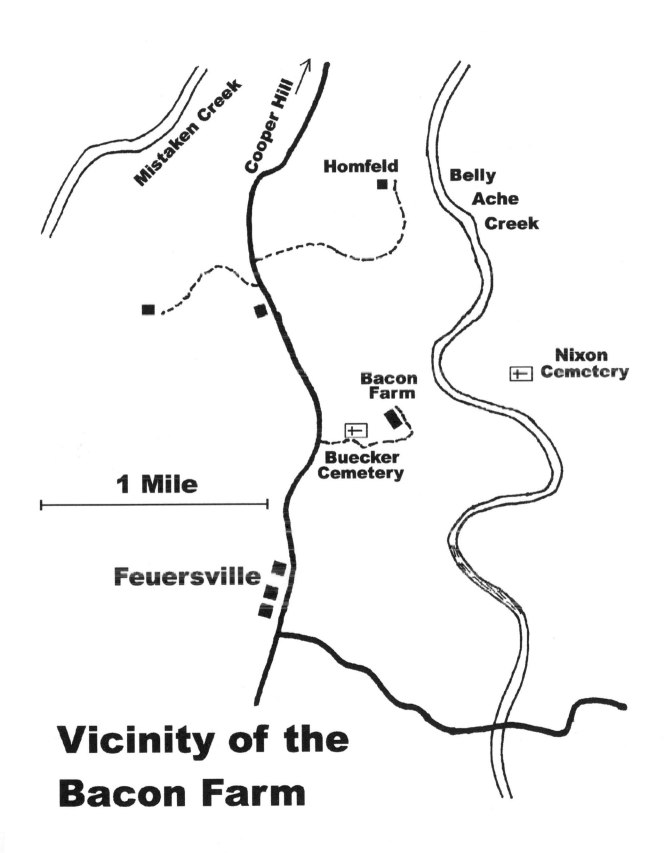

Mistaken Creek

Cooper Hill

Homfeld

Belly
Ache
Creek

Nixon
Cemetery

Bacon
Farm

Buecker
Cemetery

1 Mile

Feuersville

Vicinity of the
Bacon Farm

Dedicated to my good friend,

Chuck Lahmeyer,

without whom this book would not have been possible

Table of Contents

FOREWORD

It was a good time to live and work - our country was at peace. Peary had just discovered the North Pole after numerous failures when two Osage County school teachers decided to face life together. And so 30-year-old George Bacon and 29-year-old Jennie Lorain LeFevre rode the train to Glensted, Missouri, to have their marriage ceremony performed on February 15, 1910. This was because George's sister, "Tillie," was married to Rev. H. C. Green, a Methodist minister. After a few days honeymoon, they returned to the farm two miles north of Linn on the Bonnots Mill road to make their home. They had purchased this property sometime the year before from Mr. Ben Schroeder. All this was in February of 1910. The elderly Schroeders wanted to stay on for a few weeks to have a sale and dispose of their farm implements. They let George and Jennie have the parlor room downstairs. Jennie shared the old black range in the kitchen for cooking. She then carried the food across the hall so she and her handsome husband could eat in privacy. Before she could cook meat, she had to borrow the key for the smokehouse. That was a story Mama related often in her later life. Dad also had to share the barn with Mr. Schroeder since he had old Peg, Nell, and a couple of other mares as well as several cows. After the Schroeder sale, George and Jennie brought their new furniture to the farm from J. P. McDaniel's Store in East Linn as well as a few pieces from Jennie's home, since Jennie's mother, Mrs. Theodosia LeFevre, would soon be living with them along with Neva Pearl. Neva was the four-year-old daughter of Jennie's deceased sister, Belle. And so it was that George and Jennie Bacon began their life together. That first year brought many adjustments, much joy and one sad event. Neva's father wanted his daughter to come home to live with him, although Aunt Belle on her death bed had given her to Mama to rear. They did not wish ugly feelings. Consequently, one beautiful lazy autumn day Uncle Everett came to the farm and took his four-year-old daughter home to live with him and his maiden sister, Alice. Mama and Grandma saw very little of her in later years. It became a closed door in Mama's life, she almost never spoke of the episode. It must have been like the death of a child. The following February on Ground Hog Day, Jennie gave birth to their first child - Matilda Mae. Both grandmothers were present and they labored hard over an appropriate name. Matilda was chosen because it was Great-Grandma Vaughan's name (Matilda Schackleford) and Mae for Mama's sister (May Hancks). Now with a baby girl of her own to love and care for she had less time to miss Neva. Jennie and George doted on this baby. She was so sweet, so smart, so cuddly. Mama (Jennie) left her on the bed one summer day while she went to the orchard to pick cherries. When she came back there was no Tillie Mae on the bed - Jennie's heart jumped up into her throat - the bed had been moved close to the wall - no baby. Mama lay on the floor to see what was under the bed. There was Tillie Mae cooing and sucking her thumb as if that were the proper place for all well-behaved babies to be!

People were still bemoaning the sinking of the Titanic when George and Jennie's second daughter, Grace Virginia, was born on February 28, 1913. This baby was tiny - a mass of wrinkles and skin. Mama always described me by saying "I don't think you weighed two pounds." We doubted you would live - especially when you had 'summer complaint' the summer you were two. You probably wouldn't have if Dr. Jones hadn't insisted we feed you 'squirrel soup' and 'blackberry jelly'." Every morning Dad took his shotgun and went up into the woods pasture to bring back squirrels for my soup. He also picked the blackberries for the jelly - my illness continued for several weeks. Dr. Jones came often. Uncle John and Aunt Ida came often to help with the work and to care for me, (I did get well as you can see!) because Mama had given birth to her first son, George Jr., in December 1914. Bud (as he soon became known) was a cute, fat, good-natured baby. Aunt Ida loved to hold him. I had another episode of pain before the "summer complaint." The day I was one year old I was wearing Dad's vest. I tripped over a shoe, fell against the red hot heater and burned my right cheek and forehead badly. Mama was so afraid the deep burn would leave a scar. Again Dr. Jones came. He prescribed lots of liquids - the facial area was hard to bandage. It hurt. I cried. The salty wetness irritated the burn. I wasn't recuperating very well. One day Ed Stonner came by to see Dad. He told Mama to put unsalted lard on the wound. She did and the wound began to heal. Ed had grown up in a large family and at that time had a large family of his own. He said that was what they always used! In after years Mama would remark, "My, my if it hadn't been for Ed Stonner you might have had a bad scar on your cheek!"

Bud was so calm and serene, he wasn't much bothered about headlines in the Globe Democrat. But Dad and Mom and Grandma talked about the Kaiser at breakfast, dinner, and supper. One of the first headlines was "Kaiser Strips Heir of his Authority" on January 6, 1914. This was followed in June by "Heir to Austria's Throne is Slain with his Wife by a Bosnian Youth to Avenge Seizure of his Country." Now the war in Europe was inevitable. By August the headlines seemed big and black to Mae and me. We sat on Dad's lap while he read the news in the evening by kerosene lamp light. The paper was spread out on the dining table. He read, "Russia Invades Germany, Germany Invades France, But Does Not Declare War: England's Decision Today: Belgium Menaced, Luxembourg and Switzerland Invaded: German Marksmen Shoot Down a French Aeroplane." Mae and I asked Dad what an aeroplane was. He had trouble finding words, but he said he would find a picture of one and show us. (Remember, Dad had never seen such a thing.)

And so it is I begin a saga of a happy farm family, long warm summer days when we played childish games in the yard. We begged to help Mama set plants in the garden in spring. In the autumn we listened intently for the sound of Dad's wagon on the gravel road as he returned from Bonnots Mill after hauling a load of wheat to the railroad station. It was such a happy occasion when he returned. We felt so safe and warm and comfortable. One night it was after dark, Mama was visibly worried. She was baking a molasses cake and not just frosting it but putting coconut on it - that was really a treat. To keep us quiet until supper she cut the big dark cake and gave Mae and me a large helping. We were eating our late supper meal on the screened porch just off the kitchen side of the house. As we ate, we heard the sound of the wheat wagon way down the creek. Even though it was almost full darkness now, we raced out through the yard and flew down the lane to ride along with Dad in the wagon. He knew how we loved this - he stopped - reached down and hoisted us up into the wagon so we could ride into the wagon shed with him. Then he gave each of us a package to carry in to Mama. After putting Peg and Nell to bed, he carried the groceries and whatever Mama had sent for into the house. We sat down to supper. All I wanted was another piece of that wonderful molasses cake. Mama told me it was rich. I would get sick. I knew better, but I wanted more coconut! I ate it greedily, before long I knew Mama was right. I was feeling nausea. I was upset all night! Never since that night have I eaten molasses cake! It was always one of Dad's favorite desserts. He was always glad I couldn't eat it, or so he said with a merry twinkle in his eyes!

The twenties may have been "roaring" in some places, perhaps in the cities. That was a way of life foreign to us out on the farm. Many people felt unsettled and unstable. The war had brought better prices for farm produce, but floods and droughts and chinch bugs destroyed our entire crops. People were still talking about the war. Since our community was largely of German descent many had close relatives there. Mrs. August Langenberg and her sister Mrs. John Lahmeyer had returned to Germany in 1911 to visit their father. They came home saying there was much "talk of war" in the "Old Country." Kaiser Bill was busy training armed forces - most people did not agree or preferred to "turn a deaf ear."

But in the twenties, people were still coming to this country to find a new home and a better way of life. So it was that Fritz and Gertrude Schaeffer lived in our neighborhood for a time. They were nearly destitute when they came. They spoke no English, and they had a son perhaps a year old. I saw them at the Feuersville church on Sunday. Fritz wore a heavy black wool suit, black wide brimmed hat and high topped black buttoned shoes. The toes of the shoes were built high and seemed to turn up. Gertrude wore a black and white printed cotton dress, very long skirt. She also wore high-topped button shoes. The baby's dress was of the same material, black and white print - and guess what? His shoes were also black, high-topped and buttoned. Even with all our countrified ways and hand-me-down clothes, we hadn't seen buttoned shoes for some years.

Everyone tried to help Fritz and Gertrude a little. He wanted to work "by the day" but very few farmers hired any help and if they did it was only a few days during hay harvest or wheat shocking. Everyone sent any surplus vegetables or fruit to Gertrude. They were always so appreciative - although they spoke only German the smiles and hand motions spoke volumes.

I was so sorry when we went to church one Sunday and there was no Fritz and Gertrude and baby son. I asked Otto Wildebrandt where they had gone. "Oh Gracie - they just couldn't make it. They got their relatives up north to send some money. They've been gone a couple of weeks now." This happened to us many years ago. I've always wondered what happened to them - "Up North."

Shoes were a very important article of clothing in our lives. Usually each of us had two pair. One was referred to as our "everyday shoes," the other was our "Sunday shoes." All shoes were purchased with the idea of wearing them at least a year. They were examined over and over by Mama. She pressed hard on the toe to see how much room your feet would have to grow - then how much heel room would you have. If your stocking was heavy enough, your heel wouldn't rub and cause a blister. It was a big day in our lives when we could carry eggs to the Feuersville Store and bring home a pair of shoes. We were told to keep them in the box so they would stay nice. They did for awhile, until school started. Then we tried them out as we ran over the rocks, jumped the ditches, skipped down the muddy road and played all the running games at Post Oak. We really put them "through the paces."

Then there would be the day when the "soles came loose" or a tack would work up through the sole and through your flesh. Then Mama or Dad would feel around carefully inside the shoe. "Yes, there's a sharp tack in there all right." (As if I didn't know that. I'd been feeling it pinch all day.) "Dad needs to do some half-soles right away. We'll get some sole leather at the store." So we were told to bring 50 cents worth of sole leather. That would be a piece of leather perhaps 15 inches square and 3/8 inch thick. The last and staff were brought in from the smokehouse. The leather was soaked in water to soften it. The pattern was drawn off on the leather and then cut to fit with Dad's sharp pocket knife. Then the new sole was tacked on and we were back in business. I remember one pair of everyday shoes - black of course (What other color was there?), flat soles, laced up high tops. Mama insisted I have this particular pair because wearing flat heels would "make my instep grow higher." Well the shoes were too big - both in length and width. I wore them for everyday and Sunday for two years. My instep remained flat, and when they were completely worn out they were still too big!

The kind of shoes all the boys wore were of a very stiff leather. The toes always had an extra piece of leather stitched across the toe. This was called a cap. They must have been very uncomfortable especially after being half-soled!

Our great day arrived when Mama felt of our toes, and decided we could take our Sunday shoes for school. If not, they would soon be too small. Shoes were something we couldn't pass down to our next younger - none of our feet were anywhere near the same size or shape. I was constantly being teased about my feet. Mama would tell me I would have been nice and tall "if so much of you hadn't turned up in feet."

As soon as the threshing machine moved on down the creek, I knew the next days work would be to fill our straw ticks. These were known as poor man's mattresses. No one I knew had even one mattress for everyday use! So before rain fell on the new straw, we must hurry to carry the straw ticks downstairs and out by the chicken houses where "last year's straw" was dumped into hens nests. New straw was stuffed into the center opening, and the ticks were carried back into the house and upstairs. On these nights when there was freshly threshed straw in our ticks, we were excited to get to bed. The straw was loose and we sank down deep. Soon the straw would be packed down solid, and we would take our hands and reach down deep and stir up the straw whenever we made the beds. In winter each bed had a feather bed placed over the straw tick.

How snug we were under our home-made quilts and comforters. All the women in our neighborhood made quilts and comforters. Quilts were made from any suitable scrap of leftover dress material. Sometimes Mama pieced two or three quilts in one winter. She sat by the dining room heater and cut diamond-shaped pieces for "A Sage Bud." When that one was quilted, she cut squares for "The Sheep Fold." It was real hard to get enough scraps for a quilt top. It was common to piece as many blocks as the scraps would allow and set it together with wide strips. These were rather small quilts because the scraps were very limited, but we were so proud of them. They looked so pretty on our beds. Comforters were simpler to make. We just stitched a length of material together, put wool inside, tacked it with yarn, bound it, and in a day's time a new comforter was ready. Quilt material was so scarce no one had surplus bed clothes, but with two or three little warm bodies in each bed we furnished our own heat!

George and Jennie were blessed with good health for the most part. They worked hard, saved wherever they could, and soon had a farm home paid for. It was a good location two miles north of Linn. This is how things were in the early part of the century when we were very young and my story begins.

Chapter 1

Visiting Uncle John and Aunt Ida

Surely the children in our family must have been among the most fortunate of all times to have such kind and wonderfully caring parents as well as aunts and uncles. That is not to take any credit away from doting grandparents. In my mind our childhood memories were quite different from modern youngsters. Everything moved in slow motion as compared to today. Travel was endlessly slow. Riding behind a team of horses or mules in a buggy, surrey or farm wagon in any kind of weather wasn't always pleasant. But it seems as one recalls it in later years, it's always summertime. One is always dressed in Sunday best on the way to visit one or another of the sisters or brothers in Mom's or Dad's family.

My father came from a family of several - three brothers and three sisters. Nearly all of them were farmers and stock men as they are spoken of in obituary vocabulary. They were land loving, observant, and thrifty caretakers of the soil. My mother's family were not farmers. Her mother, Theodosia LeFevre, was a school teacher. She was always in demand in her home neighborhood of Indian Creek and Buck Elk because she had graduated from Edinboro, Pennsylvania, Young Ladies Academy previous to her marriage and removal to Missouri following the Civil War. Grandpa's business was buying land, hiring the suitable timber on it made into railroad ties, and rafting them down the Gasconade River.

In the Bacon family, Uncle John was Dad's eldest brother by at least eight years. His wife was Aunt Ida, who like our mother, was a school teacher before she married. Both were of French descent. Throughout most of their lives, they were extremely close friends. Whatever Aunt Ida said, decided, or did was without question the ultimate in wisdom. They visited us often and sometimes at length.

These interchanges (overnight visits) were not to be taken lightly. Farmers don't leave home overnight without some inconveniences. Cows must be milked early and unless we had a hired hand at the time, they would not be milked until the following evening. If we were to travel quite a distance, "snacks" must be prepared for the baby. (There was always a baby in our family.) Extra clothes for the small children, diapers and necessary items for sleeping were usually packed in a box. And so it was I remember visiting Uncle John and Aunt Ida for the first time. I must have been barely four years old at the time, because I was "big" on programs. Program meaning a series of recitations, speeches, readings, etc. as prepared and presented to our audience at school. Consequently, Mama began to plan days in advance for our "parts." Mae, my older sister, always did well in everything. I never did well in anything except reading and singing. There was a funny little school song called "Morning on the Farm" which Mae and I had learned. It went like this:

Oh, who wakes first in the morning
Oh, I wonder who
Listen and I will tell you
Cock-a-doodle doo!
Oh, Cock-a-doodle doo
Now listen and I will tell you
The rooster gets up early too
Cock-a-doodle doo!
Oh, Cock-a-doodle doo
Its morning on the farm!

This chorus was to be the climax of our program after our recitations and readings.

Bud, our brother, who was perhaps two and a half years old, was to turn somersaults forward and backward as his part of the performance. So into the box with Pete's diapers, went our books for reading stories, and a well crumpled bit of paper on which Mae had arranged the sequence of our appearances.

Anticipation ran high. The days preceding were endless. "Mama what day is this? Oh is it only Tuesday - won't Saturday ever arrive?" But it did finally. Then the hot, blazing August sun beat down upon our sun-bonneted heads as we drove down the lane away from our farm on Linn Creek, Osage County, Missouri, that fine Saturday afternoon. We were crowded in the buggy but our teams had to work in the field six days per week. In order for Old Peg and Nell to revive somewhat, the buggy would be lighter to pull. In those days most people had only two kinds of apparel - "everyday" and "Sunday." So we were attired in our Sunday clothes. Dad's white shirt front was tucked. Mama always made a special starch for what she called "Dad's bosom and cuffs." After this starching and ironing process, they stood away from the body like celluloid. A black string tie, properly knotted, with ends tucked in between the third and fourth buttons on his "shirt bosom" and good black dress pants made up his outer garments. Mama wore her best checked gingham as did Mae, Bud, and I. Bud's suit was brown-and-white-checked gingham, sort of Buster Brown style, with white collar and cuffs.

The drive was pleasant. We left the lane and turned onto the main road leading from Linn, Missouri to Bonnots Mill. We traveled east through the town of Linn and then turned southeast toward the Gasconade River. After several miles we came to Uncle John's road. Soon afterward, we saw the neat, white farm house, big red barn and what was to me an absolute miracle - a windmill to pump water for the livestock. Aunt Ida came bustling out, wiping flour off her hands, and calling "John, John Bacon, come on now. George and Jennie are here! Now Jennie, let me take the baby. My, my, how he has grown! What are you feeding these children? How well they all look! Now Jennie, do be careful, don't get your skirt close to the wheel!" (I should say here and now that these wonderful people never had a family. That was always a cause for wonderment among the other members of our family.)

Mae and I were really glad to unload because our position on a box in the front of the buggy wasn't always comfortable. We rode with our backs to each other. The lines were always jerking our ears or slapping against our cheeks as Dad guided Old Peg and Nell. Peg was our fine black mare. All of us grew up and learned to ride under her gentle supervision. Her mother was "Old Maud," Uncle John's pride and joy, so another thing we couldn't wait to do was run out to the barn to greet "Old Maud." Soon we were everywhere. As Uncle John and Dad took Peg and Nell to the barn to unharness and feed them, I tagged along to see "Old Maud." On my way back to the house, I simply had to detour by way of the windmill. Here I listened to the squeaky music of the wheel turning and wondered how in the world that apparatus up in the air could pump water for cattle. I "dawdled" a little, washed my hands in the cool water and admired the green mossy algae in the bottom of the tank. But there were so many more adventures, I couldn't tarry long. I must say "Hello" to Aunt Ida's cats - "Puss and Tom." At Aunt Ida's, cats were always "Puss and Tom," and they never seemed to have offspring either! Maybe Aunt Ida told them not to - and if Aunt Ida said "you don't" - it was understood you didn't!

The afternoon was so short. Dad and Uncle John set off to "look over the farm." This was a standard phrase used by the Bacon brothers to explain their constant observation of crops and livestock. So long as they were able, this was the mainstay for entertainment when we visited. Before they came to supper, every pasture, grain crop, cow, hog and horse would have been closely scrutinized and discussed. In these early days of the century, I'm sure this was essential to performing each day's work. Nothing was mechanized - except perhaps the miracle windmill.

While all this was transpiring out of doors, indoors Aunt Ida was trotting from kitchen to cellar to smokehouse to chicken house. Our families bought only staples. We ate our produce - home grown potatoes, tomatoes, beans, pork and beef. There were also the indirect products from the cows - milk, butter, buttermilk, cream, cottage cheese, and various foods made with these. Mama and Aunt Ida were both known for their excellent food and their ability to stretch it. The Bacons were all fond of meat and dairy products so our tables were apt to be well loaded with ham, potatoes, all of a variety of fresh vegetables in season, as well as pickles, cottage cheese, and fruit of all kinds, frequently transformed into preserves, pie or cobbler.

Mama and Aunt Ida were quite knowledgeable about nutritious food, so we were well fed on milk, fruit, and related by-products. Custard pie was a favorite staple, along with baked custard, stewed fruit in winter and fresh fruit in season. Cream was always forming on a large crock in the cellar ready to be skimmed. All were taken for granted in those carefree childhood years.

We were all very fond of chicken, too. Where Mama always preferred "stove-top frying," Aunt Ida preferred "oven-style frying." She grew heavy-type chickens which required a more extended cooking time, while Mama grew a lighter breed - usually brown leghorns. These were better layers. She was convinced of this! A meal at Aunt Ida's was always a banquet. So supper was a pure delight - chicken (oven-fried in butter), mashed potatoes, gravy, cottage cheese, beet pickles (Dad's favorite), slaw, butter, milk, cream for coffee, sliced peaches, and lemon cake were quite sufficient to fill our welcome capacities! As we ate Mama and Dad commented favorably on all the various dishes. Mom would say, "Ida, I just don't see how you make this wonderful, light bread! I must write down your "receipt" (recipes were always "receipts" in our vocabulary). (Later we were really "putting on the dog" when we began to speak of recipes!) To Mama and Aunt Ida the word remained receipt throughout their lives. Another quality they shared was their reticence to change their minds!

Now the evening had fallen, the cool concrete porch floor felt good to my bare feet. Shoes and long white cotton stockings had been shed while I was helping Uncle John "separate the milk" earlier that evening. That cream separator was unbelievable (we didn't have one of those either). I stood in awe watching Uncle John work up to the desired r.p.m.'s of the handle before the puzzling little knob could be adjusted to let the milk flow from the large holding bowl on top and out through the cream spout and the milk spout. Aunt Ida always stood by with small crocks, jars or bowls - cream in this one for our breakfast coffee - cream in this one for churning - milk in this one for drinking - milk in this one for a special calf - and the rest of it back into the big aluminum bucket to carry out to the pigs.

Now came the time for our "program." Mama and Aunt Ida were seated in squeaky wicker rocking chairs, as were Uncle John and Dad, arranged in a line along the immaculate, scrubbed board floor of Aunt Ida's kitchen. Out came our books from the diaper box. Mae was always first. I came along reading *Little One Eye*. How the adults applauded. We were in seventh heaven. Then the singing - "My Darling Nellie Gray" - "Carry Me Back to Old Virginny" and sometimes Dad and Uncle John sang with us. We completed our show with "Morning on the Farm." Uncle John thought that was really wonderful, but by then it was time for Bud's somersaults to be performed forward and backward. We called his name as we read each number from our crumpled paper. "Bud, Bud, its time for your somersaults." Bud wasn't interested, he had fallen sound asleep on a folded quilt pallet under the kitchen table! All of us took a cue from Bud's weariness. He was gently lifted by Dad and carried off to a soft feather bed in Aunt Ida's parlor. Mae shared the double bed with him. Mama, Dad, and Pete slept in another large wooden bed in the same room. I was led upstairs to sleep in the bed with Uncle John and Aunt Ida. I was lost to the world until I heard Uncle John's voice teasing me awake, "Little sleepy head, little sleepy head. I'll let you stay a little while longer." I didn't sleep though. I was too full of curiosity. On the wall was a calendar for some year long past, picturing a beautiful young lady with long, flowing brown curls running along a road preceded by a beautiful, collared collie. Aunt Ida had a great love for collies. She always had one everywhere they lived!

The morning dawned clear, bright, hot sunshine. For breakfast we had cured ham, oatmeal, thick slices of that delicious bread, chunks of cool butter, milk, sliced peaches, coffee with cream for the grown-ups, separated milk for us young'uns and lots of compliments spiced the conversation. There were arrangements to be made for the return home. Mae and I ran around gathering up our night gowns. Soiled diapers had been stored in the box, so Aunt Ida found another for us to use for our sleeping apparel and program material. All of us donned our sunbonnets - Mama, Mae, Bud, and yes, - me, Bud also wore a bonnet. Mama tried to buy a nice cloth hat for him earlier that summer at Aimee Maice's store in Linn, but he picked it off his head, threw it on the floor, stamped his little fat foot and yelled, "I don't want no old hat. I want a sunbonnet like Mae and Grace wear." So Bud's sunbonnet was a combination of brown-and-white-checked gingham for the brim and pink and white checks for the hood. Mama was using what was left over from his suit and our dresses.

The drive home was somewhat less exciting, but it was Sunday so other friends and neighbors were out on the road too. It was considered unthoughtful if one merely passed on the road without stopping, so we spent pleasant moments visiting with friends and relatives as we passed each other on the road. This also served to rest "Old Peg and Nell." On this trip Peg was wearing her blue ribbon and tassel attached to her bridle, while Nell was wearing the same in red. These honors had been won in shows at the Osage County Fair.

Long before we arrived at our lane gate, we could hear the old cows scolding us. They didn't appreciate being left overnight without any attention. So before unhitching Old Peg and Nell from the buggy, Dad hurried into the house to exchange his white tucked shirt and black tie for everyday blue shirt and dark pants. He brought the milk buckets and tin cups for Mae and me. We had also switched from our dress-up ginghams into well worn, button-down-the-back, everyday blue aprons. We took our tin cups and went to help Dad milk Buttercup and Rosie. These two cows were so gentle we could not only milk them but also ride them, whichever the moment brought first to mind.

After a while the cows and calves ceased to bawl, Peg and Nell were bedded down and well-fed, chickens and pigs were fed and watered, and our tired little family settled down to a good warm supper of Mama's best biscuits, fried bacon, and stewed tomatoes. Near the end of the meal when the biscuits were almost all eaten, Dad offered Bud the lower half of one all dripping with butter and peach preserves. Bud reached out for it, but not before he ordered Dad to "put the lid on it." Dad was, of course, wanting the top (lid) all brown and crusty for himself.

This visit left sugary, sweet memories in our childish minds for a long time to come. We were constantly asking Mama, "When are we going to Uncle John's again or when are Uncle John and Aunt Ida coming to see us?"

Uncle John was of medium build, rather stocky with large blue eyes, brown hair and ruddy complexion. Dad was a few inches taller, thinner with grey eyes and darker brown hair. Aunt Ida was a tall, dark-skinned woman who had become quite mature by the time I remember her. One of her facial features was a high, very prominent forehead, making her dark Frenchy eyes the focal point of her face. At times she did not need to speak her disapproval. She only needed to turn her slightly slanted French eyes in your direction and you read the message loud and clear. This quality she also shared with Mama. Aunt Ida had boarded with our grandparents - Charles P. and Amelia Vaughan Bacon - when she taught at Mt. Aeriel School. This is where she met Uncle John, taught Aunt Till and Aunt Alta, and learned something of the art of cooking. She faced a choice between Dad and Uncle John as a partner to spend her life loving. She and Uncle John really had a strong loving attachment, but sometimes there was cause to wonder. Her temper could explode as though a charge of dynamite had suddenly been ignited. At these times Uncle John usually took off toward the barn whistling and singing as loudly as he could and his overall legs would be flapping noisily as his feet moved rapidly past each other. After several explosive sentences, she would interject, "John, John Bacon, do you hear me?" This form of parting repartee would be repeated several times with no reply from Uncle John - who was safely out of earshot now. Then she would sink into her old, creaky wicker chair with a cool, wet wash cloth and "bathe her face" as she called it. Usually it took quite a little while for her to calm down. I'm positive now she threw some of these temper tantrums entirely for my benefit. Both Mama and Aunt Ida thought this was the proper way to keep a husband "in line."

Chapter 2

Carpenter Work and Surgery

These early years of my life were as carefree as could be. We had an extra good living on the farm. Pre-World War I prices were adequate for grain crops and livestock. Dad nearly always had a "hired hand," and sometimes Mama had a "hired girl." We built a new barn. First the Peters brothers moved their steam powered saw mill up the lane from our house and "set up to saw logs." This was by far one of the most exciting summers of my life. Standing a safe distance away, Bud and I watched the big, rough logs travel through their transformation journey from log at the beginning to beautiful boards, joists, flooring and studs as they came off the sawing floor. The sawdust was a new diversion. Mama cooked for the saw mill crew. When she purchased her extra supplies for this, she bought a new coffee mill. Bud and I immediately claimed the old one as our personal property. We spent hours in the sawdust pile grinding sawdust through the old coffee mill. Bud carried fresh dust in a large red bandanna handkerchief to me wherever I was seated grinding and grinding and grinding.

Uncle John and Aunt Ida became frequent visitors now. They were almost as excited as Mama and Dad. Every piece of freshly sawed oak had to be inspected, approved or discarded. Uncle John considered himself quite a carpenter. His father C. P. and his father before him, John Overton Bacon, as well as Uncle Jim (C. P.'s brother), were in demand as carpenters. (John Overton built furniture; our clothes press is his product. He also built the iron smelters in Meramec Springs St. Park at St. James.)

Sawing the timbers was done in early spring. By mid-summer the barn was taking shape. To me it was huge. There were four stalls along each side, a grain bin at the front end on one side and a harness room opposite. Overhead was a huge hay mow - it simply took my breath away to climb the new steps leading to this cool, airy haven. And the aroma of that new, unseasoned lumber was absolute ambrosia to my young nostrils. I can recall even now how I used to stand still and draw in deep draughts of the "rosiny," tingling air. I simply can't refrain from relating my first snake story. One beautiful bright day, I hurried down from the "rosiny hay mow" and set off for the sawdust pile to do some grinding. Bud was coming along at a somewhat slower pace. I had a favorite, deep cow track I admired greatly, so as per custom I stopped by to see how my foot would fit the cavity the cows foot had made. Just as I was lifting my little bare foot to fit it in the track a long, slender, yellowish head suddenly protruded from my favorite cow track. I'm sure this was my first encounter with a garter snake. I thought the thing rather pretty although strange in appearance. I didn't disturb it. I proceeded to my "grinding" while Bud carried plenty of sawdust in his red bandanna.

A few days later, the big, black "log eater" moved back down the cow barn lane and out onto the county road where the huge iron wheels ground over the rutted, rocky road toward Bonnots Mill. Now that the lumber was sawed, Uncle John and Dad, along with the carpenters, John Laughlin and Doris Hasenbach (Doris was short for Theodore) could begin the work in earnest. As I said previously, the barn took form rather rapidly and by fall it stood shining in the sun with galvanized tin roofing, bright red paint and even ornate red and blue ball ornaments on the lightning rods. While we were building the barn, John Whicker Mantle swallowed a grasshopper. He said he knew he swallowed it "because he felt it kicking as it went down."

The St. Louis paper was full of pre-war rumors. We watched for the mail hack to bring our paper every morning. The mail hack was a light wagon, horse-drawn of course, which brought mail and freight to Linn from Bonnots Mill and vice versa. Mae and I had no idea what war really was, but we raced down the lane to bring the mail so we could spread the *St. Louis Globe Democrat* out on the bare dining room floor and read the "war news" to Mama as she prepared the midday meal. We familiarized ourselves with Kaiser Bill, David Lloyd George, Italy's Orlando, President Wilson and other names pertinent to the news items. When Dad came in for dinner, he would grab the paper and try to absorb all the activity at home and abroad. He ate with one eye on the paper and the other on his meat and potatoes. He read some more during his short rest period at the end of the meal and then it was back to the field. In the evening after supper, he would again have time to look at maps of Germany, England, Belgium and France where the European troops were supposedly fighting. During the next winter, Dad developed a case of mastoid infection in the bone structure directly back of the ear. Seeing our usually lively and active Dad in bed during the day, eyes bright with fever and full of pain, was new to Mae and me. Dr. Jones came every day with his little black bag full of pills and powders. The kerosene lamp burned all night beside Dad's bed. Mama was not singing now, she looked pale and worn. Grandma LeFevre came to stay. Even though her shoulder pain (arthritis) was bad, she could wait on Dad while Mama fed the chickens, gathered the eggs and helped with the milking. Surgery wasn't commonplace in those days. People were fearful of it. Insurance for such things was unheard of, but it soon became quite apparent that an operation was the only logical thing to make our Dad better. Preparation was begun to take him to Barnes Hospital in St. Louis. Mama wanted Uncle John Hancks to go with him. This Uncle John was a physician, the husband of Aunt May who was Mama's older sister. They lived at Koenig, Missouri, a tiny village across the Gasconade River and to the east of Linn. Uncle John (MD) came to see Dad to examine and confirm Dr. Jones diagnosis and returned home in the evening to pack a small bag of personal belongings. The next morning he came down the road on the mail hack. They stopped at our lane gate. Uncle John walked quickly up the lane to help Dad get ready. But Mama and Grandma had probably been up all night caring for Dad, packing his suitcase and keeping the fires burning. He was all ready to go when Uncle John came to the door. Because he would be riding for a couple of hours in an open vehicle, Mama had wrapped her long, white, wool fascinator around Dad's head. The weather was cold and a stiff wind was blowing. I can vividly remember how sad his eyes were as he said good-bye to all of us. His eyes were too bright. He didn't cry, he just kept turning back to wave as he and Uncle John hurried down the lane where the hack and driver were waiting to take him to Bonnots Mill. There they would board the Missouri Pacific train for St. Louis and Barnes Hospital. I can't quite fathom a seriously ill person today riding a freight wagon on a frigid March day to get to a railroad where a train would carry them to a hospital location. Details of the days following are sketchy. There were no telephones to follow the daily progress of loved ones away from home. I do remember Uncle John and Aunt Ida coming early one morning to spend the day. Uncle John and Aunt Ida told me years later that Mama was crying when they drove up. She came running out of the yard gate sobbing, "You've brought me bad news haven't you? You don't need to tell me I already know." They were hard put to convince her they had no bad news. In fact, the surgery had been performed and if all went well, he would be home after a period of recovery. This last stage would take place at the home of "Cat" and Mayme Vaughan in the city. Mayme went to see Dad often and wrote letters to Mama to keep her appraised of his progress. Dude Bacon, Mayme Vaughan's younger brother, came to stay and help do the farm work. There was still no singing as Mama cooked, washed our clothes on a washboard, carried in wood and did all the thousands of chores farm women did as a matter of everyday living. We were anxious to have Dad home. We missed his voice, his teasing, his reading to us from books and newspapers, and most of all I missed him rocking me to sleep on a pillow every night. As long as I can remember before this episode whenever I felt myself getting tired, I would trot into the bedroom, get my pillow, bring it to Dad's chair, put the pillow on his arm, climb up on it and soon I would be off in the "Land of Nod."

Before too long Dad was really home again. He came the way he left - by train and mail hack. When we saw him alight from the hack at the lane gate, Mae and I bounded out the door and down the lane to help Dad. The driver was holding him by one arm and carrying the suitcase in the other. How we flew to greet him, our hugs and kisses were numerous. Mama and Grandma weren't far behind. Suddenly the sun came out, all the clouds disappeared - Dad was home! Soon he was resting in bed. Mama was beginning to hum softly. The teakettle was even singing on the kitchen cookstove. There was one little bitty fly in my jar of happy ointment that day. Dad had brought Mae and me each a pair of beautiful, black buttoned shoes - high topped patent leather! These shoes had the most beautiful, red, silk tassels at the top, but they were too small - both mine and Mae's - so they had to be returned. The exchanges were nice but minus the tassels. Never mind shoes or even feet - our darling Dad was home - eating Mama's best biscuits, chicken and dumplings, apple pie, and drinking the steamy mugs of cream diluted coffee. All was well!

The next morning very early, I awakened to the crowing of old cock-a-doodle-doo. He sounded full of joy too. I jumped out of bed and across the icy cold hall into the warm bed with Dad. How wonderful to be back in those warm loving arms as he held me close. Soon I was fast asleep and so was he!

Later that morning after breakfast, Mae and I thought it very appropriate to entertain Dad with a program. He was sitting up in the old oak rocker which had been draped with a warm, woolen comforter. He was very careful of drafts and anything else that threatened to chill his thin body. Since we had practiced "Morning On the Farm" so thoroughly before the visit to Uncle John and Aunt Ida's, we ran through the verses quickly and were getting ready to read a few of our favorite Bible verses, when Bud came somersaulting through the kitchen door forward - bumping his fat little rump against chairs, tables and dressers. He ended his bumpy little tour right at Dad's feet where he was helped up and held tightly for a moment until he squirmed free and announced proudly, "Now watch me go backwards," which he did all the way back to the kitchen.

Now Mama didn't have to hurry so much about her chicken feeding and egg gathering. She could sing again; the sun was shining in our hearts all day long. Dad could look after us as he convalesced in his rocker by the fire. We knew God was in his Heaven - all's right with the world!

Mr. and Mrs. Ed Anderson lived "on top of the hill" from our farm. Today this farm would be on Highway 100 or the Luystown Road as we called it then. They were such fine people, both of them tall and thin. They could have been models for Grant Wood's "American Gothic" painting. Their house was high on the hilltop. In fall and winter when the sun shown on their windows, the reflections would glance off in red and gold lights. Mae and I would dance into the kithcen and tell Mama, "Mrs. Anderson has the prettiest lamp lighted. She's burning red and gold kerosene." Mama would laugh at us and explain how the sun bounced light rays off the window panes. We weren't sure about that. I was certain Mrs. Anderson had colored kerosene.

One Sunday afternoon we walked up the cow barn lane, past our sawdust pile and on up the hollow, past the orchard and into the woods. Then we began to climb. We were good walkers (all the Bacons are!) After what seemed a long time we came out on the top of the hill - only a hay field to cross now. We arrived on the Anderson back porch, hot, tired and thirsty. Mrs. Anderson drew a bucket of fresh water from a strange contraption in the side yard. They had a sort of wishing well where the bucket on a rope had to be lowered and water pulled to the surface by a handle on the side which had to be turned. This was a new invention to me! The fresh water was soon turned into cool lemonade. No one could make lemonade early if company was expected, because it would get warm. No refrigeration. No ice cubes. Beware of the Good Old Days!

This was like heaven to Mae and me. We sat on the high-backed chairs and hooked our heels over the rungs - our legs came nowhere near the floor. We sat and sipped our lemonade and tried to act as Mama would expect us to. She had reminded us all morning that Mrs Anderson wasn't used to children. We looked at her out of the corner of our eyes. We couldn't see anything different about her. She was so clean; she had a lovely smile. She told Mae and me we could take our lemonade and go sit in the yard swing. Now that was another invention. I put that in my book right along with Uncle John's windmill. This swing hung from a frame and the seats faced each other. We pushed the best we could but our legs were too short. Besides we couldn't sip our lemonade and push the swing at the same time. The time passed quickly. Dad and Mr. Anderson walked out to the big new barn to inspect each department. (This visit might have been just prior to building our barn; perhaps that was the reason we went.)

The afternoon flew by. The yard was so cool and inviting. We could follow Dad and Mr. Anderson from one farm building to another. And there was "Shep" the big woolly dog. He was in a state of perfect delight. He ran; he barked; he rolled over on his back; he fetched sticks for us. We petted him, we rolled in the grass with him and he sat in the swing with us. We had fun!

It seemed only a few minutes until Mrs. Anderson came on the back porch and called, "Ed, you and Mr. Bacon come on in now - bring the children." In the huge kitchen was an oblong oak table set for supper. My, my what finery - white damask tablecloths, real china, and pretty glassware. We washed our hands, climbed up onto the hi-backed chairs and waited while Mr. Anderson said "the blessing." Then Mrs. Anderson set on the biggest platter of fish I had ever seen in all my life. There were other dishes too: mashed potatoes, slaw, pickles, home-baked bread and apple sauce. Nothing appealed to me but the fish. I continued to eat piece after piece until Mama began rolling her eyes and frowning at me. Nothing had any effect on me. I ate fish. The sun was sinking in the west. We must hurry home now. Mrs. Anderson put the rest of the fried fish in a small tin bucket and gave it to me to carry home. I remember how tired my legs got as we trudged across the field, scooted down the hill past the orchard, the cow barn and into our own "home sweet home." For days Mama laughed at me and teased, "Thresia, are you fish hungry? Where's your bucket? Are all your fish gone?"

Chapter 3

Love Thy Neighbor

Uncle John and Aunt Ida came to "see about us." Because Uncle John was the oldest of the brothers, he always seemed to feel a certain sense of responsibility for all the others. As usual he began to inspect the chores the hired hand (Dude Bacon) had been doing. He went down to the pig pen to see if the pigs were being fed and cared for properly, to the cow barn to see Old Buttercup, Red Rosie and Daisy with their new calves – and, of course, out to the new barn to see if "Old Peg and Nell" along with "Anton" were getting a fair measure of corn and hay. He did all of Mama's chores for the day and by the time they had to leave there was a beautiful stack of split cook wood on the screened porch, and the big wood boxes in the kitchen were running over. Aunt Ida had spent the day helping Mama with cooking, cleaning, carrying Pete in large capable arms and, of course, carrying on a constant conversation with Dad and Grandma - whom she always addressed properly as "Mrs. LeFevre." She also had dozens of questions concerning cousin Mamie and all the large family in St. Louis.

At dinner the talk naturally turned to the unrest in Europe. Young men were being inducted into the service every weekly period at the Linn Courthouse. Everywhere we went the young men were clad in khaki wool "doughboy" uniforms. Some had been to Camp Funsten or Ft. Riley and were home on furlough. There was also much discussion concerning neighbors who were "selling out." This meant they were selling their farms, livestock, farm machinery and, in some cases, households goods because farmland brought a good price. The idea of meatless, sugarless, flourless meals were not greatly appreciated by the Bacons. All of them were meat, potatoes, bread and fruit eaters. When Mama called for sugar at the store and was told the only thing available was powdered sugar, she studied a long time - then she asked to see it and taste it before purchasing "a quarter's worth." It was carefully measured out into a brown paper sack and tied with a twine string. When Mama reached home with what she referred to as "that old powdery, lumpy stuff," she put it high on the kitchen safe shelf - declaring that it wasn't fit for "man nor beast" but it might be all right for coffee - if you "put in lots of cream." Both Mom and Dad used sugar and cream quite extensively in their breakfast menu.

During this period of Dad's illness, not only the family came to "help out," but also we had wonderful neighbors. There were Henry and Regina Schroeder who lived on our "town side." Their house was just across the field from us and at that time the road ran across the fields on the opposite side of the creek from where it is now located. This was another topic of discussion almost every day when Henry came in to see if we needed anything done or if he could bring us something from town. He and Dad would wonder what the effect of the new road would have on their farms. Fences would have to be changed and the land they owned across the creek which they planned to use as pasture would be worthless, because those "danged automobiles" were running up and down "the pike" scaring the tar out of cows and horses. One evening Henry and his oldest son Fritzie came to "sack up" a load of wheat to have it ready for an early start to

Bonnots Mill where it would be sold at the mill. Long before daylight the following morning, we heard Henry come rattling up the lane with his farm wagon. The grain was loaded and he rattled off again into a bitter, cold winter morning. It would be after nightfall before he could possibly return. We were eating supper when he came stamping his feet on the screened-in porch. It was so cold, he had walked beside his team most of the way home to keep warm. He placed the envelope containing the cash payment along with the weight ticket carefully on the corner of the table where Dad sat. Henry insisted that the money be counted. When he figured all was in proper order, he inspected the wood boxes and split wood on the porch to see if we were going to be comfortable before he stamped out to his waiting team. His parting words were, "I'll send Fritzie in the morning to do some splittin'."

Mr. Bogler came to visit too. He was our neighbor down the creek toward Bonnots Mill. He had also built a new barn at about the same time as we had. In fact, that fantastic saw mill moved there from our cow-barn lane. So he and Dad talked about barns and barn paint. We had hired our barn painted while Mr. Bogler and his sons had built and painted theirs themselves. On one of his visits, he advised Dad on using "good business judgment" about spending money. He said, "Frankie is going to paint our barn, and I'll bet he'll do a nice neat job of it too."

Regina Schroeder came often. She had a large family ranging in age from late teens to small toddlers, so she understood perfectly well Mama's situation. The biggest and hardest chore country women had to do during those days was keeping the diapers clean and dry. There was the water to be pumped by hand out of an outside well, then it had to be carried in buckets to a boiler on the cookstove to be heated, and even if the diapers were soaked beforehand it was still a messy, nauseating day's work - and it had to be done every day. Farm women didn't even have enough diapers for more than one or two days supply. So at least every other day Regina came to "tend to the baby's diapers," or she would send Angie, her oldest daughter, to "tend them." As I write about these wonderful people who made up our tiny world in my early years, I can't refrain from making comparisons. How many sixteen-year-old girls would go wash soiled diapers for a neighbor just because her mother told her to and if Mama paid her for it - the comparison in money would not have covered the actual facts of the case. This in my mind is truly "love thy neighbor" love.

Spring was now approaching. We must butcher or it would soon be too warm. With all the anxiety of winter this big event had been postponed. Uncle John Hancks came one morning to assist Dr. Jones in removing the big, heavy, white bandage from Dad's head. Now all he needed was a small piece of gauze taped to the cleanly shaven space back of his ear. I was always very much in evidence when this dressing was being changed. I couldn't quite understand why that little hole had made Dad so sick or why everyone talked so much about it. Uncle John (M. D.) looked so strange to me and Mae. Now he was wearing one of those khaki suits such as we had seen the boys in town wearing. He would be leaving the next day for Ft. Riley, Kansas. They were in need of doctors to help process the soldiers for overseas duty. Aunt May was to stay on at Koenig until he could see how the war developed. She could finish teaching the term of school at Indian Creek School.

The weather was very cold when Uncle John and Aunt Ida drove into the lane one evening in early March. Old Maud was unhitched from the buggy, taken to the new barn where she was unharnessed, put in a stall and given a ration of shelled corn. Then the pre-butchering necessities began. The gamboling poles had to be set up, usually one end of this pole rested in the crotch of a tree, but it had to be high enough to keep the hogs off the ground. It also had to be very, very strong to hold three or four large fat hogs. Wood to heat the scalding water had to be dragged up near the big, black iron wash kettle, small dry chips and bark were brought in for the night to dry by the big kitchen range. This would facilitate getting the fire off to a good start in the morning. Uncle John whistled "Long, Long Ago" and "It's That Old Time Religion" as he hurried about all the preparations. He then went down to the new barn to find material to build a "scraping platform." This consisted of several flat boards nailed at one end to a log, perhaps twelve inches in diameter. At the other end, the boards were nailed to a two by four, this giving the platform a slant where the water would run off as hot water was thrown onto the pig to remove stubborn bristles. When all these things were done (of course I helped a lot - I was always with Uncle John if I could manage it), we went down to inspect the pigs. Dude was bringing yellow corn from the log granary to feed them their final meal!

Mae and I slept with Grandma that night so Uncle John and Aunt Ida could have our bed - all in the parlor room across the cold, icy hall from the kitchen and dining room. The dining room had been Dad's bedroom ever since he came home from the hospital. Everyone retired early, a kerosene lamp was left burning low on a stand by Aunt Ida's side of the bed. Uncle John would need to replenish the fire during the night, and he would be up by four o'clock to have the fire blazing under the big, black kettle full of water. I was glad to get up. Grandma always rubbed her shoulder with a black stinky ointment just before going to bed - her shoulder always ached! I loved her so much, but I just couldn't see why she wanted to rub that smelly stuff on her shoulder. So by morning I had had about all I could stand of Grandma's ointment. We ate fried bacon, oatmeal with cream and sugar, and of course Mama's crusty, flaky biscuits with home-made molasses for breakfast. Uncle John had to be called in from the log smokehouse (where he was busily whetting the butcher knives for their bloody task) when breakfast was ready.

Henry Schroeder and son Fritzie arrived just as the meal was finished, also Johnnie Williams and our neighbor who lived at the "Big Rock" farm near Linn. Now Dude was dispatched to hitch Old Peg at the rack outside the yard fence. The pigs would have to be dragged from the slaughter pen to the scalding barrel. This was Dude's job, but it took all four men to put the big, fat hog into the scalding barrel where they "sozzled and sozzled" - that is pulled the hog up and down and rolled it over in the scalding water. A place was tested by scraping with a sharp knife to see if the bristles would "slip." This was one of the most important steps in butchering - if not scalded enough the bristles would not slip, this leaving long unsightly places on the skin side - if scalded too much the outside layer of skin would be cooked - this interfered with proper curing later, and sometimes spoiled the meat. Uncle John was in his element. Everyone deferred to his opinion. I rather suspect the others had no choice! But all these men were experts at meat handling and curing. As each pig was drawn up from the pen, I felt as if I had lost another close friend. I looked into Old Red's sightless eyes and then ran to hide behind the smokehouse as I saw Uncle John and Fritzie lift him into the sozzling barrel. This was too much. I wouldn't have Old Red and his brothers to feed yellow corn tonight! Soon all four pigs were hanging from the scaffolding poles. Now they were white and wide-eyed and getting very cold. Earlier one pig had been "gutted" as we said in our plain way of speaking. The guts were placed in a tub and carried onto the side porch where Mama was waiting with the butcher knife to sever the liver from the intestines. The fresh liver was thinly sliced and tenderized. Then it was rolled in flour, salted, peppered, fried in a hot skillet and quickly devoured by hungry men, women and children for our lunch. I'm sure we had other things because Mama and Aunt Ida had spent all morning cooking and baking for the hard working men.

Just as soon as the last bite was swallowed, the table was cleared. Grandma supervised Mae and me as we managed to wash and dry the dishes. Mae always washed; she was the oldest. I always dried everything but the silverware. I drew the line there, so Grandma helped me. She put them away in the safe - the plain white plates, cups, saucers and pie plates. Grandma was six feet tall, thin and angular with the kindest voice. I never remember her ever lifting her voice or ever disagreeing with anyone. She lived by the Bible and taught Mae and me to read from it even before we went to school. (I started school at four years of age, so I had read the Bible for Grandma before that!)

When the dishes were done, Grandma took Bud and sat down in the rocker to "put the baby to sleep." Mama and Aunt Ida had lifted the heavy tub of intestines out onto the kitchen table where with the small kitchen knives they were now scraping the fat from the "guts." This fat would be placed in the wash boiler on the kitchen stove and cooked until the fat was rendered into lard. The fat off the larger intestine was finer and was cooked separately into "leaf lard" to be used for extra fine cooking such as pie crust and very best white cake. After the fat was removed, the intestines were carried out to the chicken yard where they were cut into lengths four or five feet long. Each length was turned inside out by turning one end back like a cuff and pouring warm water into the cuff until the entire length was turned. It was then dropped into a bucket of clean, warm water. On a cold day this was a dreadfully painful task, ones fingers nearly froze. These intestines would be soaked in salt water and the water changed and soaked some more. Then they would be scraped on a board until the intestines from one hog could be contained in a big white teacup. They would then be ready to be stuffed with sausage.

While Mama and Aunt Ida were cleaning the intestines, Uncle John, Henry, Fritzie and Dude were carrying the heavy dressed pigs into the log smokehouse where they were laid out on long tables. On a cold day like this, the meat "cooled out" quickly. Before long each of my friendly pigs had turned into hams, shoulders, slabs of bacon, spareribs, backbones, heads and feet. Those pieces didn't look like old "Red" or "Spot" or "Pinkie" at all. The rough carving was finished. Henry, Fritzie and Johnnie Williams departed each with a portion of fresh pork as a partial compensation for a hard days work. Uncle John busied himself awhile to make sure the smokehouse was all in order, that the animals were all fed and that Dude was taking proper care of everything. Again he whistled, "It's That Old Time Religion," as he split a big pile of wood for Mae and me to carry in and stack on the porch. The sun was nearly down now as Dude brought "Old Maud" up from the barn and backed her into the buggy shaft. Aunt Ida came out, all bundled up in her heavy coat and black fascinator which was so long she had one end wrapped over her nose and mouth. She had bad attacks of asthma in really cold weather. They climbed into the buggy quickly, assuring Mae and me that they would be back soon. Uncle John admonished us "not to eat all the stuffed sausage" until he got some and away they went down the lane and up the road. Old Maud was trotting fast; she was headed toward home. Mae and I watched as long as we could see the buggy moving into the willows along the creek, then they crossed the creek, and the willows swallowed them up. Mae and I carried a few more sticks of wood. It reminded us of whistling and singing and teasing and pleasant moments.

Mama and Dad were so pleased to have that big job done. The tasks that followed were hard and laborious but could be taken in somewhat more leisurely fashion. The meat needed to "cool out" for a few days. During that time Mama would scrape the intestines, get the sausage mill down from the "garret" room - wash and scald it. She would cook the livers - cool and grind them - add some sage, broth, salt, pepper, a smidgen of chopped onion and press the mixture into a crock. This would be sliced for a quick lunch or used for a breakfast meat with fried eggs. The hog heads would be cleaned, split in the middle and boiled in the wash boiler on the cookstove. When they were well done, they would be put on the side porch to cool. The next day the meat would be picked from the bone, ground through the sausage mill, seasoned with salt, pepper and onion, and enough broth was added to make it into a loaf consistency. This was also pressed into a crock, covered with a clean cloth and set in a cool place to be used in much the same way as the liver sausage. Sometimes Mama made scrapple or "sauce," but Aunt Ida always made it. This "receipt" required broth from the head thickened with meal and cooked as one would for mush. Mama and Aunt Ida used very little seasoning in it - salt, pepper and sage were all they ever used. This was also poured into a crock and set in a cool place. By the week end Uncle John and Aunt Ida were back. They had brought sharp knives to "trim up" the hams, shoulders, middlings, back, etc. These trimmings would be ground into sausage. So Uncle John and Aunt Ida had worn their everyday clothes. Uncle John always wore blue denim bib overalls and a blue chambray work shirt - over long underwear, of course. Aunt Ida wore a long, black skirt, gingham blouse and an apron with sleeves in it - buttoned down the back but it really covered all. She wore her black fascinator to protect her nose and throat from the cold. They trimmed and laid the hams, shoulders and sides out in long neat rows on the curing shelf. Now they mixed salt and pepper and sprinkled it over the meat to begin the cure. After a few weeks of exposure to the air, the pieces would be laid in the salt box and cured with a thick layer of salt.

That evening after supper the "sausage board" was placed on the seat of two kitchen chairs, the mill was attached to the board. The sausage meat was piled high in large pans on the end of the kitchen table. The big white enamel dishpan was placed on the floor under the mill where the ground pork would fall. Then the fun began. All of us begged to be allowed to turn the handle. Small as we were, we wanted so much to be a big part of all the work. We actually fought each other for the honor of turning that handle. Dude and Uncle John and Dad found this so funny. They laughed and laughed, but they were very patient with our trials and failures to get large pieces ground through. Mae, Bud and I soon wore out and trotted across the icy hall and into the warm parlor where Grandma superintended our nightly routine - ending with that beautiful child's prayer - "Now I lay me down to sleep." If we weren't asleep by the time we got to "I pray the Lord my soul to keep," Grandma started on "The lord is my shepherd - I shall not want." In spite of all the excitement going on in the kitchen and the happy thought of waking up to the aroma of fresh pork sausage frying in the big iron skillet, I was still aware of the strong acrid odor of Grandma's Rheumatism Ointment.

One more beautiful Sunday seems fresh in my mind. We didn't visit Uncle Vic and Aunt Alta Pinet very often. Aunt Alta was Dad's youngest sister. She, Uncle Vic and Marjorie, their young daughter, lived on a farm located in the Fairview neighborhood out of Linn. We didn't send them a postcard to announce our intention. We had made all our plans days in advance. We put on our white voile dresses. Bud wore his brown-and-white-checked gingham suit. Dad guided Peg and Nell down the lane one blazing Sunday morning in July. We traveled leisurely through the town of Linn. We passed J.P. McDaniel's store and turned down a steep hill which led us out toward Fairview. It was only a few miles out of town to the farm. Dad stopped Peg and Nell to let them drink from each small stream we crossed. Out past Fairview church and school, and across the creek (I always called it Pinet Creek).

But what had been a lovely plan turned into a big disappointment. Uncle Vic and Aunt Alta weren't home. Uncle Vic's brother, Dolphus, lived up on the hill. Perhaps our relatives were there. So we drove up the hill toward the beautiful white house. As we drew near we could see automobiles parked in the yard and everyone dressed in summer finery. Mr. and Mrs. Pinet didn't know where Vic and Alta were but we must come in and cool off and rest a while; Aunt Alice insisted. The cool drink turned out to be lemonade. Then Aunt Alice said we couldn't think of going home without eating. "Of course there is plenty," she said. The house and yard seemed full of young people. As it turned out, we spent the day. The young ladies, Grace and Anne, were helping in the kitchen. Big aprons covered their ruffles and lace. I can't remember what we had to eat but fried chicken. Aunt alice was a famous cook.

To this day I can see the big white house, pretty green grass in the yard, Ford automoblies and ruffled white dresses and young men dressed in suits. Forever after, this day was remembered as a big event. We would say, "OK, that was when we went to visit Uncle Vic and Aunt Alta." Then we would add, "but Aunt Alice cooked dinner!"

Chapter 4

Cute Little Pranks

Those were busy days for Bud and me, we were everywhere, asking questions and getting in the way. We followed Mama to the smokehouse when she went to get spareribs for supper. Our eyes fell on the pile of pig feet waiting to be cleaned. Bud turned his big brown eyes to meet mine and in his slow, thoughtful manner said, "Grace, I guess we won't 'iss year." I knew exactly what he meant, both of us were grinning as we recalled an episode during butchering time the previous year. Mama and Dad had gone to do some shopping in Linn. Grandma was supposed to supervise us but her shoulder ached, so she laid down to "rest a bit" as she called her nap. Bud and I were hunting for something to amuse ourselves. Time was heavy on our hands. We struggled with the heavy iron latch on the smokehouse door. We had to build a step out of split wood in order to reach the latch. We gained entrance. On the curing shelf was a pile of pig feet - oh what fun! What could we do with those that would be exciting - "Oh - I know - lets carry them over to the well and drop them in." Oh, how exciting that was. What a grand and glorious splash they made as each one was carefully dropped. A few days later, Mama went to the smokehouse to get the pig feet to cook - she couldn't locate them. She knew instantly whom to consult and consult she did. "Grace, Bud - what have you done with the pig feet?!!!" I was always inclined to be somewhat nonchalant, so in my best "so-what manner," I tossed her my reply - "Oh, they're in the well." I can still see Mama's eyes widen and hear her voice sharpen considerably, "In the well! In the well!" She repeated this unbelievable bit of information from her offspring. "How in this great, wide, wonderful world, did those pig feet get into the well?" Bud thought he had better come to my rescue, so he said, "Oh it was easy. Grace and me just dropped 'em in," and he pinched his little fat fingers partially together to demonstrate just how he picked them up and dropped them. Well, Mama's temper caused us to run as fast as we could to hide behind Grandma's big calico apron. She was always our source of protection, but Dad was summoned from the barn, the pump was removed, a large ladder was brought up from the barn, Dad took off all his clothes but his long underwear, he climbed down into the dark cavern and fished out the pig feet. Bud and I stood by watching this process intently. I can't remember feeling badly about this at all excepting I hated to see Dad come up in the cold, frigid atmosphere all dripping wet. He looked pretty miserable. Years later I told Aunt Ida about this prank; she had never heard it. Her comment when I finished was, "Well, I never - well, I just never - never, never, heard of such a thing. I believe I'd just as soon drink the water with the pig feet in it, as to drink it after your Pa took a bath in it!"

One evening not too long after Dad's return from the hospital, the mail hack crossed the creek and left a large wooden crate in our side yard. In it was the strangest looking big, round, wooden tub with legs and a lever on top to push and pull. Dad explained to Bud and me that it was a washing machine. We didn't see how in the world that thing was going to do what Mama had always done, but we were busy as we could be helping

Dude and Dad uncrate the monstrosity and carry it in on the porch. Oh, how proud Dad was. Cousin Mayme had one in St. Louis. She said washing was "just play" when one had a "machine." So he had ordered one for Mama from A. J. Child's and Son in St. Louis. Besides the washing machine, we ordered such things as dried navy beans, canned tomatoes, carriage bolts, heating stoves and once we got a large container of something called "black strap molasses" which none of us could eat. It was recrated and returned via hack and railroad.

We couldn't wait for Mama to wash. Bud and I would beg, "Come on Mama, we'll push the handle." I really think Mama didn't trust that thing much. She would look at it out of the corner of her eye when she passed by it. But the morning came when the big wooden tub was filled with hot, soapy water after being heated in the big wood range in the kitchen. The white clothes were sorted and pushed under the water with a broom handle, we always used for a clothes stick. The lid had to be fastened securely because most of the cogs were attached to the underneath side of the lid. Then the lever was firmly gripped and pulled - back and forth - back and forth. That was hard work too if you had the tub full of soiled clothing. The lever was too high for Bud and me, but Mama put a kitchen chair near the machine so we could take turns trying. It didn't work very well: our feet slipped out from under us. The lever was too big for our childish hands, but we were satisfied we had tried. When Dude came in for dinner he had to try it out. When he finished, most of the clothes were ready to be rinsed and hung on the line outside to dry. The machine was an improvement in our laundry situation. Mama always managed to bargain with Dude on wash day. Mama was "a great negotiator" - "Dude, how would you like a cherry pie for dinner?" - "Well it's wash day you know. If I bake a pie, I'll have to have a little help with the machine." Well by noon, the cherry pies would be cooling on the window sill and by the time Dude went back to the farm chores, the wash would be soaking in the rinse tubs.

About this time another absolute miracle came into our lives. For at least a year men had been working along the creek road, setting poles and attaching wires to them. Mae and I would stop on our way home from school and by each pole place our ear close and listen to them sing. Oh, how beautiful that sound was. Now one morning a workman appeared at our door with a big, heavy board on which a funny lever with a trumpet shaped end occupied the center. At either end of the board was a box, and on the top box were two shiny inverted metal cups with a tiny bell clapper between. Of course Mae, Bud and I wanted to know what it was. Dad explained patiently that it was called a "telephone." We would talk to our neighbors on it, and "Yes, with good luck, we may even call Uncle John and Aunt Ida on it." We didn't believe it; we had never seen a telephone. We knew better than to think anyone could hear us on that thing. We went outside and looked at those tiny wires, and went back inside and busied ourselves with playing train by lining up the dining room chairs. Anyone knew that thing hanging on that wall would never work! It required quite a while for the phone to be properly installed, but when it was finished the workmen insisted Dad call our neighbor Jim Wilson at the "Big Rock" farm just to see "if it works." So Dad took hold of the little handle on the side of the upper box and turned it quickly and to my utter amazement the bells rang - short - long - short - pause a moment - short - long - short - after a moment of waiting, a short answering jingle was heard. The receiver was carefully removed from its hook and placed against Dad's bandaged ear. "Hello – hello," Dad was shouting, "Can you hear me?" "Yes," Mrs. Wilson could hear him loud and clear. Then she inquired how he was feeling. Dad continued to shout as if he were outside. "I'm fine - getting better every day. I'm sure glad to get this new-fangled apparatus. Now I can talk to Dr. Jones whenever I need him." Well, as Aunt Ida always said, "I never, I just never." I repeated the words as Bud and I decided to go look at those magic wires again. How did that thing work? But one thing was absolutely positive in my mind; it had to do with the singing in those poles. Mama would sometimes be anxious if Mae and I were a little tardy getting home from school. We were always sure of a smile on her lips when we would explain that we stopped at each telephone pole to listen to them "sing." I was four when I started to school. Mae was two years older.

Before I go on, I must record one more rotten, mean little trick Bud and I planned out. One extremely warm summer day, Dad left the horse-drawn mower in the shade of the old oak just outside the yard while he made a quick trip to the blacksmith shop in Linn. The mower, the cool shade, our determination to do something helpful, all combined into a pleasant hour for us. Bud was still very fond of carrying anything "loose" in his red bandanna handkerchief, the same one we had used in our sawdust grinding earlier. The mower had several of the most enticing little cups with the loveliest little lids on them. They were just right for little fingers to lift up, let go quickly and enjoy the "plop" as they sprang shut again. This fun lasted a few minutes until we thought of what we really ought to do. That was to fill Bud's red bandanna with sand and pebbles left over from the barn foundation and fill all those wonderful little oil cups with it. My what fun - if we couldn't get much sand or gravel in the cups we found small sticks and poked it down deeper. That was really gratifying to see the oil mix with sand and run over on the outside of the cup. When we finished we were so satisfied with ourselves. Our afternoon had really been profitable! A little later Dad arrived. He was moving fast. A big, black cloud was threatening a summer thunderstorm. He must get the mower in the shed before the rain poured. He quickly harnessed Nell and Anton to the tongue, jumped on the seat, yelled "Giddap" to Anton and away they went - such grinding and grating - some small pieces fell off. Anton and Nell were so startled by all the noise, they took off in a run. Dad jumped to safety and let them go. Bud and I couldn't imagine why the mower made such a noise. It never had before. When Dad got the team untangled and safely into the barn, he went to examine the poor and crippled machine where it stood against the barnyard fence. It didn't leave much to wonder about when he saw the oil streaks around those beautiful little cups, and from the cups to two mischievous little faces so earnestly trying to understand why a little sand and gravel caused all that commotion. Usually both Mama and Dad were quick to work a little "psychiatry" by way of a peach limb. But if any such was administered, I've long since forgotten it. Such is the way of happy childhood memories. As I write this more than seventy years later, I can recall the expression of horror on Dad's face when those gravel filled gears began to grind. I can't help laughing aloud as I see him leap into the air to escape from danger.

A few days later when Uncle John and Aunt Ida came to visit, the story of the "mower accident" was recited while we ate dinner. Uncle John laughed merrily but Aunt Ida brought him back to earth with one of her frequent "sermons on the mount." "John Bacon, don't you laugh - George could have been killed, and besides if you laugh, those little younguns will probably try it again." But war talk soon dominated the table conversation. More neighbors had sold out for unheard of prices. Both Dad and Uncle John had been approached with almost unbelievable offers. "Good sound business" Dad termed it. Both had concluded however "to hold on a while." Just wait and see "the offers would still be there if the war became a reality." There was also a new disease in the country. It was a killer supposedly spreading through contact in the military camps. People were staying home because of it. When a funeral was held the body was taken first to the cemetery, followed by a service in the church. People were cautioned to care for themselves. Take every precaution because it was dreadfully contagious. Aunt Ida purchased that awful stuff called "asafetida," tied it in a white cloth bag and wore it on a string on her neck. When she came to visit now, I didn't like to be near her as I did before. She also forced Uncle John to wear his little cloth bag in the same fashion.

I cannot omit that chapter from my early days: the gypsies. They never failed to show. On a gorgeous autumn day we would awaken to the neighing of strange horses near by. Mama would jump out of bed, run to the window, and in a half scared, half frenzied voice she would almost yell at Dad, "George, it's the GYPSIES. They've moved in and set up during the night."

That was all Mae and I needed - the gypsies! Oh, the gypsies were our delight. We loved their pretty bright yellow, green and red wagons. We loved the bright calico and silk skirts the women wore. Some of the older women wore bright bandannas over their dark graying hair, but the young ones all wore head bands to hold their hair back. We jumped out of bed, ran to the window to verify Mom's announcement. Sure enough, there they were: camp fire for boiling water and cooking breakfast, ponies tethered to stobs driven in the ground. We hurried to get dressed because soon one of the young Romanis would be walking up the lane to ask for a bucket of cow's milk. There were always babies; once there were twins.

This gypsy camp was down the lane and across the creek from our farm house. Here was a deligtful camping site on a flat between two hills, just right for perhaps a dozen wagons and a campfire. The water in the creek was clear and fresh for washing. The men came over every day to buy hay and corn for their ponies. Every morning they watched to see when Dad finished milking so they could get a bucket of milk. Every evening they watched again and came for the bucket of milk. As much as Mae and I loved the gypsies, Mama disliked them. She was in a frenzy of anxiety throughout the whole time. "George, you've got to tell them to leave," she would fuss. "I just can't put up with them one more day. They'll kidnap the children and we'll never see them again." No matter how warm and bautiful the day, Mae and I had to stay inside. We read our story books. We read the Bible. We cut paper ladies from the Sears & Roebuck catalog and chose beautiful names for them (after long and careful deliberation). We thought Margaret, Maud, Mattie and Beulah were just the ultimate in our tiny vocabularies. We begged Mama to let us play in the yard. After several very definite "No's" we tried slipping out the hall door to the back of the house. We could at least slide down the cellar door where we would be hidden from view of the gypsies. Mama soon appeared with a peach tree switch in hand and we were right back in the kitchen. This time we were really in prison. Mae had to stand on a low stool and wash the dishes. I had to dry them!

I can't imagine to this day why Mama was so fearful of these people. To be sure, there were the stories of how they swarmed into small towns telling fortunes, crossing palms with money and taking everything not nailed down. There were also weird tales of blond, blue-eyed babies among the infants. Mama always and forever was afraid of someone kidnapping one of her children. When they came up on the porch to ask for milk, Mama kept the screen door hooked. Sometimes we would send some home-baked cookies along with the milk. Sometimes they would buy vegetables from the garden or a pound of cured bacon.

After Mae and I were old enough to go to school we were never allowed to walk if the gypsies were encamped. Dad always took us in the buggy. But the other children from down the creek walked or drove by the gypsy camp every morning and evening. They were never bothered, much less kidnapped.

There was one time I actually got close to the camp. All these many years have elapsed and I can't imagine how it happened. I suspect I slipped away from Mama on this precarious adventure. I was close enough to see the pattern of bright swinging, full-gathered skirts. I could peer into the open end of the covered wagons. I observed the pretty little girls and shy dark-skinned boys. They smiled at me. I was fascinated by the iron pot hanging over ther red hot coals. Mama yelled so I ran like the wind back up the lane.

At school every norning the other kids would be waiting for us. "Hi Mae, Hi Grace - are the gypsies still there?" The were excited too. The big boys would walk down to the camp in the evening although they always stayed on the roadsides, sometimes wandering up the lane to the houses, talking to Dad and the hired man about fishing, quail hunting and farming.

I don't think Mom (or Dad either) slept much while the encampment was in place. We sometimes gave the gypsies all our milk. We never refused them hay or corn. We had heard too many stories about what they did. So we tried to be nice to them. Usually after a couple of weeks we would hear Mama say in the gray of early morning, "George, I don't hear the horses. I wonder..." She would pull back the lace panel and peer into the early morning. As she blew out the night light and climbed back into bed we heard her murmur, "Thank God!"

There was one fall when the gypsies had been with us for about their usual length of time. Mama and Dad had been planning all summer to attend the school reunion at Chamois. That was a big occasion. The people they had grown up with and taught school with would be there. Also Uncle Harry and Aunt Lulu, Uncle John and Aunt Mae Hancks. So Dad rented a car to take us. Grandma LeFevre would stay with Bud. The day came and we went to Chamois. We had fun. For Mae and me at least, the gypsies were forgotten for the day.

It was late evening when the car rounded the bend in the Ford, ground the gears in the gravel creek crossing, and pulled up the bank. We came out of the willows where we could see the gypsy camp. "Oh my, oh my, oh my! They're gone. So are the apples!" That was Dad's voice, full of disappointment. Sure enough, the orchard had been stripped. There wasn't a Jonathan or a Winesap or a Ben Davis left. They had even taken most of the windfalls. All Mama said was, "It's better than one of the children."

Chapter 5

Goodbye Grea' Granny

In February 1918, we celebrated Granny's 100th birthday. She was Dad's grandmother, born Sarah Jane Shepard in St. Louis on February 18, 1818. She grew up there in the early days of that city with the Chauteaus and LaCledes. Julia Dent Grant was her Sunday School pupil. Sarah Jane attended the Young Ladies Academy at Steelville until she fell in love and married John Overton Bacon on her 18th birthday. Then they began their westward movement by way of St. James where John Overton built the iron smelters. Some are still standing. They then traveled on to Osage County, settling first on the Gasconade River Bluff at Rollins Ferry. John Overton operated the ferry boat at Rollins Ferry for some years. One child died and is buried on this bluff - Belle side of the river. From this rough pioneer home, they moved nearer Linn where John was employed as a carpenter and farmer. After John died, "Grea" Granny was what we always called her. "Grea" being our word for "Great." Although for a long time in my childhood, I was sure it was for "Grey Granny." Her hair was grey, her clothes were always grey or black and she was totally blind. I can remember distinctly how she would reach out toward me and say, "Come here sweet child and let me see you." This meant sitting on her lap and letting her feel my cheeks, my nose, my eyes and then she would take both hands and smooth my unruly brown curls down closer to my head. Mae and I both wore our dark brown hair in "sausage roll curls." Mae's were long, mine were short. The curl in them made them bounce back like a screen door spring and they were always in my way - bobbing up and down.

Grea' Granny lived with my Grandfather and Grandmother Bacon, Charles Porter and Amelia, on a farm about five miles south of Linn. All the children and grandchildren and great-grandchildren would be there. That meant Uncle John and Aunt Ida, of course, Aunt Vaul, Uncle Joe Wills, Uncle Will, Aunt Till, Uncle Al and Aunt Vi, Aunt Alta and Uncle Vic, Grandpa's brothers, Uncle Jim Bacon from Arkansas and their sister-in-law, Aunt Joycie, and of course our family along with various other cousins, nieces and nephews of various members of their families. These were not engraved invitation affairs, if you had received a word of mouth invitation it was all inclusive when they said "Y'all come." So we all came to Grandpa's house on that Sunday. The children were all "put out to play" in the side yard by the "doghouse." Now the doghouse was not where the dog slept at all. It was an outside bedroom where Dad and his three brothers had slept when they were growing up. "Doghouse" was a teasing nickname they gave it when Grandpa built it for them. They told him he was throwing them out of the house, and now they would be forced to sleep with the dogs. It was a large room with a cellar underneath. On this memorable day, there were three big double beds made up with numerous feather beds covered over with pieced, wool comforts in bright shades of red, blue and plaids. There was a home-made rag carpet on the floor. Rags were woven into strips and sewn together, straw was put underneath and the carpet tacked in place. While I was admiring all this comfort, Aunt Alta and Grandma came to get butter, cream, milk, pies, cakes and hams from the cellar rooms.

Because I never wanted to miss anything, I followed them down the steps and admired all that good food. They made several trips from cellar to kitchen. I tagged along. Sometimes I was allowed to carry butter because that wouldn't spill if I fell.

After dinner Uly Duncan arrived with his photography equipment - big box to set on a tripod and a black cloth to drape over the whole apparatus and over his head and shoulders when he was focusing his camera. This was another miracle in a box. It ranked right up there with the telephone and the washing machine. Grandpa and Uncle Jim began to round up everybody on the front porch to take our picture. The weather was warm, unusually warm for February. We did not need extra outside clothing. I was busy helping Mr. Duncan set up his tripod and I'm sure I was pestering him with such questions as, "What's this for? Where does that thing go? How does this work? How long does it take? Will I be able to see it as soon as you push the button?"

Everyone was in place. The front was crowded and the children were lined up outside the porch. Grandpa and Uncle Jim helped their century-old mother to her place of honor in the center of the porch. Grandpa carefully lowered her into her arm chair. As he did so Grea' Granny said to Grandpa, "Now Charlie, bring the flag. I want the flag in the picture." So Grandpa brought the flag and draped it across her lap just right. I took time off from my job as Mr. Duncan's helper to run to my designated spot by Mae in the front row. That was a day never to be forgotten, because two weeks from that very day the mail hack driver stopped by in the early morning to tell us Grea' Granny had died. We knew she was sick, she had developed pneumonia soon after the centennial celebration. Mae and I were very sad, we sat on the floor back of the old black iron heater and read from Grandma LeFevre's Bible. She helped us with big words and explained to us that Grea' Granny had lived a wonderful life as a pioneer wife and mother, but one hundred years was a long time to live. She was very tired and wanted to rest, so Grandma said. We felt better. The next day we helped Mama a great deal with dishes and sweeping and baby Pete. On the following day we went again to Grandpa's house. All was sad and grief was causing tears. Voices were muted as my father and Uncle John took Mae and me into the parlor where Granny lay all white and cold looking in her black casket. Aunt Till brought in a basin of water to sprinkle the flower sprays still in their boxes surrounded by green wax paper. The horse-drawn hearse drew up outside the front gate. It was also black, drawn by black horses - the sides of the coach were glass. Granny's casket was covered. The minister, H. C. Green (Uncle), offered a prayer. Dad, Uncle John, Uncle Will, Uncle Al, Uncle Vic Pinet, and Uncle Joe Wills then carried Granny to the hearse. All of us climbed into our buggies and followed the black hearse the five miles into Linn. The March day was cold. The funeral service at Linn Methodist Episcopal Church was short, the cemetery was on our way home on the hill west of Linn. I didn't like the open place in the ground. I didn't like seeing Grea' Granny's casket being lowered with leather straps into the space. I didn't like it at all when the funeral director, Artie Dubrouillet, jumped down into the grave and began to tighten the big metal screws at each corner of the lid to fasten it securely to the wooden box. Our Uncle H. C. Green then tossed three roses one by one into the grave and intoned, "Earth to earth, ashes to ashes and dust to dust."

It was especially nice to get home and be met by Grandma LeFevre. She gave Mae and me a big smile and a special tight hug just to let us know she understood our misery. To help us feel better Mama let us keep on our fine black patent leather high-topped shoes that Dad brought us from St. Louis and, of course, our long white cotton stockings we always wore for dress up. Both of us had to button on our big coverall gingham aprons before we sat down to a steaming pot of navy bean soup with chunks of ham cooked in it, corn bread and apple pie. We didn't talk much; Dad and Mama looked worried. When we were getting ready for bed, Grandma LeFevre gently explained that our Grandma Bacon was quite ill. She had "overdone herself" getting ready for the centennial, caring for "Grea' Granny" and then all the company during the time of Granny's being "laid out." She had developed pneumonia. Now Mae and I really were worried. Our Grandma Bacon was a tiny, little, thin woman with no surplus energy, but we were anxious because Dad was anxious. Every time he came in from his outside work, his first question would be, "Jennie - any word from Ma?" Sometimes Aunt Ida would have called or Uncle Will would come by to say there was little change.

Two weeks from the time Grea' Granny died, we had a repeat performance. The driver of the hack stopped by on his morning run to Bonnots Mill to say Grandma had died. We were all in the kitchen. I'm sure Mama and Dad knew from the moment the hack stopped over by the mailbox what the words were they would hear because they didn't hurry to open the door as they always did in an ordinary time. Dad didn't say anything, his eyes were swimming. Mama kept her back to us all; she was fighting tears but Mama never in her life let us see her cry. Grandma let the hack driver out the door. We ate our oatmeal and boiled eggs silently. Dad went out to the barn. Mama started the cooking and readying our clothes again for Grandma's funeral. She and Grandma talked in soft voices about Grandma Bacon, what a fine woman she was, what a fine a family she had reared, what a care Grea' Granny had been and most of all her extraordinary cooking talents. They said she cooked only one thing at a time, tending it with the greatest care until it was exactly right. When she baked bread, she carried the yeast mixture to the cellar room out under the "doghouse" for it to rise in a cool place. She was a master hand at curing hams and shoulders and bacon. Grandpa sometimes butchered as many as forty hogs which made quite a few pieces of pork to cure. When Dad came in for dinner, he and Dude reminisced about by-gone days. Dad recalled his childhood days when he helped Grandpa and his older brothers drive hogs from the Linn farm to Bonnots Mill, and how it was always his job to stay in the wooded areas away from the road to round up those ornery critters who sought to stray from the herd.

On the following day, Mae and I put on our black patent leather shoes, our long white cotton stockings over our long underwear and our best dresses. Mine was blue velvet with lace collar and cuffs. Mae's was a dark blue and red wool with silk threads woven through it. Our long curls were tied with red silk hair ribbons. Over this we wore our wool coats and hoods. We rode on the small box in the buggy front. Bud and Pete were left at home with Grandma. We left early but everyone else was there early too. Uncle John and Aunt Ida met us at the door. Again they led us into Grandma's immaculate parlor with the big ornate woodburning stove, the beautiful parlor organ, the red velvet fainting couch and the soft red and beige patterned carpeting on the floor. In the far corner sat Grandpa, his hands shading his eyes, his long white beard rested low on his chest today. He was devastated. For all these years he had had Ma, and "Melie" (short for Amelia) to look after. Now in the space of two weeks he had lost both. He lifted me in his arms and held me tightly as we looked down on Grandma. Again that cold, white feeling gripped me just as it had when I saw Grea' Granny in her black coffin. Again Aunt Till and Aunt Ida came in to sprinkle the flowers. Everyone was bustling to get outer garments on for the trip to the church. Grandpa gave Mae and me an extra big hug just before he was led away to follow his beloved "Melie's" casket. It was carried by sons John, Will, Allan, and George helped by two sons-in-law, Vic Pinet and Joe Wills. Another son-in-law, Reverend H. C. Green, offered prayer and read scriptures. We were soon following the black hearse along the river road toward the Linn M. E. Church. There were many tears. Aunt Ida sat with Mama, Mae and me on a front pew. Both of them found it necessary to wipe their noses frequently. They were such strong characters they were determined not to cry. Aunt Vaul, Aunt Till and Aunt

Alta, Grandma's daughters, sobbed and wept. Grandpa looked very sad and totally alone as he sat staring at the black casket.

The cemetery ceremony was an almost exact repeat of two weeks earlier. The casket was lowered, the lid was put down for the outside wooden box, and the funeral director, Artie Dubroillet, jumped into the grave and fastened the metal screws to secure the lid. Again we heard, "Earth to earth, ashes to ashes and dust to dust." We hurried home again. Grandpa left with Uncle John and Aunt Ida in their buggy, driven of course right behind the hearse and drawn by Old Maud. Aunt Till, the only one of Grandpa's children away from Osage County, would remain for a few days to straighten the house and keep him company.

Chapter 6

Flu and Goodbye Farm

The following Monday morning, Mae and I were up early. We had to get back to school. We had missed several days because of the funerals. We lived two miles north of Linn and the school was near the east end so it was necessary to leave home soon after daylight. After all we had to have time to listen to the telephone poles sing. That fall Gladys Cox had come to stay with us just to walk to school with Mae and me. She was a country girl from the Mt. Sterling area who wanted to go to high school. Gladys had become a member of our family. She was accustomed to a big family. When her lessons were done she helped Mama with cooking, dishes, sweeping, baby tending and even sometimes she took turns pulling and pushing the big, black lever on top of the washing machine! All of us had grown very fond of Gladys. Grandma LeFevre had gone to stay with Aunt May now that Uncle John had left for Ft. Riley. She was now babysitting with Aunt May's twin boys, Harry and Dorsey. They were only a few months older than I. Jennie and Nelson were some years older. Aunt May was teaching at Indian Creek. We seemed to be getting back to normal.

In school, Miss Gussie Gove, my teacher, was listening to the 3rd grade reading class. I suddenly became aware of a swimming sensation in my head, my eyes were watering, and the printed lines in my reader wouldn't stay in place. I felt sick. Miss Gussie dismissed the 3rd grade class and came quickly down the aisle to my desk. She felt my forehead and sent one of her trusty 3rd grade boys to the Intermediate Department (room next door) to tell Mae to get ready to go home with me. Another trusty from the High School was dispatched to J. P. McDaniel's Store (just east of the school) to tell Dad to come for me immediately. Dad's team, Old Peg and Nell, were hitched in front where they were easily seen from the school house. Miss Gussie bundled me from head to toe. Dad had extra lap robes he wrapped around me. He had presence of mind to tell Gladys to stay in town or go home because there was no question as to my ailment. I was coming down with that dreaded monster influenza. Dad touched Peg and Nell lightly with the end of the driver's reins. In a short time we were home. I was so sick. I felt very, very warm. Nothing stayed true in my mind - it kept slipping off center in strange dreams. For days I don't remember seeing anything or anybody. I kept seeing a black girl running up and down the New Bluff Road, her tongue was so black and swollen it wouldn't stay in her mouth. Over and over this dream re-occurred.

Finally one day I awakened, Mae was lying beside me. She was asleep. Mama and Pete were in the other big double bed across from us. Bud was asleep in the big oak rocker in which pillows had been placed. I wondered why Mama didn't get up and come to see about me. Then our elderly friend, Dad Cramer, from town came into the room carrying a large soup bowl, and smaller soup bowls on Mama's old tin kitchen tray. He seemed so glad to see me awake. He put the big Alfred Meachin soup bowl on the heating stove, ladled out some potato soup and helped me eat a few bites. He then fed Mae and Bud, Mom and Pete the same way. Dad and George Voss, who had bought our farm and was there to put in his spring crops, were sick too. They were bedded down in the dining room. Everyday Dr. Jones came bringing his little brown pills. He mashed one in a silver teaspoon, poured three drops of warm water on it and bade me open my mouth wide. How terrible it tasted, and the taste stayed in my mouth forever it seemed. Dad Cramer gave the pills regularly after Dr. Jones showed him how. I recognized then that everyone was sick. I didn't like that either. I had had a lot of things lately I didn't like - funerals, flu, bad dreams and awful tasting medicine. But as quickly as I got sick, I began to feel better. One morning I got up, dressed and slipped toward the door before Mama told me in no uncertain terms to get undressed and back in bed. She didn't want me to cross the cold, cold hall, but I wanted to see Dad just to make sure he was all right. I went around to the other side of Mama's bed to see Pete. He looked feverish and very sick, so did Mama, but I did as Mama said. Soon Dad came across the hall with Dad Cramer to bring our oatmeal and hot biscuits. I guess I didn't feel as well as I thought, I was weak and tired. Perspiration bathed my skinny, little body. Dr. Jones lectured me on the necessity of staying in bed and staying warm or I might take pneumonia! This thing, whatever it was, must be terrible, even worse than the "flu," so I believed them. For several more days, I was content to stay in bed. I was so thankful that black girl wasn't running up and down the New Bluff Road anymore. Her swollen tongue had haunted me day and night. For once in our lives Uncle John and Aunt Ida didn't come to see about us. They did call every day. Aunt Ida was sure they wouldn't get the flu - after all both of them were wearing their asafetida bags around their necks. But we had to get well soon. Our farm sale had been advertised for March 20. We had to get ready to move to our house in town. But Dad had been warned to take things easy and not risk exposure. His strength had not returned as it should following the mastoid surgery the year previous.

Dad Cramer was staying on to make the potato soup. We had bakers bread as we referred to it, because Mama wasn't able to make bread and none of the men, Dad, George Voss or Dad Cramer was a very good biscuit makers, although they were acceptable. The bakers bread was toasted in the wood stove oven. Warm milk with a bit of sugar, butter and salt added was poured over the toast. These two items were always on Dad's menu. Potato soup was first choice usually. Mama's recipe (or receipt) was to boil the potatoes until very well done. The tuber pieces must be well covered with water, a pinch of salt added. When well done, the potatoes were drained and mashed until they were fluffy with a large lump of butter. Whole milk was then placed in the saucepan, the mashed potatoes added - and chopped onion. Just before serving, a large cup full of sweet cream was stirred in - salt and butter were adjusted. This creamy concoction was one of our favorite supper dishes along with cold canned tomatoes and usually hot biscuits. Dad Cramer tried his best to follow Mama's directions, and I don't remember anyone complaining about the bill of fare. We were so, so fortunate to have such a friend! I do remember distinctly the first evening all of us were well enough to get dressed and gather around the dining room table for supper. We looked very queer in the shadow of the kerosene lamp. Dad and George Voss were not completely dressed. They had not come down with the malady as soon as Mae, Mama and I, so their recuperation would require more time. George Voss had his long blue chambray shirt over his long winter underwear. Dad had his "town grey pants" on over his long handles. Bud was still wearing his flannel gown. Mama had pulled on her flannel "dressing saeque" over her blue flowered calico dress. We were so pale, our eyes looked too large for our faces. The lamp flickered throwing shadows over the tablecloth and over our ravaged, thin bodies. But how happy we were everyone was recovering. Soon we would be basking in the warm sunshine of spring and love and excitement of living in town. That night Mae and I put an extra emphasis on "God bless Mama, God bless Papa, God bless Pete, Mae and me - and God bless Dad Cramer for making us potato soup and milk toast - and oh yes, God bless George Voss - and please make us all well."

It was time to organize farm machinery, animals, chickens, everything but some household furnishings for the sale. Again Henry Schroeder, son Fritzie and Uncle John came to get things ready. They lined our machinery up in rows out by the new barn. Red Rose, Buttercup and Daisy were curried, well-fed and given extra attention by Dude and Uncle John. George Voss had bought our grain in the bins to feed the animals he would soon bring to the farm.

Mrs. Regina Schroeder and Angie came early one morning to help "straighten us out" in the house. The big, black iron kettle was filled with water out in the side yard by the wood pile. A fire was built under it and big tubs were filled with the boiling water. Tub after tub of soiled clothing was scrubbed, well rinsed and hung on the line. Mrs. Johnnie Williams had come too. She managed the washing machine where the bed clothes were cleansed of all our influenza germs - we hoped! The March air was chilly. The wind whipped the clothes on the lines, sometimes wrapping the sheets and pillowcases around the line. Before Regina, Angie and Martha left, our beds were all cleaned and sweet smelling. The feather beds had been hung on the line to air. The floors had been scrubbed white with the big buckets of soapy water left from the laundry. Martha got down on her knees and scrubbed one small space at a time with a stiff brush. Her hands were so red and chapped looking. She did this kind of work every day for women in town.

As the sale day neared, Mae and I were busy saying good- bye to all our favorite places; the door that opened into the garret room - the slanted outside cellar door where we had spent many pleasant hours - then to the cellar to see the swinging shelf hung from the ceiling by a chain at each corner - the apple barrel - the peach tree outside the back door. We begged every day to be allowed to go to the new barn to say good-bye to Red Rose, Buttercup and Daisy, but Mama stuck to her guns - "No, not yet - perhaps on Friday (the day before the sale), we could see our beloved Buttercup from the parlor window." So we were somewhat satisfied to play paper dolls on the floor beside the warm heating stove. Paper dolls preserved our sanity. We weren't accustomed to being prisoners in our home. We were inclined to be free spirits. But we spread pages from the St. Louis Democrat on the floor. Each crease on the page was a room, making four rooms to a page. We cut furniture illustrations from the Sears & Roebuck catalog - chairs, divans, bedroom suites, kitchen cabinets, stoves, tables, etc. After carefully trimming around the outside edge of each piece, we folded the chairs where the seat joined the back and placed it in an appropriate location along the newspaper crease. In this way we furnished at least eight rooms. We were always "enormously wealthy" with fine furniture - and the Axminster carpets were usually pictured in color - so we clipped those and carpeted our floors. Naturally we had to have people, so we cut our people from the ladies ready-to-wear section, the men's ready-to-wear, children and of course the baby. In our young minds, every home "worth a hoot" had a baby. Well almost every home (not Uncle John and Aunt Ida). When we weren't playing with our catalog paper dolls (all of them had names written on their back side - fancy names we thought like Irene, Beulah, Myrtle, Amy, and Margaret), we played dominoes or read stories from our story books. The best story book was the Bible or Mae's *Tell Me a Story Book* or the comic section of the *Globe Democrat.*

On Friday, Henry, Regina, Uncle John, Johnnie and Martha Williams came to make final arrangements. We were afraid no one would come to the sale. They might fear the dreadful influenza. To many of our farm family neighbors, the disease had not been as kind as to us. We saw the black horses and hearse travel down the bluff road numerous times and return at the head of a line of buggies, surreys and horseback riders. Mae and I would stand at the parlor window and pull back the lace panel which covered the panes of glass. We would ask Mama, "Who is this procession for?" She would tell us, "This is Mr. Verdot." He was an old man and not able to cope with the disease. But on occasions, it would be a child. Then Mama would shy away from our direct questions, sometimes she didn't reply at all in exact terms. She would say only "I don't know; he was from Loose Creek, or Bonnots Mill or Frankenstein."

Sometimes crawling along the Bluff Road in these funeral processions, we would spot an automobile. Whenever we did we fixed our eyes on it and followed along until it was completely out of sight. This new means of travel completely baffled me. Dr. Cooper had a bright red run-about. He had been motoring up and down our Bluff Road to see his flu patients. Dr. Jones had a black run-about. Uncle John Hancks (the doctor) had a Maxwell. Once when they were visiting in the autumn, they were driving through the barn lot toward the lane when Grandma spotted what she thought was a fire underneath the rear of the auto. She screamed and waved her big, full-gathered, calico apron to attract Uncle John's attention. He slammed on the brakes because Grandma was screaming, "fire, fire, John, John, stop, stop." All of us reached the auto just as Uncle John kneeled and detached a bright red maple leaf from underneath the rear of the auto! However, my first ride in an auto was brought about by a near bad accident, certainly a time of great anxiety. We had gone one morning in late summer to the Osage County courthouse to see a group of our young men inductees leave for Bonnots Mill to enter military camps. We were on our way home in our surrey with the fringe on top (this was a gift from Grandpa Bacon after Grandma died). We were driving Nell and Anton. We had reached the long Mill Hill traveling west alongside the public cemetery when an automobile came up behind us. The young man driving "tooted his horn." Anton didn't like that at all. He picked up his ears, strained at the bit, leaped into the air and took off as fast as he could. Dad pulled on the lines and yelled, "Whoa, Whoa - Whoa now Anton - Whoa - Whoa." The louder Dad yelled the faster Anton traveled. There was no stopping. Mama was shouting, "All of you grab each other and hang on." Meanwhile she was gathering up her skirts in one hand and fitting Pete into the crook of her left arm. Just when Anton was going into his finest hour, Mama upstaged him. She jumped from the front surrey seat over the wheel and landed on the gravel road. Pete was totally intact although scared and yelling at the top of his voice. Mama had skinned her elbow. Anton finally stopped but Mama firmly refused to climb back into the vehicle. By this time the auto had caught up with us. They were as frightened as we were. They were also sad. The mother had been crying. One of her sons was among those we had bid good-bye a few minutes before. She insisted Mama and Pete ride home with them. When I heard this invitation, I immediately climbed down from the back seat of the surrey and announced that if anyone was going in the auto, I was going along. And so I did. Mama, Pete and I rode home in style - such fine leather seats - such intriguing doors that opened so easily. Mama kept holding my hand tightly to keep me from releasing the catch while we were moving. The auto ride was over too quickly. Mama insisted the auto owners "come in for a while" - the mother did - to see I suppose that Mama and Pete were all right. She was still crying. She insisted on helping Mama bandage her injured elbow, but Mama was always so fiercely independent she would have none of it. I think she wanted Dad to see how badly her elbow was hurt. She was also getting her sermon in mind for his arrival. Mama hated that surrey with a passion. No one else drove one of that vintage. "Old faded fringe hanging around, dangling and getting all frayed," she would say. C. P. (Grandpa) couldn't give it to anyone else, she continued. So as far as I can remember, she never rode in the surrey again. It was parked in the hallway of our beautiful new barn. Dust accumulated on the fringed top and on the seats. The only trips I took in it were imaginary. Those were numerous. Every day I took my doll (for the baby) and along with Bud, we sat in the front seat, cracked the whip and yelled "Giddap Nell" - "Whoa Anton." We visited all the neighbors and all the relatives we had ever been to in reality - until today. Today it (the surrey) had been rolled out into the barn yard to be sold along with Dad's new mowing machine and corn cultivator. Oh yes, that was the same cultivator with which Mae and Bud rolled the heavy iron wheel over my big toe. Mae had put me to bed and brought me a lump of sugar. Later she came with a scrap of pink chambray to lay over my toe.

While Dad was changing his town clothes for work clothes, Mama delivered the sermon. The sun clouded under while she stood with hands on hips and spewed her disgust. "That horse, that idiotic high-spirited horse - you knew better than to hitch him to that big, old lopsided surrey. I could have been killed having to jump out over the wheel." Dad and Uncle John had that same quality - whistling while their wives raved at them and putting distance between themselves and the voice. The surrey was another thing to which Bud and I felt a definite need to bid adieu. I wanted to feel the padded seat once more as I sat on it. Bud wanted to crack the whip and yell "Giddap" at his imaginary Peg and Nell. There was the sawdust pile and the orchard and the long summer afternoon walks in the woods with Mama and Dad. We wouldn't be singing, "Morning on the Farm" anymore. If we did, it wouldn't be the same.

Sometime earlier, before the dreadful influenza epidemic, Mama had spent a lot of time studying the A. J. Child's catalog. She would need a cook stove, because we were selling the old black range that had been Mrs. Ben Schroeder's before Mama and Dad had married and moved to this farm. Mama had also ordered a fine Axminister-Wilton rug for our parlor in the town house. The rug had come upon the hack and had been deposited in the parlor room in town; so far the cook stove had not.

Friday morning dawned, cold, grey and windy. All the grownups were so busy - getting cows and calves in pens together - setting out small implements, tools, etc. Mama was still wearing her long, white, knitted fascinator wrapped snugly around her head and neck. Dad was also wearing a warm, fur-lined cap to protect the "hole behind his ear." Our staunch, dependable Schroeder family was right there - Henry, Regina, Angie and Fritzie. Johnnie Williams and Uncle John were feeding the cattle and hogs. Dude and Fritzie were the strong young men lifting and carrying whatever needed to be moved. Regina was organizing items for the lunch to be served the next day. She would boil hams, slice the bread and clean the big iron wash kettle in which she would boil water for coffee and for dishwater on Saturday. Bud and I kept an eye on Mama. When she went with Regina to the smoke house to get the hams, we saw our opportunity - to the barn we flew. Mae saw what we were up to and came flying out of the house to escape with us. The following moments were bittersweet. We hadn't seen the surrey since we had recovered "from the flu." We just had to climb into the seat, feel it with our hands, crack the whip and "Giddap, Whoa" once more. To my great delight, I found my long, lost corncob doll. It was just what the name implies, a corncob with a doll dress fashioned on it. Mama had pacified me with it one day when I couldn't locate my real doll.

From the surrey, we climbed into the hay mow - just to draw in deep draughts of that sweet resinous aroma of new timber. We postponed as long as possible saying good-bye to Red Rose, Buttercup and Daisy and their curly little red baby calves. Old Jers had been taken to stay with Uncle Will at his farm near Grandpa's. She would be brought to the cow shed in town after we moved. There were other cows and calves and horses to be sold along with "Anton." Before long we heard Mama's voice in her most demanding tone - "Grace, Mae, Bud - come in here this very minute. Where are you, do you hear me?" Uncle John answered for us in his matter-of-fact don't-get-in-such-a-huff voice, "Yes, Jennie, they're just saying good-bye to Buttercup." Then to us he said, "Would you like to sit on her back once more?" So how wonderful that was - absolute Heaven to sit on that broad, sleek back and hold to her velvety ears once more. Uncle John let us sit briefly on Buttercup, Red Rose and Daisy. Then with a gentle spank on each little behind, he sent us off to the house. We were satisfied. The day had been too much for us. Mrs. Voss had come in the afternoon to see her husband, to bring him extra clothes and to see the house she would soon be living in. Mae and I thought she was an elegant lady. So well dressed in a three-quarter length black and white checked outer coat. Her dress was short and she wore high-heeled shoes. I could sense her relief for the welfare of her husband when the smart, sorrel mare and Mrs. Voss wheeled rapidly down the lane. Supper and bedtime were almost synonymous that night. We fell asleep almost instantly in that marvelously carefree way things happen before you mature into stress-filled grownups who search for things to be concerned about - especially after going to bed.

Morning came early, Mae and I were to stay in the parlor room with Pete and Bud until we were sent for - so instructed Mama. "Grace, you get in bed with Pete now and stay there until we are ready." Mama was dressed in one of her second best wool suits left over from her teaching days. She was carrying the kerosene lamp carefully. It was long before daylight but Henry, Regina, Angie and Fritzie were bustling about - feeding animals - currying and combing the animals. Uncle John, Uncle Will and Uncle Al were all out there setting up an auctioneer's stand and helping Regina start a fire under the kettle for coffee. This was all too much for me. I stayed in bed awhile, but the voices in the barnyard were like magnets drawing me to the window. Lanterns were flying around like overgrown fireflies. Someone came up the lane with a huge, wooden crate filled with bakers bread. He also delivered a huge roll of something I found out later was "bologna"!

When some of the important chores were done and breakfast was ready, Mama came to "free her prisoners." Mae and I were told to put on our good school dresses and our black patent leather shoes. Such a treat - wearing our good shoes on Saturday. Surely Mama made a mistake, but she dressed Bud in his town clothes - blue serge knee pants topped by a red wood sweater. Pete was also dressed in his new gingham apron.

I could hardly eat my oatmeal and boiled egg for "eyeing" that roll of bologna on the cook table. I begged to taste it but Mama said, "No, absolutely no, no, no. We're going to use that only if our ham isn't enough." So all I was going to feast from that luscious looking roll was my eyes.

As soon as we could, Mae, Bud and I ran into the side yard for a better view of the activity. Uncle John told us we would be safer if we stayed in the yard because the sale crowd was gathering. Men and women came in farm wagons, drawn by fat mules, horses or matched teams of dapple grey. There were buggies, surreys, men and women on horseback and just a couple of automobiles chugged up the lane much to the consternation of most of the horses. Promptly at 10:00 AM, the auctioneer mounted the stand, terms of sale were announced, clerk and cashier were identified and the sale began - tools such as garden hoes, shovels and small machines - corn planter, binder, plows - all the way through our beloved belongings. Old Buttercup, Daisy and Red Rose were led up to the auction block, their calves pushed along because they weren't used to halters and crowds. Their new owners loaded them into farm wagons or tied them to the rear of their vehicle and hauled them down the lane toward the New Bluff Road. Anton threw quite a fit when his time came to do his thing. He snorted, kicked up his heels and just let everyone present know his temperament. He brought a good price and was purchased by a good, kind man (Anton Backes). We saw him occasionally in later years. Another horse was David Daniel Newton Crockett Collier - all the names of his former owners - so his last name should have been Bacon. He was a gentle well-mannered black horse to be trusted anywhere. The few pieces of household furniture only required a few minutes - an iron bed - two high chairs - and a wash stand. We didn't have much to begin with. At the day's end everything was gone. We felt very alone, almost desolate - no cows to the milk shed - no pigs to grunt and knock the swill pails out of your hands. I only knew the animals were all gone; so was the bologna. Mom sent it back to town by Theron Carnes the cashier. "It costs too much" she said and furthermore "it wasn't good for children" so much for my first farming job. By a strange turn of events my husband, Buell Ferrier, and I re-purchased this farm from George Voss when he retired to town life forty years later. For two absolutely blissful weeks one summer, I lived there all by myself. I'll get to that later but for ten heavenly days I reveled in memory as I climbed to the hay mow and tried to recapture the spicy, sweet resin. I walked to the creek and through the woods and pear orchard. I could sense all these happenings. I could see the sale day. I could hear Mama's demanding voice when she lectured Dad on the day of the run-away - but time had intervened - too much time - the memories were just that - sweet, sweet memories.

Dad had not sold our farm wagon or buggy (only the surrey). We had Peg and Nell and Old Jers. Sunday was spent packing glassware, mirrors from the dresser and the bookcase. The legs were removed from the heavy top of our dining room table. As much as possible was packed into our wagon and Uncle John's, so that early Monday morning we could leave.

Chapter 7

Town Kids

That Sunday at supper, we were sad and a bit frightened at what lay ahead. Mom and Dad had more than doubled their investment in the farm. That was something they had never thought would happen! Dad wasn't able to do the farm work alone. Hired help was hard to find because all the strong, young men were in the service. Dude had answered the call of Uncle Sam and was now in camp. Gladys Cox's brother, Cecil, had died of influenza, so she wouldn't be returning to live with us. We seemed to have our young hopes dashed somewhat. The old weather-boarded farm house had been the only home we knew.

It didn't take long to "move." Some of the furniture had been taken earlier, just whenever Dad and Uncle John were passing that way. By evening the beds were up and the dining room table was in place. Our kitchen room was of no use whatsoever, because the new Bridge Beach cook stove had not arrived. We cooked our supper on the heater in the dining room. Mama fussed a good deal about no heat in a heater. The cooking surface was far from the fire etc., etc. Dad was sure the cook stove would be along in a "little while."

Old Jers was now brought to our town house from Uncle Will's, but Peg and Nell stayed there along with our buggy. Dad was helping Uncle Will and Uncle John with their farm work when he wasn't busy keeping records at the courthouse for the county clerk, Wiley Langendorfer. Recently I went to the old books and looked at Dad's beautiful handwriting - long tails on his capital letters.

Mae and I went back to school. We were glad to see our friends and teachers but the walk was so different. No telephone poles to sing to us, no dead dogs along the road for Mae to be afraid of, no Wilsons to visit on the Big Rock Farm where Mrs. Wilson would have a warm brown biscuit with fried bacon and molasses on it for our snack. We didn't have a whole farm to explore - only a yard, a house, a cow shed for "Old Jers" and a small stable for "Old Peg" when she stayed overnight with us. But there were things pleasant. We could "saunter" on our way home from school. We could stop for a few minutes some evenings with Carmen and Zelda Campbell or with Alma and Marie Tafflinger. The store windows were full of pretty materials for dresses. We would choose a piece and tell each other how Mama would make it - "a ribbon here, a lace collar, a big wide sash," we would say. We would wear it with our black patent leather shoes to Sunday School. We had been to Sunday School rather frequently, but now we could go every Sunday and take Bud with us. That was so interesting. We had beautiful, colored, printed cards with Biblical illustrations on one side and Bible verses in small, small print on the reverse side. The Intermediate Department had a "leaflet" as we called them - two pages of printed Bible stories with questions at the end to study and answer. Mae and I didn't need much help with the lessons, but if we did Mama and Dad took time to read and explain them to us. Dad had studied the Bible a great deal. He could delineate the families of Enoch, Isaac, Ham, Moses, David and all the rest! And on very special warm evenings, we would walk over to the courthouse and say

"Hello, to Poll Parrot." Poll was kept in a cage on the window sill in the basement office of Mr. Cell Zevely. (This was the old courthouse). There were iron bars over the small basement windows. Polly would fix her eye on you and say, "Polly want a cracker. Polly want a cracker." Mr. Zevely would think that was funny. Sometimes he would tease us by insisting we stick our finger through the space between the bars of the cage, but I knew better now. I had tried it once, before I became a "town kid"! I was smart now! The bakery shop was definitely on our way home - such aroma - yeasty, sugary, spicy. Really I think Mr. Frank Balkenbusch only baked bread, doughnuts and sweet rolls, but to Mae and me it was food for the Gods. And in Aimee Maire's plate glass store front there were wooden buckets filled with chocolate drops, ribbon candy, and orange slices.

But there was still no cook stove. Mama would poke and probe and coax that old heater to cook our potatoes or stew tomatoes. Bean soup had to be started a day before you expected to eat it. Bread baking and biscuits were out of the question. Every day Mama lectured A. J. Child's on why he wasn't shipping her Bridge Beach cook stove. She finally wrote a letter - it was not answered promptly - she wrote another. She must have explained the situation quite thoroughly because she received a prompt reply saying the stove would soon be ready for shipping. Meanwhile we waited - and waited.

Uncle John Hancks had now been stationed at Ft. Riley, Kansas, for some months. He liked the army routine. He had found a house in Manhattan. Aunt May was to have a sale and join him. Grandma LeFevre came to stay with Mae, Bud and me while Mama and Dad went out to the tiny village of Koenig to help Aunt May organize her sale. Uncle John had supplemented his medical fees by farming so he also had farm implements, tools, cows, pigs and horses. Since Aunt May and the children would be traveling to Manhattan on the train she would take only valuables, bedding and clothes. Mama and Dad were away several days. Grandma didn't do any better than Mama cooking on the heating stove. She was very fond of mush, so she built an enormously hot fire to boil the mush - flames ripped and roared up the stovepipe. Grandma was afraid the house might "catch" as she called it. She grabbed a basin of water and doused the inferno, throwing ashes and steam all over the dining room. Some landed in the mush, but Grandma insisted we eat it - some ash is good for you - just put lots of cream and sugar on it. It was all we had. When Mama and Dad and Pete arrived very late Saturday evening, the sale was done. Aunt May was on her way to Kansas and we were so glad to have Mama to cook for us - even if it was on the heater.

Mae and I thought our parlor room was absolutely the latest thing in luxurious living. The bright colors in the Axminster rug could keep us in ecstasy for hours. There were groups of blossoms - about the size of a rose in the center of each side and end - red, lavender and gold. The center had a crown-like design. It looked just like the fantastic room we had arranged for our paper dolls. In one corner of the room stood Dad's bookcase. He had bought a bookcase before he was married. Grandma Bacon wanted to keep it when Dad married, so she gave Dad $16 to purchase this one. In it he kept all his books, a set of Pedagogy study for a correspondence course, Margaret E. Sangsters' *Good Manners for All Occasions*, a copy of *John Halifax - Gentleman*, and a lavender bound book entitled *After Death, What?* Two thinner volumes were on a lower shelf: *The History of Osage Co.* and *The Life and Death of William McKinley*. Leaning against the bookcase was Dad's violin in its gray-green cloth case. A large wooden spare bed was made up with Mama's "woven bedspread" on it, and two or three rocking chairs were the furnishings until Dad came home from the courthouse one day and announced he had bought a piano - such excitement - a piano?? He had used the Liberty Bonds - all $300 of them. Mama's face looked a bit cloudy at first as she studied that over. She always picked up the corner of her apron and rolled it in her fingers when a new subject was broached. A couple of times she started to say, "Now,

George - Now, now George," but Dad hurried to say it was time the girls took music lessons. That was all it took to change Mama's facial expression. Mama always wanted her children to have the best advantage possible and if her girls were to grow up to be teachers then they needed to know music!

In a few days the "hack" pulled up in front of our house. How we rushed out to examine the piano. To our surprise it was crated in a big heavy box - as if the crate had been built around the piano. Dad kept saying, "I just hope its the right one. I bought a Schaeffer. I'd sure hate to ship it back." It took an eternity, I thought, to get that crate away from the piano, but when they did - how lovely. Mama called it "Mahogany" - to her "Mahogany" was the essence of fine furniture. Grandma called it "lovely, lovely." "Jennie did you ever see anything like it?" she would say to Mama.

Finally it was in place in the parlor room, a stool accompanied it. Dad sat down and played a few chords. We were all in a great humor that evening. Mama didn't even mention "Mr. A. J. Child's" or "Bridge Beach." The piano box was carefully stored out in the wood shed, because even though we had hardly settled in Linn, Mama made no secret of her discontent - no garden spot - no room for chickens - Old Jers didn't have any pasture - we fed her bran. There just wasn't the kind of things in town Mama liked. Mama wasn't a joiner. Clubs or women's organizations didn't interest her. At a very early age all of us learned Mama's wish was also the family's.

Mae and I began music lessons under the supervision of Miss Hattie Bunch. This wonderful woman had a millinery shop in the Mahon Building on Main Street. In the back she had a piano, sheet music, and crates and boxes in which the hats were shipped. Her father and mother operated the county farm where homeless or penniless people were housed. Earlier I had been here to practice a solo called "Requiem" to be sung at a courthouse rally for war bonds, so I felt quite at home when I sat on the bench. My feet came nowhere near the pedals. Miss Hattie wanted me to learn the right hand treble first, then left, then put them together. The piece was "Fox and Geese." I worked and worked on those notes. They didn't sound like Miss Hattie wanted them to. Mae was progressing nicely. She always did. Soon she was playing "Sunshine Waltz" and "Irene Waltz." Miss Hattie gave me other pieces like "Little Rondo," but she still continued to set "Fox and Geese" on the music rack. That piece was getting dog-eared. Then one morning right in the midst of "Little Rondo," I heard a threshing machine whistle. I was off that piano bench and out on the street in no time flat. A few days before that, some monstrous machine had run over a man, crushing one leg so severely it had to be amputated. The leg was buried in Dr. Gove's back yard until the victim died a few days later. It was then buried with him. I'm not sure why such gory details were always of such interest to me, but they were. At any rate that thresher absolutely ruined my musical career. I went home and told Mama "I figured I knew all there was to know about music." I only went back to Miss Hattie's to help her trim hats. The smell of that liquid lacquer in the can on the counter intrigued me!

There was the big event of the summer - the "Chautauqua." Now Mama and Dad approved of that, there was something educational about a "Chautauqua." The Chautauqua tent was pitched on the vacant lot between the public school and Mrs. Katie Yelton's house. In the morning children were invited to partake of a free entertainment. Beautiful women read stories, played games and sang songs with us. In the afternoons there were orators, debates, one act plays and song sessions for the grown-ups. Mama, Dad and Grandma always attended along with almost all of the other Linn residents.

There was always the Osage County Fair in late summer. This year a parade was held on opening day. The theme was war - sailors, soldiers, nurses and red cross emblems on each float. We went almost every afternoon. We loved walking with Mama through the exhibit hall, looking at rows and rows of canned tomatoes and pickles, peaches, plums, apples and pears. There were plates of fresh tomatoes, cucumbers, hot peppers and roasting ears. There were huge pumpkins, squash and potatoes, baked goods in glass counters also jellies and preserves. One afternoon we met Uncle John and Aunt Ida. After we had led them through the exhibit hall and the cattle barn, we headed for the ice cream stand. All of us lined up along the rough lumber counter and had a "dish" of ice cream. There were only two choices in this delicacy "cone or dish." Mama always got a cone. They cost a nickel. Dishes had a bigger dip for a dime. This was a big day, there was a merry-go-round. I don't think we rode on it, but we had a bottle of red soda late in the day. There were two choices of soda, too, - "red or white." How times have changed!

Uncle John and Aunt Ida visited us often. Aunt Ida always brought a baked treat, cake, pie or cookies. She did this regularly until the "Bridge Beach" arrived - as it finally did. We were eating dinner when the "hack" brakes sounded on the gravel road and the driver was saying, "Whoa, whoa, whoa now." Our house was on a hillside. Mama got up to see who was stopping at our house. She spied the crate and turning to Dad she said, "Well I never - I just never - don't tell me that old Bridge Beach is here at last. I've a good notion to send it back." Well it was "Old Bridge Beach" even though it was a New Bridge Beach that was carried into the kitchen and set up - and right there in big raised letters across the hearth it read: "Bridge Beach and Co., St. Louis, Mo." That evening we had biscuits. After waiting all those months we were starved for Mama's flaky buttermilk biscuits made with milk from Old Jers and eaten with yellow butter.

Another amusement for Mae and me was watching people come to the photography shop, "Weeks Studio." Everyone came, it seemed to us: newly married couples to have their wedding pictures made - babies in christening white - families for group pictures - church organizations - anniversaries - and young men and women for individual likenesses of themselves to give to their friends or relatives. Weeks Studio was owned by Mr. Charles Weeks, his wife, and daughter, Miss Ruby. The latter was really the artist. She must have made photographs of everyone in Osage County over her long lifetime. The Weeks had a Jersey cow. When our Old Jers was "dry," we would get milk from the Weeks'. Mr. Weeks brought a square board about 12 inches x 12 inches and nailed it on top of a fence post where our yard fence joined theirs. Every morning I thought it great fun to run across the yard and bring the milk bottle from the post. We would pour the cream off the top to use in Dad's and Mama's coffee and on our hot oatmeal.

Mrs. Weeks liked her milk cool. So every morning in summer she placed three bottles of milk in a little wire basket and had Mr. Weeks hang it down in the cistern. One day he accidentally caught the basket on the pump chain and turned a bottle over. It spilled into the water. Bob Mahon was sent for. He pumped and pumped - milky water flowed out the spout and down our street for several hours. Mama commented, "Guess that will teach her," but shortly after Mrs. Weeks resumed her cooling process.

The summer was extremely hot - sometimes it seemed Mama didn't feel well. One evening she condescended to let us have ice cream for supper. Mae was given a 25-cent piece and told to "ask for a quarters worth" at the drugstore. Mae went obediently up the hill and across the street and gave Mama's directions. Alas! Alas! They had no containers. If she would go home and bring a pitcher, she could have a quarters worth of ice cream. So here she came running back. Mama sent our "old Sleepy Eye" blue pitcher, and we finally sat down in style - eating ice cream out of a "dish" at home! We were getting up in this world!

Every morning Bud would beg to go with Dad if he was getting ready to farm at Uncle Will's. Sometimes Dad would leave extra early to avoid the hassle. He was the only one saved; Bud would be cross all day. "Where's Old Peg? When will Dad and Old Peg come home? Didn't he remember I told him I was going along today?" Most of the time Dad took him along. He wore his brown checked gingham shirt and blue overalls, a wide-brimmed straw hat and a big grin. Dad sometimes worked so late it would be after dark when Old Peg turned into the driveway.

Pete's dark brown curls were admired by the whole family. They were so long he was looking "girlish." Dad had been a barber in his younger days, so he kept saying "Jennie, we've got to cut that youngun's hair." To which Mama would reply, "Yes George, but I don't see how." Pete had them "buffaloed." He kicked, he screamed, he laid on the floor and slapped his ears whenever the scissors and Dad appeared. Finally one day when he was napping, Dad and Mama took each long curl to the guillotine. "Oh, what a storm" when Pete awakened and felt his head. It took days for him to recuperate. Every time he awakened from his nap and felt "lightheaded" the whole kicking, screaming, and slapping his ears was re-enacted. He also was introduced to chewing gum that summer. Mama didn't like him to have it. She was afraid that he would choke on it, because he clamped his jaw tight when anyone tried to remove it from his mouth. Even at night he kept it in his cheek.

One afternoon I was asked to come stay with Mary Marcia Vaughan while her mother and grandmother went to a "social." I was so excited. I just loved Mary Marcia. She was perhaps three and I was about six and one-half years old. Her grandmother "ran the switchboard" - a strange contraption I thought. The operator faced a board full of holes and at intervals, she spoke into a mouthpiece saying "Hello." Without any further knowledge, she chose one of the connections from the base of the board and poked it into a hole in the upper board. Nothing to it I said to myself - anybody could do that. The afternoon was so pleasant, I had Mary Marcia all to myself. We played "Kitty Wants a Corner." In our scurrying for a corner, Mary Marcia slipped on a wet spot and fell. A puffy, blue lump appeared on her forehead. Grandma Vaughan had scrubbed the board floor just before she left for the social. I got so scared; Mary Marcia cried. I cried too. I found Grandma Vaughan's dish cloth in the dish pan, poured some cool water on it from the water bucket and held the cool dish cloth on Mary Marcia's bruise. This is how Mary Marcia's mother and grandmother found us when they returned soon afterwards. When they saw it was only a superficial injury, they started laughing and laughing because I had used the dish cloth. I "dawdled" considerably on the way home. I was sure Mama would find out and scold me because I had let Mary Marcia fall. I could just hear Mama saying, "You're older. You should have known better."

This episode should have been included earlier, before moving to town. School was pleasant, Miss Gussie promised a prize to the pupil who read the most library books. Well, I had already read them all - and I told her so. She explained carefully but thoroughly that I couldn't be considered for the prize because I wasn't a registered pupil. I wasn't yet six years. I failed to comprehend that. She often left me in charge of the 3rd Grade reading classes when she had other duties such as taking care of a skinned knee or checking someone for "visitors in the hair." This process always took place in the cloakroom. On the day the prize was to be awarded, I was just sure Miss Gussie would call my name. I had reminded her several times, but my hopes were dashed when Howard Bryan's name was called. Tears ran down my cheeks - Howard of all people - how dare Miss Gussie give that beautiful copy of "Jack and the Beanstalk" to Howard. I had a very strange reason for disliking him. One morning I had walked to school in the rain. I was soaked. Miss Gussie took me across the street to Howard's mother. She removed my dress, petticoat, shoes and stockings and put one of Howard's long flannel night shirts on me. When my dress and petticoat were dry (hung on the oven door), she re-dressed me and sent me back across the street. But she insisted I wear Howard's long black stockings - and I did. I had been taught never to remonstrate with elders. The rest of the day I was miserable, trying to keep my legs hidden. Somehow I placed all this unhappy episode at Howard's door and now he was getting the prize. I can see how this must have bothered Miss Gussie. Just before recess she went to the library, selected a paper back copy of "Aesops Fables" brought it to my desk and asked if I'd like to have it. I couldn't have been happier - except perhaps with "Jack and the Beanstalk."

One more incident at school indicates how very immature I was. The previous winter during a big snow storm the big boys were sledding on the steep slope back of the school. A game the high school boys played was to see if they could guide their sled with their feet and slide under a barb wire fence safely. One of the High School boys hadn't executed the trick exactly as planned, so the rest of the winter his head was swathed in bandages - his face was almost covered. This gave him an eerie look. The only toilet facility for elementary and high school pupils, teachers, and all was a wooden weather-boarded building in the rear. It was all one building, separated from each other by a wide wall of boards. I wanted so badly many times to use the facility, but I was afraid I'd meet the boy with that unsightly bandage around his head.

As winter approached, it seemed Uncle John and Aunt Ida visited more often. They came to talk about "selling out." There was a nice house in town they could buy not far from ours. One Sunday afternoon all of us walked down Main Street and took a left on to Old Mill Road - just down the hill to the right was the house. It had been the Sullentrop house when Mae and I walked that way to school. On a level spot at the foot of the hill was the power plant where electricity was generated for the town. We thought it was perfectly beautiful to see the coal burning as the fires were stoked. There was also one of our favorite singing telephone poles near the building. So we were acquainted with the road. We didn't enter the house, we just stood in the well-shaded front yard and studied the house. Uncle John and Dad inspected the outbuilding. Could it be made into a suitable stable for Old Maud? Well, with some remodeling perhaps it could.

The next week the deal had been completed. When Uncle John and Aunt Ida came on Thursday, it was to attend to the necessary paperwork at the courthouse. Aunt Ida was still wearing the little bag of asafetida around her neck. We had all become so accustomed to the acrid odor now, it was accepted. If you wanted to love Aunt Ida, you had to love her by either holding your nose or your breath or both!

The farm sale must now be thought about. Uncle John would be selling everything but household goods and Old Maud. Mama and Dad wanted to buy the cattle, because Dad was "on a deal" for a farm near Cooper Hill, Missouri. That was in Jefferson Township some 15 miles east of Linn. Mama was already planning garden, chickens, yard, flowers and orchard. Both Mama and Dad knew the place well. They had each boarded there and taught school at Post Oak. They were almost afraid to hope they could buy it. Mr. Henry Buecker (Adelheid Lahmeyer) had lived there so long, but Mrs. Buecker had died leaving him no heirs. He had to depend on hired help. Dad made a trip to Cooper Hill. He drove Old Peg and the buggy. When he returned the next day, he was happier than I had seen him for a long time. The "deal" had been completed - $19,000. We didn't have that much, but Mr. Buecker would hold the mortgage. Some money would be needed for farm machinery. The sale seemed so positive that Mama and Dad got out the A. J. Child's Catalog again and started making lists. At the top was Item Number 1 - farm wagon. We had to have that to move our belongings from Linn to the "New Farm." After farm wagon came plows, mowers, harrows, cultivator, etc. On Mama's list were a kitchen cabinet, Dutch safe, four rocking chairs, two iron beds, etc. Both Mama and Dad had used the white, marginal, unprinted edge from the Globe Democrat daily paper to write the price of each item so it could be added in neat columns.

Mr. Buecker had set a time to be in Linn at the courthouse - 10:00 AM on Thursday. Dad told all of us at breakfast not to be disappointed if Mr. Buecker did not appear. Dad himself had certain misgivings. Mae and I went to school, praying every step of the way that Mr. Buecker would "show up." I'm sure we were not that excited about another move, but seeing Mama and Dad so happy about something meant it would be good for all. We practically ran home in the evening, tumbling in through the front door. We questioned breathlessly, "Did Mr. Buecker show up? Did Dad buy the farm?" I'm sure we knew the answer before Mama answered. Her face wore that happy expression, and she was singing "When the Roll is Called Up Yonder." I was suddenly reminded that Mama hadn't sung much since we moved to town. She kept on singing as she made biscuits and baked them on the "Old Bridge Beach." When Dad came home from the courthouse, he was whistling "Beyond the sunset's radiant glow, there is a brighter world I know. Beyond the sunset I can see, a brighter world that has no end." After the biscuits and milk gravy were eaten, Dad went into the parlor and brought out his violin. He removed it carefully from the stiff cloth-covered cardboard case, used a bit of rosin on the bow and asked what Mae and I would like to dance to. He played and we pranced - "The Irish Wash Woman," "Arkansas Traveler," "The Eighth of January,, "Soldier's Joy" and everything in his repertoire. Then we sang - "Rye Whiskey, Rye Whiskey"

> If you were the Ocean
> And I were a duck
> I'd dive to the bottom
> And never come up
> But you're not the Ocean
> And I'm not a duck
> So I'll drink to Rye Whiskey
> And hope for good luck

It also occurred to me that Dad's violin had hardly been out of the case for a year. Bud hadn't been turning somersaults. Mae and I hadn't organized any programs. We must get busy!

Once again Mama, Dad and Pete went out to help Uncle John and Aunt Ida get ready for their sale. Aunt Ida was so particular and so clean. Everything had to be scrubbed and dusted and polished. Dad and Uncle John "polished" the farm machinery, harness and tools.

On the sale day, Dad bought several cows. We called them "Old Roany," "Old Horny," "Lily Girl," "Old Whitey," and the bull "Proud Boy." "Lily Girl" was a pure white cow as was "Proud Boy" - all were "Shorthorns." Dad also bought some of the plows, harrows, mower and cultivator he needed.

Now that our farm was definitely bought, Dad was excited about moving. The farm wagon had arrived at Bonnots Mill. Dad had purchased a team of big fine mules from Mr. Jim Agee (Aunt Lulu LeFevre's father). Early one morning he met the hack driver at the livery stable. They tied the fully harnessed mules to the rear of the hack and Dad rode in the seat with the driver. At Bonnots Mill the wagon was assembled and driven home. The mules were named "Old Jim" and "Old Odie." Jim was for Mr. Agee - Odie was for Odie Cooper, Mrs. Agee's son by a previous marriage. Jim and Odie were an integral component of our family life from that day forward. We had no place to keep them at our town house, so they were stabled at Uncle Will's along with the cows until we could get them moved to Cooper Hill. Uncle John would help Dad load the animals and all the other farm implements. Each would bring a loaded wagon to Cooper Hill, stay overnight and return the following day. This was an extremely cold winter - often below zero. They had a choice of two routes. They could travel the Linn-to-Belle road and cross the Gasconade River by "wagon bridge" at Rollins Ferry, or they could travel east down the "Old State Road" and either ferry or ford the river at Cooper Hill. So each trip was an ordeal. This was during December, January and February. We were to be moved by the end of February. Mama and Aunt Ida would visit whenever Dad and Uncle John were away. They were worried when Dad and Uncle John would pull out of our driveway long before daylight on the moving days. Oh, how wonderful those evenings were when the return trip had been safely negotiated.

Saturday, February 27, 1920, dawned cold, blustery and very March-like. Our last bit of household furniture, beds, bedding, table, and "Old Bridge Beach" had been left until last. The Schaeffer piano had been a back-breaking chore at both ends of the journey. In Linn the piano box was brought in from the shed. Dad, Uncle John, Port Wills (Dad's nephew), and some of his strong, young friends then loaded the crate onto the wagon. On that trip Dad went by way of the wagon bridge. The weight of the piano might sink the ferry.

Again it was time to say good-bye to all my favorite things. I had several. The dump down the street where I had dug up beautiful pieces of pretty china plates for my playhouse. The ornate glass panel in the front door. The center panel had pink and blue leaded corner blocks set into it - a swan on a lake, a bird flying with widespread wings, and a duck with ducklings on a sea of blue. The fourth pane never seemed to fit the other three, a pink unicorn in lovely raised grass. I was also busy wondering if any more "jailbirds" would escape, and I wouldn't be there to participate in the excitement. Because the Osage County jail was an old stone structure with only a high iron picket fence around it, anyone impounded there found it relatively easy to escape. That was what happened late one hot August evening when we were sitting on the front porch to cool off.

The prisoners had been entertaining the townspeople nightly with their yelling, whooping and singing much to Mama's dismay. She was deathly afraid they might escape and bring harm to us. And so on this warm evening, we looked up to see three "jailbirds" running pell-mell down the street toward us. Mama screamed, "Into the house, into the house - all of you quickly." But I wanted to see what a "jailbird" looked like. I was truly surprised to see they were people who looked very human. I ran down the steps and out to the picket fence to see what was going on. By this time they were past the house and lost to view in the thick timber. But here came Ed Baumgartner jumping his yard fence, carrying his shotgun and here came the jailer "Foozy Boillet" with his gun and cane. "Foozy" was lame in one leg and couldn't run, but he was shouting orders to his associates, "Go get'um - they knocked me down and nearly killed me when I took 'em their supper."

By now Mama had counted her offspring and found she was one short. Here she came to the front door with a slender peach tree switch in hand. I had to go inside where I glued my face to the parlor window. Soon I heard loud talking from downhill. Here came "Foozy" and Ed and other men following along behind the "jailbirds" who were now in handcuffs. This incident served to intensify Mama's dislike of town living. The remainder of the summer we were not allowed to play in the front yard. The "jailbirds" might escape again.

Shortly before the last load of furniture was ready to be driven away, Mama herded the family to the Weeks' studio to have our pictures taken. There we were, Mae looking very prim and proper. She and I wore our best red serge dresses made with an "overskirt." Bud in his blue serge (wool) knee pants with bright red sweater looking so serious, and Pete sitting on a high stool, eyes full of mischief, wearing a blue and white checked gingham suit. His curls were hard to comb, especially today because only a day before he had removed the chewing gum from his mouth and placed it in his topmost curls. Dad had to cut it out with his barber scissors.

Now all these lovely memories had to be left behind, "jailbirds" included and we, Mae and I, would not see our school friends or teachers again. I don't remember this being too much on my mind. I do remember thinking how wonderful it would be to have a barn, sheds, smokehouse and a house that was ours.

When Dad and Uncle John drove away with the last load, we were so happy - tomorrow we would go to the farm. He and Uncle John would "bach" there tonight. For us there was the short walk down Main Street and to the "Old Mill Road" to stay with Aunt Ida until Sunday morning. Even though we were out in the cold air, I could smell Aunt Ida's asafetida. I couldn't help wishing people would stop having "flu" so Aunt Ida could throw that bag away!

Mae had a thing about feather beds, she couldn't sleep without one. Aunt Ida thought that was funny. She kept telling Mae she would have to sleep across the street with Rosie Schroeder that night because Rosie liked feather beds too. This aroused my curiosity. I knew wherever Mae slept, I would have to sleep too. So I slipped into Aunt Ida's cold, bare but very clean bedroom and examined all the beds. I couldn't see why we would be sleeping at Rosie's - all Aunt Ida's beds suited me fine - all had feather beds. Now I was satisfied. Mae, Bud and I went to play on the "steps." These were earth steps cut into the sod of the lower yard. Each one was about two feet above the lower one - all the way down to the garden area below. We had to jump from one to the other and clamber up again, but it was so much fun.

Soon after supper we were put to bed - on warm feather beds - and soon after it was daylight. The weather was still cold, damp and windy. So what - we were going to our farm. It was also my seventh birthday - February 28, 1920. Aunt Ida thought she ought to bake a cake, so while Mama cleared away the breakfast things and organized our night apparel, Aunt Ida baked and frosted a "plain cake" with chocolate icing. An early dinner was eaten because George McDaniel ("Gib" the taxi driver) would soon be there with his auto to take us to the farm. Just at the last minute Aunt Ida had a brainstorm - "Why don't I go along? - I'd love to see the place." - "Why, Ida, there's no reason at all for you not to go," said Mama. "Gib will be coming right back to Linn." The chocolate cake was wrapped in a newspaper, pinned with a large safety pin on top and Aunt Ida carried it carefully on her lap. She rode in the front seat with Gib, Mama and four wiggly children in the back. We were going by way of the Cooper Hill ferry. Now at last I'd see what that thing was. Dad had tried to explain it to me. Just how anyone could cross over deep water on a ferry was a mystery. When I saw the flat-bottomed ferry boat being brought across from the Cooper Hill side guided along by a pulley running along a cable stretched over the water a few feet above the boat and Tom Cox was also using long oars to push against the river bottom, then I did understand. Mama and Aunt Ida got out and ordered all of us out of the auto. They had heard of autos "missing the ferry" and landing into the river. although I didn't want to, I got out and walked on. Aunt Ida held one hand, Mae held the other. Mama held Pete in her arms and led Bud down the slippery bank. We were safely on. Gib sat at the steering wheel. I thought he was the only sensible person in the group. I held on to the hand rail that run the length of the ferry boat and watched Tom Cox work that oar to propel us to the opposite side. Once across we re-boarded. Aunt Ida actually left the cake on the front seat with Gib while we crossed. We were getting chilly now, the wind was gusty and the auto was open. Gib kept telling us he was sorry he hadn't "buttoned on the side curtains." Gib also chewed tobacco, the juice blew back into my face whenever he expectorated. I also wished he had "buttoned on the side curtains."

Chapter 8

Country Kids Again

It was only a short drive now to the farm. How would it look, what would the house be like, the barn? I couldn't wait. When we turned off the county road and began the descent of a very steep hill, "Gib" applied the squeaky brake. I didn't want brakes. I wanted speed. When we were halfway down that hill, I could look down on the roof of the house. I could see a big, red barn with vertical white stripes. A big, red cow barn, a smaller, square log barn. Oh, hurry Gib, hurry! The brakes continued to squeak. We seemed to move at a snail's pace. Mama and Aunt Ida were also straining. Aunt Ida was saying, "Oh Jennie, just look at that garden spot!" and "There's the spring house just like I remembered it," that was Mama. Finally, finally we had arrived. We were home, and home it was to be for our family for a long, long time. I was in absolute ecstasy. Where should I begin. Time was of the essence. First I wanted to see Dad. I raced up the incline through the white picket gate up the slope of the yard, across the concrete porch floor and through the kitchen door. There was Dad and Uncle John. The latter was standing on the cooking top of "Old Bridge Beach" endeavoring to fit the elbow joint of the stove pipe into an opening in the wall. It didn't seem to fit. It had to be taken down and re-cut to accommodate the length of pipe attached to the stove. As I hastened through the dining room, I noted the heater was in place and two beds had been set up.

The big, sturdy kitchen table was in place in the kitchen and on my first running tour I noticed the Schaefer piano standing sedately in the parlor room. The house was built in a "T" - two rooms and a huge hall in front. The same arrangement upstairs excepting the hall area was divided into two small rooms, with the kitchen and dining rooms forming the stem of the "T." There were porches along each side of the "T" angles - one was L-shaped. There was a beautiful front porch, all decorated ornately with carved panels and gingerbread trim.

In the short space of time I had seen the inside of the house. The wallpaper was very old, in the upstairs rooms it was hanging in long, ragged strips from the high ceilings. Downstairs, I ran out to the "horse barn" - oh how lovely, long dark hallway, four stalls on either side. "Old Peg" and "Old Nell" occupied two stalls. "Old Jim" and "Old Odie" were opposite. There was a nice stairway leading to the hay mow, almost as nice as the one I had left at the Voss farm. I was almost out of breath by the time I arrived at the old, square log barn where Roany, Horny, Whitey, Jers and Lily Girl were contentedly chewing their cuds. Aunt Ida would be leaving soon. I danced into the kitchen so full of adventuresome spirit, I couldn't wait to see the other buildings. Aunt Ida was testing the stove pipe to see if it fit tightly into the stove pipe hole. She patted it rather smartly with the palm of her hand as if to say it met with her approval. The fires were beginning to warm the kitchen and dining room. The beds had been made up with the usual bedding plus Mae's feather beds. Aunt Ida was pulling on her heavy cloth coat and tying her black wool fascinator around her head and over her mouth to prevent asthma. She and Gib took off in the auto. Uncle John had left with his team and wagon soon after we arrived. He was anxious to get across the ferry before dark. Arrangements had been made earlier with Tom Cox to be waiting for both parties on the Cooper Hill side. If he wasn't waiting, there was a dinner bell to ring signaling a fare to be ferried. After another race around the buildings helping Dad feed "Peg and Nell." We milked "Old Whitey" to get enough milk for our supper and breakfast. Fried potatoes, milk gravy, biscuits and Aunt Ida's cake composed the evening meal. Everything was especially delicious because it was cooked and eaten by a labor of love. After all these years I consider it my finest birthday!

Monday morning Mae and I awakened very early. It wasn't quite daylight. We felt so good. We were home. I felt so vigorous I thought I ought to sing. Nothing seemed more appropriate than the favorite "Morning on the Farm." Mae joined in, so did Bud on the chorus and so we sang, "Oh, who wakes first in the morning - Oh, I wonder who - Listen and I will tell you - Cock-a-doodle-do."

Mama and Dad were awake now, the day would be a busy one. Dad always fed the animals and milked the cows while Mama cooked breakfast. Pete Leach, the hired man, arrived from his log cabin down the cow barn road and up the hill. Most of the day would be spent getting the house in some semblance of order. The huge old heater Grandpa Bacon had given us had to be set up in the north room. Pete was dispatched to the Feuersville store, just a hop, skip and jump from our mailbox at the top of the hill, to get additional pipe. These ceilings were high. There was linoleum to be laid in this room. We had the linoleum at Linn. It was a deep red chrysanthemum and green leaves pattern printed on a beige background. The backing was burlap. During the years that followed, this linoleum was trimmed down to fit the dining room, then the kitchen and now is still under the carpeting in the little room upstairs.

The beds had to be moved from the dining room area. But before anything permanent could be arranged, the walls had to be papered. The wallpaper had arrived in Belle at the railroad depot. On Friday Dad hitched "Old Jim and Odie" to the new farm wagon and drove to Belle to bring the huge, heavy cardboard boxes of wallpaper, as well as the kitchen cabinet, Dutch cabinet with frosted glass doors and the new rocking chairs for the parlor. Everything was crated. It was nine miles south to Belle. Dad had to leave very early and didn't get home until after dark. "Old Jim and Odie" were strong but the road led uphill all the way and the mules traveled slowly. But by night the wallpaper cartons were stored in what would be the parlor room. Aunt Ida had been instructed to send Alva Tafflinger over from Linn as soon as possible to hang the paper. The following Sunday late in the afternoon, Alva arrived driving his pretty black mare and buggy with the top down. For the next two weeks, he worked steadily measuring lengths, pasting and walking the scaffolding as the long, white strips of ceiling covered the gray plaster. Then came the gorgeous, silver-striped, violet-patterned paper for the room Mae and I would call ours, silver and deep rose across the hall in the boys' room, a gray and spring beauty spray in the parlor room, gold and silver striped in the hall and north room. All were finished with a wide, wide cutout border and a narrow strip of binder above the baseboard. The dining room and kitchen had painted walls and ceilings.

There was still plenty of cleaning up to do around the outside. Mr. Buecker had also had a sale only a few days before we came to occupy the farm. He had placed a barrel of whiskey just outside the cellar door and tied a tin cup to the top of the barrel. Everyone was welcome to quench his thirst. Some evidently "over-quenched" according to our neighbors.

Chapter 9

Post Oak Sprouts

Now we were in the Post Oak School District. It was a one-room school - one teacher, three directors. I was so excited to get started, but Mama said there was only two weeks left in the term. It was six months total. Mama also said it would be too much trouble for such a short time. I'm sure she had discussed this with Aunt Ida before handing down her supreme court decision. So we helped with anything we were capable of doing around the farm. Pete became my responsibility to get up in the morning, bathe, dress and feed. All day long I was to be his constant supervisor. This wasn't much change; I had been caring for him ever since birth. When he was less than a year old, Mama would send me upstairs to bring him down when he awakened in the morning. I sat down at the head of the steps and "scooted down" while he grasped my forehead curls in his tight, little fists. I enjoyed looking after him. He was at that "who, what, why" stage. He was still wearing his baby aprons although Mama felt he should be in overalls. Baby aprons were popular then, it was a knee-length straight shirt affair made a little full in front where they were usually gathered into a yoke. They had long sleeves and were buttoned down the back. One of Mama's first purchases at the Feuersville Store was to bring home a pair of bib overalls for Pete. Oh my, how proud he was. Now he could strut around with a rolled cuff in the bottom of his overall legs. Now his baby aprons were worn as shirts with a part of the apron tail protruding like Pete Leach and Bud.

Pete Leach along with his wife and their children lived in a two room log cabin on our land. He had been Mr. Buecker's hired hand. He knew something of how the land needed to be handled. The upper field was rented to Otto Wildebrandt and August Gerloff. They had sowed wheat the fall before. This stymied our farming operations somewhat. The lower field was to be put in corn with a strip of alfalfa along the creek. Dad got out the A. J. Child's catalog and ordered the alfalfa seed. Whenever Uncle John visited, he and Dad walked along the creek and studied in particular a place in the bank where it was beginning to wash badly. They thought a "dam" should be built. I listened to every word wondering what in the world a "dam" could be. Very early in the spring, the rains began and continued throughout the planting season. The alfalfa was sowed, and Dad, Uncle John and Pete Leach began work on the dam. This consisted of a bed of rocks - huge rocks hauled down from the hills and placed against the field side, cedar trees were tied with wire in among the rocks, more rocks, more cedars, more wire all in layers - such hard, back-breaking work! It went on for several weeks. Uncle John sometimes came and stayed several days at a time. But most generally Aunt Ida came along. Their was a slat fence around the garden. These were slats perhaps four feet high held together at top and bottom by a smooth wire twisted over and under around each slat. Mama said this antiquated slat-thing "had to go," so new woven wire was brought home from Belle. Posts were sharpened and a new fence was erected under Mama's and Aunt Ida's eagle eye. Then Mama began her chicken-manure-and-horse-manure-and-"rich-chip dirt"-from-the-wood-pile parade. It was quite a distance between these two points. The garden being located up the road and across a branch from the chicken houses, barns, and wood piles. Mama just kept the buckets filled with the smelly stuff and sitting in the middle of the road. Woe be unto anyone who went in the direction of the garden empty-handed.

Along with the farm work there were the trips to the Feuersville Store. We took our baskets of eggs and "traded them out." This meant the eggs were figured at so much per dozen. We asked for "a quarter's worth of sugar - a quarter's worth of coffee - a bar of ivory soap" and these purchases were deducted from the total value of eggs. Mama always figured to purchase less than the eggs brought. Her first question when we entered the kitchen door was, "How much money did you bring home? Where's the bill?" The bill usually would have been folded and stuck under the twine string wrapped around one of the brown paper sacks holding the sugar or coffee. The bill would be carefully studied for errors, then she would count the change and drop it in the Hauptmann's red tin cigar box on the cabinet shelf. For years and years following as we grew up, and especially during the depression, we would go to the cabinet, pick up the "cigar box" and shake it to see if there just might be a nickel or dime in it. The Henry Drewel family lived at the store. There were four children at this time. Alice, a little younger than I - Arthur, Bud's age - and Elmer a year younger. Mabel was the baby. These families came near fitting my idea - there was a baby in almost every one! Sometimes when we carried eggs to the store, Mama would let us stay to play awhile. I really didn't care to play outside. I wanted to examine everything in that old-fashioned country store. Sugar and coffee, rice and salt were stored in large drawers built under the counters. Baking powder, soda, soap, etc. were stacked on the shelf. There were almost no canned goods other than sardines. There were small, glass jugs of mustard. On the counter was a small rounded glass case containing candy. Just a few varieties - lemon drops, chocolate drops, licorice sticks and peppermint sticks. On shelves opposite this grocery counter were bolts of "dry goods" - gingham, voile, organdy, silk in pink, blue and white - unbleached muslin and striped ticking for pillows and feather beds. There were cards of lace and braids for trimming, a few pairs of heavy shoes - men's, women's and children's - socks, stockings, long underwear in boxes. In the center filling a large island space was a huge, glass showcase. In it was a perfectly gorgeous assortment - women's hats, young ladies' hats and children's hats, on other shelves were men's pocket knives, men's suspenders, baby vests, white Meachin china cups, saucers, plates and soup bowls. In the rear, leather harness hung from pegs, over the front door hung a bell which rang when the door opened. These are only a few of the most treasured items stored in my memory bank.

The Drewel children were wonderful playmates. We shared our barn and straw stack with them. They shared their store and neighborhood know-how with us. On the road about halfway between our mailbox and the store lived Dr. and Mrs. Leach with their two sons, Irvin and Basil. Irvin was going to high school in Bland, Basil was in 8th Grade at Post Oak.

The Homfelds were soon met also. A couple of Sundays after our move, we looked down the road which curled around our bottom field to the north. We could see two people moving rather slowly in our direction. This gave Mama and the whole family time to straighten the house, get out the "good white damask" tablecloth and plan a lunch. We had already been advised as to the Sunday afternoon lunch when neighbors visited. Usually this was a very, simple meal, bread, butter, jelly or preserves was the preferred meal. Fruit, pie and cake were also acceptable along with coffee. By the time Mr. and Mrs. Homfeld arrived the floors had been swept and a jar of peaches had been brought up from the cellar along with jelly. The Homfelds had brought their two youngest, Chester and Louis, with them. All were well dressed. Mrs. Homfeld wore a fine, white voile blouse with a black shirt. Mr. Homfeld was wearing a suit and tie. The little boys were about one and a half and three. Now I really found myself struggling to lift these fellows. They were what you might call sturdy. After a few steps carrying them, I decided we would all stay close to the house.

The afternoon was spent in just ordinary conversation - weather, making gardens, chickens - how many and what breeds, household hints. In our case we needed to know just how things were handled, who went to which church, how many children went to Post Oak School and who lived in all the houses around. By the time lunch was over Dad had an invitation to go to Bland with Mr. Homfeld, and Mrs. Homfeld had made arrangements for Mae and me to go to church at the Feuersville Lutheran Church on the next Sunday afternoon. Yes, church was in the afternoon, because ministers had more than one church to serve. Therefore, they had one sermon in the morning and another in the evening. I think another reason might have been the long distances people drove to church. At one time, parishioners had attended church at Feuersville from as far away as Lanes Prairie.

The Homfeld's only daughter was Alma, second oldest with six younger and one older brother. Alma was thirteen, tall and thin for her years. Charlie was oldest, Clint, Clarence, George, Arvil, Louis and Chester were stair steps.

Mae and I thought Sunday would never come. Our black patent leather shoes were worn out. We now had brown leather high-topped laced shoes. Mae's were shiny leather of a finer cut than my more dull ones. Long before noon we were dressed in our red serge dresses, long black stockings and best brown shoes. When Alma came she was wearing her heavy everyday shoes and carrying her brown high-topped leather-laced shoes in her hand. She explained that the road would be muddy so we had better wear our everyday shoes and carry our dress-up pair. I was so disappointed, but I was sure Alma knew whereof she spoke. After all, it was two miles along the road toward Belle from our mailbox. We wore the heavy shoes until we were almost to the church. Then we sat down on a large, flat rock just off to the side of the road and made the exchange. Carefully we concealed our heavy shoes behind a tree and tripped merrily to the big, weather-boarded sanctuary. The people here had never seen us, but most of them knew Mama and Dad from their days of teaching. Mama had attended church there when she boarded with the Wildebrandts. All were of German descent - Dahms, Roehls, Ahrens. These families had intermarried. Four Dahms married four Roehls and together with their offspring made up the greater part of the congregation. The sermon was delivered in German. The hymns were sung in German. So what - I could spend my time looking at the most beautiful painting I had ever seen. It depicted Jesus kneeling in the Garden of Gethesemene. His robe was a bright blue with a red toga over the shoulder. This painting was held in a frame of marbleized wood, all occupied the center of the church between the lectern and the raised altar. Another thing attracted my attention, the huge wood heater in the middle of the church - but the pipe had to extend straight up for at least six feet - then elbow toward the flu hole in the southern wall - it was a long, long way. Big hooks had been secured in the ceiling and fit under the pipe to hold it in place. So while the German service was being held I was busy examining every crook and cranny, all the women's hats and pretty earrings, silk stockings and coats with fur collars. When services ended everyone visited awhile. They spoke in German. I thought it sounded beautiful. I had been deeply impressed with the sincere devotion to prayer books and hymn sheets. Their hymnals had only words - no music.

Even if the language wasn't familiar to me, the people had no trouble communicating by friendly smiles and warm handshakes. Some said, "Bring your Mama and Papa. We would like to see them. We remember." Soon we were hurrying down the muddy road, over rocky ledges, toward home - of course we had exchanged shoes again. That was truly a red letter day, we had ventured out into the new world of new friends, strange languages in which words didn't carry a message but friendly smiles and a painting bridged the gap. We now had a telephone again. The same type we had at the Voss farm only larger and older - our call was one long and two shorts. Homfeld's was a long and one short. Dr. Leach's was five shorts.

Telephones weren't used much except for business. If Mama forgot to write an important item on the store bill, she could call the store and tell me to bring a box of "Arm and Hammer Soda" or "a quarter's worth of rice." The call for the store was five longs, and the phone was in their dining room back of the store. Sure as anything if you were at the farthest point from the phone, that was when it rang!

The rain continued to fall. All spring one heavy rain followed another. The Boyce or Belly Ache Creek which ran all along the length of the farm, could be seen from our front porch as it flooded the farm land again and again. The alfalfa strip looked like a rice paddy. The corn rows looked like we were using surface irrigation.

Mama's brown leghorn chickens were "laying good." We were anxious to have good corn to feed them and our milk cows and "Old Jim and Odie." But the "good layers" were a source of weekly income. They meant we could have a luxury now and then. One day Mama went with us to the store. All three of us, Mac, Mama and I, carried a heavy basket filled with white eggs from our brown leghorns. Mama had promised Mae and me a hat if we worked "good." We had finally got to the day we were going to actually choose a hat from that huge glass showcase. Well actually there wasn't much choice to it. We had been studying those hats since early spring. It was fun trying on several. I knew which one I was going to choose. The one I liked was a black shiny straw "cloche" shape with a bright pink grosgrain ribbon band - a long streamer hung down my back. Mac chose an avocado ribbon with her straw hat. Her hat had a wider brim. Mama even had a hat "laid back" for herself. It was an absolutely stunning creation: black lacy silk over a wire frame - wide brim - deep crown. The crown was surrounded with the prettiest artificial red cherry-like berries with stems, blue silk forget-me-nots, black satin ribbons and bows. Mama spent lots of time tucking her dark hair in here, puffing it out a bit there, turning and twisting her hand mirror to see how it looked in the back. Years later I realized what an important want this must have been in Mama's life. In her teaching days, ruffles and bows and ribbons, especially on hats, were her idea of elegance. I don't recall how much my hat or Mae's cost, but Mama's cost $5 which by our "egg money standard" was unheard of. It didn't take me long to inform Dad how much Mama had spent on a hat. Mama's back was turned toward us; she was stirring milk gravy for supper. Dad whistled as he always did, "Whee, wee," then raised his eyebrows and said, "Well, by Joe, she's got to have her head covered - lots of women get sun strokes from wearing bonnets." But I could see he was really thinking how pretty Mama would look in that black lacy affair. This really gave me confidence in "egg money." Now I could haunt the gingham counter. Mama sang, "In The Sweet By and By" all evening as she fed the leghorns and gathered the eggs.

On the fourth of July, in the afternoon, Alma Homfeld came to visit for a little while. Mama made a "pitcher of lemonade." Somehow Mama thought a pitcher of lemonade was the epitome of a celebration. After Dad read the Declaration of Independence, he went to the spring to fetch a bucket of cool, cool water. Mama squeezed the lemon juice, stirred in the sugar and we quenched our thirst. We were playing "hide and seek" when the mightiest of all the thunderstorms broke. We ran for shelter into the wash house. Just as we got to the door a flash of lightning dazzled us. The lightning had struck nearby. Mama came to the door shouting, "Come in quick; go sit in the hall, I mean right now." The hall was the central location in the house and Mama's "safety zone" for storms. Everyone was herded into the hall and made to sit down: Pete Leach, Dad, Alma and all the rest of us. Then Mama sat where the door opened into the dining room and held us prisoner. The storm was the worst of the season. Bellyache Creek roared and swirled through the alfalfa patch and raced down the corn rows on its way to Big Third Creek.

After the storm cleared, the sun broke through with all the fiery fingers licking at our wet little bodies as we waded the flooded branches and tried to empty the indentations in the soil by running through them barefooted. This rain was becoming worrisome. The renters, August Gerloff and Otto Wildebrandt, came to look at the wheat. They hoped for several days of warm drying sun. This wish was granted. In a few days the Gerloff boys brought in the binder to be drawn by four horses. A crew of "shockers" followed, setting up the bundles on the cut end, capping the stack with a bundle that had been pulled apart at the head end to form a protective umbrella over the shock. This was truly fascinating to see all these men turning the beautiful, golden field of grain into a short stubble with shocks here and there. At noon Mrs. Leach, Lena Gerloff and Alvena (Otto's young bride) came in a surrey (with fringe on top) to bring the lunch. I couldn't understand why Mama had confined me to the yard that day. I was told to "keep Pete out of the way and mind company manners." Mrs. Leach and Lena spread a tablecloth on the ground under the biggest apple tree in the orchard. This tree we always called "Old Spot." The apples were red on one side with green and black spots on the other. On the tablecloth, I could see big white bowls of food being passed around. I was so full of curiosity as to what they were eating. Mama wasn't watching that particular minute so I grabbed Pete by the hand and away we went. By that time, the men had polished off everything in the bowls and it was pie time. Now I had made it to the spring house at the edge of the orchard. Mrs. Leach called for me to come have a piece of pie. I needed no further prodding. Mission accomplished! There was one great big puzzlement still in the back of my mind. Why had Alvena sat in the surrey the whole time. She was young, she was exceptionally pretty but she just sat while Mrs. Leach and Lena did all the work. Later in the day, I asked Mama why Alvena sat in the surrey so much. She looked at me as if I shouldn't have asked that. After quite a long time she answered, "Alvena is having trouble with her mind right now." Far be it from Mama to simply say "Alvena is expecting a baby" - that would have handled matters too simply! Mama loved complications! Besides Mama had convinced me a long time ago that doctors brought babies in that little black bag all of them carried. I was positive Dr. Jones had brought Pete on that extremely warm August morning - only I still hadn't figured out why Grandma took us up the lane to the cow barn. If the baby was in that black bag, why hustle us off to the cow barn. Before long I heard the sound of a baby crying - I said so. Grandma smiled her special smile and said, "Are you sure? I believe it was an old rooster crowing." Because Grandma never tried to mislead me, I found myself wondering if I really had confused a baby's cry with a rooster.

The summer was so pleasant - filled with discoveries every day - exploring fields and pastures. There were numerous brown leghorn hens bringing their broods out of hay fields and from under the building foundations. When this happened Mama would always say, "I've been missing that old hussy for several days." Every old hen was a personal friend of Mama's. She and Aunt Ida had pet names for some of them such as "Old Money Maker," and a non-layer "Old Worthless," "Old Eggless," and "Old Good-For-Nothing" soon became chicken and dumplings for Sunday dinner. The summer brought a wealth of blackberries. Aunt Ida and Uncle John spent several weeks at a time with us. Everybody picked berries. Dad and Uncle John took their big baskets and went to the patch across the creek just as daylight crept into our valley. Aunt Ida and Mama washed and scalded jars, picked over the blackberries, boiled them on "Old Bridge Beach," canned them and carried them to the cellar. In the later morning or early afternoon, Aunt Ida and Mama, Mae and I picked. Even Bud had his tin cup and worked manfully among the briars to fill the big baskets. Sometimes a bread and butter sandwich would be taken along for Pete. I usually managed to help him with this chore, supplemented with a handful of fresh berries, it was ambrosia. By evening there would be rows of Mason jars on the cabinet cooling. For supper there would be a huge bowl of fine, plump, fully ripened berries to eat with cream and sugar.

One day when Aunt Ida was canning berries a jar exploded, throwing berries and juice all over Aunt Ida's best everyday dress - white with big red polka dots. She washed and rinsed and washed and soaked and rinsed but the dress remained white with red and with big irregular purplish polka dots. Mama thought it was amusing but gave no outward indication until Aunt Ida had loaded her berries in the buggy and gone home. This same blackberry incident gave way to another. Aunt Ida thought washing her soiled dress in "good strong soap suds" might erase the stain, so the following morning the enamel-coated boiler was put on the Bridge Beach and Aunt Ida's dress put in to boil. She went out in the yard to find a "clothes stick" with which to stir the clothes. She found one leaning in the small space at the end of the wall along with several others where it joins the smokehouse. This choice stick had a cloth string around one end - like a halter. She picked up the stick and began removing the halter when Pete came along and grabbing the stick out of Aunt Ida's hands yelled, "No, No, Aunt Ida don't you know that's Old Peg?" Aunt Ida dropped the stick saying she had no intentions of "stirring the clothes with Old Peg."

Numerous times during the summer when Aunt Ida would be in Linn, Ellie Nixon would come to help out. Ellie was only fourteen and when she came she had to bring Frank and Rude along. Their mother was dead and their father worked for all the farmers in the community. They lived on Nixon's Ridge just on the top of the hill across the creek from us. Their house was two log rooms separated by a dog run. They helped pick blackberries and Mama baked pies for them. They brought dewberries and took home a cobbler. Anything we could afford to give away went to Ellie and her younger brothers. There were two older brothers Ray and Roy - just old enough to begin working for farmers. Pete Leach wanted to farm for himself so Roy began helping out. Don Shockley was now our mainstay. His family also lived on Nixon's Ridge. These people all walked to Feuersville to the store. Our house was about half way, a good place to rest and drink from our Silver Spring. This spring was renowned for miles around. The water was so clear and sparkling, covered with a spring house where we kept milk, cream, butter, buttermilk, cottage cheese, any food that improved with cooling. The air in the spring house was always cool. A cup or dipper was always hanging on the wall over the deepest part of the pool so anyone could help himself.

These "Ridge" people didn't carry eggs to the store like we did. Ellie always had some money tied in the corner of her handkerchief. Mrs. Shockley always had a flat-like wallet clutched in her hand. She and her daughter-in-law Minnie would explain, "They had to go by Dr. Leach's." Minnie was out of medicine. "The last batch" hadn't done her one "iota" of good. So one morning Mama was washing in the wash house. She was getting ready to starch dress shirts when she thought she saw a hole in the bottom of her white enamel dish pan. She took it out into the bright sunshine and held it up between her eyes and the sun. Mrs. Shockley, whom we called "Fron," short for Sophronia, had an Indian stealth about her walk. So quiet was she, Mama had no idea she was anywhere around when "Fron" poked her between the shoulder blades and laughed. Mama jumped straight up in the air and threw the dish pan in the air. After that it really did have holes. I really thought it was fun to see Mama jump.

It was fun to go to the store with Ellie. She would be by our house very early in the morning. Sometimes we would still be at breakfast. In that case Mama would set out extra bowls of oatmeal or fried squirrel and gravy. There always seemed to be an extra pan of biscuits. Mama always had a motive. After breakfast she would say, "Well, I'd just as well fix up our eggs since Ellie is 'going to the store empty handed.'" Mama never wanted anyone to go anywhere "empty handed."

At the store Mrs. Drewel would "candle our eggs." This was a light enclosed in a candle holder to which was attached a set of dry cell batteries. Three eggs would be held in each hand and run lightly over the light bulb, any inferior egg would be laid out along with cracked or broken ones. Naturally, these culls were deducted from your total count.

Ellie always got certain things - "a quarter's worth of side meat" - "a nickel's worth of salt" - "a cake of Baby Doll face soap" - "a quarters worth of coffee," etc. The coffee was in bean form, weighed out of a big bin or sometimes a burlap bag. The side meat was carefully contemplated from each side on the counter. Ellie would eye the middlin' as it was laid on the scale. "Pa likes it streaked," she would say quickly. On occasion Mama would let us get a nickel's worth of candy. What pure joy to say, "Mix it - some of this and some of this." But Ellie always got licorice sticks or sen-sen as it lasted longer. At home the candy would be poured out on the kitchen table and Mae would be appointed to divide it into equal portions, always putting back a piece or two for Dad. Dad definitely had a sweet tooth. He could hardly eat without something to "top off on," maybe just a biscuit with a bite of jelly or home-made molasses. Quite often Mama made sugar syrup - just sugar and water boiled together - sometimes brown sugar was used. We referred to this as "wipe-it-up." When we said it, it sounded like "wi-bi-dup." However we said it - it tasted good.

Chapter 10

Don't Drink the Water

Summer seemed so short. We had heard all sorts of enticing things about school opening. Mr. Allen Shockley would be the teacher. It would open the first Monday in August. That was certainly sooner than we expected, but it was the usual date for this farm community. The people wanted their children home early in the spring to help with planting. Mama had to hurry with our school clothes. Some hems had to be let down, some had to be mended. Nothing new, except Bud's overalls. When the great day arrived, rain was simply pouring down. We were up early helping with the milking and feeding, straining the milk, scalding jars and crocks, all this in the rain. Mama was frying chicken, making gravy, selecting nice, juicy, red tomatoes. Some of this was for breakfast, some for our school lunches. The rain slackened somewhat, we donned our best plaid gingham dresses, Bud his new blue overalls and ran up the rocky ledge behind the log granary, hopped over the big limestone rocks where Mae and I had our playhouses, passed the pansy patch, climbed the rail fence, raced over more slippery, slimy rocks and out onto the main road. From there it was sticky, red clay mud all the way. But it wasn't far, perhaps a little more than a half mile for us. It took longer on this first morning because we had to pick our way carefully where there was grass or a rock to step on.

We had seen the inside of the school on a very, very warm day the week before. Mae and I had gone to help Mama and Mrs. Leach "scrub" the floor, wash the windows, the blackboard and the desks. As we carried water for all this cleaning, I was constantly envisioning classes in a one-room school. I couldn't quite feature one teacher for all eight grades. I did not wait long to see how all this was done, because now the pupils had begun to gather. The Homfeldo we knew, of course, and the Kracnows - six of each - ranging from eighth grade and what we called post graduates down to first grade in each family. The Hasslers were an interesting family. Zoa the oldest was exactly Mae's age; Floy was one and a half years younger, Coy was another year younger; Buell, Carl, Mina and Dorothy were the youngest. There were the Shockleys: Areba, Eunice and Marvin. Sometimes Oma, an older sister, came for a few days. Leona Nixon, a pretty girl, and only child, was also in the eighth grade. There were Ellie, Frank and Rude Nixon, whom of course we knew and Pete Leach's children, Edgar and Mildred. And then there was Audrey Lange; she was special to me, and over the years she has become very special. Audrey was Mae's and Zoa's age but very small and dainty. She was always well dressed - much, much better than any of the other pupils. Her Dad nearly always brought her to school in the surrey - driving two beautiful, bay horses, "Bop and Barney." There were a few others who attended regularly: Virgil and Agnes Nixon sometimes, and the Drewels from the store, Lee and Elsie Vincent, and Delmar and Gladys Brown.

Mr. Shockley, as all of us addressed him, also arrived early on horseback. There was a small stable down back of the school building about halfway between those two necessary buildings for boys and girls.

Since the red clay was stubborn about being removed from our shoes and the big boys were using the mud scraper by the front step, Zoa, Floy and I found some sticks to use for scraping. This was truly a good place to get acquainted - "What grade are you in? Who are you sitting with? Where are you sitting?"

Mr. Shockley rang the bell. We trooped into the building and plopped down in our "seats built for two." Our teacher looked us over and began rearranging the first graders and shorter people in front - taller, older folks in the rear. Sometimes an older sister or brother was assigned to sit with a timid, tearful first grader. Small feet dangling in the air wasn't such a sin in those days. Mama had made it "crystal clear," I was to sit with Bud to help him get through the first few days. I didn't like it at all. I wanted to sit with Audrey, but I knew Mama would ask as soon as I got home, so I rather timidly informed Mr. Shockley that I was to sit with Bud. While I was imparting that information, Mr. Shockley asked me what grade I was in. I told him, "I don't know." Mama said I was to be in the third grade, so that is where I was placed along with Zoa, Floy and Audrey and Eugene Kraenow.

Everyone furnished his own books. They were passed down like all of our other things from the older to the younger. They were cared for by paper covers or oil cloth secured on permanently to protect from wear and weather. There were always some extra first grade readers and spellers, and some U.S. histories one could buy from those families not needing them that year. If it was absolutely mandatory, we ordered new books. Mama wrote Aunt Ida a postal card telling her to get me a copy of Easy Road to Reading 3rd Grade at the Linn drugstore. In a few days, Aunt Ida mailed the book to me. How proud I was. Such a beautiful green cover. I wanted to read everything in it all at once.

But the first day at Post Oak was one I never forgot. Mr. Shockley sorted all of us out from post-graduates down to first grade and had each class recite as we sat on recitation benches in front of the room. Halfway through the morning a recess was declared. This gave everyone a chance to "run out back," visit a little, play a game of "stink base" or "dare base" or eat a bite from the lunch box. After another round of arithmetic and grammar came one whole hour in which to eat our lunches and play various and sundry games. The lunches were all different. For the Drewels it was the finest of white bread - homemade, and "egg butter." Because of the many cracked eggs brought to the store, they were served in as many ways as Lydia Drewel could devise. The Homfelds had meat sandwiches and pie. They carried a lunch basket; the portions were "doled out" by Alma. The Browns had stewed tomatoes with macaroni and huge brown biscuits and always the fascinating dinner bucket - an oblong affair six or seven inches deep but the lid was the crowning glory. It was a sort of thermos jug, opening on top of the bucket where the lid fitted on and served as a drinking cup.

The Hasslers always had bread and meat along with fresh fruit. The Kraenows nearly always had boiled eggs which they peeled and dipped in salt wrapped in a bit of newspaper. There was very little wax paper to be had. We saved liners of cereal boxes and used it over and over. Audrey always had an extra nice lunch, fine slices of beef on buttered bread, or sliced egg sandwiches with cookies, fruit and cake. Nearly everyone had a jelly sandwich for dessert. Mama was great on "gem cakes" - small individual muffin like cakes baked while she was getting breakfast. Sometimes we had chocolate cooked frosting on them with a sprinkling of coconut. Mama always seemed embarrassed to send biscuits for our lunch (white bread was a status symbol with Mama). But the food we ate was of small consequence, everyone was so anxious to get to the games. They were totally unorganized by teachers. The pupils sometimes played "base" games in which everyone participated. Sometimes we divided into "girl groups" or "boy groups." At one o'clock we were brought back to "books" by the bell.

Geography, agriculture, physiology and extra classes for the post grads were held. Mr. Shockley watched his gold timepiece carefully so that no class would be robbed of its share.

The walk home was pure delight. There were the Kraenows, Drewels and Audrey unless her father came for her as he always did if he could manage it. Sometimes Henry Drewel came for his children in his automobile, especially if it was raining. If he did Alice would usually ask me to ride as far as our mailbox. Oh, how happy I was to climb in and smell that wonderful gasoline-and-leather scent as we dipped up and down the hills.

Each day was an exciting adventure into the unknown realm of the one-room school. We considered book learning a necessity. At home Mama drilled us continually. We went through the spelling lists - over and over - "i" before "e" except after "c" - or when sounded like "a" as in "neighbor and weigh." Then came those miserable multiplication tables - seven times seven - and six times nine. Right in the middle of a delicious bite of fried chicken, Mama would point her big wooden spoon at me and demand, "How much is six times twelve? You need to develop immediate recall." I didn't have that quality, but Mama always attributed great intelligence to her offspring, hoping, I suppose, that one day one of us would develop "immediate recall." I did develop a love for most books. We had such a meager library, only a few worn and tattered volumes in the corner cupboard. The *Dutch Twins*, I had already read at Linn. *Hans Brinker or the Silver Skates*, I read and re-read, as well as *Tom Brown's School Days*. One of the finest was *Grisilda or the Cuckoo Clock*. *Indian Legends* was a new book ordered as a text for an 8th grade class. A few times I managed to slip away from the playground and by good luck I could read a few short stories by borrowing this book from Areba Shockley. It seemed you weren't supposed to read any material not prescribed for your grade, so if Mr. Shockley caught you reading from an unassigned text it was almost a sin!

Life in a one room school was not known for human comforts. In the late days of August the big red wasps were annoyed by human beings inhabiting their domain. Post Oak had an exceptionally high ceiling, the wasps would come out of every crack and crevice, dive and dip and buzz around our heads. According to our teachers, we wouldn't notice a little thing like that if we were really interested in our learnin'. There were also "mud daubers" and the "brown-waisted wasps." They floated in and out of the windows, crawled on the walls, ceiling and anywhere they could.

Each family had a drinking cup, usually a tin 5-center, holding perhaps 1/2 pint. Each person had to obtain this cup from one designated family member who was appointed "keeper of the Holy Grail" in his desk. We usually got drinks only at recesses and noon. Anyone requiring a drink oftener was looked upon as wanting an excuse to go to the little building out back. These little houses were really hard for me to accustom myself to using. I suppose they were for the other small girls too, because we would go in groups. Floy or Audrey would approach me with a rather meaningful expression on their face and say rather hurriedly, "Let's go down by the 'horse house,'" the girls facility being located south of a small building used to house the teacher's riding animal. I was always willing to accompany anyone. Sometimes the building would be occupied by a group of very small girls. All of them too short to turn the big wooden inside latch to let themselves out. In that event we taller ones would break a branch off the silver maple tree nearby, poke it through a wide crack and free the weeping prisoners. This facility for females was always in danger of falling over backwards so in order to perform the door opening trick, one needed to lean forward considerably and pull the door up as well as out. Then getting seated required great agility because the seat tilted upward in front to such a degree that one's backside never dared touch the back rim of the seat. If you made a miscue your feet went up in the air and you might never get out alive. I attended Post Oak school through the 8th grade and this ailing building was never repaired. Girls were required to hang on the "cutting edge" and keep firmly planted on the old rough slanted floor boards in order to perform ones personal chores.

When cool autumn days approached, fires had to be built in the stove. This affair consisted of two drum-like apparatuses - one above the other. The fire was built in the lower; the heat was stored in the upper because the pipe ran through it. Then around the outside was this galvanized jacket. Supposedly the jacket served to help the heat rise and circulate more freely. But there was something amiss with this heating apparatus. It never burned properly. It smoked and smoked until it nearly put our eyes out. It spewed forth soot and ashes every time the door was opened. Mr. Shockley would send word home to Mr. Homfeld and Mr. Hassler and Dad - "The stove smoked." - the note would read. Soon all of them would appear, the pipe would be taken down, disassembled, flue cleaned, stove cleaned, reassembled, fire rebuilt and guess what - more smoke - and more smoke. How my eyes burned! Tears would roll down my cheeks. The stove went right on smoking. Sometimes it was so bad Mr. Shockley would let the fire go out and tell us to put on our heavy coats. Such fun - such nostalgia - one room schools!! All year Mama and Dr. Leach fussed about the water in the cistern. Mama had a great fear of typhoid fever. She was certain it came from drinking "bad water." Most of the time she forced the children to carry a jug of water from our spring and nearly every morning when we would be almost out of sight Mama would come out in the yard and yell loudly, "Don't you all drink that cistern water. If you do you'll get typhoid fever and die." Well nobody in our family wanted to die; we were having too much fun. Our only enemies were red wasps, smoky stoves and now typhoid carrying water!

In spite of such small inconveniences school progressed. We went through our classes: spelling, arithmetic, reading, history, geography, agriculture, grammar and physiology. No such thing as science in those days. No such thing as special education or retarded youngsters. If a child learned slowly he might be retained in that grade. Parents respected the teachers and their decisions. There were no "social promotions" due to "peer pressure." No one felt embarrassed if success were not achieved momentarily. We accepted life as it came - and loved it!

In late autumn the "big boys and girls" began to say such things as "Wouldn't a pie supper be nice." Usually this statement would be made when Mr. Shockley was within earshot. He would usually turn his back and look out the window. (It wasn't the window teacher Press Patterson had painted red over the glass to discourage children watching the road when people drove past.) Such statements continued on the playground. Charles Homfeld was a great organizer. He would say, "Teacher, we always have a pie supper - usually around Thanksgiving." So this was something new to me. I didn't know anything about pie suppers. How that could be exciting, so I interceded Mama. "What is a pie supper? What do people do? Just eat pie?" When she explained that girls brought pies in prettily decorated boxes and boys bought them and then ate pie with the girl whose pie he had purchased - well - that was a horse of another color! If that was the case I could get excited too! But Mama took the wind out of my sails by saying, "You're still too young to take a pie. I'll bake some pies. Dad will buy them and all of us will eat pie." Well, anyhow I could still enjoy the planning. There was to be a "program." I had really been missing my school and home programs. School became heaven, watching our plans develop. A "dialogue" was chosen from an old dilapidated play book and the 8th grade class assigned parts. Each person copied his speaking lines from the book onto the tablet paper and began memorizing them. Everyone was to have a part, a recitation, a reading or a song if you weren't in the dialogue.   Usually the last section of the day following afternoon recess would be relegated for program practice. Usually a tiny first grader would have the welcoming speech.

>I'm just a little girl (boy)
>And I haven't much to say.
>I'd only like to tell you
>You're welcome here today!

Sometimes a perfectly prepared speech would end in disaster. Tears and refusal would result in running to Mama and gluing oneself to her dress tail.

Chapter 11

Pie Suppers and Programs

While we were preparing our program, a date had to be established. Other schools would be having pie suppers too. Everyone preferred a night during full moon. The calendar was consulted and a date chosen. The big girls were very secretive about their box decorations. They whispered among themselves at noon and recess. When the younger girls came close, the whispering ceased. Small fry had been known to give away secrets to the wrong young man. This happened a few years later, when I was considered "old enough" to eat pie with a boy. Mae and I decorated our boxes exactly alike (excepting mine had considerably more flour paste on the outside). Delmar Brown was crazy about Mae and didn't like me at all. My pie was sold first. He bid it up to $5, he was so sure it was Mae's. As I remember, Delmar didn't eat much pie.

When the night finally came, everyone was charged with electricity it seemed. Mama and Dad scurried around, feeding the animals, milking, gathering eggs, putting the chickens in the hen house early. Supper was early. We were too excited to eat much. Mama kept practicing all of us lest we forget our lines or not emphasize a word properly. Mama was a very emphatic person. Put the emphasis on "steering gear," she would emphasize because my speech started by saying.

"The Ford Car"
I don't remember the make or year
It had a Chinese puzzle for a steering gear.

But everyone had his own personal struggles. Mae and I had to get our pies into boxes without breaking the crusts, put lids on boxes and tie with ribbon without turning the box upside down. Mama struggled with supper dishes and clothes for all of us. Mae and I had our red serge dresses laid out upstairs and our high topped brown leather shoes. Bud and Pete had a struggle with Mama over their scratchy "wool britches." Mama always won these battles - scratchy, itchy, too hot or whatever. Mama was the dictator. Dad struggled with the kerosene lantern, even though the moon was full we would need the lantern to come home. So Dad filled the little tank, lighted the wick and set it by the kitchen door. Before long we were assembled. Mae and I were armed with our pies. We were allowed to carry them even though Dad would buy them. Bud and Pete were grumbling and scratching. Mama was telling Bud to concentrate on his lines and don't forget to "emphasize," then you'll forget about your "britches." Dad picked up the lantern and we filed out the kitchen door, across the porch, out the white picket gate, up the slope behind the chicken houses, over the rocks. It was uphill all the way but we didn't notice it. We were on our way to the pie supper. Dad and Mama remarked on what a lovely evening it was. Just perfect for a neighborhood social event.

When we came out on the county road from the wooded area the moonlight was quite sufficient. While we were in the dark tree-studded woods pasture, the lantern had thrown strange eerie shapes around our feet and legs. Now out on the road we could see easily, so Dad lifted the lantern globe and blew the light out. No use to waste kerosene! As we traveled quickly down the hard-packed clay road, we could hear voices farther down the road, beyond the schoolhouse and from far down in the creek valley below. That would be the Homfelds, Nixons, Vincents and Shockleys from the ridge. Dr. and Mrs. Leach and Basil were catching up with us. Doc had a new-fangled device called a "flashlight." Another mystery had entered my young life! Mr. Shockley had arrived earlier. He had lighted the kerosene wall lamps. Someone had brought a Rayo lamp to set on a small table where bookkeeping would be done. Everyone seemed to arrive at once - horses and wagons or buggies filled the playground area - families were alighting. Children were climbing out of the wagon beds and hurrying toward the door of the school building. There were some people I didn't know. Young men with their girlfriends came in buggies. People from Cooper Hill and College Hill, neighboring school districts came because such affairs were popular with young people and were inexpensive unless someone bid against you on your favorite lady's pie. Among the final vehicles to arrive were the Lange's. Bill and Anna were always well dressed. Their surrey was always shiny and "Bop & Barney" were well groomed, fat and sleek, but tonight Audrey had on a beautiful deep aqua Crepe de Chine dress. Such a garment I had never seen except in the Sears & Roebuck Catalog. My old red serge had looked so good at home. Now it seemed dowdy and bedraggled. I couldn't waste time worrying about my appearance. There was so much to see and do.

The pies were being brought in. Someone met each young lady at the door and took the box from her. He carried it carefully to the teachers desk where a number was attached to the box. An identical number was given to the young man who purchased the pie. When the time came to start the program, Mr. Shockley called the children to attention by ringing a small bell on his desk. All of us scurried to get behind the bed sheets we had hung on wires to serve as curtains.

Our program began by singing a group of favorite school songs - "My Old Kentucky Home" - "Annie Laurie" – "My Country Tis of Thee" - then the "Little Girls Welcome" - the speeches, the dialogue. Mae and I sang "Morning on the Farm." I said my recitation about "The Old Ford Car" - striving to use emphasis on "steering gear" because Mama's eyes were drilling a hole through me. Even with the kerosene lamps flickering and dark shadows being cast by lanterns sitting on the floor, I could hear and see Mama's lips forming the word emphasize – emphasize. Soon our program was finished. Buds speech was the final emphasis.

> A wise old owl sat on an oak
> The more he saw the less he spoke
> The less he spoke the more he heard
> Why can't we all be like this wise old bird!

The sheet curtains were pushed back against the wall and the auctioneer was introduced. Terms of pie sales were announced and the bidding began. Mama gave Dad that look when "our pie box" came up. Anna Lange nudged Bill when their box appeared, and so it went, big prices were paid by young men for their favorite lady's pie. It was considered a great prank to "run the bid up" on a particular young man. After the pies were sold, contests were held - such things as the prettiest girl, the ugliest man, the dirtiest feet, also guessing games: how many beans in a jar, or what was hidden in the cake. Once Etta Hassler wrapped a small onion in layers of wax paper and kept people guessing all evening. Each guess cost one cent. After the contests, the pie numbers were called and everyone hunted a seat to eat pie. Oh how good Mama's pie tasted. It was Dad's favorite "raisin receipt." Such crisp crust and of course it had to be something with two crusts that could be held in the hands. Just across the aisle were Bill and Anna Lange eating delicious looking pumpkin pie with whipped cream topping. Behind them Edward and Lizzie Homfeld were polishing off huge wedges of apple pie. Millard and Etta Hassler had brought a huge basket of sugared doughnuts for themselves and anyone who might have been unfortunate enough as to fail in pie buying. Doc had bought Mrs. Leach's pie because Basil was considered too young to "buy a pie." And so the pie supper came to an end. Families collected on the playground. Millard and Etta drove away quickly. Ed and Lizzie led their brood across the road where they climbed through the barbed wire fence, followed by the Nixons, Vincents and Shockleys. All of them soon disappeared into the darkness, but we could hear them laughing as they descended into the creek valley. Mr. Shockley extinguished the lamps, locked the door, hitched his horses to the buggy and traveled quickly up our end of the road toward home. Dr. and Mrs. Leach, Dad and Mom, Mae, Bud, Basil, and I strolled along rather leisurely even though the evening had become crispy cool. The moon was full. The world was beautiful. Dad and Doc observed a "ring around the moon" that meant "bad weather" approaching - so they said!

After the great social event our lives settled down to humdrum everyday living. At home it was feeding chickens and gathering eggs, feeding Jim, Odie, Roany, Horny, Lillie Girl, Old Whitey and Proud Boy. Dad had bought a fine young heifer from Mr. Bill Korte. We called her "Billie." She was a red and white spotted animal - gentle to a fault. She fit in well with our old cows. Dad needed more horse stock so he took Old Peg and Nell to a breeder hoping each would foal. Neither had been bred for several years. He also purchased a sorrel mare from Bill Roesner near Belle. We called her "Flora."

That fall Dad had put the upper field in wheat. We needed a good grain crop to feed Mama's growing flock of leghorns and to take to the mill for our soft wheat flour. It made wonderful quick breads such as biscuits and muffins, but it was not suitable for "light bread," and of course we hoped to have a money crop. The alfalfa crop had produced reasonably well considering all the spring rain. So had the corn. Dad and Don Shockley were busy cutting, shocking and "shucking out" corn to be fed to our animals. Any extra was hauled up the hill behind the granary and stored in our old log crib.

By the time the "bad weather" hit us we were comfortable. The garden had produced well. We had potatoes, canned tomatoes, pickles and sauerkraut in huge stone jars in our cellar along with our blackberries, gooseberries and peaches. Our apple trees were located in the spring pasture enclosed by a fence to keep the animals from them. Apples were a staple - stewed and eaten with biscuit, baked in a pie, fresh in the lunch basket or cooked in a copper kettle until the mixture was rich and dark red (a must with nearly everyone in our neighborhood.) This apple butter was something Mama had never made in large quantities previously. But it had such persuasive powers. No good housewife would be without jars and jars of apple butter on her cellar shelves. Our neighbors ate it with the meat course - spreading an even thin layer on their bread and butter - then dunking it in their coffee. Just writing about it causes my mouth to water. Oh its so good! We also learned that "peach butter" and "plum butter" were delicious delicacies although one tires of them sooner than "apple butter."

It was such fun to get up with the chickens, milk cows, shuck corn for Jim and Odie, carry cream, butter and fresh water to the house before eating a big bowl of hot oatmeal, and polishing off a pan of Mama's hot brown topped biscuits before changing into school clothes. After all this we were admonished to "be good - study your multiplication tables" and be sure to "emphasize the principal word" in each sentence when you were reading. And most of all, don't ask permission to "go out" - do that at recess and noon.

There was one part of the day I simply "doted on." I couldn't wait until Mr. Shockley "called up" the literature class. This was composed of the 8th Grade and post-graduate students. Oma and Areba Shockley, Lee Vincent, Charlie Homfeld, Hermann Kraenow, Basil Leach and Leona Nixon. This class read the classics - *Evangeline*, *Enoch Arden*, *The Great Stone Face* and at Christmas time, Dickens' *Christmas Carol*. The students would read a passage then stop for questions and explanation. I didn't like the latter; I wanted them to finish the story quickly. I couldn't just devote full time to listening either. I had to pretend to be busy with my own assignments. In all the forty years of school teaching, I never came to the Christmas season and "Scrooge" that I didn't credit Mr. Shockley with the knowledge I had of Christmas Past, Present, Future as well as the Cratchit family.

Following the pie supper there was a Christmas program to prepare. How exciting! The tattered Christmas play books were dragged out of the roll top desk - recitations were assigned. Again we copied the lines or verses onto our "Guarantee" tablets and began the business of "memorizing and emphasizing." Alma's mother was making her a pretty brown wool serge dress by a new pattern ordered from Capper's Weekly. When I "ran this past Mama" a couple of times she replied sharply, "I heard you the first time. I guess I'll just catch a few of those old 'good for nothins' and order some navy blue serge. Those red ones you're wearing have seen their best days!"

And so on Saturday morning, "Old Good for Nothing" and old "Sharp Bill" and old "Hide Away" were caught - their feet tied securely with strips of cloth. A loop for your hand was tied into the end of the cloth and away we went to Henry Drewel's Store. Then the old hens were transformed into cash. The following Monday morning, Mae was instructed to purchase a money order, enclose it in the Sears & Roebuck envelope, seal it, place a 2 cent postage stamp on it and see that Roy Jett, our rural mail carrier, took it to Bland. Nearly every morning some one of the older pupils would need to "meet the mail." This needed to be approved by Mr. Shockley. At this time mail was still carried by horse and buggy. So at about 10:30 every morning as Mr. Jett and his buggy approached the school, the teacher would announce, "All you folks who need to meet the mail are excused for a few minutes." On this Monday, Mae attended to the business of the money order and in a few days our yardage of beautiful navy blue wool serge arrived along with a new pattern. Such complications. This pattern required extra cross over front pieces separate from the dress itself. The cross over pieces were stitched into the top of the shoulder seams and ended in a wide belt affair that snapped in the back at the waist. Mama had splurged to get a small piece of beige serge to trim, that is for collar and cuffs. After studying the navy blue stuff for several days she would remark, "That's going to be hard to sew. I'll bet it ravels like the dickens." In the end it was decided Mrs. Leach would struggle with Mae's. Mom and I would struggle with mine. Mama and I could never agree on sleeve length and hem lines. Since Mama was not a gifted seamstress, she always wanted to make my new dresses extremely long. Then as I grew the hemline need not be adjusted. There was one big trouble with that, I never grew enough to ever have the hem in the proper place. Mae was sent up to Mrs. Leach's several times to "try on" her dress. When it was all finished, Mama and Mrs. Leach thought it would "set it off just right" to have an embroidered sunflower on Mae's belt - so off went the crossover pieces to Mrs. Agnes Brown (Delmar's mother) to have the embroidery done in aqua blue wool. My, my how stunning Mae looked in her new serge. Her long dark curls falling away from her forehead. Always we wore bright red silk hair ribbons tied on top of our heads to keep the hair "out of our eyes." One of Mama's obsessions was keeping "one's hair up out of one's eyes" - you'll go blind - "and wearing glasses just ruins anyone's looks" - and don't rub your eyes with your dirty hand - you'll go blind for sure!

The new blue serge dresses released the old red serge dresses for school. How dressed up we were, or so we thought on the day of the Christmas program. And it was actually presented on Christmas day. In those early twenties a Christmas vacation was unheard of in country schools. The members of the board, called directors, met with the teacher to reach an agreement as to whether or not school would be in session on Christmas day. Often this was the only social event for many families. The teacher was expected to furnish a treat and most times a basket dinner preceded the program. On this Christmas day, the weather was warm. Our blue serge dresses were scratchy and my skirt stood away from my body in spite of my efforts to smooth it down closer to me.

Classes were cut a little short that morning. Some last minute adjustments were made to our bed sheet curtains and the safety pins which held them on a wire. We were all ready for company. A good thing because the families all seemed to arrive at once. Millard and Etta Hassler came from the Cooper Hill direction. They were driving "Old Colonel" and "Maud" hitched to the farm wagon. Etta's dinner was packed in a wash tub riding on the straw in the wagon bed. The Kraenow's drove a spring wagon, Bill and Anna Lange their well kept surrey, Mom and Dad usually walked. Soon the school yard was full of wagons, buggies, surreys and horses. Boards were laid on the desks in the center of the room. Tablecloths were spread and all kinds of food appeared: fried chicken and ham, roast beef, home-baked bread, deviled eggs, pickles, pies and cakes. We didn't bother with plates or silverware. We were the early day devisors of "finger food."

How pretty our school room looked. The tree held the place of honor in the south corner by the library. It was decorated with red and green tissue paper chains all made by hand - little narrow strips pasted together with flour and water mixed together. A few stars were cut from a cardboard shoe box and covered with tin foil saved from chewing gum wrappers. Sometimes a few cookies were sent as tree decorations. They always disappeared mysteriously. The big boys would say, "I guess the mice ate them." Today another wash tub stood under the tree, covered with a dish towel. As soon as the dinner was put away the men and boys teamed up in a game of "stink base." The big girls re-combed their hair, and tried to make themselves as pretty as possible. Alma was beautiful in her new brown serge and brown hair ribbon with brown high topped shoes. Mae was very dignified and pretty in her blue serge. I was dying to partake of the stink base game but the occasional gleam in Mom's eye meant "No you don't," so I stood patiently by, waiting for the program.

Promptly at 1:00 p.m., Mr. Shockley rang the bell. Parents and small children filed in and occupied students desks. The tall men sat sideways because desks would not permit long legs to slide under. The pupils (about 35 of us) crowded behind the bed sheet curtains. We always opened such occasions with a song sung by the entire student body. No musical accompanist - only a few really musical voices but everybody stood in place and made a noise. Gladys Brown sang quite well. She usually hummed a few opening notes then all of us joined in. Every school I ever knew had a "set" of twelve paper bound copies called Golden Book of Favorite Songs. Sometimes three or four people shared one book. At this Christmas time we sang "Oh Little Town of Bethlehem," "Away in the Manger" and "Silent Night." This was followed by speeches and readings and short one act plays - often they had no connection with Christmas at all. When the program was finished, Mr. Shockley stood up and made a short address, sometimes being very complimentary to his 8th Grade and post graduate class for having done so well in the classics and ranking high on examinations. These questions were sent quarterly from the county superintendent office in Linn. (M. O. Reed was county superintendent) These questions were always a source of great concern to me. They were printed on a long sheet of onion skin paper perhaps 12 in. x 24 in. The teacher copied the sets of questions on the blackboard beginning with arithmetic. He then waited until everyone was finished before erasing the arithmetic and copying the grammar questions. This process was repeated for at least two days until all the subjects had been examined. The papers were then collected and graded. In early days, they were sent to the county superintendent's office for the grading process.

Mr. Shockley also gave a brief resume of what each grade had accomplished and just what he was attempting to teach. Sometimes parents had questions but generally everyone seemed pleased with the progress of their offspring.

This Christmas day ended with passing out small brown paper bags of rock candy, peanuts and chocolate drops. The mysterious wash tub was uncovered to reveal beautiful popcorn balls that Mrs. Etta Hassler had brought. A box of stick candy was passed among the adults and small children. The day was more than satisfactory. It was one of those that left a sweet, sticky taste in your mouth. And sweet, sticky memories in your mind never to be forgotten. It was all done too soon. The bright December sunshine was slipping rapidly behind the hill as we hurried home to do the evening chores. There was always corn to be shucked for Jim and Odie, Peg and Nell. Corn to be shelled for Mama's brown leghorn layers and Lily Girl, Roany, and Old Whitey were bawling to be let in to their calves. Mama's voice was a little sharp as she ordered us to "Hurry up and get your everyday clothes on" and get out there and "tend to the chores." We always knew what Mama was going to say. Consequently, we were usually pulling on our everyday clothes before she remembered to instruct us. And always when the whole family had been away from home a few hours, the wood fires had burned out. Mama always ran her "stove catch" through the ashes several times to let the ashes fall into the hearth of "Old Bridge Beach." They did not fall into a hopper beneath the fire box as in most stoves. Dad was always careful to see about a supply of dry fine kindling or chips, to start a fire quickly. A sack of corn cobs was generally close by in those days. How good they smelled when the fire blazed up quickly. As soon as the fires were rekindled and our clothes were changed, Mama went out to gather the precious eggs and we had to look everywhere. Not only in the regular nests in the hen house, but under the feed boxes in the barns and in the hay lofts because in winter eggs left uncollected would freeze. Such a mess in the nest, eggs stuck together from those which had frozen and cracked. If this happened, we salvaged what we could. The damaged eggs would be placed in a bowl and Mama would announce, "Looks like we'll have eggs for breakfast." I didn't like that because eggs once frozen never cook properly. The yolk stands up in a firm golden ball and doesn't seem to want you to eat it. It can slip and slide all over your plate while you try to pin it down with your fork.

Darkness fell early. We had to hurry with the milking and feeding chores. The warmth of the day had changed quickly into a chilly windy December night. We were just finishing our supper when we spied a lantern light seeming to move all alone along our lower field. Soon Charley and Alma Homfeld, Basil and Irvin Leach, Mae and I were enjoying a merry game of dominoes spread all across the big dining room table. Of course we took time out to recall the exciting adventures of the day. Alma was still dressed in her pretty brown serge and was permitted to wear her new brown shoes. After all this was Christmas! We were even permitted to stay up a little later but all farm children knew better than to visit more than a couple of hours because its always - "Morning on the Farm."

Farm families in our neighborhood did not celebrate Christmas with great enthusiasm or great extravagance. Usually it was a one day affair either visiting or having company. Many times the Christmas dinner was postponed until the following

Sunday. Neither was there great cause to rejoice and be happy, because property taxes and interest on borrowed funds were due. These were the subjects discussed every day during December. It seems in my mind's memory bank that Mama and Dad were always worried. What did they own that could be converted into cash? This first year was especially hard on the farm. All the spare cash had been used to pay on the land, purchase the mules - Jim and Odie, some machinery, seed, and oh, there's so many things needed to start a farm. Besides the heavy rain of the spring had not been conducive to the best of crops. All these things, added to the fact that we had not had access to our upper field, had culminated in a rather bad year financially. Every evening at supper the discussion would be sure to go something like this – Mama: "Now Dad I've been studying about the taxes - we can get along with less meat - we'll just sell one of those hogs we saved back to butcher." Dad's eyebrows would draw closer together at first then he would raise them and frown - "No, now Jennie -I've been studying too - I think we had better sell another calf and maybe some corn. Someone in the Belle or Bland community will be wanting a fine bull calf. We'll run an ad in the paper." Always it was a sacrifice. Always lots of discussion. What could be turned into cash with the least detriment to the family. Somehow, some way, the taxes got paid - only to be replaced in our supper conversation with the word "interest." Always on March 1st Dad had to pay a visit to Mr. Henry Buecker who now lived in Cooper Hill (in the Ed Leach house). Minnie Kopp took care of him as she had on the farm. But on the farm she had helped with farm work too, such as driving a horse to the hay fork, splitting wood, feeding the animals, shucking out the corn and shocking wheat in the field.

But December through March were lean months with never a spare cent in the cigar box. Mama would squeeze the egg money to pay for sugar, coffee, navy beans, rice and as a special treat, a quarter's worth of raisins to eat with our rice. This dish, a favorite for supper, was served warm with sugar and Old Jers' cream. Often Mama made a pan of biscuits to eat with the rice and that was it! Perhaps a glass of milk or a few warmed over scraps leftover from dinner made up most evening meals.

John Hodges, born Sept. 5, 1787. Father of
Theodosia Lorraine Hodges, grandfather of
Theodosia Mitchell LeFevre, great
grandfather of Jennie LeFevre Bacon, great
great grandfather of Grace Bacon Ferrier.

John's wife, Theodosia Alford Hodges,
great great grandmother of Grace Bacon
Ferrier.

Sarah Jane Shepard Bacon - Our great Grandmother, wife of John Overton. Lived to be 100 years old, born in St. Louis on Feb. 18, 1818. Called Grea' Granny.

Charles P. Bacon family group around 1895. Front from left to right: Alta Josephine Bacon, Charles Porter Bacon, Amelia Vaughan Bacon, daughter Viola Belle Bacon Wills, her son Logan Prescott Wills. Rear: John Rueben Bacon, William Joseph Bacon, Mary Matilda Bacon, Allen Menefee Bacon, Joseph H. Wills (son-in-law), George Bacon (age 16). Some of the young men, Al Bacon and the Wills boys had planned to go exploring for land in Texas, as grandma's sister Mary Jane Thornton lived in Texas. Later they planned to go prospecting for gold in California. But before they got organized, both families came down with typhoid fever. As a result, Uncle Al had his hair shaved. The trip never materialized.

The one hundredth birthday of Grea' Granny, Sarah Jane Shapard Bacon, celebrated February 18, 1918. She died only two weeks after this occasion. Sarah sits in the center holding the American flag, surrounded by her relatives and descendants. To her rear standing are her two sons James Bacon, Charles Bacon, his wife Amelia and Joyce Bacon, widow of Joseph. In the front row left side are the children: Eleanor Green, Grace Bacon, Mae Bacon, Russell Bacon, King Bacon, Charles Bacon. Behind them are: Till Green, Viola Wills, Logan Wills, Will Bacon, Joseph Wills. Back row: George Bacon Sr. holding George Bacon Jr., Charlie Laughlin, Jennie Bacon holding Ellis Bacon (infant), Alta Pinet, Marjore Pinet, Tip Laughlin, Ida Bacon, Viola Bacon. On thee right sice are three boys in front: Herman Fisher, Tom Fisher, Kenneth Berry. Middle row: Allen Bacon, Richard Bacon, Cora Vaughan, John Bacon, Charles Vaughan, Lafe Vaughan, Porter Wills. Back row: May Vaughan, Eda Fisher, Eva Fisher, Eveline Fisher, Fred Fisher, Mrs. Branson. The inscription on the face of the photo reads: Centennial Birthday Celebration, Mrs. Sarah J. Bacon, Linn, Mo., Duncan, Belle, Mo.

Mama, Jennie Lorraine LeFevre,
shortly before she and Dad were
married, around 1909

Dad, George Bacon, around 1909

Uncle John Bacon around 1905

Aunt Ida Bacon around 1905

Allen Bacon and Viola Branson
wedding picture, 1904.

Uncle Will Bacon with ducks and
heads of ducks he had killed on the
Gasconade River

Wedding picture of Uncle John and Aunt May Hancks, taken around 1898 when John was a medical student at St. Louis University.

LeFevres and Bacons. In the rear from left to right, Mrs H. M. LeFevre Mrs. Theodosia LeFevre (grandma). Children left to right: myself, Russell LeFevre, Mae. Taken in 1917 or 1918 on a long hot summer afternoon. We had been to take Reta to her boarding place (maybe when she taught at Plattner's). On the way home we had a flat tire so while Everett patched the tire, Buell took the picture. The LeFevres were still living at Aud, Missouri and Mae and I were visiting.

Mama, Jennie Lorraine LeFevre at age 4 around 1884. Mama wasn't in a good humor on the day this picture was taken. Aunt Belle had let the water get too hot for bathing and had almost burned Mama's feet. To further infuriate her, she had seen some ripe cherries on the way to Linn and Grandpa wouldn't stop to pick them for her. Aunt Jennie Greaves sent the material for the dress she is wearing. Aunt Jennie was Grandpa's sister and lived in Cambridge Springs, Pennsylvania.

My mother, Jennie Lorraine LaFevre. I call this photo "Mama and her hat."

Dr. Harry Mitchell LeFevre, Mom's brother, when he graduated from Louisville, Kentucky medical school in 1898.

The Louisville College of Medicine, graduating class number 3, 1898.   Student number 9 is Dr. Charles T. "Doc" Leach, number 10 is Dr. Harry M. LeFevre. Yes, that's a **cadaver** they're standing over.

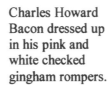

Four Bacon children in 1920, left to ight: Mae, Grace, George Jr., Ellis.

Charles Howard Bacon dressed up in his pink and white checked gingham rompers.

Charles Howard Bacon as a young man, standing on a chair.

Mae, Bud, Grace Bacon around 1916.

Indian Creek School around 1908. Folks who taught there included Mom, Dad (the teacher pictured here at the left), Grandmother LeFevre, Harry LeFevre, Belle Pearl, Aunt May Hancks.

Uncle Harry LeFevre leaving Belle to ride horseback to Shelbyville in the spring of 1925 in order to transfer his medical practice to that city. He made this trip on horseback because he was never very comfortable with automobile travel.

Post Oak School children in the spring of 1924. First row left to right: George Bacon Jr. (Bud), Bernard Kraenow, Buell Hassler, Elmer Drewell, Troy Vincent (behind Elmer), Elwood Patterson, Louis Homfeld, Carl Hassler, Ellis Bacon (Pete), Wilbur Vincent, Arvil Homfeld. Second row: Adolph Kraenow Jr., Virgil Nixon, Harvey Redden, Eugene Kraenow, George Homfeld, Coy Nassler, Audrey Lange, Lillie Redden, Grace Bacon, Alice Drewell, Floy Hassler. Back row: Delmar Brown, Clint Homfeld, Paul Patterson (teacher), Clarence Homfeld, Mae Bacon, Zoa Hassler, Esther Kraenow, Amanda Gerloff.

Belle High School class of 1924. Front row left to right: Willa Johns, Orval Lehnhoff, Ruby Travis, Harry Travis, Hazel Ridenhour, unidentified boy, Reta LeFevre, John Licklider, Iva Decker, James Johnson, Marguerite DeLap, Hazel Johnson, Pearl Dingley, Buell LeFevre. Second row: Opal Hasty, James Rethemeyer, Mildred Manicke, Hursley Rogers, Gladys Rohrer, Alfred Dreysse, unidentified girl, Mabel Love, Ray Biles, Lillie Swanson, unidentified girl, Vic Langenberg, ?? Thompson. Third row: Paul Breuer (superintendent), Clinton Woffard, unidentified girl, unidentified girl, Orpha Gieck (teacher), unidentified boy, Alex Tellman, Wade Wallace, Bryce Jett, Earl LeFevre. Back row: Virgil Breuer, Lavada Mee, Boyd LeFevre, Zelma Mitchem, Chauncy Pointer, Oda Duncan, Earl Milam.

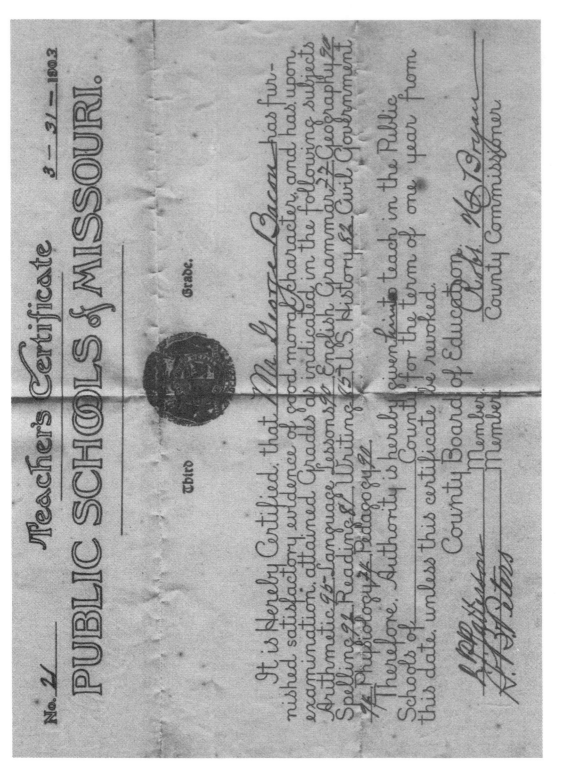

No. 2

Teacher's Certificate 3 — 31 — 1903
PUBLIC SCHOOLS of MISSOURI.

Grade.

Third

It is Hereby Certified, that Mr Gustie Bacon has furnished satisfactory evidence of good moral character, and had upon examination, attained Grades as indicated in the following subjects. Arithmetic 95 Language Lessons 96 English Grammar 95 Geography 95 Spelling 95 Reading 97 Writing 95 U.S. history 95 Civil Government 95 Physiology 94 Pedagogy 92

Therefore, Authority is hereby given him to teach in the Public Schools of _____ County for the term of one year from this date, unless this certificate be revoked.

County Board of Education.

L P Pittman _____ Member.
A. A. A. Peters _____ Member.

Geo. McBryan
County Commissioner.

Teacher's certificate for Papa, dated March 31, 1903. Valid for teaching a term of one year.

Certificate of Promotion

This Certifies that *Grace Bacon* has completed the work outlined in the S Course of Study for the *1a* Grade, and hereby promoted to the *2nd* Gr

Gussie Gove tea

R. H. Bryan, Co. Supt.

Needs practice in writing

BOOKS TO BRING

If promoted you will be expected to bring opening of the school next year, 1919, the books cated by the teacher in the blanks below.

Reading _____
Writing _____
Spelling _____
Language _____
Grammar _____
Arithmetic _____
History _____
Civil Government _____
Physiology _____
Agriculture _____
Drawing _____

OSAGE COUNTY
1918 — PUBLIC SCHOOLS — 1919
R. H. BRYAN, Co. Supt.

REPORT CARD

Report of *Grace Bacon*

a pupil of *Linn* School

Age *5* Grade *1* Class "D"

STUDIES	1st Quar.	2nd Quar.	3rd Quar.	4th Quar.
Reading	E	E	E	E
Writing	P	M	M	M
Spelling	E	E	E	E
Language	E	E	E	E
Grammar				
Arithmetic	G	G	G	G
History				
Civil Government				
Physiology				
Agriculture				
Drawing	M	M	M	M
Music	E	E	E	E
Attendance	E	E	M	E
Deportment	G	G	E	E

INDUSTRIAL WORK

GIRLS	1st Quar.	2nd Quar	3rd Quar	4th Quar.
Sweeping			G	
Dusting				
Ironing				
Sewing				
Washing Dishes				
Keeping House Tidy				
Bread Baking				
Cake Baking				
Churning			G	

BOYS				
Feeding Stock				
Feeding Poultry				
Milking Cow	✓			
Providing Fuel				
Currying Horses				
Keeping Yard in Order				
Clean'g & Bed'g' stalls				

TEACHERS' SIGNATURE

I Quar. *Gussie Gove*
II Quar. *Gussie Gove*
III Quar. *Gussie Gove*

NOTICE TO PARENTS

You will assist the teacher very much by co-operating during the school year in the following plan:

Under "Industrial Work" please report to the teacher each quarter the progress made by your child home in some of the different divisions there out ed, using the letters E, G, M, P, to denote excellent, good, medium, poor, respectively. Let each child have more of the it s his own work on which ill be grade. grades on op side with

RE

I

II

My report card from first grade, in 1919. The teacher was Gussie Gove. Mama had <u>stitched</u> the aged report card together to preserve it. Note the "industrial" skills that were stressed in this country school.

Belle High School sophomore class in 1928. Front row, left to right: Irene Phelps, Wilbur Matthews, Grace Bacon, Harold McQueen, Hazel Pointer, Mary Love. Middle row: Lorene Morelock, Lillian Litton, Sophia Lehnoff, Edrie Strain, Irene Morelock, Reva Hartley, Fern Morelock. Back row: Right Smith, Mable Branson, Clarence Klaas, Reba Lore, Erma Garner, Mildred Harris, Narvin Groff, Sylvia Picker.

Belle High School class of 1930. Front Row left to right: Eunice Newbound, Iva Owens, Logan Steen, Ollie Rogers, Leona Picker. Back Row: John Owens, Howard Maddox, Vernon Travis, Ralph Tynes, Hadley Strain, Sammie Licklider, Wade Harris.

School fair in 1929. Front row, left to right: Florence Poor, Sylvia Picker (Harris), Grace Bacon (Ferrier), Buelah Ridenhour, Irene Jett (Pendleton), Reva Hartley (Picker), Iva Owens (Cook), Anna Isenberg (Verhoff), Opal Smith (Branson), Ruth Tynes (Paschel), Mildred Mason, Jewell Kocnig (Smith). Back row: Lillian Litton (Epstein), Mabel Branson (Hinson), Lorene Morelock (Nicholson), Reba Lore (Dingley), Anna Wieman, Hazel Pointer (Boesch), Hazel Castle (Biles), Fern Morelock, Mabel Ridenhour (Harrison), Mabel Rogers (Garver), Mary Love (Pearon), Sophia Lehnhoff (Biehl).

Orpha Picker Keeney, our high school friend.

H. C. Green and wife Till Green,
Alta Pinet and husband Vic Pinet,
Allen Bacon and wife Viola.

Ida Benson Bacon, Alta Bacon Pinet in a buggy drawn by Old Maud, just prior to John and
Ida Bacon moving to California around 1908.

Charles P. Bacon's birthday in 1937. Viola Bacon, Papa, Mama, Lena Bacon, Janet Bacon, Mae Leach holding Yvonne, Bud, Alta Pinet, H. C. Green, Stella Bacon, Till Green, Allen Bacon, C. P. Bacon, Russell Bacon, Scott Bacon, Will Bacon, John Bacon, Birdie Wills, Paul Bacon.

George Bacon, Allen Bacon and unidentified man around 1900, when they were working on the construction of Rollins Ferry Bridge.

Four generations of Bacons. George Bacon (2), Mae Bacon Leach (3) holding Yvonne Leach (4), Charles Porter Bacon (1).

This the ship that brought John Albers from Germany to America. It is named the Vaterland, which means Fatherland in English.

Uncle John with his team,
"Belle and Katie."

Hershel Rogers, Earl LeFevre and Boyd LeFevre. Earl taught at Post Oak School 1924-1925

Post Oak School in 1914

A group of Royal Neighbors of America, the chapter from Cooper Hill, shown here in 1920. This organization was a major part of the social life in this small burg. Royal Neighbors was the sister organization of the Modern Woodsmen of America. Left to right: Elsie Renfrow, Dora Baker, Wilhelmina Baker, Katherine Brown, Anna Brown, unknown, Cynthia Enke, Lena Leach, Emma Busch, Margaret Elsner (Aunt Mag), Nora Rogers, Eliza Leach, Amanda Branson, Ida Elsner, Mary Smith, Farida Langenberg, Loretta Jett, Elizabeth Reuter, Anna Langenberg, Dora Reuter Bock Lange, Nettie Miller, Viola Branson, Della Miller.

Chapter 12

Fourth of July – New Ground and Ticks

When March arrived with its blustery winds and interest worries it also brought the end of the school year. Great excitement had accompanied the preparation of another program. But this time there would be 8th Grade graduation for Charles Homfeld, Basil Leach, Leona Nixon, Lee Vincent and perhaps others. This "last day of school" has stood out in my memory for all these seventy some years as one of the happiest events in my young life. Again we had prepared skits, recitations, one-act plays and songs. But it was different in one respect. There was to be a big basket dinner and parents were invited to spend the day. Most parents were glad to respond. They came early to listen to classes recite. Some like Millard and Etta Hassler came before 9:00 AM since they had at least one child in each grade - none should be slighted. All morning parents and visitors arrived: Mr. and Mrs. Bill Lange, Mr. and Mrs. Ed Homfeld, Mr. and Mrs. Henry Drewel in their automobile; they were the only family in the whole neighborhood to have such a conveyance. About noon, Mr. and Mrs. Jim Nixon drove onto the playground, found a post oak tree along the line fence and tied up their sorrel mares. Mrs. Nixon better known to all of us as Aunt Lizzie, was carrying a package carefully wrapped in newspaper. I found later it contained Leona's coral silk dress she had made herself especially for her 8th Grade graduation. Also Leona's fine brown leather high topped shoes were in the original box. Somehow Leona managed to trade her school gingham for the beautiful coral silk and her rough everyday school shoes for the shiny brown leather. All the grown-up girls, Leona, Oma and Areba Shockley, re-combed their hair in the "latest style." This was quite an art. Most parted the hair in the middle, drew it down over the ears at which point little pads of black gauzy material was fitted over each ear, the hair combed over them and then the hair was drawn into a bun at the back. These humps over the ears were referred to in our plebeian way as "Cootie Garages."

All morning Mr. Shockley had gone from 1st Grade reading to 2nd Grade to 3rd, 4th and on to his 8th Grade and post graduates. Each one stood, faced the room full of visitors, read a paragraph and re-seated himself on the long recitation bench. Now that all students had "shown off," Mr. Shockley looked at his gold pocket watch and announced it was 12:00 noon. Again the boards and table cloths appeared and out of baskets and buckets and tubs came the platters of fried chicken, fried or boiled ham, baked chicken, home-made bread, pickles, deviled eggs - food easily handled without plates. When it was time for pie and cake, Dad eyed Mama's gooseberry pie, but it was somewhat juicy. He made a remark saying he would drip juice. Liz Owens, who was Mr. Shockley's sister- in-law, was quick to remedy the situation. She picked up a slice of bread, placed a good-sized portion of pie on it and handed it to Dad. His eyes bugged out and he said "Liz, do you mean I have to eat the bread to get the pie?" Liz thought this was funny - she laughed loudly and asked Dad if he could figure out a better way. Dad ate the pie/bread sandwich carefully considering each bite as he did so. Just where could he manage to get pie without so much bread?

As we ate our crispy chicken and coconut cake, the rain poured down. At times it seemed determined to pound holes in the metal roof. Thunder and lightening made conversation almost impossible. Many of us longed to visit the "little leaning room" out back. Mae, Alma and I all three were wearing our good brown leather shoes. Mae and I had on new gingham dresses made by the same pattern as our blue serge. We certainly didn't want to risk getting our shoes muddy or our gingham wet. Gingham shrank and puckered. My gingham was a red, yellow, brown plaid thread woven into an off-white background. The raised threads looked funny when damp. We waited as long as we could for the rain to slack. When it did a bit we all made a dash for the "leaning tower." The afternoon was pure Heaven listening to the final rendition of "My Shadow" - "Old Dobbin and Me" - "America Tis of Thee" - and "I'm Just a Little Girl," etc. The final glory came when Mr. Shockley stepped forth in his army uniform and presented diplomas to Leona, Basil, Charlie, Lee and Areba. Leona then recited a long, prosy speech concerning Missouri's Centennial - "A Golden Smile and the Folks Worth While." This ended our first year at Post Oak. Mr. Shockley had been contracted to teach another term. Now it was time to begin another crop year. We would likely not see the Hassler children, Zoa, Floy, Coy, Buell, Carl and Mina, through the summer, or the Vincents, Reddens and all those who lived on the Cooper Hill Road.

Even though the rain fell and the creek ran bank full, the "dam" held. Uncle John and Aunt Ida came often, he and Dad plowed the fields, built fence, split fence posts, cut more cedars, sledded more rocks and tied them into the dam. They helped Mama and Aunt Ida put in the garden; they seeded the meadows for better hay; they painted the buildings; they repaired foundations and from daylight to dark, all of us flew from one task to another. Once when this wonderful uncle and aunt came, they brought me a copy of *Paddy Muskrat*. They thought it great entertainment in the evening to listen while I read the whole book to them. There was one chapter where Paddy's uncle and aunt came to visit. They expected Paddy to furnish sweet tuberous roots from the creek bank where he lived, for food. One day Paddy grew tired of digging sweet roots, so he asked his Uncle how long he intended to stay. Uncle replied, "Auntie and I intend to stay until the fall rains come." So apropos for all of us and the rain. Uncle John would laugh and whistle and say, "Ida, I guess that's how long we'll visit in Jeff Township." But right at that time he had his eye on a good farm just across the Gasconade River from us.

The following summer was an adventure from beginning to end. Along the school path on the gentle slope of the hill was an outcropping of big, flat limestone rocks. There Mae and I spent hours furnishing our rock playhouses. Mae's rock was the living room. Mine was a combination kitchen and dining room. One smaller flat rock balanced on top of another larger flat rock became an imaginary cabinet, dresser or piano, and a rather large flat rock balanced on four small rocks at each corner was the dining room table set with bits of broken china and glassware. How time would fly as we lived in our make-believe houses. The afternoon shade was cool. The breezes helped us sweep leaves from our rocky floors, but Mae's living room was almost completely carpeted with dark green moss. I envied Mae her dark green moss, but her rock slanted so much she had trouble keeping her piano set up. The top of that piece of furniture was always toppling off and rolling downhill. These marvelous make-believe playhouses furnished many hours of joy in the years of our blessed childhood. When Zoa, Floy and Coy Hassler came to visit or Audrey Lange or Alice Drewel - in good weather - the playhouse was where we could be found.

Dad was also clearing a patch of new ground on the tip top of the hill across the creek from the house. Clearing new ground is no easy task. Trees, stumps, logs, sprouts all had to be removed by human hands and mule team strength. All of us worked at it, piling brush, carrying tree limbs, doing anything our small hands could handle. One extremely warm spring day, our work was rudely interrupted by a heavy thunder storm. Mama, Aunt Ida and all the children took a shortcut down the steep hill hurrying to get across the creek. Dad and Uncle John and Pete Leach were close behind with Old Jim and Odie. As the rain came down, we began to try to brush away the huge drops from our arms and legs. It was then we found all of us were simply covered with both large and small brown wood ticks. When Mama and Aunt Ida saw them on us they began their usual - "How in the world" - "Where did you get ----" then they looked at their own arms and legs. Then their Frenchy eyes did a double take, they too were covered. When we reached the house, we were soaked and the ticks were crawling all over us. Mama herded us onto the back porch where we were ordered to stay until she could change her own clothes. Then we would be properly cleaned, de-ticked and re-clothed. The new ground was planted with sugar cane to make molasses in the fall. Also new ground was wonderful for tobacco so dad also put in a few dozen plants.

March and April were "hen setting months." Early chickens always did better. So Mama began laying aside extra nice large, well-shaped eggs. She would chose an egg she thought well-shaped, hold it a moment, turn it over and around and if it failed Mama's criteria, it was placed in the basket to be carried to the Feuersville Store. If it passed the test it received the "sign of the cross" marked on each side with a piece of charcoal picked out of the ashes in "Old Bridge Beach." When Mama had found fifteen eggs and given them the sign of the cross, we toted them out to a nest where a sharp-billed old brown leghorn was waiting for just such a chance to cluck and peck our hands and try to peck out my eyes. Our nests were built like a long, flat trough just on eye level the length of the hen house. By now, 1920, the puzzling old wooden washing machine had seen its best days and was now serving as a fine hen's nest in the left front corner of the hen house. The old hen who chose the washing machine nest had a large, roomy compartment with no danger of baby chicks falling out of the nest and getting chilled before we found them. Usually we had twelve or fifteen hens setting in the hen houses and barns. Then there were always those who "hid out" - some in the deepest hole in the leftover hay in the loft, some under the floor of the corn crib. They gave us exciting surprises all summer long. After three weeks of waiting, we would begin taking a sample egg out from under each hen, look to see if it had been pecked from inside and if not, hold it close to our ear to listen for the pecking that told us a baby chick would soon be forthcoming. The egg would be oily slick by now and very warm against one's ear. Baby brown leghorns are precarious bits of beautiful brown and buff fluff. So smart, they are out of the nest eating and drinking almost before they're dry. Until several years later we had no brooder house to keep young chickens housed. So now we must put them in coops built of slats and placed in a cool shady spot. When the chicks were older they would be permitted to range freely. The black ones were so soft to hold in your hand or brush against one's cheek. Mama discredited them immediately - "Make a good fryer in a few weeks." I couldn't believe that darling bit of black down was going to become fried chicken. However they usually did. Whenever Mama sent us out to "get a nice fryer" she never failed to call after us, "There's a nice black one just the right size." It's strange how the bit of black or brown fluff seem to be far, far away from that nice fat broiler you're preparing for the dinner! Must be stomach logic!

Early in the summer the big boys in the neighborhood began to talk about the Fourth of July picnic to be held at Bland in the city park. It sounded so exciting! Basil, Charles Homfeld, Ray, Roy, Willie, and Chrissie Nixon planned to start early and walk. There had been another strange phenomena near Bland that summer. A huge "sink hole" had appeared in Mr. Gleize's field. It was the conversation piece of the entire countryside. Not only conversation but people went to see it. Mama thought that was dangerous - "More earth might cave in. Who knows when another sink hole might appear and everybody would fall in with it." All sorts of dire predictions were forthcoming whenever the sink hole was mentioned.

The picnic was uppermost in all our minds. Finally one day when Mama was in a "good humor," Mae, Ellie and I managed to muster up enough courage to say timidly, "Mama, why can't we go to the Fourth of July picnic?" We knew the answer: "No, of course not. We can't afford any picnics this summer." - so no more was said. No one ever argued with Mama, but she had a method in her madness. All the time she was thinking that this was a good way to get some extra chores done, so after a while when Ellie and Frank and Rude were getting ready to go home, she said, "Now if all you kids work real good, I've been thinking it over, maybe we can manage some way to go." Mama was a sly conniver. Ellie came early and helped with everything: cooking, dish washing, laundry and housecleaning. Frank and Rude, along with Bud, pulled weeds in the garden. We took turns feeding and watering the baby chicks. We carried milk, water, butter, buttermilk, and cream to and from the springhouse. We milked the cows. We fed the pigs. We carried eggs and some old roosters to the store. Mama was figuring out how much "change" she could afford to dole out. She reminded us every day that just going ought to be enough fun because we would pack a "nice lunch," "wear our best summer clothes" and "see all the sights along the way." I really couldn't see much to get excited about on that last one.

The long, hot days seemed to go by at a snail's pace. We had worked so hard and walked miles and miles feeding the animals. But arrive it did - clear and cool in the early morning. Because it was nine miles to Bland, we were up before daylight to milk and feed and strain the milk and fry the chicken and pack it in the big old split basket along with a loaf of home-made bread, a pie and a cake, deviled eggs and other good things, such as Early June apples. There was a jug of milk for Pete to drink on the way. Very early we were on the road. Mae and I wore our best gingham dresses. Our voile dresses were packed in a box along with Pete's gingham suit and Bud's Sunday shirt. We would put these things on after we ate dinner. Dad was proud of his new farm wagon with A. J. Child's & Co. written along the side. Jim and Odie were the biggest mules in the country. So we moved along the road over Nixon Ridge where Elsie, Frank and Rude climbed over the wheels and sat with Mae, Bud and me on the straw covered bed. We were so excited - actually on our way to the Fourth of July picnic at Bland! The sun grew warm; Mama raised her parasol to shade Pete. He sunburned easily. About half way to Bland, we rounded a curve and spotted the group of young men up ahead. Charlie seemed in good shape, but all were willing to climb in and ride for awhile. Not all rode at once. And so it was we entered the town of Bland. Others were arriving too. We met Jim and Jessie Phelps and their children. Dad wanted to stop and visit awhile - Jessie was his cousin, but we couldn't give him time for that. Where was that wonderful picnic? Now Bland wasn't that big, it was no trouble to find the park - cars, wagons, buggies, horses with saddles - were all over the place. We found a good shade tree, tied Jim and Odie to a low limb and placed our lunch on a tablecloth spread on the ground. We weren't especially interested in Mama's good lunch. We knew there was ice cream or a red soda awaiting us a little later. Mae and I found a clump of trees where we could exchange our ginghams for our voiles. Pete's new gingham suit was fresh and clean. Now for the real stuff! We started our inspection tour. Ellie had some nickels and dimes tied in her handkerchief. We wanted to see what looked best for our money. We had to intercede Mama for each nickel. That way she kept us in eye sight. She had found a bench under a shade tree where Pete could sit on the quilt or lie down and rest. Frank and Rude were never far from Ellie. Neither was Bud far from Mae and me. It was a great place to be on the Fourth Day of July - lots of people, bands playing, people eating ice cream and drinking red or white soda from bottles; some others were eating from their own baskets as we had done!

There was so much to see. I had to study the color and design of each young lady's dress, shoes and hat. Some of these were very fancy - flowers, satin, ribbons and lace. All were simply stunning in my eye. Although I thought none of them could match beauty with my mother who was also wearing her beautiful black lace and satin ribbon hat with the red cherries surrounding the brim. My afternoon was busy finding out people's names. Ellie knew lots of the folks there.

Then I was at the soda stand wishing I could have a red soda. They were so tempting lying there in the ice water. All of a sudden out of nowhere, Amanda Gerloff was standing next to me. She was our neighbor and also attended Post Oak school. Amanda was looking for someone to share a soda and as we drank she unfolded our next move. Would I like to ride out to the Gleize Sink Hole - Ernest and Charles Feuers were just about ready to take off. Would wonders never cease!! Red soda and now the "Sink Hole." The Bland picnic was really paying big dividends - and a car ride thrown in. It wasn't far out of town to the gorgeous hole in the ground. Lots of other people were there viewing and offering their opinions as to what caused it. We drove up close and walked up to the barbed wire fence to speculate with all the others. It was a sight for my childish young eyes. Where had the ground gone - in the bottom of this huge "sink hole" was water. I began to think Mama was right - that thing could "cave in" some more. I was ready to get back to the picnic. We didn't stay long; all we wanted to do was see the actual size. I figured I'd better report to Mama. Just when I was nearing Mama's bench under the shade tree, I saw her give a start, jump up and almost run toward Dad just a few steps away. I found out that Bud had just dropped a bombshell. He had reported on my whereabouts and for a moment Mama was "having a fit." When she saw me and Amanda approaching, I could sense the relief she was experiencing - yet the other half told me to just wait until I got home. For the rest of the summer, I was teased unmercifully. Mama would say, "I guess Grace will go to the sink hole again today" - or Bud would ask, "When are you going back to see the sink hole?" I just couldn't see why it was such a big deal. You were supposed to have a good time at a picnic, weren't you?

After the picnic came more hard work. Weeds in the garden grew fast. Our calf pasture was big and we had to build a new fence around it. On hot summer afternoons, I always had to carry a fresh bucket of water to wherever Dad, Uncle John or Pete Leach were working on fence. Sometimes all of us would go to hoe the cane in the patch of new ground or to pull weeds out of the corn. Lots of work was done as a team. Mama would assign each of us a row and have us race to see who could clean a row quickest. How our backs ached! How hot the sun shone on our hands and arms as we snatched at the mean old weeds!

Sunday was always a day of rest. We still went frequently to the Feuersville Lutheran Church with Alma Homfeld. We had made friends there and found their services interesting - even in German.

But the best Sundays were those when I was permitted to go spend the afternoon with Audrey. She was an only child. Her parents were so kind, so patient, and so courteous. Audrey had numerous dolls and stacks of doll clothes, games we had never seen, puzzles, cards, and Erector sets. All so exciting to me! Mr. and Mrs. Lange treated me as a truly grown-up guest. Anna always set the table nicely, brought out the home-made bread and butter, apple butter and nearly always cake, pie or cookies with a dish of fruit. The adults had coffee, Audrey and I had milk. They, too, had a spring.

Sometimes just before we ate, Audrey and I would be sent to bring the cool milk and butter from the spring. They didn't have a house over the spring. It was like a big box built into the side of the creek. I always stayed as long as I possibly could playing games with Audrey or conversing in "grown-up" vocabulary with the adults. I hated to leave, but Mama always set a time when I was to be home. Time to gather the eggs, feed the baby chicks and see they were safely housed for the night, time to help with the milking and carry milk, cream, butter and fresh water for supper and some time left over for sitting on the front porch listening to Dad play "Soldier's Joy" and "Irish Washer Woman." "The Eighth of January" was guaranteed to cool us off on the warmest summer eve and then to bed - and to sleep - no insomnia in those days!

Chapter 13

Got to Go Visit "Pa"

We were now several miles from any of the brothers and sisters in Dad's and Mama's families. I'm sure they missed seeing them often as we always had when we all lived in the Linn area. At intervals all summer Dad would refer to "goin to see Pa sometime soon." I liked the idea. Visiting was nice; putting on our best clothes, wearing my hat with the pink ribbon, what could be finer? Mama never got too enthusiastic about long trips in the farm wagon. In order to visit "Pa," who lived with Uncle Will, Aunt Stell and their children, Paul, King, Scott, Janet and Nelson, we had to go south to the Rollins Ferry Bridge, then a short distance along the river road toward Linn. This was the route we took one extremely warm August Saturday. It was school time again so if we were to go visit "Pa" it was now or wait another year. Again Jim and Odie were harnessed to the wagon, straw was scattered over the bed, an old clean quilt was placed over the straw.

Now "Pa" was our Grandpa Bacon (Charles Porter). Since the death of our Grandmother, he had lived with Uncle Will and Aunt Stell Bacon. Grandpa was dearly beloved by all his grandchildren. He was always patient and kind and seemed to truly enjoy the company of his family. He was a man of great physical stamina. In his late eighties, he walked from Uncle Will's farm near Linn to visit us at Cooper Hill taking what he referred to as "nigh cuts" through woods across farms and wading the Gasconade River - often using a shallow crossing at Lake Ford. Grandpa had grown a beard sometime earlier and now when I remember him the beard was snow white and rested on his chest. He always wore blue bib overalls and a blue chambray shirt - both seemed to always be immaculate.

In order to make this trip from our farm to Linn in daylight we had to leave home early in the morning. The previous day had been spent washing, ironing, pressing and getting a "batch of bread baked" because we would have to take a lunch with us.

This wasn't considered a dress-up occasion, so Mac and I wore our best gingham school dresses. Mama had a new gingham, too, with lace collar and cuff set. But Pete and Bud had only wool knee britches as a "best" with blue checked gingham shirts. Consequently, they were forced into their "woolies." We hadn't got to the top of our hill until Pete was scratching and complaining bitterly about his pants "rubbing all his skin off." Mama reminded him in no uncertain terms that he had them on and there was no alternative. Pete screamed, cried, tried standing up, lying down, and fussing at Mama - all to no avail. Pete wasn't happy with his wool pants!

Even though the day was scandalously hot, we didn't notice. We were going visiting. Lunch under a shade tree was delicious - fried chicken, home-baked bread, fresh tomatoes dipped in salt and fresh peaches for dessert were especially good. It was like a picnic. While we ate lunch Old Jim and Odie rested. When we crossed a creek or branch Dad always stopped so they could drink and cool a bit in the spring fed streams.

It was late evening when we arrived. Uncle Will's house was a large frame, painted white, four rooms up and four down. I call them "box" houses. His farm was well tended, neat and clean. His family was what we would refer to as "extended." Aunt Stell was his second wife. Aunt Bashia had died when Paul was a very small child. Aunt Bashia's first born son, John William, had died earlier. So there was King (my age), Scott, Janet and Nelson in addition to Paul, Grandpa, and Aunt Stell's mother, Mrs. Scott.

This farm and visit was almost equal to the excitement of visiting Uncle John and Aunt Ida because there was also a windmill grinding and squeaking along as it pumped water for the cattle. And Uncle Will had a Model T. Now that would have to be explored for sure!

When I finally got around to inspecting the big square kitchen, there was an aroma of freshly baked bread, fresh fruit pies, and on the big old wood range, something was cooking in a huge blue granite-ware dishpan - covered by another dishpan - I knew it was beef and when Aunt Stell removed the top dishpan to probe the meat for tenderness, I saw what looked like a whole quarter of beef. It was huge! On the back of the stove was a huge pot of potatoes and one of green beans. All nine children were instructed to "run on out and play" - supper would be ready soon. With nine children it was almost like school. We could play "hide and seek," "Ante Over," and "Froggie in the Meadow." Dad, Uncle Will and Grandpa had gone out to "look over the farm" - including the cows, calves, horses and crops. Mama "pitched in" to help Aunt Stell mash the potatoes, make the gravy, set the table, make dressing for slaw - all was ready. Milk was poured for all nine children, but we had to wait on the "beef." Finally the men came in. They washed up on the back porch. Grandpa combed his beard and hair, and set the high chairs at the corner of the table where he and Uncle Will would feed Nelson and Janet. First course was "beef soup" - good hot, clear broth with great thick slices of Aunt Stell's famous white bread. Finally the beef was done. The main course was served and by this time heads were heavy. Nelson and Janet were asleep in their highchairs so the beds were turned down and the babies were washed a bit and plopped into bed. Pete was finally relieved of his "itchy britches," but he swears to this day he didn't sleep a wink because there were four little boys in a rather small bed. He says the other three had their feet in his face all night.

All too soon it was "Morning on the Farm." We scurried around putting our night gowns in the cardboard box. Breakfast was a substantial meal - biscuits, bacon, oatmeal, eggs, fresh peaches, preserves - all the usual food items found on the Bacon family tables. Aunt Stell sliced another huge loaf of bread for "beef" sandwiches to take along for our lunch on the road home. Of course, Mama remonstrated (that was the proper thing to do) but all the time she was busy really helping prepare the lunch. Mama would say, "Now Stell, we really don't need this - we'll be fine until we get home. We had such a big breakfast." To which Aunt Stell would reply, "Now Jennie, those children will get awfully hungry and cross. They need something to eat." The "beef" needed to be put on a plate or else it would soak into the bread. So saying she went to her sideboard and chose a dainty thin china plate. I was very interested in the beautiful piece. As Aunt Stell piled the thinly sliced "beef" on the plate, she explained it had belonged to Grandma Bacon and she made it extra exciting by telling me I could have the plate for myself. Now that made me ecstatic!

Again Dad, Uncle Will and Grandpa took off for more inspections of the ridge field. Dad instructed all of us to be ready to "jump in and go" when he got back.

I remember carrying the cardboard box very carefully to the wagon, climbing up by means of the spokes in the wagon wheel and placing it near where I planned to sit on the way home. In the box was the precious china plate, the beef, bread, tomatoes and peaches. (People much younger than I may not appreciate the fact that wax paper, plastic bags and foil were not found in farm kitchens of 1920 and 1921.)

After a hurried lunch of leftovers supplemented by a huge plate of sliced tomatoes, fresh slaw and cherry cobbler, we "jumped into the wagon" and Old Jim and Odie "champed at the bits" anxious to be homeward bound. They were no more anxious than Pete. His lower section was again encased in the brown wool cocoon he hated with a passion. He scratched and fussed and stood up and finally solved the problem by removing the offensive article entirely. There he sat, his bare legs looked peculiar sticking out in front of him on the old quilt! Mama's face got red. She demanded he put his pants on. She tried shaming him - "What if we meet someone and we're driving along with a half-naked young one? George make him put his britches on." Dad would sing and whistle and pretend to see or hear nothing. I rather suspect his own woolen britches were itching him too. He just wasn't as brave as Pete. So we proceeded along the river road, crossed the bridge and headed toward Cooper Hill. Jim and Odie were headed home too. Their ears wiggled and they weren't much interested in drinking or resting or Pete's naked legs. We were home by dark. Years passed - Mama was nearly ninety - we were talking about the weekend visit to Uncle Will's. I said I had always remembered the roast beef. Mama looked at me in disbelief, "You big goose - that was venison!"

That summer had been fun. Our wheat crop had done really well. Several times Mae and I had been permitted to ride the "wheat wagon to Belle" with Dad. That was a real treat. First I had to "hold the sack" while Dad scooped shovels of grain into it. Each farmer owned several canvas bags holding a bushel of grain. When you had it about half full you lifted it up and let it fall on the granary floor with force two or three times to settle the grain. When it became too heavy for me, Dad would take it and bounce it hard. Wheat was weighed to determine the number of bushels. Usually a wagonload was about 20 bushels. The bags were loaded the night before and the wagon was pulled into the shed adjoining the granary.

Mama had not forgotten all about music lessons as I had hoped. She had seen an article in the Sears & Roebuck catalog called a music roll. This peculiar thing she ordered for Mae to carry her sheet music in. It was just a piece of imitation leather laid out flat to place your sheet of music inside, roll it up and fasten with a strap and buckle. It had a handle to carry. Mama was so proud of this handsome way of carrying music; Mae didn't share Mom's enthusiasm. Her books for finger exercises wouldn't fit. But Mama was not to be daunted. She had found Mrs. Carrie Wooten in Belle who Mama insisted was "most proficient" in teaching music. She had also purchased a fancy brown wool coat at least two sizes too large for Mae and for each of us "brown beaver" hats, wide brims, flat crowns, wide brown ribbon bands with streamers which hung down our backs. We thought these hats were wonderful at first, but there was no way you could keep them on your head. The crown was so flat and my hair was so curly. The curls and hair ribbon kept popping the hat off my head. The brim in back kept hitting against my shoulders. If the wind blew the least bit you spent all your energy holding the thing on. But Mama thought she had us elegantly attired, especially Mae with the fancy brown coat ordered from National Bellas Hess. This item of clothing had a collar the like of which I hope never to have to struggle with again. The material was stiff. I think it was called "velour." This collar was a very large wrap-around, in front there was a wide buttonhole through which one pulled opposite collar point to button over in a sort of butterfly effect. The belt buttoned in the same way, for small rather awkward fingers, the collar and belt were very time consuming and exasperating.

When I informed Mama at Linn earlier that I was sure I knew all there was to know about music, she had somewhat deferred my musical training. After all I had mastered "Little Rondo" and "Fox and Geese." I had also sung "Requiem" as a solo for a war rally at the courthouse when I was four! But Mae was now a fully outfitted, properly dressed music student so she was dispatched every time Dad went to the wheat market. Sometimes I cried and begged to go along - but it was no use, unless I condescended to take a music lesson, I wasn't permitted to go. Everything had to serve a purpose in Mama's opinion!

School began again. We resumed our studies with Mr. Allen Shockley for our second year at Post Oak. I renewed my friendship with the corner bookshelf - we called our library. I re-read *Hans Brinker or The Silver Skates*. It was cooling to my warm little body on a steamy September afternoon, while the big red wasps buzzed and hit their heads against the grooved wood ceiling. This year I was permitted to sit with Audrey. Mama had finally agreed I didn't need to sit with Bud any longer. Bud was always a quiet, docile child. With me just older and Pete just younger, he had no chance to be otherwise!

Games were so much fun. We had a new one, "stealing sticks." It was the same principle as "base" excepting that in addition to just choosing two opposing sides, we had at least three rows of short sticks stuck into the ground in front of each base. Base was usually a couple of rails borrowed from Otto Wildebrandt's fence. The idea was to steal the sticks from the opposing side and run to home base with them. The side stealing all or most of the sticks by the time the bell rang was declared the winner. The big boys thought it was great fun to cut some very, very long sticks and really push them deep in the ground. When some of the small children grabbed them they wouldn't budge. Everyone joined in the games. There was no thought given to division according to grade or size. Big brothers and sisters were accustomed to looking after the younger ones. We also played harmless pranks! Mr. Shockley didn't often join in our games as he had the year before. He frequently remained in the schoolhouse with his feet propped up on the small table he used as a desk. His face had a high color. Sometimes he wouldn't get through all the classes recitations which seemed to irritate him. He was also driving his team of horses hitched to a surrey instead of riding horseback.

We got through August and September hot days, rainy days, red wasps, red mud clinging to our shoe soles and the peculiar odor of boiled eggs when our lunch boxes were all opened at the same time. It was popular now for all the girls to gather under the shade of the silver maple tree in front of the schoolhouse near the road. This year Mae and I had persuaded Mama to stop packing our lunch in a basket for all three of us. Because Bud didn't like eating with the "big gulls" as he called them. So a bucket was purchased for Bud, and Mae and I had the basket all to ourselves. Esther Kraenow's boiled duck eggs fascinated me. They were never hard boiled. The white would be solid but the yolk was runny. So much so Esther would suck the yolk from the small hole she made through the white with her forefinger. Of course, I watched intently, fixing my eyes on Esther as she attacked her duck egg. Sometimes she would look straight at me as she was sucking and explain, "Mama says that's good for you." That didn't appeal to me or change my opinion.

On a cold, cloudy late October morning, Dad came upstairs to rouse all of us. He was carrying a kerosene lamp which he sat on the small stand by our bedside. He told us to put on our school clothes and to see Bud was dressed for school. What seemed strange to me was that it was still dark outside and stranger still he admonished me to dress Pete in his "brown britches" and blue sweater. The same "itchy" britches he had worn to Uncle Will's. Mae and I did as we were bid. When we were dressed, we hurried downstairs only to find some more puzzles. Mrs. Leach was cooking oatmeal and frying bacon and eggs on our faithful "Old Bridge Beach." As soon as it was light enough to see, all four of us were pushed out the back door. I was told to "walk slow so Pete can keep up." I led him by the hand, steadying my oil cloth book satchel as we maneuvered our way over the big limestone rocks, climbed the rail fence, slipped over the green mossy rocks and shuffled our feet in the crackly brown leaves. We were well ahead of Mr. Shockley so we sat on the big square cistern rock and waited. It looked like rain. I hoped it would hold off until our teacher came. It didn't. We ran for the stable. There we stayed until Mr. Shockley arrived and unlocked the door. No one seemed much surprised to see Pete at school. It was common for the pre-school age children to visit a day now and then. When I explained that Mama was sick, too sick to get up and fix our breakfast, the big girls giggled and made knowing gestures with heads and eyes.

For several months I had been begging Mama to have Dr. Leach bring us a baby. After all she told me Doc brought them in that funny black leather bag he always carried. She would laugh and think it was so funny. I believed her.

When I burst into the kitchen door that cloudy, cool October evening, Mrs. Leach was still holding fort. She had a big pot of steaming vegetable soup ready for us, but I was simply ecstatic when she said, "Guess what your Mama's got - a baby brother for you." A baby! A baby brother! My fondest wish had come true! I made a dash for the front bedroom - seeing is believing. There he was, a little blonde bundle all wrapped up in a white blanket. Such joy, now I had a real baby brother. Pete had now outgrown his baby ways. He was 4 1/2 years. He was big enough for overalls and "itchy pants."

After supper, Doc gave the baby a final check. Mrs. Leach helped Mae and me with the dishes. Then they donned their rain coats and walked up the hill to home. The following days were busy for Mae and me. We had to cook, wash dishes, keep the fires going, wash diapers, wash our clothes, keep the house and wait on Mama. She had spoken for a "girl" to come from Cooper Hill to be our hired girl but she had a felon on her thumb. She just couldn't do any work, so we settled for Annie Jett, another Cooper Hill girl. Annie came. Dad went for her in the buggy. She was a small thin girl, well-dressed in a red wool serge dress and high topped shiny brown leather shoes. Her small box of everyday clothes was placed near her bed in our parlor room. But I suppose we astounded Annie; she had to ask Mama what needed to be done. Well, as I remember, everything needed to be done. For a week, Mae and I - eight and ten years old - had been doing the work, or trying to do it. Mrs. Leach came every morning to bathe the baby and attend to Mama's breakfast. She would put something on to cook for our supper or leave it ready for Mae and me to cook. She would also clean Mama's bedroom and tidy the house. This was a fringe benefit received by many, many neighborhood families in times of need and Doc's fee was $15.

Annie spent the weekend with us. At the breakfast table on Sunday, she announced she was sick and had to go home immediately. So Dad hurried to hitch Jim and Odie to the buggy and take Annie home. In the interim, Mrs. Leach and Ida Elsner had persuaded Olga Baker that her thumb was well enough to take us on. So when Dad came home, he had Olga in the buggy. She jumped out, grabbed her bag and walked quickly toward the house. Olga was of medium height, slightly plump, very talkative, knew how to handle children and certainly didn't have to ask Mama what needed to be done. She said "hello" to Mama, inspected the baby and then began giving orders. "Mr. Bacon let's get that big wash boiler on and fill it. I'm going to scrub these floors." Mae and I took turns sweeping. We dusted and brought potatoes and turnips and sauerkraut from the cellar. Dad brought in a cured ham from the smokehouse and bacon for breakfast. Olga scrubbed all the floors downstairs, cooked potatoes and mashed them, fried ham and fried apples with hot biscuits and made a meal such as we hadn't had for a week. We knew we were going to love Olga. And we did! The wash boiler was kept going all day, soiled diapers and clothes were scrubbed on the board. She kept our house warm and clean. She was an excellent cook, usually limiting the meal to two or three food items. If she baked pies as she often did, we might have soup, bread and pie. Everything she cooked was well prepared and hot. Mama's tray was made so attractive that all of us begged to carry it to her. Soon the nine days were accomplished that Mama had to stay in bed. She promised I could hold the baby as soon as she could get up.

For several days all of us had been suggesting names. We didn't know Mama had already selected Charley Howard. Charley was for Grandpa, who's birthday was October 29. Our baby brother had arrived on the 28th so of course the name had to be Charley.

Things were much brighter now in several ways. Mae and I weren't very adept at keeping even fires. We were forever having to re-build them, letting lots of smoke out into the rooms. Mama would smell it and when we went into her bedroom, she would ask, "Are you getting the wall paper smoky out in the dining room?" To which we of course tastefully replied "No, Mama, of course not. What made you think that?" She would sniff the air and retort, "I've got a good nose for smoke." But with Mama sitting in the rocking chair, holding Charley and rocking him gently, and with Olga's expert management, Mae and I were also relieved of the cooking and cleaning chores. Dad could get back to his outside chores. He had had a young man from the ridge, Don Shockley, to do the feeding and milking. Don came every morning and worked all day at shucking corn, feeding cows, calves, cleaning barns and running errands for anyone who needed them. Pete had sort of attached himself to Don like a leech. He would be ready and waiting when Don came to work. When Mama tried to keep him near the house he would yell at her that Don didn't know how to do anything. He had to "show him how" - so Pete went out to the field and to the barn and followed Dan like a shadow. He often took his afternoon nap on the hay in the loft while Don threw down large bundles of timothy and alfalfa for Peg and Nell, Flora and, of course, Jim and Odie.

We had continued our education at Post Oak during all this excitement. No one got terribly excited about the new baby boy at our house. All the students came from large families where a new baby appeared at regular two year intervals or less.

On Sunday Olga wanted to go home to spend the day with her small daughter and her father and mother. She invited Mae and me to go with her - that day was another great event in my life. The Bakers were a large family. We knew all of them. We had gone to church and Sunday School at the Cooper Hill E & R Church rather frequently for a year or so. There we had met Mr. and Mrs. Charles Baker, Olga's parents. Ida and Edith were her two youngest sisters, slightly older than Mae and me. Dick and Arnold were grown young men. Lydia was Allen Shockley's wife. Farida was married to Ted Langenberg and Charles Jr. was married to Opal Rice. Emma Nunley Busch was a half sister as was Lizzie Owens and Henry (called "Heinie"). Heinie and Dora lived in a big old house on the hill above the ancestral Baker home. Emma's house was only a few feet away. Since Emma wasn't living in the area just then, Lizzie and Jess Owens lived in Emma's house. Olga's small daughter, Nora Belle, was a cute little fair-skinned red head. I had seen Nora Belle at Sunday school and picnics. Earlier in the week, I had spent my small hoard of pennies at the Feuersville store for some small parawax kewpie dolls. These were filled with a thick, sweet liquid. They came in white, pink, yellow and black. I can't remember how many I got but I carefully stashed one away to take to Nora Belle on Sunday. I couldn't wait to give it to her. She ran away to her Grandma Baker who lovingly hugged her and told her to put it away until after dinner. The day flew by. Family and neighbors stopped in, some stayed to visit "Just have a cup of coffee," Mrs. Baker would say - her hospitality knew no bounds. It seemed her table was always set for extra people. Two or three extra were of no consequence. While Mae and I visited with the Bakers, Dad had spent his hours with Mr. Henry Buecker, who now lived in the Ed Leach house. In rather early afternoon, Dad came for us. After all Mama was home by herself with three little boys, one only 10 days old.

For three beautiful weeks, Olga brightened our days. She was up early preparing our breakfast, getting bread dough set to rise, putting the wash boiler on and filling it with soft water to heat for sheets, clothes and diapers. When evening came and we trooped in from school, there would be fresh white laundry on the line, fresh white bread from the oven and a dark cake made from bread dough with raisins. It was wonderful, sweet and warm. I begged every night to sleep with Olga. (We called her "Doodle." She said she earned that title from watching the big, big black "doodle bugs" work in the sawdust at the mill.) Olga also had a boyfriend, George Czeschin. He came to see her several times during her three week stay with us. Once he walked from his farm several miles away. He wore his knee boots made of rubber because he would have to wade the creeks. Olga loved to waltz. She persuaded Dad to bring out his violin that he had played for parties and dances in his younger days. Soon Olga took George's hand, pulled him into the center floor and they were waltzing; rubber boots, however, were something of a handicap! My big moments were helping Olga dress for an evening out. Her best "dress up" was a soft georgette blouse very, very sheer, worn with a black silk skirt. She also possessed a box of fine pink face powder purchased at the Feuersville Store (when I was with her, helping her of course). In those days one just asked the merchant for a box of face powder - that simple - no matching with skin tint. Olga used lots of powder. Her rouge was a bit of red crepe paper moistened with a drop of water then rubbed against the upper cheeks. You can't believe how well this works! When Olga got all dressed up she was the prettiest thing in this whole world. So I thought! Among her personal possessions was a curling iron. In order to use this item a kerosene lamp had to be lighted, the iron hung down inside the globe to heat, and in a few minutes she took the iron out, tested the heat by spitting on her left forefinger and touching the iron quickly. If the "spit sputtered" it was too warm. That meant it would burn and scorch the hair, but Olga could judge the heat exactly right to lay nice even waves in her soft brown hair.

Olga's laugh was merry and ready. If things didn't go quite right it wasn't the end of the world. She could perform miracles with simple food! She had a "pied piper" effect on children - even Pete. Sometimes Mae would play hymns on the piano - all of us joined in; sometimes George came to spend the evening. Usually we played dominoes. But the crowning glory was Thanksgiving! Mama's only brother Uncle Harry LeFevre had moved his family from Aud to Belle. The LeFevre children were of high school age and Belle was reputed to have a good school. Mama was astounded when Dad came home from town one evening and announced that Uncle Harry was moving. "Well, I'll vow, doesn't he know there's already one doctor there?" Mama never gave any member of the family credit for using good judgment unless her opinion had been included. But that gave us something good to think about. Mae and I had been permitted to visit with Uncle Harry and Aunt Lulu a few times at Aud where he had been serving a large rural community as a country doctor. They were the parents of Everett, Reta, Earl, Boyd, Buell and Russell, the youngest was a little older than I. Everett and Reta had gone to high school at Chamois for a year and both had taught school for two or three years. Now they needed to have four years high school. Once when we lived on the farm at Linn, Everett and Reta came to the school there to take the teacher's examination to qualify for teaching certificates. They stayed a couple of nights with us and took Mae and me home with them. They drove a team of horses hitched to a buggy. Aunt Lulu's house was run something like a hotel in her younger days - always a hired girl - sometimes two or a good stout woman. Her linen tablecloths were ironed smoothly, her china was beautiful, and her living room had one of those new fangled machines called a phonograph. On her library table was an Aladdin Lamp - really a mystery to me! I liked going there to visit. All those big boys teased me, chased me, told me wild scary tales and I loved it all. Sometimes Grandma was there too. I knew I was safe wherever Grandma was.

But now since Mama had Olga to help, she would invite the entire LeFevre family for Thanksgiving, and they came driving Uncle Harry's long, black Dodge touring car.

The menu was nearly always the same for Mama's company dinners. Two or three fat hens (old good-for-nothins) were caught, dressed and placed in a large baking pan in the oven. Irish potatoes and sweet potatoes were prepared, a vegetable or two and always the crisp succulent cucumber pickles. These were difficult to make. First we grew the cucumbers, put them in a 20 gallon stone jar, covered them with soft water, measured out a couple of cups of salt from the barrel in the granary, and weighted them down so all would be under the brine. When we wanted fresh pickles, we would go down to the cellar and bring up a dishpan full. They would be freshened by soaking in soft water until most of the salt had evaporated from them. She would then drain the pickle pieces and pour over them a mixture of vinegar, brown sugar, molasses and pickling spices. After a few days, they were ready for the table. This year Olga made the pickles, baked the bread and pumpkin and apple pies.

On this day of thanks our dining room table was extended its full length - about 12 feet. Our best damask cloth was spread on it. Our company silverware was brought out, the food was placed on it and the rest is history. The big LeFevre boys seemed to have good appetites. Since they were so much older than we, they looked about for a game suitable for their grownup state to fill the afternoon hours. They found it in some hickory sticks and a tin can. They called it "hockey." Soon there were at least three games going. This was my first introduction to this popular game. Everett, being the oldest, served as official referee for all three games.

When Olga left us at the end of a month, life returned to routine. Of course, I had the new baby brother to hold and love. I soon appointed myself his nursemaid. He soon learned to recognize my voice. I sang him to sleep, I changed his clothes and principally his diapers. He and I were forming a lifelong friendship.

At school Mr. Shockley moved more slowly. He couldn't spin on his heel nearly so fast when he had his back turned and wanted to catch someone passing a note or throwing a spit ball. His face looked so flushed. He almost never came to the playground. He even left a big boy in charge while he went to the boy's room down in the back. His patience wore thin easily. We had no pie supper, no Christmas program. Soon after Christmas Mrs. Shockley came to teach for a day or two. This I loved. Lydia conducted her classroom in an easy, well-disciplined way. She had two babies at home, one almost the same age as Charley Howard. During Christmas the Shockleys moved to a two-room house just south of the Feuersville Store. Lydia came more frequently to teach now than her husband. Ida Baker came to stay with them and care for the babies. The pupils seemed to adjust to the situation. I don't remember questioning why Mr. Shockley wasn't coming to school. I just knew he was sick. There was no basket dinner for the parents and neighbors on the last day of school either - although we had one of sorts. Each family brought a basket and we put all the food on a tablecloth spread on the ground. When we put the food out, Alice Drewel set out a bowl of sliced pineapple. This was the first time I had seen the fruit and naturally I couldn't wait to taste it!

I think I probably grabbed a slice and downed it Johnny-on-the-spot. I thought it was absolutely food for the Gods. When I grew up and had "lots of money," I was going to indulge in a whole can of it every day! Alice's basket also contained Vienna sausage - such a treat - who wanted fried chicken and sugar cured ham when store bought food was available?

After school closed the Shockleys moved back to their farm. Dr. Leach called on them almost daily. Allen was very ill. One day when Dr. and Mrs. Leach came home they had the little boys with them. Doc had put Lydia and Allen on the train in Bland to go to St. Louis to the hospital. They would take care of the boys while Lydia was gone. It wasn't long until word came that Allen had died. We felt very sad. I had absolutely no idea how ill he must have been. This wonderful, knowledgeable teacher who had given me the impetus to be a student of literature. I remembered the pleasant days under his supervision. I also did a flashback to the "memory gems." We would stand and recite something like, "If at first you don't succeed, try, try again." or "Never put off until tomorrow what you can do today." Delmar Brown had a favorite - "Strike while the iron is hot" - that was always funny to me. I knew what he was going to say every morning. We also had the wonderful memories of our first pie supper, our first basket dinner and our first acquaintance with a one-room school.

We went to the funeral - again it was cool, rainy spring day. There were Bakers and Leaches and Owens and Shockleys all gathered at the cemetery (Baker-Leach) to pay our last respects. Mae and I made small flower arrangements from wild roses and ferns plucked from among the limestone rocks where our playhouses were! We walked solemnly to the open grave and placed our little wilted offerings on the damp earth which would soon be scooped into the open grave. The family stood nearby. There was Olga and George at Lydia's side, Mrs. Elsner and Ida, Dr. and Mrs. Leach with the little boys, Leon and Arthur, Buckshot and Eliza - just a few. The rain was coming down in big drops, a short scripture was read, a prayer was offered and that was all. We turned away and hurried to where Old Jim and Odie were tethered to a big oak tree. I looked back to see George and Olga leading Lydia away toward George's car. In a few weeks, Lydia and her little boys moved to Cooper Hill to be near family and friends. For many years, they occupied the parsonage on the hill above the church.

Chapter 14

Circus and Cake

During all this time, we had kept in touch with Grandma LeFevre who was living with Aunt May and Uncle John Hancks in Wamego, Kansas. She wrote long letters in her trembly hand - every letter in a word seemed to have little ruffles around them. How she must have slaved over those letters. Every time she wrote it was to tell us how much she would like to return to Missouri, especially now that Uncle Harry lived in Belle, which was "right on the railroad." Just about every week, Mama would have Mae and me sit at the dining room table and write Grandma a letter. We would report on the weather, how many eggs we were getting per day, the price per dozen at the store, how many little chickens we had, how many baby calves, Old Nell had a mule colt, we had named him Charlie, and Old Peg had a foal named "Minnie." We told her about visiting with Uncle Wills and how often we saw Uncle John and Aunt Ida. Aunt May had boarded at Grandpa Bacon's, too, and knew all the family when she taught at Mt. Ariel.

Late in the spring, Grandma came on the train to Belle. Some days later she came out to the farm. I hadn't seen her for a long time. Not since we had moved to our present home. I was so happy. Grandma was such an elegant lady in her black taffeta dress and long silk black gloves. When she arrived of course she had to hold the baby and see how wonderful he was - blonde curls and brown eyes. I had to wait until she went upstairs and changed into her everyday brown cotton dress and ankle length blue calico apron before I could hug her properly and sit on her lap. She thought our house was just wonderful. The garden was the nicest she had ever seen. Our spring water was just bound to be the purest and best in the country. Maybe it would help her rheumatic shoulder - it just might! Things always seemed to go a bit smoother when our wonderful Grandmother lived with us. She seemed to have a soothing effect on Mama. At least Mama wasn't quite so quick with her scolding and the "treats to peach tree tea."

In August, a circus was coming to Belle. A real honest-to-goodness circus. Uncle Harry was worse than the little kids. He sent word out to us; we must come in for the day. There would be elephants, tigers, lions, and circus clowns. The chance of a lifetime. We couldn't wait and although Aunt May and Uncle John Hancks didn't know about the circus, they wrote they would be visiting us at the same time. Goodness, gracious! Would wonders never cease!! How Mama did get mileage out of that circus. All day, every day, she held it over our heads - "All right if you don't get out of here right now and feed and water those chickens, we won't go a step to Belle." - it worked for the garden, for carrying eggs to the store, for housekeeping chores, even doing the laundry including Charlie's soiled diapers. But for him I didn't mind. I looked after him by the hour. Carrying him everywhere I went. He never slept long. He seemed to want someone to be nearby. So I rested with him, fed him, bathed him and sang to him. I loved him with all my heart!

This circus was to be a red letter day for all of us! Mama was so busy getting all our clothes ready - Mae's pretty sheer pale blue Japanese silk, my pink voile, the boys "itchy britches." Charlie had by now become "Bant" (short for Bantie Rooster). Dad doted on nicknames. All of us had one. Bant had a couple of pairs of pink and white checked gingham rompers. Mrs. Leach had made them. The morning dawned hot, blazing hot. Dad was out early to catch Jim and Odie and curry them in style. The farm wagon was rolled out, straw placed in the bed. Mae and I were running from spring to house, to the upstairs obeying Mama's orders as she cooked eggs and bacon on "Old Bridge Beach." We needed to leave early because the circus parade was to be at 10 AM. Pete was pretty excited about the elephants. We had been looking at pictures of them in books ever since we heard the word "circus." We got Pete into his "brown wool itchy britches" rather easily. Mae and I got into our gingham dresses and carried our blue and pink dress-up dresses in a box. Then a calamity befell us. We were all in the wagon, ready and waiting for Mama. All of a sudden she appeared at the front door, her face wore a storm cloud. She was dressed in her shoes, hose, corset and corset cover. Her voice left no doubt that the journey was still in doubt. She announced that unless "someone came in and found her good black lace hat right now, no one was going to any circus today, tomorrow or any other time." Mae and Dad climbed out somewhat dejected and instigated a search of the house, every possible place that hat had ever been kept was probed. I stayed in the wagon to attend Bant and Pete. I could hear Mama screaming at Dad and Mae. Why hadn't someone laid out her hat. She wouldn't go one step without her pretty black lace hat! She finally had to give in. Since the sun was so scandalously hot she had to have something on her head. The only thing she could think of to replace that mischievous hat was Grandma's black taffeta bonnet, but here they came finally. Dad and Mae looked very subdued. We were very quiet most of the way to Belle. Pete didn't dare complain about his "itchy britches."

We were only slightly late for the parade. The elephants were coming up Main Street just as we drove into Uncle Harry's alleyway and brought our own circus wagon to rest in the barnyard. Pete was over the wagon wheel and out in the street. He was going to inspect those elephants up close. Bud and I were close behind. Mama snatched up Bant and hurried into the house, bonnet and all. Uncle Harry had seen Pete's antics, had rescued him from the elephant's legs and appointed all five of his sons as overseers for Pete's welfare. The lions and tigers were in cages. It took only a short time for the parade. Then into Aunt Lulu's kitchen where she, Aunt May and Grandma were bending over double laughing about Mama's hat loss. Can you imagine poor Aunt Lulu - there were eight in her family - seven of us - five of Aunt May's plus Grandma and Aunt Lulu's parents, and Judge and Mrs. Jim Agee who had also come to see the circus. Mrs. Agee was Jim's second wife. Aunt Lulu always referred to her as "Pa's wife." Jim had also been the former owner of our mule team. Before much time passed, Mr. Agee took off for the barn to renew his friendship with those two fine patient animals. We would all eat dinner and then go to the picnic grounds out at the Wallace Park.

That day I wasn't the least bit hungry. I can't remember what Aunt Lulu's menu was - that's strange since my mind has been involved with food all my life. We were sent upstairs to change into our dress-up clothes and to get Bant into fresh clean clothes. After what seemed an eternity, Everett brought the Dodge touring car around to the front. I made sure I got to go in the first car load. There were three cars: Uncle Harry's, Uncle John's and Judge Jim Agee's. Somehow all of us crowded in. It was less than five minutes to the Wallace Park - much too short but then I had to see who was at the picnic and where the circus tent was set up. The animals had gone into hiding. Pete and I knew where they were but there were ropes and wire enclosures forbidding our close examination. Uncle Harry never grew up when it came to circuses, merry-go-rounds, ice cream, soda, toys and child's games even though he was six feet four inches and very much an adult. So the nickels and dimes flowed freely from our dear Uncle's pocket and into the circus owner's all that afternoon. I didn't worry about the method of payment. I only knew I was in seventh heaven. If only Mama had her pretty hat and if her face weren't so red. She just wasn't in a good humor at all all day! Grandma and Aunt May just laughed and teased her considerably about losing her most precious piece of decorative dress. I look upon it now as an unusual "streak of good luck." She was so upset she paid almost no attention to how many times I rode the merry-go-round or threw the balls at birds on a wire to win a kewpie doll or how many ice creams I ate. Uncle Harry's pockets were bottomless. After a time a large fat man appeared in front of the tent and cried out through a bull horn - "Form your lines to the left - form lines to the right. The circus is ready. Don't miss this beautiful sight." Well, about time! My patience was almost exhausted! Uncle Harry "rounded up" all the young ones - four of us - his two youngest, Buell and Russell, and the Hancks twins, Harry and Dorsey. This entrance fee cost no more than a nickel or a dime but how happy Uncle Harry was. Maybe that was why he liked circuses so much - watching young faces as they observed animal antics for the first time. Mom and Dad, Uncle John and Aunt May, and Aunt Lulu went in to watch too. They sat on the bench just higher than all the kids.

The circus manager came out and recited the virtues of each animal. Of course each one was "world renowned" as the best in his field. At long last the tigers were paraded and put through their tricks, then the "fierce lions." They looked old and ragged and somewhat thin - not very fierce - but they were alive! Finally the elephants led around by men dressed up in monkey suits. All this time half-naked young ladies were standing around cracking whips and interspersing animal acts with songs, dances, invitations to have your fortune told. Mama made a reference to them as "looking like gypsies" to her - maybe that's why Dad and Uncle Harry liked circuses so much.

When we came out of the circus tent, Mama had had enough - too much for one day. "George we've got to get started home." Everett guided us to the Dodge, took us into town and we re-loaded into the farm wagon loaded with a paper bag full of "all day suckers" from Uncle Harry.

We had much to look forward to though - Aunt May, Uncle John and their sons, Harry and Dorsey, their daughter Jennie who was sixteen, and of course, Grandma would be coming out to the farm to visit. So after any such a heavenly day as we had just experienced, I couldn't believe there was more to come.

The next day was extra big - extra big in work that is. By now we knew the routine pretty well - fix extra beds, do some extra laundry for Bant (especially diapers,) catch at least four black roosters, shut them in a coop until morning, bake bread, dig potatoes from the patch behind the barn, and bring in cabbage and green beans from the garden. Roasting ears would be picked fresh early in the morning. Apples had to be brought in from the orchard. Sweet cream was carried from the springhouse. The churn was scalded, the cream poured in, and we took turns with the crank. When the butter was worked with the paddle and molded in the wheat sheaf pattern, there would be perhaps six beautiful one-pound molds to put in a crock and sink in a deep, cool, pool of water in the springhouse. Ellie had come to help out. All day we ran our legs off. Since we had been gone all day the day before, the old hens with young families had to be looked up, fed extra and watered. You also had to report to Mama just how many chicks each old biddy had with her. That gave you a "use for arithmetic - especially subtraction," she said. When night came, we were in pretty good shape for Aunt May and Uncle John.

Mama was up early making biscuits because she had to get started on the pies for dinner. Mae, Ellie and I each plucked a big, black rooster. We then submerged them into a dishpan filled with cool water. We peeled apples and "looked over" fresh plump blackberries and dewberries for pie. Dad had picked an extra nice patch of berries when he brought the cows in for milking. Ellie had picked the dewberries on Nixon Ridge the day before.

When the Hancks family and Grandma arrived, we had dinner almost ready. Aunt May praised our cooking, our choice of wallpaper, our house, the farm land, the garden - everything. Today she had time to hold Bant and comment on how different he was from the rest of us with our dark hair and eyes. He was a brown eyed blonde! Harry and Dorsey had explored everything. They tried burying themselves in the loose wheat in the granary. They had discovered the ledge around the wall over our stair steps. By some strange sense of balance, they could hold to the wall and walk the two inch molding. Aunt May soon put an end to that!

Later in the evening Aunt May wanted to see the creek. She asked if we could perhaps go "swimming" - that was a very complimentary term. Nowhere along the creek could anyone really swim, the water was never more than 2 feet deep at the mouth of the spring branch. But this appealed to Jennie and Mae and Ellie. None of us had bathing suits. We found old dresses for ourselves and overalls for the boys and away we went. It was a lovely show, splashing in the cool, clean water, sitting on the warm sand, wading in next to the bank where perch and small mud cats scurried into hiding. The minnows simply defied all our efforts to catch them. Harry and Dorsey had to be dragged out and marched home - they were determined to capture one minnow!

The next morning Aunt May was going to bake an angel food cake - she had baked one for Aunt Lulu. "They are so easy to make," she said. We had to have special cake flour called "Swans Down" - a box of this had been purchased when we were in Belle. I jumped out of bed very early, just as soon as I heard Mama rake the stove catch through the ash trap in "Old Bridge Beach." We sliced thick slices of tender cured ham. We always had ham when Aunt May came; she simply "doted" on home cured ham. For years Mama wrapped one of our finest in brown paper, packed it in a cardboard box and off it went to Wamego, Kansas. When it became illegal to mail meat products across state lines Mama would label the box "books and clothing." Aunt May would write in a few days saying the "books and clothing" had arrived in good shape.

After breakfast Aunt May assembled her baking equipment. Separating the eggs fascinated me - we had never in all our lives used a whole dozen eggs in one cake. Aunt May assured us we would love the "Golden Glow" layer cake she would make with the yolks. We had only a wire whisk beater, so Aunt May and Mama took turns beating the whites. Nothing much happened - they got frothy and foamed in a very lazy manner. Mama thought the kitchen was too warm, so they carried the bowl and beater into the yard. They beat and beat and discussed the possible trouble. Finally they were exhausted. The frothy mess was brought back to the kitchen; the wonderful Swans Down flour and sugar which May and I had been sifting over and over was added. The angel food was shoved in the oven and the two exhausted experimental cooks flung themselves down in the rocking chairs on the cool north porch to fan with newspapers and discuss what was the matter with "that" cake. Aunt May was sure it was the wire whisk. Mama was sure the heat in the kitchen was too much for the eggs. The cake didn't rise much and it was tough - it stuck to the pan but we ate it and even called it "angel food" - after all, that was the name. After dinner they just sort of threw the Golden Glow together, and it did turn out beautiful, light and fluffy.

Uncle John spent most of his time sitting on the front porch, reading the Globe Democrat or some of our books and magazines. Jennie made herself useful in many ways. She had always been a nursemaid for the twins - they were a handful to manage - and Jennie loved babies so she helped watch and amuse Bant. That freed me for trips to the spring, to the garden, and to the henhouse.

It wasn't until later, when I was sent to the dining room to bring a footed bowl for Mama, that I spied a strange tri-cornered newspaper parcel on top of the safe. Immediately I knew what was in that package. "Oh Mama, come here, see what I've found." In a minute she was unwrapping her beautiful black lace hat and memory came flooding back. She had worn the hat to an event in Belle earlier that summer, and on the way home it began to rain, so she stopped at Tom Walker's and left her hat. A few days later Dad stopped by and brought the newspaper wrapped package home. Mama was busy so she put it in a "good safe place" on top of the safe. Again Aunt May and all of us had a good laugh. Mom had proved she really did have a hat!! All our excitement brought Uncle John in from the porch, he laughed too as he stood in the hall door twirling his fine gold watch chain. Uncle John dressed in dress-up clothes: fine starched shirts, some with removable collars. He always used cuff links, his suits were matched with the seasons, and he wore his gold watch every day. Dad had a fine gold watch but he only wore it when he dressed up.

Aunt May's visit was over too soon. Uncle John couldn't be away from the hospital any longer. But Jennie stayed on for a couple of weeks. Even though Mae and I were years younger than she and Rita, they were very gentle and considerate with us. They invited Mae and me to stay at Belle for several days. I was almost consumed with excitement. Grandma went back to Belle. All of us would be staying at Uncle Harry's for a time while we visited around. One day we went with Grandma to visit Aunt Kate and Uncle Tom Groff. Aunt Kate was Grandpa LeFevre's half-sister.

Aunt Kate and Uncle Tom lived on a farm in the Summerfield area. They were so glad to see Grandma. There weren't many of their relatives in Missouri as the LeFevre's had come from Pennsylvania soon after the Civil War. They told wonderful stories that day about their families and what they had heard from Pennsylvania and New York relatives. Aunt Kate went to the field and brought in roasting ears. She made custard pies and fried ham. We sat on the wonderful cool screened in back porch and laughed a lot. Jennie Hancks spent the day with her father's youngest sister, Aunt Tavia Goodman, who lived nearby. Everett came back for us late in the evening.

The next morning Aunt Lulu got us all organized and off to spend the weekend with Aunt Lou and Uncle Ed Mee. Uncle Ed was Grandpa LeFevre's half-brother but so different in appearance. Grandpa was short and stocky. Uncle Ed was very tall, over six feet and very, very bald, twinkling blue eyes and a wonderful sense of humor. Aunt Lou was a very special woman, had she been alive today she would have been presidential timber. She was so innovative - anything she saw or heard of that she wanted, she figured out some way to get it. Work was something she dissolved as easily as the sun melts ice in August. She knit socks for men who steered the steam boats up the Gasconade River. She also dried apples to sell these same people or to carry to country stores in exchange for sugar, coffee, and more yarn. In winter she set up her loom and wove rag carpeting for anyone who brought her the balls of rags. Her cooking was superb. They lived on a fine river bottom farm above the Rollins Ferry Bridge on the Belle side of the river.

They had always been prosperous farmers. At times Aunt Lou would go long distances from home to buy hogs at a sale. Often she would get quite a bargain. Once when she had succeeded in getting a good buy, she heard a big rough man who had been bidding against her say in an undertone - "Oh, I always feel sorry for poor widder women. That poor Miz Mee lives way over yonder acrost the river."

During this particular summer, Aunt Lou had turned her attention to boarders. This was a business she really enjoyed. Once she bought a hotel in Belle and served meals to the town's people (and relatives who came in hungry). She and Uncle Ed had moved to the state of Washington and set up a hotel business. Now for several years, they had been back home farming and keeping summer boarders. When Grandma, Jennie, Mae and I arrived, Aunt Lou was busily engaged in cooking dinner. Her hands were flying around as she mixed a huge "wad" of pie dough. She had a dab of flour on her nose as she came flying to the front door to welcome us! She was very pretty this morning in her blue checked gingham dress with white collar and cuffs. She put all of us at ease before returning to her domain. There were people all over the place. The front porch was the length of the house, upstairs and down. It seemed full of people, all busy doing nothing. They were on vacation. Some were sitting in home-made chairs on the beautiful green grass, some were lounging in their cabins built in the back yard. In the kitchen all sorts of food preparation was going on. It was by far the biggest operation I'd ever seen. Chicken and ham were frying under the supervision of Mrs. Eva Freshwater, Aunt Lu's mother. Slaw and potatoes were being managed by Mrs. Robertson. The table was being extended to its fullest in the big dining room by Levada and Dorothy, Aunt Lu's daughter and granddaughter. The kitchen work was so streamlined, little talking went on. Each knew exactly what her duties were, so the food would all be ready at one time. Now this was really living! Aunt Lou came to the dining room buffet and struck a small bronze bell with an accompanying bronze rod and everybody sprang into action. Someone on the porch called, "dinner's served" to those in the yard. Someone in the yard called, "Hey Ed, dinners ready" and everyone found their places around the biggest dining room table I had ever seen. Talk about good! The chicken and ham were the best, and there was home baked bread, mashed potatoes, green beans, pickles, slaw and corn - even a huge plate of sliced tomatoes. We hadn't had any of those yet. But dessert was the crowning glory, angel food cake and sliced peaches. Aunt Lu's Angel Food was a far cry from Mama's and Aunt May's. This one was high, light and so full of air, I hardly knew I had eaten a piece, so I asked for the cake to be passed please. Grandma's face fell. She looked at me as if I had committed the Cardinal Sin, but someone passed me the cake. I took another piece, but I noticed Grandma politely declined. I'm sure she had counted the pieces!

That afternoon left lots of times for exploring all these new hideaways. I peeped into the cabins out in the back yard. Each one contained one or two beds, a dresser, a wash stand with bowl and pitcher, a chair or two and rag rug strips on the floor - clean and neat!

Mrs. Shanks came to the store. Yes, Aunt Lou kept a small stock of goods such as sugar, coffee, flour, meal, chewing and smoking tobacco, canned goods, a few bolts of gingham and unbleached muslin and lace on cardboard wrappers. On a shelf were men's and women's everyday shoes, socks and stockings. All these were stored in the "old house" - a much smaller structure than the one they now lived in. Aunt Lou carried Mrs. Shanks' eggs to the basement in the new house and shut the fat Plymouth Rock hens in a big slatted shed along with several others she was feeding extra for the slaughter. The exchange of goods went on while I examined everything in the store. This was like living in Paradise!

After the boarders had taken their "siestas," Aunt Lou asked who would like to go to the Gasconade River. They could swim or go wading or fish or just have a nice shady tree to sit under. Grandma said she would really like to go but it was a little too far for her to walk. "I'd like to see that big river bottom field where Ed's working." Aunt Lou immediately exclaimed, "Oh, Dosia, I'm going to drive you down there in that car." Well, again if anybody was going for a ride in a car I wasn't going to be left out! I even tagged at Aunt Lu's heels when she went out to the shed and while she cranked up the new, black, shiny Ford. I climbed in the front seat. Aunt Lou backed the car out and pulled up in front of the house where Grandma and Judge Graham climbed in. Judge said he was still too full of fried chicken to walk. He was huge, he almost filled the back seat! But off we went, around the ridge field, then began the descent - at first gentle slopes then down a rather steep hill and there we were right on the river bank. Uncle Ed and son Jim were "laying by" the corn. Uncle Ed was using a beautiful team of matched sorrel horses. Jim was using a tractor. We had a couple of beautiful hours. Grandma and Aunt Lou walked down the path to the wooden steps that led to a rowboat tethered to a sycamore tree. Grandma dipped up some water in her long, thin, blue-veined hand and remarked, "Its just as I remembered it. I've wondered many times if I'd ever see it again" (the Gasconade River).

Soon was Aunt Lou was grinding the gears back up the river road toward the house. I went with Levada to gather the eggs. I watched Uncle Ed and Jim milk their Jersey cows. They carried the milk to the cellar in the old house, they separated the cream from the milk. Aunt Lou then took over and set out pitchers of cream for breakfast, milk for drinking, and cream to churn.

Supper wasn't quite as elegant as dinner because we were to have home-made ice cream later. While we went to the river, Mrs. Robertson had been busy mixing the cream, chipping the ice and, along with her daughter Melinda, had cranked the old wooden freezer in order to prepare this delicacy. In the dusk of early evening, dishes of this beautiful, cool concoction were passed around. Plates of angel food and chocolate cake were on a picnic table nearby and Judge Graham recited poems, such as I had never heard. He pointed out constellations, something else I had never heard of. Now it was off to bed, to sleep with Grandma and to rub that smelly liniment on her shoulder before we slept. The smell didn't bother me long, I had had a really big day.

The next morning I had the run of the place. I decided this was exactly what I would do when I grew up. I would have a big, new house and an old house where I could keep store. I'd cook for summer boarders and drive a Model T and cook and cook and freeze ice cream and, and, and. And all these happy, care-free hours came about because of Jennie Hancks visit, and I don't remember one thing about what she or Mae did. I only see Aunt Lou going from kitchen to cellar to store to chicken coop, upstairs, downstairs to the garage. Yes all those and in the evening playing hymns on the parlor organ. I found out that the parlor was also where she kept the Angel Food Cake!

It was early afternoon when Earl came for us. How sorry I was to leave, but Aunt Lou was sure Mama would let me come back soon. Maybe I could help her with the work - that was my idea! She followed us to Belle taking a load of boarders to "catch" the Rock Island train to return to St. Louis. I wondered if they hated to leave Aunt Lou as much as I did.

That evening Reta and Everett had planned a "little spread" in honor of Jennie. While we were away Aunt Lulu had had time to clean house and rest, and on this evening they had asked some young folks in for a light lunch, games and fun in general. Luckily I was to sleep on a day bed just outside the dining room on the cool back porch. I lay propped on my elbows peeping through Aunt Lulu's lace curtains. They were feasting on sandwiches and fruit salad. I soon rolled over and fell asleep. That afternoon we said goodbye to Jennie. We hated to do that; Jennie was such fun to be around and it would be a long time before she came back. Earl drove Mae and me to the top of our hill. We climbed out and started our homecoming. How I had missed my baby brother! I couldn't get enough of holding him, loving him. Mama wanted to hear all about Aunt Kate and Aunt Lou and Uncle Tom and Uncle Ed, and I was ready and willing to talk. I had met Aunt Lou once before when she was keeping hotel at Belle in the Gieck Building. Once when I went with Dad to Belle, he had turned me over to Aunt Lou. I was nearly frozen. She thawed me out by removing my shoes and setting a chair in front of the wood stove oven door. She placed a board over the door, then a folded towel over the board, she said, "I could borrow the oven until her 'stir cake' was ready." She bustled and rustled about in her starched checked apron. Her helper that day was Sadie Branson. Sadie needed a pair of new shoes. Soon after dinner, she invited me to walk up the street with her to look at the shoes. She counted out four one dollar bills in case she found a pair that fit. She tried on several pairs of stout laced oxfords, and we went back to the hotel. She put them on to show Aunt Lou how nice they looked. Aunt Lou stooped way down and felt the toe region. She pressed hard and said, "They may look nice Sadie, but they are too small for your feet." So back we went with the pretty brown shoes, we even had to leave the shoe spoon in the box. I'd never seen one of those before.

Coming home was quite a letdown after of several days in town. The eggs were waiting for me to carry them to the store. Bant was waiting for me to carry him any place he wanted to go. The thing I missed most during my visiting was his little loving arms around my neck, and the feel of his soft blonde curls against my cheek as we spent our days together! But now it was time to get on with routine.

The old hens, the famous brown leghorns, had been busy while I had been visiting Aunt Lulu, Aunt Kate and Aunt Lou. Mama said Bud and I could make several trips up the hill to the store. "We wouldn't need to carry many at a time." But the baskets were always heavy - no matter what Mama said. I nearly always carried a basket full of the precious money crop. Bud's load was put in a light-weight tin bucket. We would stop to rest several times while pulling the hill, then pick up our "burden of life" again. Sometimes we were permitted to stay an hour and play with the Drewel children; they were always fun. Often the play was supervising the younger Drewel children, but that was fun too. Sometimes Bud and I made two trips in one day, one in the early morning and another after the sun was set behind our hill.

Soon school would begin. Bud had to have new shoes and bib overalls. Mae and I had to have gingham for school dresses. So when all the eggs were delivered to the Drewel store, the new stout shoes had been purchased and gingham was waiting for Mama's cutting shears. There was actually a piece of beautiful yellow and brown plaid gingham for Mama and enough white organdy for collars and cuffs.

And to top off an absolutely perfect summer, there was to be a Modern Woodman picnic at Cooper Hill. Again when we begged Mama to go, Mama's answer was always the same - "We'll see, depends on how good all of you work." Well, we all understood these words. In fact, we knew what she was going to say before we asked, but we also knew our chances were excellent if she didn't say "No" in an emphatic tone of voice.

And so - o - o - o Bud and I carried eggs to the store, carried wood from the wood pile to the wood box on the porch, and carried fresh drinks to Dad and Don in the field. We carried buckets filled with chicken manure and buckets filled with rich chip dirt from the wood pile to the garden to use for compost. We carried water from the spring for household cooking and drinking. We carried fat old "good-for-nothings" to the store to exchange for coffee, sugar, flour, Calumet Baking Powder, Ivory Soap and always a "plug" of Horseshoe Chewing Tobacco for Dad that cost fifteen cents and had a small tin horseshoe stamped into each piece. By the time summer ended, Bud and I had bucket calluses on our tough little hands and quite a little bit of mileage on our fat little legs.

But the picnic materialized on a very warm August Saturday. The Modern Woodman had selected a cleared space just beyond the Cooper Hill schoolhouse as the location. There was to be red and white soda pop, home-made ice cream and also manufactured ice cream. Great was the anticipation. We felt we had really earned our nickels and dimes. Since there were no artificial lights (as Mrs. Elsner called them), picnics were daylight affairs. People began gathering in the early afternoon, just the neighborhood people. But in addition to the lunch stand and the soda and ice cream stand there was a dance floor, a "fancy work" table where embroidered pillow cases and bureau scarves, dust caps, sun bonnets, baby bibs, aprons, crocheted centerpieces and all sorts of items hand-made by Royal Neighbors who were wives, sisters, mothers, etc. of the Modern Woodman. We heard all about these plans from Dr. and Mrs. Leach who were active members.

Ellie had told me there was always a "fish pond." That was something I couldn't quite picture in my mind, so I lost no time inquiring where the fish pond was. Ellie pointed toward two saplings to one side of the picnic grounds. Around the two saplings a large brown tarpaulin was wrapped and tied to the lowest limbs. This didn't look like any fish pond I had ever seen. Some good friends, Zoa, Floy and Coy Hassler, were lined up to "fish." A pole was attached to a small syrup bucket. Zoa dropped her nickel into the bucket with a beautiful plinking sound I thought. Then a deep masculine voice was heard to ask, "Boy or Girl?" After the question, there was no doubt as to who the fisherman was inside the "tent" - Mr. Ed (Buckshot) Leach, who was very, very deaf. It didn't matter boy or girl, Mr. Leach had a small hole at eye level where he could check on the sex before putting the appropriate ball, doll, top or small toy in the bucket.

These were also the first hot dogs I ever saw. People were eating and laughing and drinking soda pop, either red or white. I suppose they were laughing because Mrs. Elsner said she was told to "cut the wieners" in two in the middle, so instead of splitting them down the long way, she was cutting them crossways. Therefore, they rolled off the bread easily. Someone explained to her how it was done properly. She drew her lips firmly up over her teeth and muttered, "Can't see how that helps a bit."

The dance floor was a popular attraction, especially for the young unmarried people. The young ladies had such beautiful georgette dresses in such luscious shades of coral, green and blue. The skirts swirled and swished when the music was fast. The scraping sound of shoe soles against the fresh board floor fascinated me. It fascinated Pete too - during a lull in the dancing, he jumped up on the floor and did his own interpretation of the dance. He swung his arms and skipped along much to the amusement of the entire picnic crowd.

In my childish opinion, this was a fine picnic. Mama's nickels and dimes were being doled out very carefully, but Bud and I had fished, we had eaten home-made ice cream and drunk red soda. We had watched the dancing with great interest. Now all of a sudden a distant roll of thunder startled everyone. Cooper Hill is located in a valley surrounded by hills. We were all so very busy having fun, we hadn't noticed a summer electrical storm approaching. Soon big drops of rain were splattering on the dance floor. The lightning flashed and the thunder roared. Those who owned automobiles ran towards them, because there was a deep branch called "Goose Creek" between the picnic and the parking lot. Luckily the fancy work had been auctioned to the highest bidders earlier and most of the food had been sold!

Those of us who were traveling by team and wagon or "shanks pony" had no shelter, but we needed to get to the wagon and head for home because there was no bridge across Big Third Creek at that time. A heavy rain would bring a quick rise and leave us on the Cooper Hill side - stranded.

When we left the picnic scene nearly everyone was rushing along with us. The last look I had was amusing - someone thought the fish pond tarp should be used to cover the ice cream and soda tub. With a couple of swift movements, Henry Baker and Tom Cox had the tarp down and were running toward the food stand with it. Mr. Leach, who was totally deaf, was standing there in stark amazement - holding a fish pole and bucket in his hand and shouting his favorite prefix over and over - "Well, I'll be G--Damn." -"Well, I'll be G-- D---"!!

We hurriedly climbed into the wagon and Dad let Jim and Odie do their best pace until we reached the creek. It was rising rapidly, tree limbs, chips, and debris were floating on the surface of the muddy water. Dad studied the route he would take for a minute, then slowly and carefully urged the big stout mules to get on with the business of crossing the creek. Jim didn't like the deep water. He looked down at it and pushed his big ears forward. Just when we were in midstream, the double tree came unhooked and dropped into the swift water. Before anyone could see what was happening, Dad had jumped over the wheel and into the water almost to his waist, retrieved the double tree, re-hooked the connection and how relieved we were to pull up the muddy bank and be out of the reach of the dark brown water.

The wind was whipping trees and saplings around vigorously as we came down the road past the Elsner and Baker homes. Grandpa Leach's rocking chair was sitting on his grave simply galloping along, moved by the strong wind. This rocking chair had been placed there by his request soon after his death. It remained there, rocking along with the wind and weather, shaded by an apple tree until after many years it disintegrated. The stone marking the grave is still there, but not in the same location due to road changes, death of the apple tree, etc.

This all happened so quickly Mama didn't have time to give Dad any "counseling." I can't remember her saying much on the way home. There was no way to stay dry; we just laughed at each other as our hair glued itself to our scalps. Our clothes stuck to our skin like Saran Wrap. The old quilt under us became soggy and the straw stuck to it. Worse than that, the hail came down in big stones, pelting us and the mules. We stuck our heads under the quilt until the storm was done. The hail and rain had cooled the atmosphere to such an extent that we were almost shivering by the time Dad drove team, wagon, wife and offspring into the shed. We ran to the house. So glad to change our wet clothes, build a nice warm fire in the cookstove and eat our scrambled eggs along with Mama's Calumet Baking Powder biscuits and climb into bed. After that I was sure I knew all about "Modern Woodman" and "Royal Neighbors." They had fine picnics but they should have interceded the weatherman!

Chapter 15

Bud's Homework

On Monday morning it was back to school! Again the lunch basket appeared at the end of the long table in the kitchen. Fried chicken, fresh tomatoes, and bread and butter were put into it as we scurried about getting dressed and running to and from the springhouse and the henhouse. Mae and I were filled with curiosity. Mr. Paul Patterson was to be our teacher this year. We were acquainted with nearly everyone now. Mildred Leach was a beginner. Pete had moved his family from our small tenant house to a three-room unpainted weather boarded abode just down the road from the schoolhouse. I felt called upon to help Mildred and Edgar, especially Mildred since she was a "beginner."

Mr. Patterson was quite different from Mr. Shockley. We found him soft-voiced, very patient and deliberate in his decisions. He didn't "spin on his heel" to catch a culprit throwing a "spit ball" or keep his gold pocket watch lying directly in front of him on the oilcloth-covered table. He was careful and thoughtful of the small children. He spent much of his time teaching them. Sometimes he had to postpone an "A" or "B" class until "after recess" or "first thing after noon."

We progressed about as usual. There were more pie suppers, more programs, more fun with base, stealing sticks and high jump. Mae was now in Milne's *Arithmetic* instead of fighting with fractions and "the Preamble to the Constitution." She was now mastering "square root," "cube root," and "cylindrical mathematics." "How many inches of 3 inch rope can be wound on a cylinder 6 inches by 8 inches by 18 inches," etc. I'm sure Mae has used the knowledge gained by solving that problem many times!! Such reading problems were designed to strengthen our powers of concentration and ability to reason.

She was also having to memorize the names of the bones in the body and know where they were located. We had to recite them in some such order as "knee cap - patella - shoulder blade - clavicle - finger phalanges - arm bones - tibia and fibia," etc. until you had mastered all two hundred and six including the five small bones at the base of the spine called the coccyx. Mama wouldn't let us say "tail bone." She said the book should have never used that expression; it was a poor choice of words. I thought those names of the bones were simply wonderful, even coccyx. I studied them and recited them along with Mae, "clavicle and patella - tibia and fibia." How I loved to let them roll off my tongue. In agriculture, Mae had to draw a diagram of a cow's stomach and label the compartments. Then the horse's skeleton had to be drawn and bones identified. Our way of drawing was to place tissue paper over the drawn illustrations in the text book, trace over it lightly with a pencil, place the tissue paper on your fresh tablet paper, press hard enough on the tissue so you could see the outline and then fill in the outline with the pencil. Teachers disapproved of this method. Everyone should be able to draw a horse "freehand." But judging from the fact that nearly every horse picture had nearly been cut from the text page, I'm reasonably sure very few horses or cows or chickens were "freehand." And furthermore, if freehand is so easy, why didn't teachers demonstrate more of it?

Bud had quite a time with "head marks" that school year. "Head marks" cut quite a wide swath in Mama's book. They were small strips of colored construction paper in several colors - red, blue, and yellow. You were given a list of spelling words. Each day the list was pronounced. If Bud was head of the class on Monday - he got a yellow slip, Tuesday - a blue, Wednesday - a brown, Thursday - a green, and if he held on until Friday - the reward was a red head mark. He got to keep it until Monday and of all things take it home to prove to Mama he had actually held on to the lead all week. This was accomplished by having a daily spell down. Instead of praising Bud, Mama preached at him and emphasized he had done it once now, he had better "bear in mind," he could do the same thing every Friday.

It was that same autumn that Bud and Mama had another "meeting of the minds." Mama and Dad had registered our shorthorn calves and when the "papers" came through the mail, Mama placed the big brown envelope on the dining room table to be put away in the strong box later. After several days, she remembered to go get them and "lo and behold" - there was no envelope - no paper, no nothing. When we came home from school, a search was instituted for the missing registration certificates. There was a fee for the certificates, and duplicates would cost double. We searched, we talked about when the envelope was last seen, who brought the mail to the house that day, etc., etc. Mama preached about how everything should be "put away properly" just as soon as it came into the house. Several days went by - the paper certificates were almost forgotten. Dad would have to ask for duplicates. Then it was wash day. Bud changed his new overalls for an older pair. Mama felt a big wad of paper in one pocket just as she was stuffing them in the soap suds. The big wad turned out to be the long lost certificates. Bud had folded each one and put them in a Bull Durham tobacco sack. He had carried them in a safe place every day to school. I guess he compared them to head marks.

I seemed to always get myself into trouble with Mama. She warned me to stay away from Annie. Just let her alone, I would be reprimanded severely, but Mae always felt it was her duty to report on my school activities. I didn't understand why I was supposed to "stay away from Annie." Mama would yell at me when I left for school, "Don't ask questions - just do as I say." Well it wasn't long until I found out why. Mama always combed our hair using her comb full force through my thick curly mass. All of a sudden, she gave my top-knot curls a quick painful jerk, "Well of all things - I told you to stay away from her." But by that time, she was jerking me through the kitchen door and out into the back yard as if I would soon contaminate the whole house. Such shouting - "Dad, come here and see if this child of yours has what I think she has." I was stunned - what in the world did I have. I felt around carefully. I couldn't feel any holes; there wasn't any blood. What could it be - something deadly I was sure! Dad came and poked around through my curls. I was crying loudly now, but Dad was always comforting when Mama wasn't around. He was laughing as he hugged me and told me to stop crying - "You've got a few visitors. Mom will soak your hair in a mixture of coal oil and turpentine - they'll soon disappear." All this time, Mama was mixing a big tin cup of this terrible concoction. She ordered me to come around the back of the wash house. I was ordered to "bend away over" and "hold your head down." She slowly poured the sticky stuff over my head, massaging it in thoroughly as she scolded some more - "As if I haven't got enough to do - my kids have to go to school and bring home cooties."

I was made to stand in a head down position for at least an hour, every little while Mama would come by and inspect. She decided I needed another application - so she prepared another tin cup of coal oil and turpentine. I tried to tell her I had to stand up awhile. I knew now how chickens felt when you carry them to the store heads down. Mama wasn't at all concerned about my aches or pains - it was my head she said that needed attention. Anyhow the treatment was repeated several times during the week that followed - kerosene, turpentine, shampoo, and thorough inspection.

About the middle of the week, Aunt Ida and Uncle John came to visit. Mama forbid any of us to mention my "head trouble." I was absolutely feeling ostracized - having to sleep by myself - being under constant scrutiny. Aunt Ida didn't seem to notice anything unusual. She and Uncle John had closed the deal for their farm on the Gasconade River across from Mt. Sterling. They were on cloud nine. But on Saturday morning Uncle John was splitting wood, and Bud and I were carrying the split sticks to the wood-box. Just as I came back for another load I heard Bud say "Uncle John, you know what?" ... long pause ... "Uncle John you know what?" Uncle John paused in his splitting and said "No, Bud, what is it I don't know?" Bud was always very deliberate in his speaking but he had decided to divulge his secret knowledge. "Well Uncle John, Mama said not to tell you but Grace has got 'its.'" (Nits was a common name for the eggs of lice.) Uncle John let out a long low whistle. It almost sounded like the low rumbling of the train whistle passing through Belle on a muggy morning run. "Grace has got what, Bud?" "Its, Uncle John, Its." Bud was getting upset with Uncle John now. Didn't Uncle John understand plain talk? Well no doubt Uncle John understood all too well. Somehow he got the word to Aunt Ida and before anything more could be said "Old Maud" was hitched to the buggy and Uncle John and Aunt Ida were headed up the hill. Now came the Inquisition. Mama was judge, jury and sheriff all rolled into one. "Now, just which one of you gave out the information?" There was no earthly use to deny anything with Mama, so in a few minutes Bud had confessed to the crime. He told Mama, "Mama, I was just trying to talk sense to Uncle John." Mama was constantly reminding all of us to "talk sense."

Things seemed to settle down for a while after the "cooties" and "calf registration papers." Uncle John and Aunt Ida were soon to move to their farm. But before they did Mae and I had one more wonderful, delightful weekend with them in town. The Osage County Fair was in session. We would go with Dr. and Mrs. Leach in "First Meyer" (this was an early, early Model T) with brass radiator and tool box on the running board and all the fixin's.

The morning of another great adventure arrived. We got up extra early, put our best dresses in a box with our "night dresses" (Grandma's terminology) and donned our long white cotton stockings and Mary Janes and our "Beaver Hats."

So on this Saturday morning late in September, Mae and I walked up the hill to meet Dr. and Mrs. Leach. We waited at the mailbox, and soon they came. Doc was in fine form - he hadn't driven "First Meyer" to Linn. He was really "barreling down." Mae and I climbed into the back seat. We soon learned we had to hold on to the "Beavers" with both hands. When we came to the Gasconade, we had to ring the bell for Tom Cox to come ferry us across. We could rest our weary arms a little. The road up from the river on the Linn side was so rough we jolted around on the back seat considerably. When your legs won't touch the floor and your back can't touch the back of the seat and one must hold to a beaver hat the scenery is of little interest. Doc just drove and smoked his cigar and cussed every time we met a wagon or buggy, it picked up a little when he met a car. "Damn fool, damn fool, don't know who he was but he's gonna get killed." Mrs. Leach always accented, "He sure will - My, my just looky how fast he's goin' down that road."

I suppose it never occurred to Mae and me to remove those awful "beavers" from our heads. We sat and held on to them patiently all the way to Linn. Doc and Mrs. Leach were to visit Doc's sister who was married to Dr. Jett. They lived in a fine two story house on Main Street. That is where Uncle John and Aunt Ida met us. They took us home to their house on the Linn hill. This is where we had spent the night just before moving to the farm.

Later that afternoon Mae and I changed into our dress-up dresses and again donned our beaver hats and went to the fair with Uncle John and Aunt Ida. The day was extremely warm. The sweat poured off our faces. Our dark brown curls were plastered to our foreheads. My bright red silk hair ribbon kept pushing the "crown" up, dare I remove it? No, no, no, Mama would surely find out I hadn't displayed all my finery to the fullest extent!

Mae and I met our friends from our school days in Linn - Carmen and Zelda Campbell, Alma and Marie Tafflinger, Ruth and Mary Ellen Peters. I saw Howard Bryan and was reminded again of those awful black stockings and the rain storm.

Sunday morning we attended church and Sunday School at the Linn Methodist. Again the Beavers took precedence over everything. It was a long walk from the church back down hill to Uncle John's but Mae and I enjoyed every step of it. It had been our daily trek when we walked to school from the farm on Linn Creek. We renewed acquaintance with jewelry on display in Andy Kliethermes' glass front jewelry store and the beautifully attired women and men pictured in a sample suit book at the Linn Mercantile window. There was the Old Corner Restaurant, the Courthouse, the Telephone Exchange and on down past the Livery Stables to Aunt Ida's. She was waiting dinner for us because Doc and Mrs. Leach had sent word for us to "come as soon as we could" to start home. We just had to run down once more to hear the telephone poles sing and to say good-bye to the wonderful high grass steps on the lower side of Aunt Ida's yard where we had spent such delightful hours. All too soon Aunt Ida was pushing us toward the door. She was carrying our cardboard box. It now contained our new gingham dresses that we had worn the day before and a piece of yard goods, a medium blue background cotton with black polkadots and lines in it. I always suspected Aunt Ida bought it for herself and decided she didn't like it. Anyway Mae and I met Doc and Mrs. Leach at the Jett home. Doc was chewing impatiently at his cigar. As soon as Mae and I were in and seated, Doc took off. Old First Meyer jumped and bucked around and acted as if he might not go at all. But Doc chewed and cussed and chewed and cussed and finally Old First Meyer turned his old brass nose up and headed toward Cooper Hill. Mae and I pointed out familiar landmarks. There's the road to Grandpa Bacon's. There's where Grea' Granny used to live. See the pond. What a pretty brick house. When we passed the small black community Aunt Lucy was out in the yard. We waved and called "Hi Aunt Lucy." She waved her voluminous blue apron at us and smiled in greeting. Aunt Lucy had helped every family in Linn when they needed someone to do extra housework. We saw no color - she was just Aunt Lucy - beautiful!

Again we fought our beaver hats from the wind, Doc's spit and our aching arms. It was good to get home. Mama's first words were "Now put those nice beaver hats away carefully" and in capital letters she always added "be sure to stuff the tissue paper in the crown real good." For a long time Mae and I fought battles with those awful things. In winter our ears froze off. In early fall and spring, we drowned in our perspiration. One thing is sure and certain, we never dared take them off if Mama said, "Wear your beaver hat!"

In school, I was now a fifth grader and, joy of joys, I was now old enough to study history. I inherited Mae's *U. S. History*, a well-worn brown cloth-covered volume picturing Columbus with the "Nina," the "Pinta," and the "Santa Maria" in the first chapter. There were no colored plates. We were assigned three or four topics per day to study. Topic headings were in "bold type." We were to read, re-read, study, know the content and be able to give every detail contained in the reading if asked to give a resume'. "Tell in your own words" were the instructions most teachers used. There were always dozens of questions to be answered at the end of each chapter. Bud was now using my 3rd Grade *Easy Road to Reading*. I could hardly stand it but Mama always put everything in proper perspective. "You're using Mae's books so Bud has to use yours. Now shut up and go fill that water jug." This year Mama was really hung up on "rain water." "If you drink that rain water at school you'll get typhoid fever and die." These words rang in our ears, so every morning when we carried fresh spring water into the kitchen for coffee, cooking and teakettle. An extra jug was filled and set on the cool concrete porch floor for Bud and me to carry to school. The jug itself was heavy, one of those white-based brown-top stone affairs. Everyone used them for vinegar in those days. Mama tied a long strip of blue cotton (like our new dresses) through the jug handle to carry it by. Bud was not very tall; neither was I. Carrying the jug was very difficult, it dragged on the ground. Holding it up clear of the ground made your arm ache fiercely. In addition to the jug we carried "book satchels." Mine was fashioned from oil cloth, a beautiful fruit pattern. Mae's was blue and white checked. These satchels were in the form of an envelope. A strap was attached to hang over the right shoulder so the satchel was rested against the left hip. All of us had one. Mama and Dad took an audit every evening to see what we brought home. Mae usually drew the duty of carrying our lunch basket. Bud and I had satchels and the jug. Egg baskets and buckets seemed light by comparison. Occasionally we would purposely walk by the jug. We would almost be out of sight in the deep woods over the big rocks when we would hear Mama. "Bud - Grace you come marching right back here this very minute. I guess you must want to die of typhoid." Everyone who came to school drank the rain water from the cistern so I started looking at them closely every day. I would not have been surprised to see any one of them "keel over" and die right there. I would have known beyond all shadow of a doubt what had killed them. Even Mr. Patterson and his young son Elwood drank the "cistern rain water" - without any noticeable ill effects!

In the spring we had another fine surprise. Uncle Will had bought the Nath Branson farm just across a couple of hills from us in the College Hill neighborhood. This farm had lots of acres - good pasture - on Mistaken Creek. Now Grandpa Bacon would be closer to us. We were very happy. We were sure Aunt Stell would miss her big roomy farm house because the living quarters on the Branson farm consisted of one large log room, one small side room, a rather large log kitchen, over the big room was a loft which was reached by means of a ladder in the back corner. Uncle Will was full of enthusiasm. He would cut timber and have it sawed for a new barn and house. All he needed was a little time.

It was a cold windy day in March when Dad set out to "help Will move." Uncle John and Aunt Ida had come on Sunday evening again driving "Old Maud" hitched to the buggy. He would ride with Dad in the wagon and drive Will's team hauling a load of household goods to the new home. They needed to be on their way long before daybreak. Old Jim and Odie weren't much for speed but they were dependable. By the middle of the week Uncle Will and Aunt Stell, their four sons and one daughter along with Grandpa were living across the hill.

It was by the same method Uncle John and Aunt Ida were moved to the Giedinghagen farm across the river from Mt. Sterling the previous spring. Now we had family nearer to us: Uncle Harry at Belle, Uncle Will's family across the hill, and Uncle John across the river. This was the beginning of many happy times. We traveled by farm wagon when we visited, always pulled by Jim and Odie. Mama felt the sting of not having an automobile. We were the only ones on either side of the family not possessing one of those things - even Doc had "Old First Meyer."

But we were always short of money - very, very short! Every day we heard interest, mortgage, taxes, drought and flood. Mama's liturgy would begin with "When the Role is Called Up Yonder" as she raked the ashes into Old Bridge Beach's hearth. At breakfast she held forth on interest and mortgage. After school and at supper we would bear up under Mama's government speech - taxes were too high - only God loved poor people and he was sending droughts and floods. What were we going to do? Usually the only answer was raise more chickens, carry more eggs to the store, move more old "good-for-nothin's." March was always potato planting time, on St. Patrick's Day if at all possible. This was another family affair. Dad plowed a big area out back of the horse barn. The soil was black and loose, just a little bit damp. Mama sorted potatoes - those with "good eyes" were cut into pieces - each containing at least "one good eye." Then the whole family trotted out to the patch and the back breaking work began, placing a piece of seed potato - eye up - in a row. Carrying a bucket, putting in the seed, Dad and Mama followed, covering the eyes with good loose soil hoed over the seed. They kept an eye on how we spaced the pieces not too far apart or too near. Row after row had to be planted and covered. It made a long afternoon. Sometimes it was very cold. Our fingers got stiff picking up damp potato eyes and putting them into the furrow. When we got a bit tired Mama would say something like "My, my won't all these mashed potatoes taste good next winter. And just think of that hot potato soup on a cold winter night." Our salivary glands would start working overtime and on and on we would go until every one of the "good eyes" had been interred in the potato cemetery - row upon row of them!

Tomato seed was sown early in wooden boxes and kept warm under Old Bridge Beach. Mama usually baked the soil in the oven for several days to kill the weed seed. Then tiny rows were laid off and seed planted. Every morning the boxes were pulled out and sprinkled with warm water. These plants were later transplanted to the garden.

If the weather permitted planting potatoes on March 17th, we could also make early garden but usually not on the same day. Gardening was big in Mama's book too. She always made a raised bed for short rows of lettuce, radishes, onion sets, beets, carrots, etc. We always left some rows in which to sow cabbage seed and some extra tomato seed to have our own plants. Peas just had to be planted early or they "won't make."

After potato planting came the setting hen routine. After this came pulling weeds out of potatoes and garden and yard. That summer Mama had heard sour milk and cottage cheese were good foods for baby chicks. Since we nearly always had a goodly supply of sour milk a big jar of "clabbered milk was kept on the back of Old Bridge Beach where it could warm through slowly. About mid morning Mama would lay out a clean white muslin sack and say " Now, Thresia (my nickname) dip out the cheese curds and hang the bag on the clothes line to drip." I didn't like this assignment very much. It was watery, drippy and messy - but everyone who might suffer reading this realizes no one argued with Mama. So I dipped and dripped out to the clothes line. By the time dinner was ready the cottage cheese would be dripped dry. I would fetch it in, turn it into a bowl, salt it lightly, dip some sweet cream over it, stir it up a bit and perhaps add a small spoonful of sugar to please Dad. He always referred to this dish as "schmere case." When dinner was over the remainder of that dish was carried out to the baby chicks. They looked so funny pecking around in that "schmere case." It stuck to their bills and their feet as they waded around in it. The old hens clucked and ate it, just like our Mama telling us something was good, we ought to eat it, when we knew all the time how it tasted! That summer I really had had it with cottage cheese and baby chicks, also potato bugs. Every morning as soon as we had finished our last bite, Mama or Dad would be sure to say, "Now, Thresia, you and Bud get right out there and bug those potatoes. Go on now before the sun gets any hotter." I disliked picking those fat yellow striped beetles off the potatoes too. It was slow work - up and down the long rows. Usually Pete and Bant went along. They sat in the shade of the big old horse barn and built corn cob houses. When the bugs got real bad, Mama would dispatch Bud and me to the store with eggs and a list. One item would read a dime's worth of "Paris Green." How she would admonish us to not dare touch the paper containers, it was deadly poison, and would "kill you before you could say Jack Robinson." I really thought I'd prefer "rain water typhoid" but Bud and I certainly didn't touch the Paris Green sack. Early in the morning Dad would mix the Paris Green with water and with the old galvanized garden sprinkling can go quickly up and down the potato rows leaving beautiful bright green water spots on each potato plant.

I'm sure the potatoes thought St. Patrick had returned to perhaps turn them into shamrocks. Mama's garden and the potato patch turned out rather well that year. By the time school opened, there were all kinds of preserved and canned vegetables sitting in an orderly fashion on our cellar shelves. The potato crop produced so well Dad and Mama decided to bring the piano box into the cellar and use it for a potato box. I suppose it was definite by then we wouldn't be moving any more. We loved the farm, the neighborhood and the school. Mae and I were still singing "Morning on the Farm" just as enthusiastically as ever. (That piano box became the potato box and was not removed from the cellar until I retired in 1976 - there were still pieces of it serving time.)

This second year at Post Oak under Mr. Patterson's supervision was Mae's 8th grade year. Mae was studying extra hard because she would enter Belle High School in the autumn. That year brought many tears. Common fractions had given way to decimal fractions. Simple interest now became compound interest and such unheard of arithmetical tables for the exchange of currencies, duo decimals and something called arithmetic progression. The bones of the body were nothing compared to the presidents' names and terms of office, all the United States and their capitals, all the European countries and their capitals, all the major bodies of water, rivers, lakes and outlying possessions. All these names and spellings kept Mama's mind occupied for a winter. Before school in the morning she pronounced any name that popped into her head - out of a clear blue sky when Mae was contemplating a delicate bite of biscuit and honey. Mom would interject "Spell Massachusetts." "Bound Missouri" - that meant name the states bordering. "Spell the five Great Lakes and name them in order of size." "Can you still repeat the Preamble to the Constitution?" Mae would attempt to bite into her still tempting biscuit and honey. "Now spell 'clavicle.' What's the proper name for those five bones at the base of the spine? Now don't you dare say 'tail bone,' that is a poor choice of words; shouldn't be in the book. And before you go, lets be sure you can do that cube root problem you finally got through your head last night. Now where did Dad go? I knew he'd give me the slip." This meant Dad was supposed to go through the cube root procedure with Mae. "Well, now spell Minnesota and let's hear the capital of Michigan again. No hesitation now." All the way through on bright, sunny, autumn mornings our kitchen must have sounded like a flock of parrots - repeating, pronouncing, repeating. Frank, Rude and Ellie would join us frequently for a fried egg, a Calumet biscuit or a bowl of warm oatmeal. Mama didn't spare them either, "Frank, let me hear your spelling words for this week." Frank would find the page and point out his list to Mama. Mom would lay the book on the end of the kitchen table where she was fixing the lunch baskets and pronounce words to Frank and remind him to "emphasize" the proper syllable. Then came Rude and Ellie and Bud and me, words were pronounced, and our syllabication improved upon. Mae's cube root was finally judged "passable," but why was it taking Dad so long to milk. Dad had learned long ago to steer clear of Mom's kitchen school room.

Somehow in the middle of all this, we would change into school clothes, feed Charles Howard his oatmeal and milk, feed the kittens, chickens, pigs, mules and puppies and away we would scurry over the big rocks, past the pansy patch, over the green, slimy rocks beyond the rail fence and arrive at school jammed full of preambles, capitals, cube root and clavicle, drop our jug of "pure spring water" on the board floor and race outside to play a round of bull-pen before the bell rang.

In March of that year, we had tears of another kind. Uncle Harry and Earl came out from Belle early in the morning to say Nelson Hancks had been killed in a train accident near Newburg, Missouri. Nelson was Aunt May's and Uncle John's oldest son serving in the Navy. Tears came to Uncle Harry's eyes, then rolled down his cheeks. He and Mama were conferring - who would go? Mama didn't see how she could leave Charles Howard, but the decision was made; she thought she had to go. So Earl came back for her in the evening. She, Reta and Earl left on the 8:00 p.m. train for Kansas City and on to Wamego. For the next week, Mae and I struggled with all the housework. We weren't very good at keeping fires even for baking biscuits. The dining room stove smoked. We weren't very adept at slicing meat evenly and cooking it properly. We could do pretty well with potatoes and stewed tomatoes. Dad helped all he could but he was never a good cook either! Charles Howard cried day and night. Mama had never, never left him alone before. Before she left, Mama had instructed me to "miss school" and "take care of Pete and Bant." Now in some ways I figured that would be a real treat - no fractions, no preamble, no capitals and no clavicles. But I was also appalled at all the things to do - wash dishes, scrub floors, cook, fix lunches. And the big chore was the laundry - scrub the clothes on the board, rinse, hang out - wash diapers, rinse, hang out - and fix lunch for Dad and Don. Charles Howard needed lots of attention. Dad brought in big bags of corn cobs for the little boys to use in buildings. Pete was good to help amuse Charles. He also liked carrying wood from the wood pile and filling the wood box for me. Those were dark days.

I didn't like thinking of Aunt May and Uncle John and Jennie in tears - red eyed and sad as Dad was, and I pictured the trouble in Mama's face when she admonished us to be "good children" while she was gone. But the days were dark and dreary. It seemed strange to stay home for a week. It was very strange to have Dad around the house, telling me how to make potato soup for supper, sweeping, making beds and putting Charles Howard to sleep. Mama was supposed to do that!

When Mama returned late one evening about a week later, we were so happy. She looked worn and tired and pale, but to us she was the dearest, prettiest person alive. She rocked Charles Howard as she sat in her big chair by the dining room stove and told us all about Nelson's funeral. There were such beautiful floral arrangements. One was a flower piece made up like a replica of the US flag because he was in the Navy. He had not been terribly disfigured in the accident. Uncle John had been almost inconsolable. Aunt May had to be strong. Then there was Grandma. Our dear, loving, kind Grandma was bedfast now with an incurable disease. Mama was sure she wouldn't ever be able to return to Missouri again.

Mama didn't sing much that spring. Dad's violin lay quiet in the beautiful grey-green case. Even Mom's stove catch was more quiet when she raked down the ashes in the morning. We didn't remember Nelson very well. He had lived with us one winter and gone to high school in Linn before we moved to Cooper Hill. He had carried his books in a leather strap slung over his shoulder. He used the same strap to bring wood in for the cooking. In the evenings, he did algebra and Shakespeare both of which Mama didn't understand and considered "absolutely a waste of time and money." However, he was the one and only person who could bring that old wooden-tubbed washing machine into full play. As Mama said "he could really make that thing hum."

All these things we recalled as we ate our potato soup in the flickering light of our kerosene lamp. Just before we went to bed, Mama opened her suitcase and presented Mae and me each a small package for being such "good little girls." We snatched off the wrappings and found a sampler of "Three Flower Toiletries" powder and perfume. Oh, such a delight. We were in ecstasies. I carried mine upstairs and put it on our bedside table where I could see it first thing in the morning!

For several weeks, Mom and Dad had been promising us we would drive to Mt. Sterling on Good Friday to see the new bridge under construction there. School was out. Mae had her diploma now and her gold pencil on a chain around her neck (8th grade graduation gift). She had sewn her gold-and-white-checked gingham dress. All of us had "passed" (advanced to the next grade). Consequently, some great treat was in order. All week the weather had been cold. Not just cool for March, but down right bone-chilling cold. Friday morning nothing had changed. Mama tried to beg off, "We'll all freeze and probably take pneumonia." (I figured we would just take a jug of good pure spring water and pneumonia wouldn't be anything like typhoid.) But we knew Mama. If not today, very likely never - so soon after breakfast we packed our lunch (salmon croquettes) and we would treat ourselves to a loaf of Bakers Bread and away we went. We now had a spring wagon. Jim and Odie knew it was too cold to go anywhere today, but they kept still too. It was seven miles to Mt. Sterling. Today it seemed fifty-seven. Dad's hands were blue as he held the driving lines. Mom's hands were blue as she held Charles Howard on her lap. Her head was swathed in her long, white fascinator. We arrived at the construction site. No one was working. We ate our salmon croquettes and fried apple pies. Bud and I amused ourselves for an hour or two by crawling through the long sections of piling lying on the river bank. Mama had her hands full keeping Pete out of the river. He wanted to "see the bridge." All of us kept telling him the bridge was just being built. "But where?", he'd yell "where is it?" It seemed to me Pete was right. Where is the bridge? After all, that's how we had spoken of it - "Going to Mt. Sterling to see the bridge." We had never said, "See where the bridge will be built." That day left an indelible impression on us. When we wanted a cold day for reasons of comparison, we equated it with "as cold as" or "colder" than the day we went to Mt. Sterling to see the bridge. Dad referred to it as "a day cold enough to freeze the ears off a brass monkey."

After our freeze-out to Mt. Sterling, all us stifled our demands for away-from-home treks. I'm sure Mom was glad. She was real worried about Grandma. Our letters were frequent. Mae and I wrote several times per week. We told Grandma about our chickens, egg production, butter and egg prices, our garden, school - what a lot we learned - never anything sad or depressing. Jennie and Aunt May replied to our letters but informed us how sick Grandma was. She was slipping. They were keeping her as comfortable as possible and Uncle John had access to any medicine or hospitalization if need be. This was a great comfort to Mama.

Again very early on a warm June morning, Uncle Harry came out to the farm with his eyes brimming over. His sad duty was to tell Mama that "Mother has passed away" early the evening previous. Aunt May would be bringing the body back to Osage County for the final rites. Uncle Harry didn't stay long. His medical practice was demanding, but he would send Earl out for Mama so she could be there when Grandma's body arrived. Now there were all sorts of things to get done. Mae had to finish sewing a blue silk mull dress for Mama. We had to bring in the big tubs and do laundry for all of us. We pressed Dad's black wool suit and the wool knee britches for Bud and Pete. There was extra cooking to do. Mama would take pies and ham and fresh garden produce to Aunt Lulu when we went. Since Mae was busy with Mama's dress and Mama was doing the cooking, we sent word for Ellie to come help with the laundry. All afternoon she and

I soaped and rubbed and rinsed and hung on the line. After the clothes were washed, we used the hot soapy water to scrub the floors in the dining room and kitchen. The two back porches and the wash house. The next day Ellie came back to help with the ironing. She and I also laid the slices of apple into the bottom pie crusts Mama had set out for us to fill. We made chocolate pies for our own dinner and an extra for Ellie to carry home that evening.

Just before dark, Earl came for us as Uncle Harry had promised. This time Mama took Charles Howard with her and me to look after him.

Aunt Lulu's living room was strange looking. The folding bed had been moved out into the dining room. The shades were lowered and the lace panels were freshly laundered. Everything was painfully neat and clean. Charles Howard was tired and cross, so very early I was sent upstairs to put him to bed and Mama said "emphatically," "Stay with him." I didn't like this at all. I wanted to be with the grownups who were waiting for the train. I did undress and lie down to keep Charles quiet. I wondered for a time how it would seem to see Grandma lifeless in her casket and what would life be like without that wonderful, kind, gentle person in my life.

I seemed to have been asleep only a few minutes when I heard voices on the sidewalk outside our upstairs window. There was a great rumbling of railroad cars and grinding of steel on steel. I could see Mama, Aunt Lulu, the tall LeFevre boys, their friends, Dr. and Mrs. Johnson and a few dozen neighbors gathered there waiting for Grandma's casket to be brought up to the two blocks from the railroad station. I dressed quickly in the early morning darkness and ran down the stairs to join the mourners. Aunt May was there now; she and Mama and Aunt Lulu had been crying. Grandma's casket was moved from the auto drawn gray hearse up the walk and into Aunt Lulu's prim living room. The tall stout LeFevre boys and their friends had carried Grandma and all the pretty mountain of flowers and placed the casket on a funeral roller affair.

Aunt Lucinda Mason and Ima Lloyd were making coffee. It was now daylight but Charles began to awaken so it was upstairs again for me. Soon Aunt May came up with Harry and Dorsey. She tried to get them to rest awhile. They had been on the train for a whole day and most of the night. But the twins weren't tired. They were wide awake. They slid down the stair banister and ran out the front door and across the side yard to Uncle Harry's office. Uncle Harry gave them a dime and sent them across the street to Tom Lloyd's store to get "all day suckers." The morning passed by quickly. I wanted to be with Grandma. There were too many people in the house. Grandma was well known. She had been a successful teacher for many years in Osage County and postmistress at LeBouef, Missouri.

About the middle of the morning Dad, Mac and the boys arrived. Dad had hired a car because the burial would be out at Pilot Knob, several miles from Belle. Uncle Everett Pearl came with Neva from Chamois. Dad's eyes were red, so were Everett's and Earl's. Everyone was busy waiting on everyone else. Aunt May wondered if her brown wool dress would be uncomfortably warm. Reta said she only had one thing to wear, a wool suit, so they would suffer together.

Our lunch was carried in by friends and neighbors. Mama donned her blue mull dress. I had one of much the same material and made much the same with panels gathered over the hips and reaching to the hemline. Grandma's body was moved to the Methodist Episcopal Church. I had watched closely as Reverend Walker from Linn said a prayer and read the 23rd Psalm. Reta had arranged a small bouquet of "clove pinks" and put them in Grandma's hands. Pinks were always her favorite flower. I knew now I wouldn't really be able to see Grandma anymore. I carried Charles upstairs to change his soiled clothes for clean ones.

All too soon we were at the church. Hymns were being sung - prayers - eulogy - and tears. My tears flowed freely as I sat wedged between Mae and Reta. Charles began to fret. Mama turned halfway around and signaled me to take him outside. I did. He became quiet. It dawned on me if I didn't return to the church I wouldn't see Grandma again. So I returned to the church and turned him over to Mama. This time he was quiet and we sat through the service. Then we all followed Sam Licklider's gray hearse out to Pilot Knob. There were several people gathered there who hadn't been able to come to town for the services. So again the casket was opened, under the big oak tree. The sun was bearing down unmercifully. I'm sure Aunt May and Pete were much too warm in their wools, but I got one more chance to see Grandma. I took special note of her high necked, tucked, gray silk burial dress. It had lace and pink ribbon on the bodice. The pinks in her hand were wilted now. Like Grandma their lifeline had been severed. After another prayer, Grandma's casket was lowered into the grave between Grandpa and their oldest daughter Aunt Belle Pearl. Because we were using a hired car we came directly home from the cemetery. Aunt May would visit with us for a few days before she and her twin sons returned to Kansas. We said good-bye to Uncle Ed and Aunt Lou, Uncle Tom and Aunt Kate, their families, more of Mama's cousins, and we were on our way home.

Tears did not end with the funeral. I cried as often as I thought of Grandma. I noticed Mama' eyes were often blurred too. But we were never a family given to mourning. We couldn't afford to lose the time. We didn't take time for tears but one can remember how she taught Mae and me to read the beautiful Bible stories - "Joseph and the Coat of Many Colors" and "Daniel in the Lion's Den." The times she had comforted me and wrapped me in her big, blue calico apron, an apron with a constant supply of raisins in the pockets. When she picked out a raisin she would offer it to me with an admonishment, "Now chew it a long time" - emphasis on long. There was the struggle with the knitting needles. Grandma's needles simply flew. They clinked and shone in the sunlight as she toed or heeled a sock. My needles got all hung up. The yarn was always in the wrong place. I'd forget to count stitches, how patient Grandma was! She never scolded. She just ripped out my mistakes and started me all over. And she smiled - always a smile. She always smelled of lilac scented talcum powder and Ivory soap. Grandma's entire wardrobe and personal possessions were carried from place to place in a trunk. In the tray of the trunk was always the talcum, the Ivory soap, her long black silk gloves, and the lace for her black silk taffeta blouse. The box of raisins was kept hidden in the bottom of the trunk. Some time later in the summer Aunt May would ship this trunk to Mama.

If spring and early summer had brought dark clouds and tears, July now brought sunshine and long happy days. Uncle John and Aunt Ida had now bought a Model T Ford so they came rather frequently to visit. They were very busy getting their new farm in shape. They would like Bud and me to spend a week with them. Oh, such a joy! A whole week to help Uncle John and Aunt Ida - ride in a Ford car - maybe go to Linn. So we packed our clean everyday clothes and our dress up clothes in a cardboard box and climbed in the rear seat of the Model T. Uncle John gripped the steering wheel hard and Aunt Ida watched and shooed the chickens out of the way as he worked masterfully to turn the car around. Up the hill we went, through Cooper Hill, across the new bridge at Mt. Sterling and soon we were pulling up in front of Aunt Ida's pretty, neat farm house. Once inside the huge kitchen I took a quick inventory of the furnishings. I saw the pretty dining room table and six chairs with cushions on the seats, a new dark green enamel wood range was in place. There was also a new cabinet holding Grandma Bacon's set of china. There was a sink where only cold water was available and two comfortable wicker rocking chairs to be pulled up later near the center of the room where Uncle John read the Globe Democrat under the one bulb light in the center of the room. This wonderful house had a Delco plant and there were wires along the walls and ceilings to carry the power.

Aunt Ida sent me upstairs to take our box of everyday clothes and changes. We then took the big shiny milk buckets off the shelf of the back porch. Aunt Ida took her small bucket and a clean wash cloth to wash old Jers' bag and we were off to the barn. All four of us milked after watching the little calves plant their hind feet firmly on the dry lot and roll their beautiful big eyes while they got their supper. Our buckets were soon full. Uncle John and Aunt Ida carried the big foamy buckets of warm milk toward the kitchen. They let Bud and me detour through the garden and on out to the henhouse to close the door and to see if we could recognize "Old Whitey" sitting on the roost pole snuggled up to "Old Rooster Boy." We closed the chicken house door and latched it carefully. We always performed our chores carefully when we were visiting Uncle John and Aunt Ida. They never scolded if work was done sloppily, but somehow you weren't permitted to do that particular thing again.

When Bud and I came into the kitchen Uncle John was turning the crank of the big DeLaval cream separator. The cream was pouring out one spout into a clean blue crock. Milk was pouring out another spout into a big white crock to be set in the cellar to cool for drinking. Last of all the skim milk was carried out to the noisy pigs in the pen by the barn. Uncle John and I sliced thick slabs of home-made bread, spread them with butter, placed them on our rose-sprayed china plates and sat quietly and waited while Aunt Ida sliced yellow cheese and put it on our sliced bread. Such a treat, eating store-bought cheese in Aunt Ida's kitchen under an electric light - such luxuries!

After breakfast on Monday morning our work began. I helped Aunt Ida with dishes and swept kitchen and walks. I watered her cinnamon vine growing in the flower box out by the back porch. I went to the garden to help pick vegetables for dinner - green beans, carrots, lettuce, onions and potatoes. I washed them all and brought them in to the cold water sink. Aunt Ida churned fresh butter because Mrs. Henry Kopp had called to see if she could get some extra cream, butter and eggs by tomorrow. Aunt Ida hung up the receiver with a puzzled look on her face. "Well I never. I just never. What in the world is she (Mrs. Kopp) going to do with all that cream and butter?" All the same we churned, washed, and molded yellow butter, skimmed cream and put it in clean scalded jars in the cool, cool cellar. This fruit cellar opened off the end of the cool, cool back porch. The shelves were like concrete steps to hold jars of fruit, vegetables and Aunt Ida's famous peach preserves and strawberry jam. Uncle John's big job for the week was to clean the barn. The name we used was hauling manure. That was about the smelliest job a farm could produce. There were no machines, just pitch forks and a manure spreader. Bud had a fork and worked alongside Uncle John all day. He would come to the house to get a drink while Uncle John hauled the manure to the bottom field. He sat in the shade and petted "Old Shep" until he saw the team and spreader come back up the hill. I sometimes sat a minute with Bud and drank a cup of cool water. I petted "Puss" and "Tom" and then I went back to weeding the strawberry patch. By the time evening came my hands were feeling prickly, dry and blistered. I was feeling real sorry for myself until Bud stuck his little chubby hands out and said. "That ain't nothing. Look at this." And sure enough he had blisters too. We were trying too hard to please. Aunt Ida and Uncle John looked wise and helped us bandage our injuries with comforting Cloverine salve. By the following morning some soft cotton gloves were found for us.

Chapter 16

Chris and Clara

Tuesday morning early, Adalia Kopp appeared at the back door to get the cream and butter spoken for on the day previous. Adalia brought a flat bottomed basket which she set on the cook table awaiting the cream, butter and eggs. Aunt Ida was filled with curious questions. They were in her face, her eyes and especially in her ears. There was something going on. No one in an ordinary country community would use six pounds of butter and 2 quarts of cream and 3 1/2 dozen eggs unless big company was expected. Adalia just visited along about the weather, gardens and chickens. All grownup talk. Adalia was about 14 years and a perfectly beautiful blonde with that typical Scandinavian skin, eyes and thick gold blonde braids. After an hour or so of this country conversation, Adalia got up rather deliberately, tied her bonnet carefully, retrieved her basket and started toward the door. Aunt Ida was completely flabbergasted by now. She had done her best but there were no answers. Her eyes were puckered. She was running her forefinger over the end of her nose. At the porch door Adalia turned to Aunt Ida and said, "Oh, Mrs. Bacon, you folks are all invited to the wedding on Thursday afternoon. Chris and Clara are getting married." Well finally we had found out what all that cream and butter was for. Aunt Ida's face relaxed somewhat.

But now we had to re-arrange our week. Aunt Ida thought we ought to do the laundry. As soon as Bud and Uncle John went back to the barn after dinner we put the big, black wash kettle on to heat the water. We took turns scrubbing the clothes, carrying water, rinsing and hanging up on the lines. None of us needed to be rocked to sleep that night. I dreamed of weddings and lots of whipped cream and butter and Adalia's honey butter braids. Now the work flew. No tub was too heavy. We scrubbed the kitchen floor and the upstairs bedroom where all four of us slept. We mopped the back porch and the cellar steps.

Aunt Ida sent me out to the barn late in the afternoon to tell Uncle John we needed to go to Mt. Sterling to the store. We needed most of all, I explained, to buy a wedding gift. Uncle John gave a long shrill whistle. He seemed to always use one for special occasions. Today he followed it with a lot of soft chuckles. So we got "Old Jers" and "Red Rose" and all the other cows in and milked them early, and after washing our faces and hands we put on clean everyday clothes and jumped into the Model T. Aunt Ida took a big basket of brown eggs. Ordinarily she took a basket filled with beautiful yellow butter, but not today. After Mr. Fritz Schaeperkoetter counted out the eggs he took a grocery item pad and computed how much the eggs were worth in cash. Aunt Ida consulted her shopping list carefully, 50 cents worth of sugar, two pounds of yellow cheese and a bar of Ivory soap. And now it was time to look at the household items - coffee pots, tea pots, cut glass sugar and creamers, berry sets, pitchers and glasses, beautiful bowls and plates. Aunt Ida chose a colorful bread plate. In gold letters it read "Give us this day our daily bread." And for Bud and me, a small cut-glass footed compote. That should have completed our shopping but Uncle John had been inspecting the show counter. Bud tagged at his heels. Uncle John examined every pair of shoes on the shelf. Bud saw only one pair he liked. They were buckskin, light in color, and trimmed with fine brown leather circles over the ankles. The tongues and toes were brown too. Real dress-up for country kids like us. When Uncle John told Bud he could have the shoes if they fit properly, Bud's big brown eyes got a bit misty. He insisted he didn't need them. Uncle John told him he had done a man's work pitching manure. He must have something in pay. The shoes fit. Bud's face beamed. Aunt Ida selected a pair of long cotton stockings for him to wear with the shoes. Aunt Ida and Uncle John settled the account. Bud and I were in ecstasy. We sat on the back seat of the Model T, Bud clutching his shoe box closely and I clutching the cut-glass compote.

Wednesday we ironed. The big green enamel range ate big meals of Uncle John's carefully split wood. Bud and I carried armload after armload as Aunt Ida cooked our dinner and ironed Uncle John's best white shirt. By evening our dress-up clothes were pressed and hanging in the downstairs closet with Uncle John's suit and white shirt and Aunt Ida's best blue silk dress (she had made it for the State Fair the year before). In the evening the wash boiler was brought in and filled with water for baths. The wash tub was brought in and placed behind the big range. While one of us bathed the other three sat with their backs to the stove. No one peeked. Bud and I were first, then we were sent directly upstairs to bed. Then Uncle John came dashing upstairs in his long white nightshirt. And finally Aunt Ida came smelling clean but slightly of asthma smoke. For a while she sat on the side of the bed with a straight backed chair covered with a pillow to rest her head. Asthma was her enemy. She suffered with it a great deal. Several years earlier they had spent a year in Bakersfield, California, hoping the smothery disease would go away. I tried to stay awake. Aunt Ida might need me. Youth knows anxiety but shortly, and so I slept.

Thursday morning, Aunt Ida forbade any manure hauling. Bud and I could help her weed the corn and beans and if there was time left over we could finish the strawberry bed. It wouldn't have mattered if she had ordered us to move boulders of mountains we would have done it or died in an attempt. Weren't we going to a wedding? Neither of us had ever attended a wedding and we knew Chris Gerloff, the groom, very well. He was our neighbor, Mrs. Dr. Leach's nephew, and was known for his strong muscular ability to work on a farm. We knew Clara Kopp too. Her father, Henry, helped Uncle John with farm work. Her Aunt Minnie Kopp had been Henry Buecker's housekeeper when the Bueckers owned our farm. So while we weeded the garden and fed "Old Whitey" and trotted to the cellar and the wood pile Uncle John thought it was a good day to charge the Delco plant. He brought the glass fuel container out to the wood shed and filled it. He replaced it in the holder, pulled a few strings, poked a bit here and there, then all of a sudden the motor started. Pop - pop - pop - bang - bang - bang . There was no conversation now unless one shouted. We ate our noon meal in silence. Delco was directly under the kitchen. It was to be an afternoon wedding. No special time because the bride's father Henry had to help thresh at Buscher's. About 2:00 p.m. we began our grooming. Again spit baths were taken. We did a good deal of yelling. "Aunt Ida, where did you lay our clean underwear?" That was Bud in the stairwell. His voice sounded strange. "On a chair in the attic room," Aunt Ida shouted back. She was behind the range.

"Ida, surely you don't expect me to wear my best bib and tucker." That was Uncle John in the front bedroom where his very best suit was laid out. "Yes, I do, and I want no further inquiries from you or Bud. And John Bacon get down there and shut that pop - pop - bang - bang machine off so we can talk like civilized people." Uncle John came out of the bedroom wearing his B.V.D.'s and ran out the side door and disappeared for a minute into the Delco cellar. Old pop - pop - bang - bang began to die down and was soon quiet. Uncle John soon appeared in suit, white shirt, tie and silk socks. Aunt Ida was splendid in her blue silk print. Her hair was neatly combed up in the back and held by a tortoise shell comb. Bud had found his underwear and was wearing his navy blue serge knee pants and white shirt. I had my blue mull dress, white cotton stockings and black patent Mary Janes. Bud of course was wearing his new buckskins. He and I sat in the back seat of the Model T. I again held on to the cut glass compote. It only took a few minutes to drive up through the beautiful walnut grove. Out to the road, a few minutes more and we were crossing Highway 50. We descended a steep slope and there was the Kopp house.

Already it was surrounded by cars, riding horses, a few buggies and people everywhere. As Uncle John hunted for a place to park the Ford, I took a bird's eye view of all the people I knew. The Gerloff family was very prominent. Chris' parents, August and Annie, were sitting on the front porch. Grandpa and Grandma Wildebrandt were also sitting there in the shade. Chris' brothers and sisters were all dressed in their best dark suits and starched white voile dresses There were Ernest, Lena, Gus and wife Gusta, Martin, John, Herman, Annie, Amanda and Orilla. There were Clara's married sister, Alma, with her husband John Linhardt and at least six small children. There were Fred Kopp and his wife and daughter, Alford and Adalia. The latter led us through the kitchen and into the big all-purpose room. In one corner was a big wooden bed covered with a white, white cotton bed spread. The small table by the bed was covered with wedding gifts. None were wrapped, so Aunt Ida and I placed ours along with other plates, embroidered pillowcases, a pieced quilt, pitcher and glasses. This was the room where the marriage ceremony would be performed. Some chairs were already arranged in a semicircle facing the two west windows. Aunt Ida and I wandered back to the kitchen where Mrs. Kopp and other neighbors were busy finishing the slaw, peeling potatoes and putting more wood in the stove to keep supper warm. Fred's wife was slathering whipped cream on the wedding cake and putting tiny purplish blue blossoms from some wildflower on the edges. It was so pretty!

In a flash all was aflutter. Henry Kopp came blustering in, all hot and sweaty from the threshing. Mrs. Kopp reached behind the stairway door. Her hand brought out a clean, freshly ironed blue chambray shirt. She handed it to Henry who took it out to the yard pump with him. He pumped a big bucket of cool water, carried it to the shed in the back yard and in a few minutes reappeared - clean shirt, clean pants, hair combed and inquired if the reverend had arrived. "No - No -- Oh yes, here he is now." So chairs were brought in from porches, yards, kitchen, everywhere. Mr. and Mrs. Kopp, Mr. and Mrs. Gerloff, and Grandpa and Grandma Wildebrandt sat in the front row. Some of the aunts and uncles found chairs. The rest of us stood. The reverend took his place, looked solemnly at the little group, checked his watch and turned his eyes toward the kitchen door. Soon Chris came through with a flourish. He looked very happy as he moved to a spot on the floor in front of the minister. A rustle of taffeta and stiff starch smell let us know Clara was approaching. No Music. No slow sedate wedding march. Clara just tripped down the stair steps, paused a minute to oversee the food on the stove, tripped on through the kitchen and took her place by Chris' side. The Reverend was Lutheran, so the marriage took a while. Bud and I "grew fidgety," but made it. As soon as the wedding was over, the principals sat down to eat - Chris and Clara, their parents and grandparents, uncles, aunts, then neighbors and friends. That took quite a while. Almost as soon as we swallowed our last bite, Aunt Ida said we must be going. As we left, Chris and Clara were sitting very, very close to each other on the wash bench just outside the kitchen door. Later I figured out Aunt Ida knew there would be dancing. She didn't approve of dancing. Young people got too close together.

But my, what a day. What a week. As we came home in the twilight, "old Jers" and "Red Rose" were bawling to their calves, who were trying their best to get their heads through the board fence.

The remainder of the week was delicious. On Friday we all drove to Linn. We ate dinner at Mrs., Lantene Benson's, Aunt Ida's mother. Aunt Ida had cut a fine cured ham and prepared the center slices. Mrs. Benson fried it along with potatoes and wilted lettuce from Aunt Ida's garden. We had a feast. After lunch she and I walked up town to Aime Maires Mercantile where Aunt Ida told me I could choose a piece of gingham for a new dress. I chose a beautiful piece of mostly pink with some sky blue. Aunt Ida and I together settled on a piece of predominantly red for Mae because she was going to high school in the fall. All summer she had been busy getting her sewing done. She and Mama and Aunt Ida were very proud of the half dozen or more simple projects. There was a blue voile, a natural linen, a yellow gingham, a pink silk, a red-and-white-checked gingham and a white linen. She had a middy and black skirt for basketball games. Now she would have another "change." If she could get it "made up" nicely.

Saturday was always a "clean-up" day at Aunt Ida's. We swept and dusted the sitting room. I loved to run the dust mop over the smooth shiny new congoleum rug. A big vase of printed flowers on one corner of the linoleum always fascinated me. There were two fancy rocking chairs. A picture of President William McKinley, his wife and mother hung in a beautiful frame on one wall. A maidenhair fern held down one complete corner. There was a fine black heating stove and a small couch covered by a bright cretonne throw. I was then sent to sweep and dust the front bedroom. That was fun, too, because it was there Aunt Ida kept my two favorite amusements, the stereoscope with lots of scenes to view (all brown and white, of course) and the ostrich egg. This object d'art was kept on top of the folding bed. Quite out of the reach of small hands. The wash stand held a complete set of china: bowl, pitcher, small pitcher, hair receiver and covered soap dish. The pattern was a ferny green vine and all edges were gold leaf. Mama's wash bowl and pitcher was plain white. So I spent time admiring this one. In addition to the folding bed was an iron bed painted gold, a rocker, an axminster carpet with pretty flowers and a small stand table. On the lower shelf of the table were some books, a celluloid covered small volume entitled *Lucille*, and a red leather with gold letters *East Lynne* that I read again and again. Hester, a character in it had been Aunt Ida's part to play in an enactment when she attended Clarksburg Seminary. (Aunt Lulu was in the same class and same play.)

In the middle room was a high wooden bed. And nearly always it sported a blue and pink Double Irish Chain Quilt. Aunt Ida had bought it at the Freedom Picnic bazaar. The dresser matched the bed. On the stiffly starched dresser scarf was a small bright blue glass cradle for matches. Next to the ostrich egg, I thought that the most magnificent of all earthly beauties.

In one corner next to the sitting room was a small clothes closet where Aunt Ida kept Uncle John's suit, white shirt, overcoat, her best dress and coat and their dress-up clothes. Things were not crowded in that closet. There was a small wood heater, a chair, a dull gray and blue congoleum rug. A sewing machine and that was it. There were no superfluous pieces of furniture, bedding or clothes around. Everything was clean and comfortable. It had its use and its place. After lunch I was sent upstairs to dust and mop the bedroom where all of us slept. There was a low wooden bed where Uncle John and Aunt Ida slept. There was a metal framed folding bed for me and a rather small cot-like affair for Bud. The only other piece of furniture was a high wishbone marble top dresser (that had been Granny's), a straight back chair, and a makeshift clothes closet. There were no doors just a cretonne curtain to keep dust out. The linoleum up there had seen better days; there was no print left on it at all - it was just plain brown. But I mopped and dusted and made the beds. I finished my day's cleaning by wet mopping the stair steps. Aunt Ida praised my work. She had been busy all morning with pies. She could never have done all that herself, she said.

Uncle John was busy cutting the grass, using a push-by-hand mower, of course. Bud had been busy watering the chickens, weeding the garden, pulling weeds out of the yard and cinnamon vine, feeding the chickens, and running to the cellar and wood shed for Aunt Ida.

When Sunday morning came we packed our cardboard box and again climbed into the Model T with a mixed feeling. We loved to stay with this dear aunt and uncle but it just wasn't home. We met Mom and Dad at church at Cooper Hill, this had been arranged previously. Richard Gerloff and his family attended this same church. He was heard to remark, "George Bacon's children sure do look like John Bacon's children don't they?" Dad and Uncle John got quite a chuckle out of that. He had seen us at the wedding.

August was a series of whirlwinds. Earl LeFevre was to be our teacher at Post Oak. This was another of Mama's brainstorms. If Earl could teach and stay with us, then Mae could stay with Aunt Lulu and Uncle Harry. All would be equal. So early in the spring, Earl had submitted his application to the school board. Dad was a member. Ed Homfeld and Millard Hassler weren't hard to convince that Earl needed that job (not with Mama working on all possible channels). When the school meeting was over, the contract signed, and Earl had returned to Belle, Mama practically danced a jig. My, my how lucky we were. Now we wouldn't have to pay board for Mae to stay in town, there would be a little money for spending and a little for music lessons. We could even furnish Aunt Lulu some potatoes and she could come out to the farm and pick blackberries to can. We could send a few eggs, extra butter and a jar of cream now and then. Uncle Harry was very fond of pure cream over comb honey. He liked that for breakfast and would eat it every morning when it was available.

In July Aunt Lulu came out and picked and canned blackberries. Ellie managed to find a few dewberries for pie and jelly. Aunt Lulu went early in the morning. Dad took a bucket when he went out to bring in the cows. Mae and I went in the afternoon. We came home with full buckets, red faces and stained, pricked fingers. By the week's end we had rows and rows of jars on the cellar shelf and when Earl came to take Aunt Lulu home we had boxes of the dark luscious fruit packed up for her to take home.

Saturdays had been set aside for Mae and me to go to Confirmation school at the Cooper Hill Church. We were part of a rather large class. The material consisted of a very small thin Catechism containing scripture, the Ten Commandments, Church Creed and numerous portions of ritual. We had to memorize this volume in its entirety in order to pass an examination on Confirmation Sunday. We also studied in detail a book of Bible stories, most of which were already quite familiar to Mae and me - thanks to Grandma's daily tutoring as we sat on the floor behind the wood heater when we lived at Linn.

Most of the time we walked to these session at the Cooper Hill Church. Audrey Lange, Clarence Homfeld and Eugene Kraenow were in this class too. So if the weather was too rainy, too cold, of if Big Third Creek was running wild, one of our parents drove us. I liked the days when Audrey's father drove us in this shiny black surrey drawn by the fat shiny horses - "Bop and Barney." We moved so slowly that flies, bees, mosquitoes and horse flies buzzed in and out of our surrey realm. Sometimes they perched on us, sometimes on Bop or Barney. We had time to speculate on their eye structure and wonder about their wings and feet. The woods and pastures were beautiful in summer and fall. Frequently we drove or walked "down the creek." This was terminology for the shorter route. From the Kraenow place Eugene walked over the hill and crossed Belly Ache Creek at the Polk field. Audrey and Eugene then proceeded down our lane. Past our garden, Mae and I joined them to make a group of four as we wound around our lower field, through the rickety gate, jumped the mud or waterhole which was always there. Again we crossed the creek, on a fine exciting swing foot bridge this time, coming out on a high bluff almost in front of the Homfeld house. Clarence would come running down the steep slope, always clean and neat in blue bib overalls and blue Chambray shirt, standard garb for farm boys. From Homfelds we followed the creek road again through the big bottom field, usually growing corn or in the picking, fodder or stubble stage. At the edge of this field we nearly always had a decision to make - definitely if we were walking. How to get across Big Third Creek? Sometimes we could walk up the bank quite a ways and find a place shallow enough so we could wade. This creek was noted for deep pools. If you waded, one had to feel carefully before placing your full weight on the forward foot. Other times we used long poles to vault ourselves across. This method worked fine from our side of the creek but was not wise on the return journey because we couldn't attain the height necessary to vault from the gravel bar to the high bank. This meant we walked home "around the road." Most of the time Mae and I were told to hurry home so we could help with the work. We didn't dare tarry with our friends in Cooper Hill. We knew we would have to account for our time. This Confirmation study continued for a period of three years, mostly in spring and summer.

In the fall Mama and Aunt Lulu put their exchange plans into place. Mae rode into Belle with whichever one of the LeFevre boys brought Earl out to our farm on Sunday evening. I'm not sure after all these years which end of this deal I found most interesting. Earl was tall, six feet four, thin, quiet, rather studious. He organized us into our proper status as to grades. He ordered several new library books, and played those usual games with us at noon and recess. The big boys thought it was great fun to gather hackberries, eat them and place the round slippery seeds on the schoolhouse floor just where they were sure Earl would be walking. Several times he was taken unaware. Being tall and a bit awkward Earl rolled and grabbed for support. The big boys giggled and laughed and continued to put more hackberry seed in his path. One day Earl stepped on the hard rolling seeds, as they cracked, Earl rolled. As Earl grabbed out in space for a hand hold, his long thin fingers came in contact with Delmar Brown's long thick red hair, a perfect cushion. Earl went down in the aisle. His hand was tight in Delmar's hair. Delmar was corpulent. Earl's hand in his hair was pulling. Delmar got twisted between seat and desk. He yelled "Ouch - Ow - ow - leggo my top knot." In the midst of his screams and twisting he accidentally did something considered the most embarrassing episode that could possibly befall a big boy! So loud and clear there was no mistaking that for anything else. Earl got his land legs back. Delmar put his head down and covered his face with his hands. That was the end of the hackberry seeds. Delmar was one of the "planters." Somehow it wasn't fun anymore!

Earl liked Mama's biscuits. She insisted he sleep a little later in the morning. Mostly so she could get early morning chores out of the way. When he came downstairs she baked a fresh pan of biscuits, had fresh eggs, ham, bacon, applesauce or something for him alone. This arrangement afforded Mama the perfect opportunity to visit with Earl to find out just how much homework to assign and just about what he could expect from his daily charges. Earl owned a clarinet, too. That was the finest thing of all. He shared his north room upstairs with Bud, Pete and Roy Nixon, our hired hand. In the long autumn evenings and sometimes in the mornings he sat on the upstairs portico and ran the scales. Mama wanted everyone to know music but running scales wasn't musical. She would be busy silking corn for supper or peeling potatoes - the high notes were particularly exasperating for her. After she reached her saturation point she would go to the foot of the stair steps and call out "Earl, now if you can't play me a tune I'll sing one for you! How would you like me to sing 'When the Roll 'll 'll 'll is Called up Yonder?" Then Earl would come down the steps laughing, and together he, Mama and I would solve the crossword puzzle in the St. Louis Globe Democrat. I loved that. Before Earl lived with us I had never known the proper technique. It gave Mama great pleasure to come up with a good word. I recall one evening we were engaged in supper preparation when Earl "got stuck" on a word meaning "to travel about." It started with a "g," had 9 letters, etc. One of Mama's favorite expressions was to say, "I'll go out now and 'galvanate' around," in the hen house. So she suggested the word might be "galvanate." Earl worked with that monstrosity for a while, looked up with a puzzled expression and said "Aunt Jennie, could that word be 'gallivant?'" Mama said "Well it might be; seems as if they spell and pronounce everything different these days." Mama was never one to acknowledge a bit of erroneous pronunciation on her part!

Our evenings were entertaining, too. Usually we had lessons to do. I was now entering that wonderful world of common fractions; adding, subtracting, multiplying and dividing. Why not just leave it whole? Teachers and Mama were always using apples as examples of halves, quarters or eighths. Halves were equal they said, two halves made a whole. Yes, they did but one piece was invariably larger than the other. Quarters weren't equal either, even though they did fit together to make the whole; one piece was always bigger than the other three. Fractions were now written vertically rather than Mama's method of writing them horizontally. So now I had a big problem. To please Mama I had to copy the fractions from the text onto my tablet paper in a horizontal fashion, find a common denominator and proceed to add or subtract. I was stymied; all my teachers expected me to add vertically as per the book. Mama was determined I must do it horizontally. I couldn't see that it was the same thing. Therefore I cried and worried because I simply could not solve fractions. One evening Mama was being especially adamant; she was adamant all over the house. Earl came in and found us with fractions in all positions. He quietly sat down on the end of the bench behind the big home-made kitchen table and said softly. "Now Aunt Jennie, you just look here a minute. It's the very same thing. These new books have simplified the methods." He proceeded to teach Mama how to add and subtract fractions vertically. Mama's face was flushed. She resented anyone who attempted to change her thinking, but she really did want to understand this "new fangled" way of solving fractions. After a few simple problems she seemed satisfied that it really resulted in the same solution. When she understood, she arose from her chair, dusted her hands as she did when putting extra flour in biscuits and announced, "Well I never - I just never" and because she never in her life admitted to any wrong or misunderstanding she looked straight into Earl's eyes and questioned, "Now, how good are you at doing algebra?" That subject had always fascinated her even though she had never attempted to study it!

Not every evening was devoted to books. We played rook or dominoes. As winter came on, Earl mastered some "tunes." So Dad played the violin, Earl played the clarinet and Roy tried hard to master the mouth organ. Sometimes in the evening, Earl shelled corn for Mama's "layers," shucked corn for the mules or threw hay down the chute for the cows and horses. Sometimes he took his .22 and brought in young squirrels for breakfast.

Mama continued to suffer from imaginary "typhoid fever" all year. That particular year it was really bad. Many mornings she would not have Earl's lunch basket ready when he was ready to go to school, so she worked out a bargain. "Now, Earl, you take the water jug to the spring and fill it. Then you take it and go on to school. I'll fix your lunch and Grace will bring it." That suited me fine. Earl's legs were long; he didn't have to hold it high over the big rocks and struggle with it as he climbed the rail fence as I did. Mama made lots of blackberry jam that year. We had bought new glass jelly jars at the Feuersville store. Mama believed in canning without sugar (because if the berries didn't keep, you didn't lose the sugar). So nearly every morning she put a big pan of berries on to cook, added sugar and boiled them hard. We ate this on hot buttered biscuits for breakfast and had plenty left over for our school lunch. There was one big fault in this method. If the metal lid was placed on the jar while the jelly was still hot the lid sealed tight - really tight! Sometimes we spent most of our noon hour struggling with that "darned lid." So there came a day when Earl couldn't get lid off at all. He gave up, brought the prized jam home unopened. This disturbed Mama, so she solved the problem by putting the lid in our baskets separately. I was instructed to "put the lid on the jar during recess." I never figured out just what the motive was here but I always performed my charge at recess, after the jelly had cooled!

Chapter 17

Educational Reels

That was a big, big year in our education. Mae came home every Friday evening in the LeFevre car. She brought her soiled clothing for weekend laundry. She also brought her text books to study - English composition, general science, citizenship and of all things, algebra! That pleased Mama and Dad. They eyed the strange symbols and I heard them discussing the big question. "How in the world could you add A's and B's and C's? What did raising to the 2nd power mean?" It was a puzzlement. Something else puzzled Mama too. On Friday afternoon the entire high school gathered in the auditorium for something called "educational reels." Now that shook Mama. What in the world could that be? She was certainly not going to let Mae know that she wasn't fully aware of the course content. All weekend Mae spoke frequently of "educational reels." It seemed she really enjoyed that hour. After Mae had returned to Belle on Sunday evening, Mama was ready to go to the henhouse. With a big bucket in hand, she turned to me and said, "Grace did you find out what that is Mae calls 'educational reels'?" Well I explained it was moving pictures dealing with some news items from around the world. Mama sighed deeply. "Well I'll vow - I just never - I was afraid it was dancing." I could see the relief fall out of her face. She swung her bucket almost child-like as she went out to collect the "hen fruit." I peeled potatoes and kept wood in the stove so supper could be finished quickly when Mama came in from "galvanating" around gathering eggs.

That school year was mostly happy and comfortable. We had a successful pie supper. Mama made lots of extras to be sold as "bachelor pies," that meant men or boys who had no wife or girlfriend. They just bought and ate pie. Mae and Ellie and I trimmed our boxes and had fun carrying the one that didn't belong to us. To fool the boys.

Uncle Harry and Aunt Lulu provided home comforts for Mae. Only Buell and Russell were home now during the week. Buell was a senior in high school. Russell was in grade school.

At Thanksgiving, Aunt Lulu invited us to dinner. Everett, Boyd and Reta would be home from Warrensburg Normal School. She also asked her father, Mr. Jim Agee, and Lucinda (Pa's wife). All of us were delighted to accept. Earl came out in Uncle Harry's big black Dodge touring car and took us into town. Uncle Harry, remembering Mama's fondness for oysters, insisted Aunt Lulu serve oyster stew as the first course. After the stew came the turkey platter. It was decorated with red and pink roses, green leaves and gold leaf edging. I was much more interested in the platter than the turkey! I also remember sitting next to "Pa's wife" at dinner, her stiff brown taffeta skirt rustled with every move she made. She helped Reta carry the bowls of oyster stew to the table. All of us were careful to avoid meeting Lucinda in a doorway because she filled it alone!

In the afternoon Uncle Harry took all of the youngsters to the Belle drugstore for an ice cream cone. We gazed at the wonders in the glass fronted stores. We closed our eyes when we passed the dental office. We had paid a few visits to Mr. J. S. Tellman in his upstairs office over the Belle Bank. In that same block between the bank and Uncle Harry's house was Wash Nassif's store. Wash wasn't well organized. He had no plan for beautiful attractive displays. There were shoe boxes with one shoe in and the other upside down, buttons, thread, black lace veils and ladies' umbrellas all in a heap. There was also dust and a few dead moths left over from summer.

Our day was wonderful: dressing in our best, riding in a car, eating oysters and turkey (not to mention ice cream cones) gave us days of pleasant memories. Soon it was time to crowd into the Dodge and head for home. In November, there was the school fair too. This was a really big event. There were parades and floats, basketball games and dinner served. I dreamed about this event day and night. Mama said we would "try to go." We did. It was on Saturday. We were all excited. I rode into town on Friday evening when Buell came out to get Earl. So I stayed all night with Mae. We got up early to help Aunt Lulu get beef roast ready to serve over at the school. Then we got dressed. Buell drove us over to the school where all the activity was. We visited all the rooms to see displays of art, agricultural products, algebra and geometry solutions on the blackboard. All of these Mama studied intently when she, Dad and the boys arrived later in the morning. In the afternoon "educational reels" were shown in the auditorium. Mama and Dad sat with their eyes glued to the black and white pictures flashing on the home painted screen. The explanation of what we were seeing had to be read from the screen too! Mama and Dad approved of educational reels. When any of those came to Belle and were open to the public we would be sure to go! The basketball games appealed to Dad and the boys. That was our first chance to see such an activity.

Mama and Dad were excited to see all these displays. They thought high school a fine thing. Their own education had consisted of rural schools plus a three week course in subject matter to be taught. This was called an institute and usually held in Linn or Chamois in August. If examinations were successfully negotiated, one was granted a first, second or third grade certificate, depending on the difficulty and number of subjects pursued. So this day of exploration was full of new learning experiences for all of us.

Mae was a beauty that day. She was wearing her new plaid flannel skirt and a beige sweater as a top. The plaid flannel had been discussed at length one weekend. Mrs. Manicke had this gorgeous bolt of blue and beige plaid one-hundred percent wool. Mae said the girls who had already bought material were "only buying one yard." If you made a straight skirt with only one pleat in front, one yard would do it. The cost was exorbitant - $4.50 per yard. So Mae came home the following weekend with her yard of one-hundred percent plaid wool and went back on Sunday evening with her skirt finished. (This piece of wool did duty for many years. Mae wore it to the school fair and for all the years intervening until 1934 when I went to Warrensburg for the winter. Then it was turned inside out, re-seamed and made to fit me somewhat. I wore it for many, many years following.)

On the way home we were full of the new things we had seen. Mama and I liked the "educational reels" best. Dad and Pete liked the math and science displays. Bud studied quite a while and announced he liked the dinner best! The dinner was served on long tables set up at one end of the gym. Tables were put away in order to play the basketball games - first the girls then the boys. The floor was natural earth and there were no seats for spectators. We just milled around on the high concrete walk-way that rose above the players heads. This building was not designed by Frank Lloyd Wright! So it wasn't any wonder we didn't enjoy the basketball much. Moreover we had no idea of rules and regulations governing the game. Everett LeFevre refereed the games. Mama made a mental note to have Earl explain it to her sometime the next week. This school fair furnished us with conversation material for weeks to come - right up until

Christmas. After much discussion Mama finally consented to let me have one whole dollar to spend for Christmas. I knew Mae wanted a compact so I studied the Sears & Roebuck catalog diligently. I desperately wanted a copy of *Little Women.* We had a copy of *Little Men* at Post Oak but I had never succeeded in getting any of our teachers to purchase *Little Women.* The Sears order blank contained the two items: one compact - 39 cents; one copy of *Little Women* - 39 cents. That left a very, very small amount for the boys. There was no sales tax in those days. On Christmas Day, Uncle Harry and Aunt Lulu and all their big family came for dinner. So did Uncle John and Aunt Ida. Both aunts had graduated from Clarksburg Academy in the same class. Mama had intended serving turkey for the feast. Dad had won a black turkey hen at a shooting match in the early autumn. We had kept her in a coop and fed her specially on shelled corn to fatten her. That is until the day Mama had a brainstorm concerning raising turkeys. From that day forward the Christmas dinner menu changed to chicken with dressing and beef roast with all the usual things. And so it was that one evening when I was preparing to go feed "Old Blackie." Mama interrupted my preparations by saying "You don't need to feed that old hussy - just turn her out." That was hard to do. I had been contemplating rich, fat turkey and dressing for days. Even minus the turkey, the dinner gave a pleasant prospect. We dressed chickens, baked bread for dressing and we brought up a dishpan full of Mama's famous crispy cucumbers from the brine jar in the cellar and began the freshening process. The day before, we made the mincemeat for pies. Mama's mincemeat was heavenly - full of chopped apples, raisins and spice.

That Christmas morning was one out of Hans Christian Andersen. There was snow on the ground, the tree was decorated with strings of popcorn and tissue paper chains. The big surprise was the arrival of the Christmas package. Uncle Harry brought the mail from the box. Yes, we had rural mail delivery on Christmas Day. I suppose the postal department knew many stockings would be unfilled without their services. The package was small. Was *Little Women* in that small container? I hastily tore open the box, sure enough there it was, a wonderful dust jacket announced *Little Women.* I glanced at the opening paragraphs, such a delightful introduction and I peeped into the small brown paper bag containing Mae's compact. I only got that far before Mama called me to K. P. duty - potatoes to peel, pies to be watched as they baked, pickles to be sliced, and table to be set. There was also a big yellow cake. Mama was making cooked chocolate frosting. The stuff got too hard. She had to put in on "Old Bridge Beach" and re-heat it in order to get the last bit of frosting out of the spoon. I got a sharp knife to pry it out. In the process the knife slipped and I cut my left forefinger just above the knuckle. How it did bleed and hurt. Uncle Harry took some soft bandage from his medical case and fixed it all up nicely after the bleeding stopped. Aunt Ida felt sorry about my injury. She took over the K. P. duty. I sneaked a few more paragraphs from "Little Women." I wished everyone would go home so I could really get into that book! Aunt Ida and Uncle John stayed overnight. They had to find out about Mae's studies in high school." They examined her text books. When Uncle John came to the algebra he looked quite a long time at the algebra equations. After a time he closed the book, carefully gave his own particular shrill whistle, got up and went outside. But in the course of the evening's conversation Aunt Ida inquired how Mae was measuring up scholastically. Mama looked at Mae knowingly and said, "Just tell your Aunt Ida how well you're doing." We also had to explain to Aunt Ida about "educational reels." She listened intently until we ran out of adjectives to describe the wonders of this subject. When we finished she used her favorite expression "Well my foot! I just never - just never heard of such things - educational reels - My foot." Evidently Aunt Ida was not impressed!

Usually Christmas was a one-day celebration for us. A few of our neighbors celebrated a second day. They referred to this as second Christmas. If those holy days fell in a school week Audrey always missed school to visit with relatives. I would be quite envious of Audrey's achievements - getting to miss a whole day of school - dress up in beautiful clothes. She got to wear her aqua crepe-de-chine dress that I thought was absolutely the ultimate in the luxurious garment department. The sorrel horses "Bob" and "Barney" were groomed so nicely as they pulled the buggy or surrey. They traveled very slowly past the school house on their way to Cooper Hill to visit the Langenbergs. Another time I went with Uncle Harry to visit a patient on second Christmas. Mrs. Chris Lange was very ill. When we came to their place, the yard was full of cars, buggies and people all dressed in their holiday clothes. Boyd was driving that day. He and I sat in the car and discussed Christmas and second Christmas. He said the reason our folks didn't celebrate the second day was because they hardly had enough gifts for one day, much less two.

So most times it was back to the salt mines for us. In those early days at Post Oak we did not always dismiss school for Christmas - not even one day. It was usually a mutual agreement between teacher and board members. The decision hinged on whether the teacher was anxious to enter the spring term at one of the state normal schools.

After Christmas, Earl practiced his scales more and more. He actually began to "play tunes." Mama continued to threaten him with "if you don't learn a tune, I'll sing 'When the Roll is Called up Yonder.'"

"Old Blackie" now had a partner. Mama had found a "suitable gobbler" at the poultry house in Belle. Now we were in the turkey business. Mama was also considering geese and ducks. Tom Turkey didn't like Charlie Howard. Whenever he came out of the house Tom strutted, dragged his wings and gobbled furiously. He would peck, flop and gobble until all human beings got out of his way. For several weeks Charlie Howard remained a prisoner behind the white picket yard fence.

Pete's chore that winter was to keep the kitchen wood box filled. He worked at it diligently. Sometimes Earl helped him by splitting the big pieces into smaller sticks. Pete took great pride in his accomplishment. He was now in second grade. He needed a jacket or sweater badly. I had a pretty light blue sweater I had outgrown but I was reluctant to give it up. Finally Mama promised a "new one in the spring" when the old hens were laying good if I'd consent to let her dye this one dark red for Pete. Well we found a time when Pete wasn't around. The dye pot was put on "Old Bridge Beach." The pretty blue sweater was now a delightful dark red. Because Mama recognized some difficulty in fooling Pete she even wrapped the box and had it brought in with the Globe Democrat and other mail that day. Pete unwrapped the box and under the tissue paper was the pretty "new" red sweater all pressed and folded in apple pie order. Pete was pleased and my lips were sealed.

Earl was anxious to get to spring term in Warrensburg, so early in March school closed. I had studied hard that year. I finally had gotten the fractions straightened out, vertically and horizontally. Bud had gotten several headmarks and Pete progressed satisfactorily through his second grade reader. Earl had survived hackberry gymnastics, pie suppers, blackberry jelly jars and biscuits for breakfast. One morning he ate fourteen, according to Mama.

But this joyous sunshine was not to last long. The Drewel family had become special friends. Alice was my age; Arthur was near Bud's. The other children were Elmer, Mabel, Lora and Hilda. Now there would soon be another.

Lora and Hilda were our children, Alice's and mine, whenever Mama gave Bud and me permission to stay a few minutes to play after we carried eggs to the store. No matter what we played or where we went all the younger ones had to go along. I had been invited when Lora and Hilda were christened. This ceremony was held at home. A beautiful cut glass bowl of water was placed on a pretty stand table in the big middle room behind the store. Aunt Pauline and Uncle Louis Drewel were sponsors. The minister sprinkled a few drops of water on the babies heads and said the proper words. A nice lunch with fine light white bread and canned peaches were the foods I remember. I always had fun at the Drewels. Lydia, the wife and mother, did everything well. She managed the store, her family, and her work extremely well. The last time I went to the store was on a Saturday morning. I knew they were moving away. They had bought a farm near Belle. August Gerloff had bought their store. I was dreading their loss on this Saturday. Irvin Leach was there. He wanted a couple of gallons of gasoline for his father's Model T. We went out to the shed across the road to get it out of a barrel. I thought Lydia looked tired and worn. She wore a large full gathered apron over her printed dress and a big fuzzy gray sweater. We got the gasoline. Bud and I picked up our egg baskets and started home. We decided Mrs. Drewel wasn't feeling well but I don't think either of us knew why. The next morning we heard there was a new baby at the Drewels. We were so happy - another baby - but they were moving away. I wouldn't get to know this one very well. For a few days all was well Then one afternoon Dr. Leach came by. That was strange. Dr. Leach came frequently in the evening but never in the afternoon. Doc could hardly talk; he chewed on his cigar instead of smoking it. His eyes were full of anxiety. They looked glassy. Lydia had a fever. This was something no doctor ever wanted to encounter. Child-bed fever Doc called it. Mama changed into a clean everyday dress and walked up the hill. She and Mrs. Leach spent the evening and the night cooking, cleaning, caring for the new baby and the other children. There were two hired girls, Lizzie Redden and Annie Gerloff, who did laundry and cleaning. From that day on for three weeks the routine continued. Mama went every day; so did Mrs. Ed Homfeld, Mrs. Leach and occasionally other relatives and friends. When Mama couldn't go, she baked bread or pie or sent food already prepared. Dr. and Mrs. Leach divided their time between the Drewels and us. I'm sure Doc knew from the outset that there was no hope but we didn't. Mama's face was full of lines. She and Mrs. Leach began to look into dress clothes for the older Drewel children. I couldn't see why. Mrs. Dahms, Lydia's mother, took charge of the new baby and stayed by her daughter's bedside constantly. Her blue eyes were bright with tears. Mama let me go with her during the day to be with Alice and to help with the little ones. That was a hard time. Doc came more frequently to talk to Dad. Lydia died in the afternoon - a dark, damp, cloudy March afternoon. Doc sat on the hay frame out under our big elm tree and cried. He couldn't see why the Lord would take a mother away from a bunch of little children. Dad quoted Bible scripture to him. Mama said she couldn't go to the funeral. She would go in and help a little later at home. Bud and I went. Arthur was sitting on the store front looking sad and forlorn. It was his birthday. Bud pulled a little pocket comb out of his hip pocket and said, "Here, Arthur, this is for you."

We went with Alice and Arthur into the "back room" where their mother lay in her casket. She looked beautiful, but I didn't want her to be so still and white. I wanted her to be in the store weighing up sugar and coffee. Her casket rested on the seats of two dining room chairs. Henry came in where we were. His eyes were overflowing and he said, "How wonderful it would be, Gracie, if she could smile at you now."

I rode to Bland with Ernest Gerloff and Amanda for the service at the Old Bland E & R church. We sat in the pew with the Drewel children. Many tears were shed. Lydia's mother wept over the casket. She wept as she hugged the children and held them close. There were many aunts and uncles. In Lydia's family four Roehls had married four Dahms. In the sad dark days following, Mama permitted Bud and me to go visit frequently. I spent hours helping Alice attend to Lora and Hilda; they were just babies, perhaps two and three years old. Mrs. Dahms attended Calvin, the baby. Annie and Lizzie were kept busy with laundry, dishwashing, mopping and scrubbing. I was there one afternoon when Calvin was very cross. Grandma Dahms was getting very tired; her eyes were full of tears as she struggled with all her young grandchildren.

Alice and I finally got Lora and Hilda to bed and asleep. Calvin of course was being fed by bottle. I had a particularly sad moment when Mrs. Dahms said to me, "Oh Gracie, if only Alice's Mama could be here, how happy we would be!"

After a couple of weeks the Drewels moved away. How we missed them! The Gerloffs came to live at the store. Their family was certainly different. The eldest son Ernest was still living at home. Martin, John and Hermann (twins), Annie, Amanda and Orilla all were grown except for Orilla who was perhaps seven years of age. They had bought the stock of goods from Henry Drewel. They continued to buy eggs and sell sugar, coffee, baking powder, soda, rice, a few cans of corn, and some smoking and chewing tobacco.

The big glass hat case in the center of the store was nearly depleted now. Only a few culls remained. But the Gerloffs were friendly people. Amanda and I had been good friends ever since the day we went to see the "sink hole" at Bland. Now we became special friends. Annie did nearly all the cooking, housework, laundry and general homemaking. Amanda helped her and worked with her father in the store. Mrs. Gerloff sat in a rocking chair; she only did such work as could be performed sitting down. She had a large abdominal tumor. I'm sure this made movement difficult. She was Lena Leach's sister. Anyhow, Bud and I continued to carry our heavy baskets to the store. Mama had a new trouble now. She had always examined the store bill carefully. The first question when we came home from the store was always the same. "Where's the bill?" Previous to the Gerloffs, Mrs. Drewell always folded the slip and slipped in under the twine string which held the sugar or coffee. Now August Gerloff just threw the slip of paper in the basket. The wind could blow it out. We could lose it as we sometimes did. Then Mama would lose her temper. "Now just march right back up that hill and keep looking until you find it." Bud and I didn't like that one bit. But now the bill posed a big problem. Mr. Gerloff wrote all the items in German. Mama even had trouble with the price of eggs. So she fell into the idea of calling first and asking the price of eggs. She always knew exactly how many dozen she sent so she could tell if the "money came out right." Mr. Gerloff also set up a "cream room." That was exciting to Mama. Now she could sell cream. I wasn't nearly so enthusiastic. More heavy buckets to lug up that hill. Mr. Gerloff tested the cream but his prices never pleased Mama. She was always positive August Gerloff didn't do the testing properly. As I remember the test was made by using a glass test tube. Holding one end in his mouth Mr. Gerloff drew up some cream into the tube, then added some acid. He then shook the two together in the tube, read the graduated weight on the tube and that was it! He and Mama never agreed on the cream weight or price! After a while Mama went back to selling butter. I was real glad!

Earlier that spring Mama had a really big brainstorm, she had seen a radio advertised in Capper's Weekly. She studied the picture and read the material over and over. She kept the magazine on the kitchen table. All of us were well aware that Mama was studying that advertisement. For some reason "educational reels" had whetted her appetite for something more than the daily "Globe Democrat." One evening she caught Earl alone sitting at the dining room table. "Earl, have you had any experience with radios?" Well he and Everett had built a crystal set and yes, he had assembled one for "Pa's wife." So off went Mama's letter to "The Crosley Radio Corp." No money, just a letter. In a few days I brought the mail into the kitchen. Mama almost snatched the letter out of my hand. It was from the "Crosley Corp." From that day forward Mama took over the mail box trek. I have no idea how many pieces of communications were exchanged. All of us were instructed in no uncertain terms. "If there's a letter from the Crosley Corp., now you march straight home with it." As if we dared to do otherwise! After much waiting, much correspondence and great stress (none of knew what all those letters concerned) two boxes arrived at our mailbox. It was about all Mama could do to lug the two big boxes to the house. She was so excited. We had a radio. She had promised to act as an advertisement agency in order to get a set for us. In the evening she turned the boxes over to Earl. We were all in the big north front room. Earl read the directions for assembly carefully. He attached the fine wires. The fuse was also removable. He attached the big tall horn-like speaker. Then came the third step. Attach the batteries. "Batteries - batteries - who said anything about batteries?" Well that was Mama exploding in the background. In all that correspondence, never once had batteries been mentioned. In a few days we obtained some dry cell batteries. So again we all got excited; we would hook up the batteries and just sit back and listen. Not so easy. We did attach the batteries. The little "turn on" button was pulled. We turned the rheostat for tuning. All we got was a weak whiney squeal. Everyone was down. We had hoped to "sit back and listen." Irvin Leach was home, someone suggested. Irvin knew all about radios. So Dad dispatched himself to the horse barn to fetch in the big feed basket. The radio was bundled into the basket. Dad, Earl and Bud were appointed to carry it up the hill to Dr. Leach's. Mama was mad, yes, real mad. How hard she had worked - and even promised to be a sales representative and now the darned thing wouldn't work. She wasn't sure she was going to scour the neighborhood and try to sell Crosley radios. About that time our "one long and two shorts" sounded on the telephone. Irvin wanted the batteries, so I had to hurry up the hill with the old heavy dry cell batteries. Earl and Irvin decided that was the trouble; the batteries had lost their spark. So back we trudged with our precious Crosley in the feed basket, resting in a rather undignified fashion, I thought, on a wrinkled burlap sack. After a few days we secured different batteries. The radio worked fairly well when we had fresh batteries. We did get to "sit back and listen" to the "Old Fiddlers Contest" on Friday night, "Lum and Abner"' and "Clara, Lou and Em." There was also Harry Smith, "King of the Ivories," who was a convict in the Missouri penitentiary. He played the piano in an artistic manner we had never encountered before. We were never permitted to turn the radio on in the daytime. No one had time to listen, and besides, that room rarely had a fire in the heater until evening. How we did enjoy our evenings! Chores were hurried just a little bit now. Supper was a little earlier. If Bud and I had to carry eggs and cream to the store we walked a little faster so we could "sit and listen."

Sometimes when Mama got supper she made a "batch of molasses taffy." Dad loved sweet things. He often picked out walnuts or butternut meats to put in it. I was instructed to wash my hands real clean so I could pull. We pulled the taffy until it was white, laid it out on tin pie plates. In the evening we carried these plates to the "radio room" and broke off chunks to chew or let it glue our jaws together. If the batteries were low we played rook or dominoes. Many, many evenings Doc and Mrs. Leach walked down the hill to spend an hour or so in pleasant conversation. Mrs. Leach nearly always wore a pair of men's rubber knee boots. She was afraid of snakes, so in summer the boots gave her security from that fear and in winter they kept her feet dry. She always slipped her feet out of the boots on the front porch and walked in little socks made for boots. Dad and Doc both were avid readers; every day they read the "Globe Democrat" and in their spare time history books and magazines. We subscribed to "The Pathfinder" and "Youth's Companion." In "The Pathfinder" we were following the excavating of King Tut's Tomb, "The French Murders," and items of daily interest. Mae and I read every story and article in "Youth's Companion." Many of the stories were such exciting serials we couldn't wait for the next month's issue. We would discuss what happened and what could happen next. One summer we had a mystery called "Scratches on the Glass," then it was "The Gathering Storm." Another was "Haps and Mishaps at the Old Farm" by C. A. Stephens. These I saved to read aloud in the evening. Dad loved for me to read for the family and these stories were about young C. A. Stephens, his brothers, sisters and cousins growing up in his grandfather's and grandmother's home in Maine. They were nearly always escapades with happy, ridiculous endings. Later we got a copy of the book containing numerous stories not published in "Youth's Companion." Then we limited my reading to one chapter per evening or one new one and one already read from the magazine. Dad listened intently, he laughed in all the right places as he kept wood in the big old A. J. Child's heater so we would be warm. Such pleasant evenings were brought up short when Mama said, "Bedtime - tomorrow's a school day and we'll all be up early." Then it was upstairs to undress in the bitter cold darkness and then curl up in the big double bed. We always slept on feather beds. Before I knew it the sun would awaken us to a bright new day.

Chapter 18

Tramps, Peddlers, Etc.

On occasion, our quiet farm life was spiced by a complete stranger. Some of these were tramps; some were peddlers. In those slow, endless days of the twenties we welcomed strangers. They were always invited to spend the night and share our table. One of these so-called "tramps" stands out in my mind as clearly as if it were yesterday. In the early evening twilight, a small clean-shaven man dressed in blue bib overalls and blue chambray shirt appeared at the kitchen door. He introduced himself. He told Mama he had stayed with the Bueckers when they lived here. He would split wood, help with the feeding and whatever else there was to do. Mama sent him to the barn to consult with Dad. But she already knew the answer. She sent me to the cellar for more potatoes and to the spring house for extra cream, butter, and milk. The stranger's conversation was invigorating. He had visited all 48 states and capitals. The evening was one of great pleasure. This fellow drilled us on state capitals, their spellings and every hard-to-spell state, country, river, mountain range and city in the world. He asked us if we could kiss our elbow and could we lock our knee joint back of our necks. He promptly sat down on the dining room floor and demonstrated his agility but he didn't kiss his elbow. He praised Mama's cooking. He said "please" and "thank you" and insisted we do likewise. At breakfast the next morning Mama set the box of shredded wheat on the table. The stranger remarked quickly, "Well, there's a Niagara biscuit." I haven't seen one of those since I ate breakfast in Niagara Falls two years ago!" After a substantial breakfast, Mama insisted he take an egg salad sandwich for his lunch. He said, "Thank you kindly. I shall be eternally grateful," and was on his way. Years later he returned, stayed all night, visited again as if it had only been a few weeks and hurried off again to visit more capitals. There were others. Some we never knew about. Some just wanted a bite to eat and preferred to sleep in the hay loft. They were nearly always gone before sun up. One of the strange men was very quiet, but certainly hungry. He ate so many biscuits Mama got up, refilled the plate, set it directly in front of this man, told Dad to "push the butter and molasses over closer," while she was doing this she gave us "the eye." That meant "no more for you until this poor fellow is filled up." We didn't care much for him. He not only had no states and capitals to drill us on, and no agility, he simply ate all our biscuits! He was carrying a long-muzzled musket; it was really old. Dad traded him a straight razor for it. After that it rested on our attic floor for many years. (If you girls wonder what happened to this Revolutionary War relic, Paul Allen found it when he was doing some work and talked Mama and Dad out of it along with a beautiful picture frame which had contained Grandpa LeFever's large picture and which he had found in a trunk upstairs.) Then there was Peddler Joe - a short, thick, stocky Syrian. He carried a huge packing case on his back and another case held with straps in his hand. He must have walked thousands of miles carrying yard goods, needles, pins, a few pieces of ribbon and lace, buttons and other notions. Mama rarely bought from Peddler Joe. She thought his goods were shelf-worn and faded. But we always fed and bedded him. Once he nearly frightened Mama out of her wits. He was sitting on the side porch when we came home from town. She didn't see him until he got up to open the door for her. She was never friendly to Joe after that. There were also Watkins men who drove teams and buggies and sold vanilla, lemon, peppermint and wintergreen extract, ointments, salves, black pepper and cinnamon. There were many other visitors too. Dad Cramer who had cared for us during the flu epidemic in 1918 at Linn came in his fancy buggy and stayed for weeks. Bant Carnes, who was the son of one of Dad's best friends, Theron Carnes of Linn, came to spend a few weeks just visiting and helping Dad with whatever he was doing. The county officials at that time (such as assessor) were required to visit each property owner, so this was also an anticipated overnight visit. Guy Vaughan, Dad's cousin, was holding this office when Charles Howard was a very small boy. One evening Guy appeared and was sitting on the front porch. Charles with the usual curiosity of a small fry asked how long he was going to stay. Guy understanding childish questions perfectly said, "Oh, about six weeks." Charles ran screaming loudly to the kitchen and reported to Mama. She and Guy thought this was a huge joke. For years when we met they would make a reference to "coming to visit for about six weeks." It made no difference who came to our door, our latch string was always on the outside. (Our dining room door leading into the new bathroom has actually been a latchstring door.)

The spring of 1925 brought many changes. Uncle Harry was thinking about making a move to north Missouri. He was making exploratory trips to towns like Auxvasse, Mexico and Paris. Now that March was nearing an end, he settled on Shelbyville, Missouri. Once he had made the decision, his medical practice in Belle was for sale.

In a quick move, Dr. Rhodes Ferrell had bought the house, offices and practice from Uncle Harry. He had packed his small traveling bag, mounted his fine riding horse and headed for Shelbyville. This left Aunt Lulu with the sale of household goods, milk cow, two boys and Mae to get through school. Now that Earl was no longer boarding with us, we were obligated to pay board for Mae. Money was something imaginary; something we never had. So Dad hauled a big load of his best alfalfa hay to Belle to pay the last month's board.

Aunt Lulu had to clear out two rooms so Dr. and Mrs. Ferrell could move in. An invoice inventory of Uncle Harry's drugs had to be made. She also bought a piece of beautiful beige wool flannel. This she took to Mrs. Alice Branson and her daughter Kate who "took in" sewing for the Belle community. To trim the new dress she bought brown silk braid to bind the front opening and buttonholes. At the waist line it was to have one large beautiful glittering button about 2 1/2 inches in diameter. Mae told me all about how Aunt Lulu's dress would be made. We couldn't wait for Mrs. Branson to finish the dress.

Mama said I could go to Belle to spend the last week of school. Now Mae, Aunt Lulu and I slept in the folding bed in the front bedroom. We had already cleaned and papered that room and dining room. Both families shared the kitchen. Buell and Russell had a corner in an upstairs bedroom. Nothing was in order; packing boxes and crates were everywhere. Nearly all their clothes and household appliances had been sent on ahead. Our breakfast was a bowl of oatmeal and a slice of toast made on the big wood-burning range. Lunch was usually sardines and crackers; supper was a good meal with at least one substantial dish - potato soup or navy beans and meat. We were trying hard to use what Aunt Lulu had on hand and not buy more. Everyone wanted to come out just even. (No leftovers.)

Mae was in the last week of the school play. It was one of those three-act comedies. Mama thought that was simply great. She had also squeezed out enough egg money to buy a gorgeous piece of sea green satin for Mae - a "dress up" dress. Mrs. Branson and

Kate made this garment. A simple straight pattern, short sleeves trimmed with a lace collar and cuff set. With Mae's long dark curls she was pretty as a picture. So that is exactly what Mama had done - a beautiful photograph wearing her greenish blue satin dress with her curls falling over her shoulders.

That week was exciting to the ninety-ninth degree. The play was perfect. Graduation night was the prettiest ever. Basil Leach was in that class so was Levada Mee, Aunt Lou's daughter. During the ceremony a huge bouquet of pink roses arrived for Levada. The speeches were interrupted; all became silence while the bouquet was put in place. It was from Judge Graham.

One evening Henry Drewel and all the children came into town for me. I went out to their farm and spent the night. I was so happy to see all of them. Alice and I had so much to talk about. They hadn't lived in their new home long enough to be settled or to have made friends. Lora and Hilda wanted to sit on my lap, both at one time. Elmer and Arthur took me to the barn to see the mules and their cows, all of whom seemed to know me as an old friend too. Henry had found a middle-aged woman to stay with the children. She was very heavy and didn't move around very fast, but she managed to feed us. Alice and I did the dishes. All the others sat around the table and asked questions. How were "Jim" and "Odie"? How was "Old Billy," our spotted heifer we bought from Bill Korte? How were all the Homfelds and the Hasslers and especially Dr. Leach? Did they come to see us real often? How was Mr. Gerloff doing with the store? Sometimes I could see tears in their eyes. I was well aware of where their thoughts were! In the morning on our way back to town we drove by Grandma Dahms' house. She was still caring for Calvin the baby. I thought he had grown a great deal. Alice and I both were permitted to hold him. Arthur and Elmer tried to "boo" at him and make him smile. Henry said it was time to go. He had work to do, so it was back to Belle to Aunt Lulu's.

The end of the week increased our fury to pack, sort and work out all the details of the sale. Aunt Lulu's new dress was finished, she wanted it to wear for the graduation exercise. She put it on. She looked down, there was a huge bulge around the big button in the region of the lower abdomen. She pressed it in with her hand. Aunt Lulu was very thin, out it popped again. Aunt Lulu repeated the process - out the pouch popped. After a time she took the shears and cut away the big button, she was sure that would remedy the situation. It didn't. The pouch looked as if Aunt Lulu was carrying a football under her new beige flannel. But it was all she had in the way of dress-up clothes. So away we went to the school pouch and all. But Aunt Lulu kept moaning - "that pouch, why did Kate press so hard around that button?" During all the time the dress was being sewn Kate remarked, "When it's finished I want to press it." And, I might add, she really pressed.

The rest of the week was a flash. On Friday morning Dad brought Mama and Charles Howard into town to help with last-minute sale preparations. He carted heavy boxes and crates to the railway depot to be dispatched by rail to Shelbyville. Aunt Lulu had contacted every railroad line in the area to find the best route. She said she was sending them via the "C B & Q" (the Chicago, Burlington and Quincy RR). I asked her what those letters stood for and she said "Carbolic and Quinine" of course! I stood corrected. Mae was out of school at noon so she and Dad departed for home after a bite of lunch. I was to stay and take care of Charles Howard. I also knew where everything was, after a week of helping. Aunt Lucinda Mason came to help that afternoon and again the next morning. Mama had given orders that Dad should get there early so he could help with the heavy lifting. On Saturday morning Dad arrived as we were finishing breakfast. Everyone was standing up eating oatmeal and toast and crisp fried bacon. Dad joined in. Then the carrying began; heavy beds and cupboards and dressers and wardrobes, some lighter weight chairs and wash stands and some china. Mama had her head set on several nice dining room chairs, the huge gold edged red rose patterned turkey platter and a few other things. Since Aunt Lulu couldn't take fruit canned in glass, she gave Mama jars and jars of peaches, apples, berries and cherries along with jellies, preserves, pickles, tomatoes, etc. Dad loaded all he thought he could haul into our wagon. At noon Aunt Lucinda fried more bacon, wilted a big bowl of lettuce from the garden, and baked what she called a "pone of cornbread." We put the bacon inside a wedge of cornbread and again ate standing up around the cookstove. Soon after noon, people appeared in Aunt Lulu's back yard. The auctioneer climbed onto a small kitchen table and in a short time the fine old pieces were disposed of and carted away by the people of Belle. Mama and Dad hurried away in the farm wagon. It would soon be dark. Aunt Lulu, Buell and Russell would spend the night out at our farm. We swept the floors and back porch, packed the remaining dishes in between the feather beds and quilts in the back seat of the Dodge touring car. We then sat down on the back steps to rest a little before heading for our farm. It would take Dad and Mama three hours to drive the nine miles - so we could wait quite awhile before starting. Aunt Lucinda cried. She was very fond of Aunt Lulu. Aunt Lulu's eyes looked red and very, very tired. She put her thin hands up and covered her eyes to rest. After a while, Buell said he thought we had better go. He and Aunt Lulu climbed wearily into the front seat. They didn't know what to do with Russell and me, but we weren't planning to be left behind as Buell suggested. We climbed on top of the mountain of feather beds, pillows and quilts which we had packed in earlier. It was fun sitting or lying on top of all those bed clothes. In a little while we were home. Mama and Dad were already there with a "good biscuit fire" going in Old Bridge Beach. Everyone was simply exhausted. We had biscuits, ham, milk gravy, fried potatoes with more garden lettuce, and some of Aunt Lulu's peach preserves with milk to drink, and we all fell into bed. Early the next morning, Aunt Lulu and the boys bid us a tearful good-bye and motored off to Shelbyville, Missouri. There Uncle Harry and Aunt Lulu lived out their lives.

Now that Mae was home for the summer, we could ask questions about her teachers and her classes. She brought her books home. In those days each student bought his own books. Occasionally, Mama would sit down with the algebra text and try to figure out how you could add or subtract A's, B's and C's. I was infatuated with the citizenship and English or American literature. She related comic happenings in class. She often spoke about study hall, too. And of course she described what she saw in "educational reels." Mama was so pleased with the teachers: Miss Lawson taught English, Miss Flola Cater - math, Miss Fannie Irene Logan - social studies, Professor C. R. Johnston – science, and John A. Miller - vocational agriculture.

All this end of school excitement was marred with one more unpleasant happening. One Friday morning we couldn't find Old Peg. All of us searched and called. We came in at noon. No one had found her. Surely she would answer with her soft whinny if she could hear us. We went out again. Dad and I found her. She was across the creek in the Polk field. She had stepped into a hole and broken her left front leg. She was lying in a crumpled heap - moaning. Dad was heart broken. Peg and Dad had been through years and years together. She had won blue ribbons at the Osage County Fair. She had been our buggy mare. She had given us fine colts. She had been our loving old riding nag - patient, loving, knowing Old Peg. Dad fell to his knees and held her head in his lap. When he looked up he had tears in his eyes. "Thresia, run to the house. Call Kraenows and ask if one of the boys can come and put 'Old Peg' out of her misery." I said "Dad, lets see if we can get her up. Maybe we can fix it." "No, Thresia, there's no use. This means the end." I didn't argue - I ran. Dad knew best about these things but Old Peg! How could anyone do that to Old Peg? I called Kraenows after explaining to Mama, of course. I then stood out in the side yard and listened. It wasn't long until I heard the shot - just one. I ran upstairs put a pillow over my head and cried. The tears were for Old Peg, for Dad, and for all kind, gentle farm animals who work and live with mankind. (There's one of Old Peg's bones in a small box upstairs in the trunk.) Old Peg left us a horse colt, probably a year old at the time. This was "Spark Plug."

That summer "Sparkie" thought he was human. He missed his mother so he tried to stay close to the people. When we went out to the chicken house or the garden or the barns, Sparkie tagged at our heels. He nudged us when we stood still. He couldn't imagine why we wouldn't let him in the garden or yard. There were also other mule colts: Lonnie, Gert and Bill. Bill was Old Flora's colt. He was a twin. The other was stillborn. Dad bought Flora from Bill Roesner, who lived on our side of Belle.

In addition to the colts there were Mom's and Old Blackie's turkey poults. Our hopes were high to raise turkeys to sell in the fall. That would mean dollars in Mama's cigar box on the cabinet shelf. We treated Old Blackie like royalty. We fed her and her young several times per day. We got them in at night and kept them in a warm spot. We had also invested in some goose eggs. Mrs. Hassler promised to "save" Mama a setting of eggs. After school one day in early March, I brought the goose eggs home from school. Zoa had carefully brought them from home that morning. When we went out to gather eggs that evening we took the goose eggs and placed them under a "good setter" in the old washing machine tub in the southwest corner of the hen house. We couldn't wait for the goslings to appear. Chickens lost all interest for us. We would now have "goslings and poults." Charles Howard caught our enthusiasm. He begged to be lifted up so he could peek in the washing machine tub and see if there were any "little gooses." After about a month the fuzzy little downy goslings began to break out of their shell houses - their bills were too big for the rest of them. So were their feet. We were fortunate to have hatched nine fine healthy "little gooses." We kept them warm and dry for several days. When they were old enough to turn out, the silly little geese simply ran for the chicken branch. The old hen flapped her wings and clucked, flapped her wings and clucked some more. The goslings were in goose heaven. Water - water to swim in. They stuck their heads under. They quacked, they paid no attention to the mother hen. Soon they were downstream all the way to the spring branch. Mama was quite disconcerted. She ordered Bud and me "Above all that's holy, don't let those goslings get to the creek." Well Bud and I had quite a summer. We spent our days beating the water in the branches as we drove goslings upstream.

We didn't like the poults much better. The Old Blackie turkey hen was long-legged, rough and rangy. We had to hunt her at least three times per day and feed her corn and cottage cheese. She acted as if we were intruding on her privacy. She would continue to run about the hillside and catch grasshoppers, beetles and small insects. Then she would scratch in the leaves and grass until she covered all the corn and cottage cheese completely. The goslings were the bane of my existence that summer while Charles Howard tagged me everywhere. He was my pet. He talked and questioned and laughed and giggled. He was so much fun.

Sometime within the year, Grandma's trunk had arrived as Aunt May had to have time to pack and ship it. In it we found treasure. Mama took Grandma's plush winter coat and with some new fur made Mae a warm garment. She took a couple of Grandma's good dresses and made them over for herself. Reta needed the trunk; she was in school at Warrensburg. I fell heir to two lovely items - A tin of Grandma's lilac scented talcum powder and her blue calico scrap bag. It was in this scrap bag I found her Blue Jay notebook where she had written a prayer, asking the Lord to forgive her. She had confused Saturday with Sunday and had carried and hauled chicken manure to the garden on Sunday when she lived with us. She had sinned doubly because she had inveigled Bud into helping her. Her handwriting was trembly. She could hardly make her letters legible but oh, the sincerity in that Blue Jay notebook. It gives me the faith I had as a child, a deep nostalgia for my dearly beloved Grandma. These items are still around. The calico bag is in the bottom of the big box in the playhouse. The tin talcum can is in the same box with Old Peg's bone. (This is hard work - emotionally - it concerns another era. Before we were the recipients of responsibility - such happy carefree days.)

Ray and Roy Nixon were helping Dad on the farm now, so Ellie, Frank and Rude stayed with us a lot. In order to make them feel at home, Mama assigned all of them chores, just as she did for us. Frank was about Mae's age. Because his mother had died when he was very small, they did not know exactly how old Frank was or his exact birthdate. Bob said he knew it was in the fall of the year. At this time Frank was a good hand. He could replant corn, help shock wheat, pitch hay and shock it. As you can see, all these processes are no more in existence. All our machinery was horse-drawn. The labor was by hand.

Ellie was good help in the kitchen. She loved to help Mama with the pies - slice apples and place berries in the crusts. She was good at stirring things on the stove and keeping wood in the stove. Rude was always sort of on the sidelines; in a very busy time he carried wood for the cookstove (Old Bridge Beach). He played with Charles Howard and he could take feed and water to the hens, turkeys and goslings. We were happy and carefree and also, at times, anxious and ambitious. We felt by carrying our fair share of the work we could share the spoils.

Mama was especially anxious to raise lots of extra chickens, turkeys and geese to pay Mae's board now that Aunt Lulu no longer lived in Belle. Early in the summer arrangements had been made for Mae to stay with Mr. and Mrs. Travis for $20 per month. That was $1.00 per day for 20 school days, extra for weekends. Mama explained to Bud and me that we must work hard to help defray Mae's expenses because we would soon be in high school and Mae would help us. Miss Lawson the English teacher was staying at Travis' too. Naomi, the Travis' daughter, was at home teaching sixth grade. All in all, it promised to be a good year for Mae.

Chapter 19

Pete and "Old Watch"

One evening in the autumn, Mama and Dad attended a "speaking" at Cooper Hill. They went in the surrey with Bill and Annie Lange. Audrey stayed with Bud, Pete and me. For some reason Charlie wasn't feeling well. He cried all evening. I carried him around and around the dining table. He cried and cried and cried. I tried every trick I knew to quiet him. All to no avail. When I saw there would be no time to do the supper dishes, I persuaded Bud and Pete to do that chore. Audrey helped them. I was at my wits end. I think he, Charles, just wanted Mama. But there was no way to stop his constant crying. I walked miles. After Bud and Pete went to bed I walked around the dining room table. Round and round I went, over and over. I sang to him. He would stop for a minute. I'd sit down. Immediately he would startle and begin crying again. How my arms ached. How my shoulders and legs ached. I was sick all over. What Audrey and I had looked forward to as a pleasant evening with our books had turned into a fiasco. I didn't know what to do. Audrey, being an only child, had no idea how to help. I suggested she go in the living room and go to sleep in the spare bed. She did. How I longed to crawl in beside her, but I had to walk Charles Howard. I was completely exhausted. Hours later I walked to the front door and heard Bill and Dad talking as they came through our lower gate. Finally the surrey wheels crunched up the lane from the cow barn. Mama hurried in to rescue her screaming offspring. I stumbled upstairs to bed after waking Audrey and escorting her out to the surrey. The next day at school I was so tired I couldn't hold my head up. In this day and age one never explained one's troubles to a teacher. Irvin Leach told us it was a little weak-kneed excuse for not knowing our lessons.

I could do nothing right. We were studying German history that day - Chancellor Bismarck to be exact. Floy was to recite the topic of study. She stammered, stuttered and stopped. Irvin prompted testily, "Well, well, what happened to Bismarck?" Floy didn't know much about Bismarck. I turned aside slightly and whispered to her. "Tell him he died." Floy hesitated and finally turning to Irvin she said in a low voice, "He died." Such an explosion. "Well, well, well, most people do, you know. Take your books and return to your seats. When you're able to recite on Bismarck, raise your hands." We crept to our seats in disgrace. I can't remember anyone ever raising his hand, not that day or ever, to recite on Bismarck!

That was one year Mama forgot all about typhoid fever, water jugs and various and sundry things. She outlined my morning: spelling, math, springhouse, dishes, churning, tending chickens and Charles Howard. I was to leave home at five minutes to nine - in five minutes I could hardly get to the rail fence. I ran, I panted, I ran, sometimes through mud and rain, lots of times through snow and through slush and over ice. She always let Bud and Pete leave about 8:30. I always had to carry the lunch, too.

The whole year was one bad, bad mistake. Mama told me every morning what to tell Irvin. Most of the things were critical. He was spending too much time on math. Tell him I wasn't going to memorize that poem. I was going to use another one for the pie supper. Tell him I needed special help in math. Tell him this, tell him that. Well, nobody ever told Irvin anything - especially a timid, scared child. When I came home she grilled me. Did I tell Irvin what she told me to tell him. "No Mama, I didn't." Then the battle with Mama began. "All right, just pitch in and do that tub of clothes, get them hung on the line before you start supper." She would go out to tend the poultry.

I think Mama was beginning to see the handwriting on the wall. Irvin liked Mae. He was meeting her at Kraenow's road on Friday evening and carrying her suitcase home as they walked together. Mama didn't like this at all. Mae was only in 2nd year high school. Irvin was seven years older. She started sending Bud and me out to the intersection to walk home with Mae. Mae didn't care for this arrangement; we wouldn't carry her suitcase. Besides Irvin usually showed up anyway. A few times we only went as far as the mailbox and waited for Mae and Irvin. These evenings were fun. We played rook and dominoes and listened to the "Old Fiddlers' Contest," "King of the Ivories," and "Lum and Abner." We made molasses taffy. Irvin laughed with us. I wondered why Mama didn't tell Irvin the things she always told me to tell him - somehow she never did.

Monday morning we would all fall into step again. Dad would carry Mae's suitcase and walk with her to the Kraenow road, about 100 yards south of the Feuersville store. They had to leave very early long before daylight in order to drive a team and spring wagon to Belle. But at Post Oak schoolhouse we were reciting and spelling and studying something called animal husbandry and trying to become master hands at math and physiology and finding out "what happened to Bismarck."

Late in the fall Pete became very ill. He had worked so hard cutting corn for the hogs and sliding over a rail fence he had bruised the inside muscle of his left groin. A large infected area appeared, red, tender, feverish. He lay in bed in the front bedroom, obviously in great pain. His big blue eyes were often red from crying. He rolled from one side of the bed to the other. The weather was warm - the nights were well nigh intolerable. Mom and Dad sat up with Pete. They laid cool wet cloths on his head to cool the fever. Doc Leach came every day. All he knew was to let the infection come to a head and lance it. Days went by, the pain and tenderness intensified. Pete rarely slept. I stayed with him at night so Mama could rest a few hours. I'm sure Mama's chickens and geese suffered. I had more kitchen chores than ever and much more responsibility for Charles Howard. There was almost no time for school work. There seemed to be huge tubs of clothes awaiting me almost every evening when I came home from school. Pete liked for me to sit with him and put the cool cloths on his head. I went to the spring to bring him cool drinks of milk.

Finally Doc said the area was ready to be lanced. He wanted Dr. Seba to help him. Sunday morning was set up for the surgery. Sunday dawned clear, hot and dry. Breakfast was hurried and skimpy. I was told to scrub the bedroom floor. Before long Dr. Leach arrived with Dr. Seba by his side. They came to the kitchen and took at least a dozen queer-looking silvery surgical instruments from a black leather case. Doc inquired for a pan. We found a bread pan for him. He put the instruments in it then lifted the teakettle and poured boiling water over them before setting them on the cookstove to boil.

Just then we heard a car in front of the house. There was the Henry Drewel family, come to spend the day. There was nothing cooked for dinner. Mama was so busy getting bandages for Pete's leg. The surgery was to be performed on the big kitchen table. Dad carried Pete from the bedroom. Some ether was sprayed on the red swollen groin. Dr. Seba reached for his scalpel. About that time I figured the surgery would have to proceed without me. I grabbed Charles Howard and ran for the cow barn. All the six Drewels and Bud ran with me. Mae soon followed. We stood around looking at each other, speaking little. It seemed hard to talk, smiling was next to impossible. We heard Pete scream when the deep incision was made. After what seemed an eternity Dad came out in the yard and called to us. We hurried up the lane. I'm sure Mae and I were mulling in our mind what we could fix for dinner. There was a side of cured bacon in the old log smokehouse. Dad sliced it up nicely for us to fry. We peeled and boiled some potatoes to mash. It was late fall so we still had tomatoes to slice. Somehow we had a big bowl of stewed apples and Mama took time away from Pete to make a huge pan of her famous buttermilk biscuits. I remember Dr. Seba bragging on the latter. I also remember how he picked up his dessert dish and drank the apple juice from it. All of us were so busy we had little time for the Drewels. Alice was used to cooking by now. She helped Mae and me get it on the table. Their father Henry held Pete while the surgery was being performed. It was not a pleasant day but Pete began to recover. Other than great tenderness, the throbbing pain was gone. He couldn't get out of bed. He was very weak but he no longer cried out in pain. He could sleep through the night. He began to worry about his pigs. He was sure no one was feeding them. After about six weeks, he came back to school again and took up the spelling, reading and language and, of course, math.

As spring approached, I was real excited about going to high school. It was true I knew my grade cards had not been good but not failing either. However, everything seemed to depend on the final exams.

Some more pleasant things were ahead for the summer. I was allowed to go to Belle to spend the last week of school with Mae at Sam Travis' home. I had a new gingham dress - blue and pink and yellow plaid with white collar and cuffs. It was to have been my graduation dress. I enjoyed all the activity in town. We went on the grade school picnic to Meramec Springs. Mrs. Travis and I went along to help Naomi with the lunch. The evening before we had ground meat and yellow cheese through the food mill. Now grinding cheese is not easy. The men couldn't see why we needed to grind it. Naomi insisted it would go further, so we ground and ground and how our arms ached. One evening Ruth and Ruby Travis came by. They cut Naomi's hair, shampooed, dried and waved it with a new fangled curling iron. It didn't turn out as Naomi had hoped. She tried to take the waves out by steaming over the tea kettle, then with wet towels. She cried and fussed. She had a date and hair was important. Finally she shampooed it again. She promised me a quarter if I would dry it with towels for her. She was all worn out. When it was dry we lighted the kerosene lamp and laid in one small wave to turn the ends of her hair slightly. She thought that was fine!

We went to graduation. We went on the high school picnic to Meramec Springs also and the week was over. It was back home for the summer. We would set the hens. Now we had some female geese so our chicken hens were not frustrated by goslings anymore. We also had a dominating gander. He dominated the entire region between our picket fence and the hen house granary region. He considered the chicken branch his private territory. Charles Howard couldn't step out of the yard. If he did, the old gander came hissing and fussing and flapping his wings to see that Charles made a quick retreat. Once inside the yard, Charles talked back and hissed at "Old Fuss Budget." One day Charles kept begging Mama to "fry a chicken for dinner." Mama was too busy. She had no notion of frying a chicken so she told Charles Howard if he could catch one she would fix it. (Safe as all get out she said.) In a short time Charles appeared at the kitchen door carrying a "just right black rooster." Mama's face fell, "Charles Howard" she screamed. "How in the world did you catch that chicken?" "Well, Mama I dist frewed a little wheat out of the dranary and drabbed him by the knee." Needless to say, Charles Howard had fried chicken for lunch.

Times were getting hard. It seemed as if every growing season was a bad one. Too much rain, not enough rain, farm prices were low. Never, never enough money to buy anything we really needed. The only sure income was the chicken and egg money. Bud and I continued to carry eggs, cream and chickens to the Feuersville store. The geese, ducks and turkeys we took to Belle when the price was good. We truly had to stretch and pinch. There wasn't always enough egg money to bring a nickel's worth of candy when we went to the store. August Gerloff continued to puzzle Mama with his German figures and writing. She got so curious about the figures and cream testing she went along to the store sometimes to see if things were done "according to Hoyle." She decided he was right. He was just using German numerals and letters in listing items. That was a big relief. The disagreement was making me miserable. There was also the three big words hanging over our heads -"Interest, Mortgage and Taxes." In smaller letters was "Mae's Board Money." In later years when I saw young Junior High pupils waving $20 bills around just to buy lunch I couldn't help comparing our economic situation during our childhood years with the later years of "government dole."

There was one especially fine day that summer. We went to Uncle John's to pick gooseberries. It was a picnic day on the river. All of us picked the huge green globes. It was actually fun knowing that there would be a fine picnic lunch laid out at noon: fried country ham, slaw, potato salad and deviled eggs along with Aunt Ida's thick sliced home-made bread. For dessert, fresh gooseberry pie! Later in the afternoon we went swimming in the river with Dad and Uncle John.

There were several days spent at Uncle Will's. One stands out with special clarity. They were sawing lumber for a big new barn. All winter and spring, Dad, Uncle John, Uncle Will and, of course, Grandpa had searched out good stout suitable trees for logs. The timber had been cut and "snaked" out of the woods. It was then piled at a good location for the sawmill. Ed (Pate) Wittrock, Herman (Wes) Wittrock and their father Henry Wittrock were the operators of the sawmill. These men came to do the sawing with their steam powered engine and they also came to stay until the job was finished. Several times I was permitted to go with Dad on the days he could spare away from home. One warm spring day, Dad and I arrived very early. Breakfast was just finished but a fire had been stoked in the belly of the steam engine much earlier. Sawing could begin. Mama had exacted a promise from me that "I would work good and help Aunt Stell with dishwashing and cooking - whatever else had to be done." So I pitched in. Since I was available for dishwashing, Aunt Stell was going to bake custards for dinner. She got out a gallon milk crock and mixed up the dough for the crust. We must have had a dozen or so crusts. We had some in pie tins, some in skillets, some in cake tins. Then came the egg, sugar, milk mixture, the beating and stirring and judging how much sugar, how much milk for a dozen eggs. At last after much of "not enough" and "just a little too much" we got them into the oven and baked. How pretty they looked. Aunt Stell was an excellent cook. She had studied cooking at a school in Kansas City. In addition to custards we had a huge pot of potatoes to mash and chicken and dumplings. Uncle Will and Grandpa dressed the chickens while Aunt Stell was busy with the pie. She made a huge bowl of dumpling dough, cutting them out round like biscuit. Mama always cut squares of dough. They all tasted the same - light , fluffy and delicious!

While Aunt Stell cooked, the men sawed boards, rafters, sills, siding, floors and facings. It was stacked neatly with air spaces between. Uncle Will wanted it to season for some time before building the barn. He was also planning a house. The one they were living in was a good, stout, log house but not what they wanted to live in for years to come.

Uncle Will was very fond of his dogs. He always had good hunting dogs. At this time his very favorite hound was "Old Drum." He and "Old Drum" were to be found along the creek banks fishing or hunting every spare moment. One day "Old Drum" was stretched out asleep on the freshly sawed boards when Pate Wittrock heaved a huge slab of timber in that direction. Poor "Old Drum." I suppose he never knew what hit him. All of us mourned with Uncle Will over the loss of "Old Drum."

It occurs to me I've said very little about our own pet dogs. We had various "Fidos" and "Spots," all of which we loved dearly. There was one we grew attached to. We wanted a "watch dog." Jess Carwile said his female would soon be giving birth to good quality "watch dogs." As soon as the pups could be taken away he would deliver one to us. Jess called one evening and said he would bring the pup the next day. The boys and I were so excited. Our "watch dog" pup would be arriving. We ran home from school. Where was the "watch dog"? Mama was sitting by the heater mending blue denim overalls. "Jess didn't bring him," she told us. Our faces fell. No Pet. No watch dog. "No," she said. "He may bring him later." About that time we heard a whimper and a tiny attempt to bark coming from the vicinity of Mom's rocker. All of us fell on the floor and pulled out our "watch dog." He was so tiny, black, curly and lovable. We fed him. We petted him. We loved him. We named him "Old Watch" of course, what else? Even though he was only a few weeks old, he was "Old Watch." I've never solved the name "Old" as attached to animals. It was always "Old Peg," "Old Nell," "Old Maud," "Old Jim," "Old Odie." The same was true of our dogs and Bob Nixon's "Old Ketch," Bill Lange's "Old Shep," and Uncle Wills "Old Drum."

Well "Old Watch" grew to maturity with us. He was never a "watch dog" other than in name. He had one wonderful attribute. When we needed to catch chickens all we had to do was call "Old Watch" and say, "This one, Watch, sic 'em" and away he would go. The rooster would soon be cornered. Watch would hold him firmly but gently in his front paws until Mom or I came to take the victim to the guillotine. He never lost sight of the exact fowl or confused the chosen one with another.

He also had a couple of painful habits, painful for him that is. He loved to swing onto the mules tails, growling and pulling back. Numerous times a mule would kick him. He would fly through the air and lie unconscious in the barn lot for a time. Depending on the severity of the blow he'd get up, shake his head, scratch his ears and more than likely go right back to swinging on the rear appendage of Jude, Lonnie or Dinah.

"Watch" nearly lost his life in an escapade with our sheep. In order to bring in a small amount of cash, Mama decided to try sheep. The wool brought a good price. We knew something was disturbing our sheep. They bleated and ran for the barn in the early morning hours. Dad was determined to kill this wolf or fox or whatever it was. So he took his double barreled shotgun one morning just before sunrise and sat on a log near the flock of sheep in our "hog pasture." It wasn't long before the sheep bleated and ran for the barn. Dad spotted an animal chasing them. The morning was foggy. No matter, he fired his shotgun. Immediately he saw it was "our pet watch dog." He was badly wounded - bleeding profusely from the mouth and chest region. Dad was crushed, our own dog, our pet. Dad carried "Old Watch" tenderly to the house, laid him on a pile of sacks on our cool north porch near the bedroom door. Watch didn't lift his head. We gave him up for dead. Mama sent us off to school saying she would watch him and feed him a bowl of milk if he woke up. This was at the same time Pete was so sick with the leg infection. Every time I'd go to the cistern to get a pan of fresh water for the cool cloths, I'd glance at "Watch" lying in the corner. I can't recall the exact length of time but it seems to me it was two or three days later I went to the cistern for water. Bud was standing guard over our beloved pet. Bud was always very matter of fact

Henry Buecker.   Mr. Buecker and his wife reared Augusta Lahmeyer (Langenberg) and Anna Albers (Langenberg).   The Bueckers owned and occupied the Bacon farm for about 50 years prior to it being purchased by our family.

Henry Buecker in his buggy, photo taken behind the Langenberg Store

Fred Albers, brother of Lena
Lahmeyer and Anna
Langenberg.

Lena Lahmeyer, wife of
John Lahmeyer, born
Adelheide Albers.

August Langenberg and his wife
Anna with their children. Clockwise
from left rear: Alfred, Amanda,
Siegfried, August Jr.

Photo taken in front of the Buecker/Bacon house around 1895. From left to right: Dick Lahmeyer's son (probably William), Henry Buecker, Augusta Lahmeyer, Mrs. Henry Buecker, Dick Lahmeyer. This is thought to portray the time when Augusta came to live with the Bueckers and was traded for a mule. This is a good photo of the Bacon house about 25 years before the Bacons acquired it. It looks much the same today.

Cooper Hill Ladies Aid Society at the old parsonage in 1925. The Ladies are, front row left to right: Loretta Jett, Margaret Leach Elsner, Lizzie Schneider Reuter, Wilhelmina Schneider Baker. Second row: Eliza Leach, Georgia Rice Volk, Lydia Mickey Steinbeck, Bertha Buescher Enke, Dora Kerley Baker, Lottie Schneider Peth, Ida Elsner, Amanda Tschappler Schneider, Dora Reuter Bock. Back Row Lydia Baker Shockley, Mrs. William Stuekel, Martha Lange Wildebrandt, Lizzie Korte Homfeld, Cynthia Owens Enke, Lena Wildebrandt Leach, Anna Kottwitz Bentlage, Jennie LeFevre Bacon.

The neighbors along Belly Ache Creek, taken one Sunday afternoon when we all gathered at the Kraenow's. Left to right: Mrs. & Mr. Adolph Kraenow, Mrs. and Mr. Jim Nixon, Mama, Papa (with Charles Howard), Mrs. & Mr. Herman Valentine, Mrs. & Mr. William Lange.

Confirmation class, Cooper Hill Evangelical and Reformed Church, 1927. Left to right girls: Viola Schalk, Boesch, Audrey Lange, Grace Bacon, Irene Enke, Mae Bacon, Edith Baker Armstrong, Ethel Eaton. Three boys in center: Clarence Wildebrandt, Raymond Berger, Eugene Kraenow. Boys in back row: Elmer Tschappler, August Steinbeck, Richard Schmidt, Clarence Homfeld, Henry Hunke, Rev. Telfair Boesch.

Uncle John and Aunt Ida Bacon with unidentified young woman at left. Taken just outside the Giedinghagen Farm, in front of the garage. This must have been a very special occasion judging from the best clothes, perhaps going to the state fair as they did occasionally.

Minnie Kopp, Mr. Buecker's housekeeper. She was an unmarried lady who was our friend at Cooper Hill. She cared for Mr. Buecker after Mrs. Buecker's death.

Edward Franklin Leach, Uncle Ed, called "Buckshot" Leach. Photo taken when he was sheriff in Osage County.

Taken in 1919 when we lived in Linn. Ruby Weeks was at home helping her father and mother in the photo shop on Jeffeseon Ave. One very warm summer day, Ruby and Mrs. Weeks invited this group of young ladies to "come up for tea." We were all related in some way. The Vaughans were our cousins and Hazel and Grace Gove were also Aunt Ida's nieces. Virginia Vaughan was later my sister-in-law, Earl Ferrier's wife. From left to right in front: Grace Bacon, Cora Seay Vaughan, Virginia Vaughan. Back row: Grace Janet Gove, Ell Vaughan, Ruby Weeks, Hazel Gove, Mae Bacon.

Annie Meyer Caroll Wyss at the Bacon spring house sometime before 1920.
The Meyer family lived here and rented the farm.

Students and parents at the Feuersville Lutheran School around 1910. Some are identified others not. The four women at left rear are Mrs. Pufogle, Mrs. Carl Wildebrandt, Mrs. Adolph Kraenow, Mrs. Ed Homfeld (in fancy hat). Young man at far left in sailor hat is Martin Gerloff, with Gus Gerloff next to him. Next to them are unidentified, Lena Gerloff, Alma Homfeld, Esther Kraenow, Charles Homfeld Clint Homfeld, Clarence Homfeld. The man just to left of door is Ed Homfeld. The three young boys in white shirts are Basil Leach, Irvin Leach and Otto Wildebrandt. The two women directly behind these boys are Mrs. C. D. Leach (dark coat) and Minnie Wildebrandt.

Grandma Baker's funeral at the Cooper Hill cemetery. Bill Schneider, Mrs. Baker's brother, is the old man on the left.

Charlie Homfeld, Clint Homfeld, Clarence Homfeld, Alma Homfeld, Leona Nixon and Ella Nixon on their way to Post Oak School about 1919.

This a group of the Post Oak sprouts one Sunday afternoon in 1923 at the Kraenow home. From left to right in front: George Homfeld, Adolph Kraenow, Jr., Arvil Homfeld, George Bacon Jr. (Bud). Sitting on fence: Eugene Kraenow, Audrey Lange, Mae Bacon, Grace Bacon, Alma Homfeld, Esther Kraenow, Bernard Kraenow, Alvin Kraenow.

Steam tractor in use around the turn of the century. Pictured are, left to right: Harrison Barbarick, George Crider and Herman Wittrock.

Dad, Charles Howard and Mama on the porch of our house, around 1924.

Dad plowing corn with a riding plow and the team of Old Jim and Odie. This is a part of the cow barn field which we called the "frog pond."

Grace (left) with Alice Drewell, in 1925

Mama, Pete and Bud in front of the old horse barn which was destroyed by a tornado in 1959. The birds are Brown Leghorn chickens, Canada geese and White Indian Runner ducks.

Audrey Olga Dora Lange

Allen Shockley, husband of Lydia Shockley. He taught at Post Oak School for two years, 1920-1922 and was our first teacher.

Audrey Lange and Grace Bacon, young playmates.

Mr. and Mrs. Charles Baker, she was formerly Wilhelmina Schneider. Their home in Cooper Hill was home not only to their large family but to anyone else who needed a place to stay for a while.

Ernest Gerloff operating a tractor at a threshing event. August Gerloff may just be seen in the distance at the right

Mattie and Charles Bacon, children of Allen and Viola Bacon.

King and Scott Bacon, sons of
Will and Stella Bacon.

Wedding photo of Chris Gerloff and Clara
Kopp (seated), in 1925 or 1926 (described in
Chapter 16.) Standing are Louis Wildebrand--
t, best man, and Anna Gerloff Crider, maid of
honor, cousin of the groom. Clara was the
daughter of Henry Kopp and the niece of
Minnie Kopp.

Dad and Pete with springhouse just visible to the right.

Me, George Jr., Mae and Ellis, around 1924. This is Grandpa Leach's back yard and a squirrel cage is visible in the left background. This pet squirrel bit my left forefinger later that same day. It recalls a painful memory. I wouldn't tell anyone what had happened because I had been warned numerous times to keep my fingers out of the cage. This squirrel was released but returned three years later.

Rex Bacon and Logan Wills dressed for threshing and shocking in the early 1900's. Rex and Logan went to the wheat farms in Kansas and other western states, as did many young men of that era.

Aunt Belle LeFevre Pearl, Mom's sister.

Sylvania Smith. Her mother was Aunt Lucia Hodges Smith, Grandma Mitchell's youngest sister, only slightly older than my grandma LeFevre. They were great friends, Lucia and Grandma.

Alta Josephine Bacon, (married Victor Pinet), seated, and Mary Mathilda Bacon, (married Rev. Harry Green), Dad's younger sisters.

Wedding photo of Otto Wildebrandt and Alvena Drewell.

The Will Bacon children. Left to right: Scott, King, Paul, Janet (Scheel) and Nelson.

Here I am holding Grandma Hodges' rolling pin. Carved from yew wood by Grandpa Hodges in the early 1800's as a wedding gift for his bride.

A proud Pete at work with his wheel barrow.

The Cooper Hill Evangelical and Reformed Church, now called the United Church of Christ, as it appeared around 1982.

Interior of the old granery at our farm, showing original log construction and an antique manure spreader.

Pete and I at home nowadays

Mae Bacon Leach as she appears today, at home with her cat.

Me signing copies of my first book, *Teacher, Teacher, I Done It, I Done It, I Done Done It*.

The five Bacon siblings on June 11, 1988. Left to right: George Jr. (Bud), Mae, Grace, Pete, Charles Howard (Bant) at a Bacon reunion held at the Linn Fairgrounds.

The Buecker/Bacon house where Pete and I live, as it appears today.

about everything. He was looking intently at Watch when he said, "Grace, come here. I think he wagged his tail at me a little." I stood and watched. We spoke to him. "Here Watch. Here Watch. Look here. Look here." Sure enough there was no mistaking it. His tail wagged feebly. We reported to Pete that Watch was beginning to wag his tail. I went to the springhouse and brought up a generous supply of cool, sweet milk. Pete had a glass full to drink and Old Watch was helped up so he could drink a bowlful. Watch made a good recovery except for the loss of one eye and scars from the shot. He never bothered our sheep again but other things did. Our sheep venture was short lived. Old Watch was our family pet for many years afterward. He lived to a ripe old age, always willing to "run down a fine black rooster" for our dinner.

In August, we were busy as could be getting Mae ready to go back to Belle High School for her third year. Mama was always great on fractional parts. Now Mae was "one half through" she would say. We just about had it made for in another year she would be three-quarters through. This year Mae would board at Mr. and Mrs. George Slinkman's where nearly all the out-of-town teachers boarded. Mae needed new clothes. If she (Mae) would paint the white picket fence around the yard, Mama would buy enough satin for a real dress-up dress, she would also buy a couple of other pieces of less expensive material. So Mae began the monotonous chore of painting the pickets. She used Tom Sawyer tactics, telling all of us how good we would feel to get it done. So Bud and I helped her. Grandpa came for an extended visit and he helped her a lot. Grandpa gave all of us lessons in paint saving methods. You barely touched the brush to the paint. You worked the primer coat of paint into the wood. That was the preservative method. You held your paint can directly under the brush and surface to be painted so that if a drop dripped it could be caught. The first coat must be very thin on the wood and worked in well. That must dry thoroughly before applying the 2nd coat. But we got the fence painted. Mae got a gorgeous blue satin dress, even a rhinestone buckle for the belt and lace for the collar.

In August we always entertained the Ladies Aid from the Cooper Hill Church. That was always the first Wednesday in the month. We had no idea Aunt Till Green was visiting all her relatives in Osage County. So on Wednesday morning we were running our legs off, cleaning, baking bread, coffee cake, getting out the best table linen and silverware. We wouldn't have much dinner because lunch would be served about 3:30 p.m. Noon was fast approaching. Our first guests would be arriving soon. Lo and behold we looked up the hill and it seemed full of Bacons. There was Aunt Till and her three children, Harry, Eleanor and Charles, Uncle Will , Paul and King, Grandpa and Aunt Vaul Wills – Dad's oldest sister who had never visited us before. They had left their car at the top of the hill and were walking down. Mama's face fell. She knew we must prepare dinner now. "Grace, take 'Old Watch' and catch two chickens, quick." "Mae fill that tea kettle and get the fire going in a hurry." "Bud get some kindling split, fine." "I'll peel some potatoes, we've got some cottage cheese and we'll have some slaw and sliced tomatoes. We'll fix a couple of Pennsylvania cream pies. I can have them ready in two minutes." All hands fell to the appointed tasks. Pie crusts were made and fluted. Pennsylvania cream pie was made by sprinkling sugar on the unbaked crust. Top it with cinnamon and nutmeg, dot it with large bumps of butter and pour a cup or more of thick rich cream over the top. Bake in a quick oven until cream and butter bubble with the sugar. This becomes a soft caramelized pie mixture. It isn't a thick pie but its very rich and filling. All the Bacons were very fond of it. By the time our dinner was finished, our living room was full of "Ladies Aiders." They set up the quilt for quilting and almost grabbed the dining room chairs out from under us as we ate! Mae and I had to run our legs off all afternoon: wash the dinner dishes, clean the table, put on the best linen tablecloth, set the table for the Ladies Aid Lunch, go to the springhouse, go to the garden, sweep the floor again, squeeze lemons for lemonade, skim cream for coffee, keep the fire going to boil water and bake fresh coffee cake. Dad was in his element - showing Uncle Will and Grandpa and Charles Berger (who drove the Ladies from Cooper Hill) around the farm. Aunt Vaul and Aunt Till were right at home. Aunt Till was the wife of a Methodist minister so she knew all about such things. Aunt Vaul was at home in any situation. People who knew her better than I used to say, "Volley Wills is one of those women who can work all the way through," meaning she could do any kind of tasks. Some would say she was a "kitchen to parlor" worker.

Finally the day was over. The Ladies had all quilted and eaten lunch; therefore their mission was accomplished. Uncle Will had to take Aunt Till and Aunt Vaul back to Linn before dark so they had to leave early. Mama instructed Mae and me to "set out" leftovers for supper, gather the eggs, strain the milk, get the old hens and chickens into the chickenhouses, put the good silver away and take the leaves out of the dining room table and restore it to normal size. Then Mama went upstairs to bed. Mae and I did our chores, again we washed the dishes and when we thought we had everything done we tumbled into bed. No reading from "Youth's Companion" tonight. Our eyes were closing even as we pulled our gowns over our heads. You who read this (if you ever do) may wonder why no telephone calls were made to tell us company was coming. Telephones existed, sure, but conversations were very unsatisfactory, even in one's own immediate community. If your phone rang you hurried to answer. The voice might be weak and far away. Our communication system was battery powered. Mama was famous in our neighborhood for "watering the ground wire." If the voice was far away. Mama would shout into the mouthpiece, "Just wait until I put some water on the ground wire." So just because one had a telephone hanging on the wall did not mean instant communications. Sometimes we had to go through switches, that meant calling Mrs. Leach or if the call was to Cooper Hill, we called the store there. They then called the party you asked for. Then the message had to be interpreted by the middle man. That way there were no secrets, just business strictly. There were also some peculiar misunderstandings, even on our own party line. Mrs. Bill Lange, Audrey's mother, called the Homfeld household one summer afternoon and after the usual courtesy questions. She said "Could we borrow your 'cattle'?" Now it was considered crude to call the male cow the bull. Some referred to him as the gentleman cow. So Mrs. Homfeld said she would go find out. She was gone a long, long time. When she finally returned to the phone she said, "I'm sorry, Annie but Ed doesn't want him to go off the place." Annie was taken aback. She said "Oh, no, I wanted to borrow the apple butter kettle." Both women thought that a bit funny. Annie was sorry Lizzie had to go all the way to the bottom field to intercede Ed.

Well, the rest of August was spent chasing chickens, geese, ducks and turkeys, canning tomatoes and peaches. The Frederichs had so many little soft summer peaches they sent word for us to come get some. Mama and Dad took the wagon and brought home a wagon load. We peeled and cooked and seeded, trimmed out the brown spots. We made peach butter. We filled jars and jars with it, even crockery jars. Those we had to seal with wax. I hated sealing wax. I despised the smell of it melting on the stove. We were still canning tomatoes in tin cans too. They had to be sealed with wax. Every time we went to the store it was a prime item on the list with Horse Shoe chewing tobacco and 25 cents worth of coffee (Peaberry in the bean stage). Mama and Dad always had good coffee. They used sugar and cream in it. It looked good. The children were never permitted to drink it unless we had to be given a dose of Castor Oil. Then Mama would pour a cup of black coffee, put sugar in it and have it ready the minute the oil went down. The coffee did not appeal to me any more than the oil. How I dreaded that process and Mama's follow-up questions, after a few hours she would inquire.

"Has the oil gripped you yet?" She thought the effort was worthless unless the patient suffered some pain. I soon learned to tell her. "Yes, it's gripping something awful." If I didn't, I'd be given another dose.

In September, Mae began her third year (so she would be three quarters through in the spring). She had a good year. She had been taking music lessons all these years from the best teachers Mom heard of. But now she could take lessons from Mary Sweeney; that was top notch according to Mom. Hazel Castle came to Belle that fall to teach math. She was a stout young woman, brown eyes, dark, red, curly hair, fair skin, a crippled left hand, and a merry sense of humor. Miss Lawson was in her third year at Belle High School as the English and social studies teacher. Her younger sister, Lucille, was teaching sixth grade. Mrs. Slinkman was one of the finest cooks we ever knew. Her menu was elaborate; every meal was a delightful adventure into taste treats. Mae was a beauty; she had always been a very attractive young lady. Now she had grown tall; she was slender. Her beautiful long curls had become well shaped, bobbed hair. She also had lots of boy friends. Mae did very well in her studies. Usually she was on the honor roll. She played basketball. Mama bought Naomi Travis' fine black serge bloomers for Mae to wear with a white middy trimmed in red tape. This was standard uniform for girls basketball. (The bloomers cost $6 - part of the turkey money.)

School at Post Oak was business as usual. Bob Monroe was the teacher, he was just out of high school, an exceptionally good basketball player and married to our cousin Mattie Bacon. It seemed as if I'd never get away from my relatives as teachers.

Zoa, Floy, Eugene and I again took up our studies in the eighth grade. We weren't the least bit interested in anything. We had memorized all of it the year before. Audrey had gone to Bland to high school. I missed her a great deal both at school and the walks to and from school. We did see each other often. We visited every chance we got. We had fun recalling our doll wedding a few years before. Audrey was the proud owner of numerous dolls, one of which was a boy doll named Hermann. My doll was named Elizabeth so Audrey and I planned a wedding for Sunday afternoon. We were so excited we sorted through all the marvelous doll clothes Audrey owned. We found a pink lace dress suitable for Elizabeth. A veil was fashioned out of a lace scrap Audrey's mother found for us. She, Annie, was also to bake a wedding cake. All was going well until we went to church at Cooper Hill on Sunday morning Surprise - Eva and Irene Enke announced they were coming home with us. I worried all the way home about how we would manage the wedding. I figured I could take Elizabeth and slip out the back door - not much. Mama caught me and demanded to know my business. I explained that the wedding just had to be solemnized. She thought that was all right but Eva, Irene Enke and Mae ought to go along. I didn't think so. I wanted it to be private but Eva, Irene and Mae thought it would be fun! Well, it really was. Audrey and I walked Hermann and Elizabeth to the altar. Together Audrey and I read the words out of a German Bible. I knew what Reverend Leischeidt had said at Chris and Clara's wedding. Just as I reached the end of the ceremony, Mae, Eva and Irene slipped out the back door and began pounding on the metal gate post and on the weather boarding. Time for a "shivaree." Bill and Annie thought this was funny. They also had a fine lunch. Along with wedding cake, there was Jell-O, bread, sliced beef, and fruit. Annie permitted us to have half a cup of coffee with cream and sugar. I thought it proper to leave Hermann and Elizabeth together, so I left Elizabeth at Audrey's house for several days. She then loaned me Hermann for several days. We considered them married the rest of our doll days.

Chapter 20

Hogs

Mama's vow to see all "educational reels" that came to Belle was realized that fall of Mae's third year. Superintendent C. R. Johnston had rigged up a silent movie apparatus. He scheduled such films as "The Covered Wagon," "54 - 40 or Fight," "Oh, Susanna," and "The Trail of the Lonesome Pine." We went to see all of them. We didn't understand how the picture was thrown on the screen but we enjoyed the stories. Gabby Hayes nearly always played in the westerns. He was my ideal mountain man - Dad's too.

Although it seems I have failed to speak as much of Dad as I have of Mom, he and I were the best of friends. I never missed an opportunity to be with him if I could manage it. I held the grain sacks while he scooped the wheat or oats in them. I turned the grindstone while he sharpened the farm implements: sickles, hoes, corn knives, etc. I begged to ride the wheat wagon to Belle. He loved to have me. Once in a while Mama would consent. But usually I had to take a music lesson if I went. Dad would let me out on Main Street to walk up to Beulah Shockley's. She was Dad's cousin. She never knew when I was coming but she would put her work aside and patiently go through scales. My hands were awkward on the keyboard - my thumbs were always in the way of my fingers. I visited more than I learned music. Her daughter Marjorie was about my age amd I usually stayed to play a while. Beulah would send me on my way. I had made no arrangements for meeting Dad any time or any place. We just knew we would meet up somewhere.

There was another day when I spent the day at "Cat" Vaughn's. Cat and Dad were first cousins (Cat was Grandma's nephew.) Cat's wife Mayme was also Dad's first cousin with whom Dad had stayed when he had the mastoid operation so Dad felt right at home with "Cat and Mayme." On the day I rode the wheat wagon, Dad drove a block to the south off Main Street, dropped me off and went on to the mill. But he had an invitation to dinner even though Mayme wasn't home. Sis (Lelia) was home. She would have dinner for us. I thought their house was beautiful - filmy lace curtains, shiny furniture in living and dining room, a piano, a divan and an axminster rug furnished the living room. In the kitchen I helped Sis shuck and silk the roasting ears Dad had brought. We peeled potatoes and fried ham. Sis baked a blackberry pie from the bucketfull of berries Mama had sent. We set the table in the dining room. We drizzled fresh butter over our roasting ears, lapped up our mashed potatoes and gravy, finished off on berry pie. I thought Sis was a mighty fine cook. She had trouble all day keeping her slip from showing. Every hour or so she would pull up her skirt and roll the top of her half slip several times. It fastened with a drawstring. But I also thought it was a mighty pretty slip. It was made of dark green taffeta. Mama must have slipped that day too: I didn't have to take a music lesson!

The day I went with Dad to haul hogs was a mistake - almost too warm for the hogs. We took a load of the fat, muddy, smelly things to sell. At every creek or branch we had to stop in the shade, take a bucket and dip up water to pour over the pigs. They grunted and squealed and rooted each other all the way to Belle. Their noise interfered with our singing. Besides Dad was too worried to carry his best bass that day. If a hog got too hot, he could die and there went one's profit!

I suppose we couldn't muster up any relatives to visit with that day. Because Dad stopped the mules in front of Mannieke's Store where I spent the entire day, except for a few side excursions looking for Dad. It was supposed to be a short trip. He was to sell our hogs and reload some he had bought from Sammie Licklider Jr. Unloading ours went smoothly, but the Licklider hogs didn't like leaving home. The mules, Jim and Odie, didn't like the smell of the hogs. The day was warm and all in all Dad had a bad time.

Mrs. Mannieke was a fine conversationalist. We visited and visited and waited and visited. She gave me some cheese and crackers for lunch. I had 50 cents to spend, so naturally I went to Jess Birdsong's drugstore and had an ice cream sundae. Finally much, much later Dad came by. He only paused long enough for me to climb over the wheel and land on the spring seat. Dad was worried. The hogs were too hot. We would drive as fast as Jim and Odie could go sensibly. The road was rough. My teeth chattered. My jaws shook. So did Dads. Our new load of hogs grunted and squealed and rooted each other just like ours had that morning. We went through the same process of jumping out and pouring water on the fat, smelly pigs. It was late when we got home. I had to help Dad unload the pigs, carry water for them from the spring and get corn from the granary for them. That day something as unpalatable as a music lesson would have seemed rather pleasant!

The first year Bob Monroe taught at Post Oak, Uncle Al and Aunt Vi Bacon visited us frequently. Bob was married to Sis Bacon, their daughter. On Sunday p.m. before school began on Monday, Uncle Al delivered Bob and Sis to the Otto Wildebrandt home where they were to board. Monday morn school opened. Sis came with Bob and stayed all day. She was so pretty, tall, slender and fair-skinned, so typical of people with dark auburn curly hair. She helped Bob organize the classes, especially "the beginners." She played with us at noon and recess and she knew some new games to teach us. We were infatuated with Bob and Sis. Bob was a good basketball player. He was going to ask the "board members" for "some proper equipment." His ability to perform in all athletic games was amazing to us. He could run the fastest, jump the highest and catch more kids in our games of "base" and "stealing sticks." He was also a fair teacher of the academics.

At the end of the first week, Uncle Al and Aunt Vi came to our house to spend Sunday. Naturally Mama called Wildebrandts and Sis and Bob soon came walking down our school path. We had Mama's famous fried chicken, mashed potatoes, sliced tomatoes and apple pie for dinner. Uncle Al was so full of stories. He had inherited the drawl and accent of our Virginia ancestors. These factors alone made it worth your while to listen. Once when we had much too much rainfall in early summer, Dad asked Uncle Al how his river bottom corn crop was coming along. Uncle Al considered his reply for some time. Finally, he said, "Well sah, now I reckon it's doin' just fine. I can tell you for sure its got plenty of water and a pretty good pasture."

During the afternoon Sis announced she had a toothache so when Uncle Al and Aunt Vi left for home Sis went along. Some of the sparkle went out of our school life, but we managed. Bob was young enough to laugh with us and really laugh like he meant it.

In the spring an epidemic of measles invaded the Belle High School. Mama got all upset. Should she have Mae come home and stay until the contagious disease disappeared or should she go to Belle and take care of Mae? She conferred with Dr. Leach. Doc bit his cigar, blinked his eyes and gave Mom some sage advice. "Kids should have had 'em before now. Measles don't kill many kids anymore. Just better get ready." Mama and Doc's conference was held too late. We got a pitiful little card from Mrs. Slinkman. All it said was, "Just a line to let you know Mae has come down with measles" signed, Mrs. George Slinkman. Mama was frantic now. Mae was sick and away from home. How sick was she? Should she go? Well, Doc said it was time all of us had measles. So maybe Grace had better go visit Mae and "bring them home." Poor silly Gracie. I knew nothing about measles. Basil was going to Belle on Saturday. He would be glad to let me ride along and visit Mae. I got dressed up in my red dress. The skirt was made from Jennie Hancks' white skirt (dyed red) with a new piece of red silk for the blouse part. Basil dropped me off at the bank corner. I almost ran the half block to the Slinkman home. I knocked and Mrs. Slinkman couldn't believe her eyes. I had actually come to "catch the measles." She said I really shouldn't. Did my mother really know I was there? Measles were ugly things to have, she said. I insisted it was my mission to get the measles. Mama and Dr. Leach said so!! "Well, well, well, I never heard the like. Mae is in the room to the right of the stairs. Just go on up." So up I went. There was Mae, lying in bed, looking feverish and ill, red spots covered her face and arms. She wasn't very pretty now. She, too, was amazed to see me. I found a chair and sat up close to the patient. I chattered about home and school, anything new in the neighborhood, what I had heard on the radio. Mae lay very quiet. I did help her to the bathroom. We bathed her bumpy face and arms. We changed her gown. I gathered up her soiled clothing to bring home with me. I really went out of my way to bring home the disease.

For several days I inspected my face and arms for bumps and eruptions like Mae's. Mama instructed us to be careful about taking cold. Measles with pneumonia "was deadly." I decided this must be worse than typhoid. But after the incubation period was accomplished the bumps appeared. I felt nauseated, warm, prickly and ill. I stayed in bed. This just wasn't any fun at all. I couldn't eat. I couldn't sleep well. Doc Leach told Mama to pull the shades in our room. Light was bad for eyes when we had measles. So the room was totally dark. The kerosene lamp was lighted on the dresser and a paper envelope was bent around the lower part of the globe to keep the direct flame from glaring into one's eyes. Doc also visited us every morning to give the little nasty tasting brown pills and the teaspoon of red pepsin liquid. As I go back in retrospect to all our childhood diseases, everything was treated with brown pills and red pepsin. The latter was mixed in a water glass and set on the dresser with a teaspoon nearby.

About a week after I came down with the measles, the boys fell heir to the malady. Bud and Pete were in the white iron bed directly opposite me. Charles Howard was put in the big wooden bed with me. He was feverish, cross and very unhappy. So was Pete. He grumbled and scratched and disturbed Bud greatly. Bud wanted to sleep. If you had to stay in bed you may as well make the most of it. Mama really had her hands full now, cooking and carrying our meals from the kitchen to the bedroom, keeping our beds clean and sleepwear clean. We were forbidden to get out of bed excepting to use the "pot." "You'll get pneumonia and die if you don't stay warm." Dad sent for Roy Nixon to come do the outside chores so he could help Mama. Ellie came almost every day to wash dishes, wash clothes and help wait on us. Dad was down in his back.

Because I had continued to attend school until I actually had to go to bed I contaminated several Hasslers, Homfelds and I suppose, others. It seemed strange to see the Kraenows go by on their way to school and I had to stay in bed. One morning we awakened and found our world encased in a crust of ice. During the night I heard trees cracking and creaking. I had no idea what it was. It must have started with very light rain which froze as soon as it touched the ground, trees, telephone wires, everything. The ground was covered with a thick slab of ice. The old cows slipped and slid. Old Watch scooted along behind them. When Don or Roy had to go out to do the milking, they pulled old rough socks over their shoes.

We heard from Mae by postal card. She was better. She was almost well and finally she was back in school. Mr. Kraenow brought news, too, when he took Alvin back to Belle. All of us got pretty tired of this thing called measles. It was no fun to be sick, no appetite, this strange awful odor, this dark room, this constant threat of pneumonia, this awful brown pill and red pepsin and this awful creaking of ice. Sometimes I'd pull the window shade back and look out at the beautiful glistening world. Every time I did this I expected to be blinded immediately. That's what Mama and Dr. Leach said would happen!

One morning, I awakened feeling much improved. Charles Howard had had a good night. He didn't feel so warm anymore or look so bumpy. I waited until Mama had served us breakfast, good warm oatmeal with thick cream, wonderful brown fluffy biscuits with thick slabs of butter melting inside them. There were soft boiled eggs sprinkled with salt, pepper and lots of butter. After such a good meal I felt my strength returning. I got up and dressed, all the time thinking how good it would be to see the hall, the dining room and kitchen. So I dared the adventure. I actually got all the way to the kitchen before Mama heard my steps. She came in from the porch where she had gone to get wood. She saw me and I knew what was coming. "You get back into bed this minute. You'll take pneumonia and die." Her voice carried that commanding tone meaning "no monkey business." She went on with the usual, "After I've got all of you this far I'm not going to let you die of pneumonia now. Don't you dare cross that old cold hall again until I say you can." So it was back to bed for me. I kept telling Mama I felt all right. I wanted to get up at least and sit in a chair. When Doc came that morning I told him I felt good enough to get up. He blinked his eyes and chewed his cigar quite awhile. Finally he said, "Gracie, if you stay in bed today and if you wake up feeling rested tomorrow morning, you can stay up half a day for two or three days and we'll see how you feel then." But as a final blow he added, "You must continue to take the brown pills and red pepsin liquid." Never did the world look so good. At least I could get out of that dark room and breathe air free of measles. I could now take care of Charles Howard. I could hold him and rock him in the big oak rocking chair. Mama had thrown a heavy wool comforter over the chair to make it warmer. I could place a pillow on the arm and hold him to rest his back. When Pete saw this arrangement he wanted to be held too. So I was busy. In a few days all of us were out of bed. It was so good to gather around the big kitchen table for our meals. Mama made big kettles of potato soup, stewed big pots of breaded tomatoes. Biscuits with bacon and ham were standard fare. It was good to smell the boiling soapy water in the wash kettle as our smelly "measly" bed clothes were washed and hung on the line. Ellie was still helping with the extra work. Frank and Rude came along to help in any way they could.

Soon after our measles episode, Boyd LeFevre came to spend the weekend. He was teaching the Horse Shoe Bend School and just happened to have his brother Everett's Model T Ford roadster borrowed for a week. Boyd had a toothache so Everett had loaned Boyd his car in case he needed to see a dentist. All of us were glad to see Boyd, especially Mama. We didn't hear much from Uncle Harry's family since their removal to Shelbyville. So we had lots of questions for Boyd. He answered them patiently after careful deliberation. Boyd was very methodical in his speech pattern. Mama always recalled a story about Boyd. When he was a very small child he attended a dance in the Aud neighborhood. The next day he was explaining the activities to Grandma. He said "Earl Lamb was there with a fiddle and he had a stick to play it with and Boyd Lamb was there and he had a fiddle and a stick to play it with."

Boyd had often helped Dad in the summer with hay. Bob Nixon would be helping too. Almost every day at noon while we were eating dinner, Bob would explain how he had to take the "second hitch at it" to get out of bed in the morning. Boyd was amused at this expression.

But the weekend was especially good. We visited, we played dominoes and rook. We listened to Boyd's stories about teaching and the people of the Bend. He seemed in no hurry to leave. Mama wanted him to get home before dark, but Boyd explained he had good lights and planned to leave at nine o'clock. To us that was the middle of the night, but we enjoyed every minute of Boyd's visit. Everett was superintendent of schools at Linn that same year. He sometimes came to spend Sunday with us.

Just as soon as Dr. Leach pronounced us well enough, we went back to school. Some of us looked pale and we felt weak but attendance certificates were much coveted in those days. Thus the recovery from illnesses was sometimes speeded up.

Charles Howard begged Mama to let him go to school. Mama finally promised he could go on Washington's Birthday if he would learn a commemorative line to say in the morning exercise. This was our opening ceremony almost every morning. As our name was called we stood and recited an old adage or memory gem we sometimes called them. Delmar Brown always used the same one - "Strike while the iron is hot."

Well Mama drilled Charles Howard on his line. "George Washington was 6 feet 4 inches tall" - that was it! He said it over and over. Mama thought she had it drilled into him letter perfect. He said it numerous times to me as we walked along the snowy path to school. He was quite timid but he felt he knew Bob Monroe well enough to stand up and say his line. After most of us had recited our memory gems, Bob said, "Now folks today we have a visitor. He has prepared a line to say." Charles marched up to the front of the room. I can see him yet - thumbs hooked in his brown knee breeches pockets. I thought I detected a disturbed expression in his big brown eyes. He didn't say anything for a moment. Then turning his eyes directly toward me he said, "Dracie, I done forgot how long he was." That just broke up the entire student body. Bob laughed until the tears ran down his cheeks. So did everyone else. I really didn't see anything so funny about it. I was embarrassed for Mama. As soon as I could, I told him how long George Washington was. He repeated it quickly and almost ran to his seat beside me.

This idea of letting the five-year-olds go to school a few days the spring previous to entering in the fall was common. We had no kindergarten. Big brothers and sisters were very protective of their younger siblings. We tried to see that they enjoyed their day.

Before school that morning some of the big boys suggested we go visit the Cooper Hill school since it was a holiday. George Washington's birthday should be celebrated in some special way. The idea caught on like wild fire. Bob Monroe and Troy Smith, the Cooper Hill teacher, were cousins. So we began to plan. We would eat our lunches early and get to Cooper Hill in time to match them in outdoor games during the noon hour. The afternoon would be spent in arithmetic, spelling and perhaps a geography match.

Lunches were devoured quickly. Naturally Mama sent chicken since Charles Howard was a visitor. Then we set out. I wondered how Charles Howard would do, a five-year-old walking 2 1/2 miles to Cooper Hill and back. He was a pretty good walker. We moved at a rather slow pace. There were several six-year-olds. We arrived just as Cooper Hill was dismissing for noon. Those who lived in Cooper Hill hurried home to eat. They returned quickly, some eating as they ran. Clarence Wildebrandt was just finishing off a fine thick slice of home-made bread with butter and apple butter. Just as soon as lunches were eaten, we took our places for a fine game of dare base, followed by stink base. There was very little difference in these two games excepting when you were caught by the opposing team you had to stand on their "stink base" until somebody from your side could run in and successfully rescue you. While you were a prisoner all the players held their noses and chided, "Oh my, how you stink - stink, stink, stinky, phew, phew, phew." When the bell rang we trooped inside, found a seat with our best Cooper Hill friends and proceeded to match in arithmetic. The teachers paired us off with a student of the same grade or intelligence. We were sent to the blackboard and the teachers read out a problem which we copied on the board. We waited for the word "go" before beginning our process of adding fractions, long division or whatever the visitors choice was. We continued with arithmetic down to the very youngest first grader. Even they could add "two plus two." We then went on to spelling - Cooper Hill lining up along one wall, Post Oak along the other. Words were pronounced according to the difficulty of your grade. It gave one a proud moment to "spell down" several older more advanced pupils. We were a bit disappointed when Bob decided we ought to leave by 3:00 p.m. because we ought to be home at the usual time 4:00 p.m. or our parents would be alarmed. The walk home was not half so much fun. The Hasslers lived near Cooper Hill so they soon dropped out of our troop. The Reddens too: Lillie, Opal and Harvey lived about half way home so by the time we got back to Post Oak, we were few in number. And if you're asking what happened to Charles Howard, he got tired, very tired. He said his "legs wouldn't go," so Bob carried him, George Homfeld carried him and I carried him. Fortunately he was small, so we made it. Mama and Dad couldn't believe he had walked all the way to Cooper Hill. We didn't have any trouble sleeping that night. But, oh, the delicious memories. It furnished us with conversation pieces for days. Who was fastest at arithmetic? Who was best in spelling? Who could run the fastest and jump the highest? These visits were not without the usual benefits, social and amorous. Big girls and boys cast admiring glances across the aisles. Sometimes they wrote notes to ask addresses. Sometimes a love letter was passed when the teacher wasn't looking. Some boys kept letters written ahead, so if a letter was received from a young lady all one needed to do was put a pre-written love letter in an envelope, address and mail it.

School ended in March; we had a basket dinner and a program. Eugene, Zoa, Floy and I got our diplomas and our summer vacation began once more.

Uncle Joe Wills died that spring. He had been so sick for some months with cancer. Uncle Will and Dad had been to see him several times. The Wills boys, Joe, Dell and Ira had grown up near the Bacon home. They had been inseparable friends. Joe had married my fathers oldest sister Viola (Vaul) Belle.

Dad hired Otto Wildebrandt to take us in his Model T Ford to the funeral. The day was cold, cloudy and wet. We went by way of Belle where we picked up Mae at Slinkman's. That made eight people in that poor little car. We went down the river road across the Rollins Ferry Bridge and out the Linn road to Uncle Joe's house. There were all the Bacons again with their families and the Wills brothers, also Aunt Vaul's sons, Logan and Porter. Uncle Joe's black mustache looked very black today against his white skin. It was quite evident he had been very, very ill. After a short service, he was taken to the Mt. Ariel cemetery for burial. We went back to Aunt Vaul's where Dad, Uncle Al, Uncle Will and Uncle John visited for a while with Ira and Dell Wills who now lived in Colorado. They recalled their boyhood days and the dances where they had played the fiddle. We returned by way of Belle where Mae was dropped off at Slinkman's.

I seem to remember lots of rain that spring - the creek was high, washing gullies in our hill pastures. When Uncle John and Aunt Ida visited, the men walked out to the creek and talked of methods to build dams. When it dried out enough, more cedar trees were cut and tied into the big indentations in the creek bank. Huge boulders were hauled off the hill along the chicken branch and used to weight the cedars. The corn turned yellow from too much moisture; it was hard to cut the wheat. Our big mules had to strain to pull the binder. When we got to the frog pond field, Dad hitched four mules to the binder and Roy Nixon rode one of the lead mules. All of us worked at shocking the wheat. Mama, Mae, George Jr., Frank and Ellie. We were out in that humid wheat field from early until late. There were all the other early summer chores to do morning and evening. Mama now had two more turkey hens to keep "Old Blackie" company. Turkeys have no sense whatsoever. They will bed down right under the runoff from the eaves and stay there until every one of their poults drown. We had two chickenhouses but not much room for turkeys and geese. It was up to Bud and me to see that they were safely in a building at night. People tried so hard to grow some money crops without anything to work with. It seemed every year we worked harder only to have floods, droughts, chinch bugs and grasshoppers complicated by low farm prices. There was never a time when we could relax. The wolf was howling at the door and three big words stood forever in front of our eyes - INTEREST, MORTGAGE and TAXES. If we complained mildly about some work Mama would turn to us and remark sharply, "Do you want to move away and just leave the farm? Do you think you'd like living in a tent? That's what a lot of people are doing. Now you just march!! March right out and gather those eggs. You can have a dime for candy." A dime bought quite a lot in those days. We got a mixture but always some chocolate drops for Charles Howard. The first thing he ever said was "Hen Drewel's Store - Get choc candy." Now that Charles Howard was five, he begged to be allowed to carry eggs to the store with Bud and me. One morning Mama counted out a dozen in a small bucket for him to carry. He was so proud. He started out, got as far as the big stump behind the smoke house when his feet slipped in the wet clay and down he went. Not one egg escaped. How he cried. He wanted to sell his eggs and "get choc candy."

That was a long, hot dry summer following the cool wet spring. Mae, Audrey, Eugene, Clarence and I all went back to confirmation school - our third summer. We would be confirmed in late summer. Because the days were so warm we went early in the morning, walking down along our lower fields and along the creek. Then across Big Third Creek and along the high bluff where the sun never shone. This was all fine in the cool mornings. But walking home in the noonday sun wasn't so pleasant. Mae, Audrey and I all had "bordered dresses." Sears & Roebuck had a special offer, a dress length where the width had border along one side. One had to cut it so the smaller pattern made a straight sleeveless sack dress. Mae and Audrey chose pink. I had a green. It was hard to tell which color faded most or fastest. But we wore them to confirmation class no matter how faded they were.

For a year I had been begging Mama to let me have my long curls cut short. I wanted "bobbed hair" like everyone else. Mama cut me off short. "Well, not much am I going to let you have your hair cut. It just ruined Mae's looks when she had hers cut," and on, and on, and on. But now I would be entering high school. My hair was hard to work with, so thick and curly. Mama always combed it, no matter how busy she was. Sometime during the morning she would set a pan of water on the stove to heat so she could dampen our curls and "comb our topknots" as she teased us.

That was quite a year, great strides had been taken in growing up. I had finally graduated from the 8th grade. We had survived the measles. We had not developed pneumonia or typhoid or "galloping consumption." Well horses were the only thing I knew of that galloped. And there was that illustration in our *Literary Reader*. "How They Carried the Good News From Aix to Ghent." That horse was certainly going at a gallop. So surely galloping consumption must be carried by a very fat man riding at a gallop on a horse. For several years I shied far to the side of the road and got far, far away from any fat man riding a horse swiftly down our country road. Now that description didn't fit Jimpsey Weir. He often rode past the Post Oak School house riding the slowest, fattest, blackest old mare I've ever seen. Jimpsey always came out of the Wildebrandt road. He lived across Mistaken Creek on a small farm. It took him an age to pass the school and out of sight. The big boys said you had to line Jimpsey up with a fence post to see if he moved at all.

August arrived in due time. The usual things were done, tomatoes were being canned. We canned and dried peaches. I never liked the drying process. Stepping out on the burning hot tin roof to bring them in at sundown ruined my appetite for them. Mama loved them. She preferred the dried flavor to canned. By autumn we would have a big flour sack full of dried peaches stored away for winter. There would be at least a 20 gallon jar of sauerkraut and another one or two full of cucumbers put down in salt brine awaiting freshening and a sweet, spicy vinegar mixture. Mama made the best pickles.

Late in August came Confirmation Day. Every Wednesday all summer Mae, Audrey, Clarence, Eugene and I had again trekked our way to the Cooper Hill church to receive our instructions in church creed, the Ten Commandments, the Apostles Creed and many necessary beautiful passages from the Bible. We might have learned quite a few things not found in the Bible, too.

The Sunday morning dawned hot as a fiery furnace. The hot sun beamed down on our heads and backs as we drove the mules and wagon "around the road" to Cooper Hill. Mae and I were dressed in our white finery. I thought Mae was the prettiest creature alive. Her dress was white silk broadcloth. Made with a slightly flared skirt, plain waist and a long straight collar ending in a tie. My dress was white cotton voile, low waist, white lace medallions in vertical rows on each side front, ribbons ran through these medallions. Each of us had white buckled pumps and white silk stockings, standard dress for this Confirmation Day. Audrey had a white silk broadcloth made just like Mae's and the same identical white pumps. All the other girls had white "uniforms" too. Eugene and Clarence had new suits. Eugene was small for his age so the first suit brought home for him had to be returned because Mrs. Kraenow said "It just was entirely too big." Everyone in the class was dressed to the hilt. It cramped our style. Boys weren't accustomed to Sunday trousers, coats and vests, especially on any such a day as this. All the boys suits were scratchy, dark wool bought for practical purposes; all had younger brothers who would grow into the suit, and maybe be confirmed in it too, who knows.

The church bell rang. We marched in and up on the raised podium. Girls to the right, boys to the left. We sang. We recited Bible verses, church creed, the Commandments. It seemed to me I got all the long verses. Finally it was over. We marched out, stood in the vestibule and shook hands with the entire congregation as they welcomed all of us into the membership and into the warm hearts of the Cooper Hill people.

Every family in Cooper Hill had outlying country cousins for dinner guests that day. We went to Baker's because soon after noon, all of us would gather at Huxold's Studio in Owensville to have a group picture made. This was the big event for me - a car ride. All the way to Owensville, seeing all the confirmands again. I knew I would miss them terribly. Soon after our dinner Henry Hunke pulled up ready to load Mae, Edith Baker and me. Audrey and her parents, had eaten lunch with Mr. and Mrs. August Langenberg. Fritz Berger, August Steinbeck, Irene Enke, Ethel Eaton and Elmer Tschappler were in the Steinbeck Ford. We set off to meet Eugene, Clarence, Richard Schmidt and Viola Schalk at the studio. We simply barreled along over the dusty dirt road. I thought we were flying. Then Henry hit the upper Third Creek crossing too hard. Water flew in all directions. Up, in, all over the top of the car, all over us, the motor spit sputtered and died. We sat. We were dazed. The boys looked at Henry in amazement. No one knew what to do - except crank - that would require getting out in the creek bed with one's very best clothes on. No one volunteered to crank. So we sat and sat and sat some more. After what seemed at least a millennium we heard a car. It was Clarence Meyer coming to look for us. They had been waiting and waiting at the studio. Clarence insisted we hurry. So all of us took off shoes, hose, etc. Boys carefully rolled up their trouser legs and we splashed our way to the creek bank. In a few minutes we were at the studio, seated on a long bench staring into the eye of the camera. Before too long we were back in Cooper Hill. Mom and Dad had gone on home leaving Bill and Annie Lange to bring Mae and me home. It was past milking time when we arrived. Bob and Barney moved at about the same rate as Jimpsey Weir's old black mare. Every once in a while Barney would turn around and seem to admire Bill in such loving adoring terms. He would almost laugh and talk to Bill. Bill and Annie never raised their voices in speaking to Audrey or to each other. Barney and Bob were never scolded. Mae and I took off our confirmation finery and after a bowl of cool milk and bread, fell into bed. Now to get ready for the next big event - Belle High School.

All summer I was contemplating high school. How would I be accepted? I had a mortal fear of teasing. Would all the other freshmen tease me? I actually trembled when I considered vocalizing. Could I actually speak out and be "clear and concise"? I knew my clothes weren't right either. I had two printed percale dresses, both home-made, my confirmation dress, which I considered too fancy for school, and a black taffeta dress made over from something in Grandma's trunk. There was a very childish-looking blue silk I had worn for good in summer for a couple of years. For winter I had a pullover sweater and a skirt makeover from one of Jennie Hancks'. I hated the skirt. Mama had sewed a top on it with built up shoulders. No one with any common sense wore a shirt outside of the skirt. I wore the shirt as Mama said, but it never satisfied me.

The winter coat was the one Mama had also made over for me from one of Jennie's - a black wool, but now it was too short. Mama had studied the Sears & Roebuck catalog all through late summer and fall. I knew the exact page - yard goods, silks, cottons, satins, unbleached muslin and the heavier goods for coats and trimmings. One item on that page was "gray astrakhan." Mama had studied it so much the page was well worn. Mama wanted that half yard of curly wool so bad for my coat. I studied the description intently, grey with tints of black, warm, drapes well. The price was $2.98 per yard. That was expensive, terribly expensive. Just before the winds of winter blew freezing cold we mustered up enough money to order the half yard of "astrakhan." I remember well the day it was delivered to our mailbox. How could such a wonderful piece of material be wrapped up in such drab plain brown paper? But when the brown paper came off there it was. The beautiful gray astrakhan. I loved it, I picked it up, held it in my hands, and in my eyes I saw it as a full length coat. In a few days, Mama and Mrs. Leach had lengthened my coat several inches. The sleeves had gray astrakhan cuffs and there was a narrow strip left for a trim around the collar. Mama had accomplished another dream. The astrakhan was a reality. How she skimped and saved to make our clothes look nice! Mae's winter coat was still the one cut down from Grandma's - plush and with a new fur collar. Our clothes were far from luxurious and far from fashionable, but we wore them. We tried to keep them clean and neat. We were just like our friends. We wore what was available. When I went away to high school there was one thing for sure I would not be required to wear anymore - high-topped rough shoes or black cotton stockings. Mama was sure I was going to freeze my feet off. But she had noticed on our trips to school fairs that none, "absolutely none" of the girls wore high shoes or black cotton stockings. So she reluctantly bought what she referred to as "silly low-cut shoes" and silk hose for us.

Chapter 21

Airplanes, Balloons

1927 was quite a year. In May our daily paper ran a tall black headline - "Lindbergh Does It! To Paris in 33 1/2 hours. Flies 1000 miles through snow and sleet. French carry him off field. Ate only 1 1/2 of his five sandwiches" - etc. etc. Such an occurrence, such courage, we read the story over and over. We put the paper away for future reference. It was bigger and more exciting than "King Tut's Tomb." That was a big story in *Pathfinder Magazine* for a long time. To read about Lindburgh made me feel right at home. Sometime earlier in the spring, Colonel Bill Stuever who owned a clubhouse at Cooper Hill had flown a very small passenger plane from St. Louis and landed in John Volk's ridge field. The news spread like wildfire. Colonel Stuever had flown a plane to Cooper Hill. He would leave for the return trip at about 10:30 Monday morning. Everyone in the community could come see the "takeoff." Such excitement! We walked on air all weekend. When Monday morning came we jumped out of bed, did the milking and chicken chores in no time, swallowed our biscuits whole, climbed into the farm wagon and followed "Old Jim and Odie" to John Volk's farm field. There right in the middle of the whole world was the airplane. I ran as fast as I could to get a close up view of wings, landing gear and cockpit. It looked like a green and yellow bird just poised for a graceful flight. Everyone we knew was there. It was like a picnic. The women were visiting at respectful distances from the plane. They were acting as if this happened everyday! The men were a little closer to the machine. Some speculated on the power in the motor and just what made it fly anyhow. All too soon, Colonel Stuever appeared in his long black automobile. He climbed in. Miss Billie Mariner, his private secretary, also climbed in. They had the regulation beige dusters on and Billie's hair was tied back by a beautiful bright green scarf. The motor sputtered, the props whirled and away they went. We were quite deflated. The air had suddenly gone out of our tires. We watched as long as we could see a speck in the sky. Then the picnic broke up. Everybody climbed in their horse drawn vehicles and we headed on our way home.

There had also been a balloon episode in our lives one beautiful summer morning. Bud and I had been sent to the springhouse to get buckets of cream for churning. There, hanging over our beautiful blue grass pasture, were various colored balls - bright, bright reds, greens, yellows and blues. We followed the ropes attached to the balls up, up, up and there was a balloon floating lazily overhead. We dropped our cream buckets and grabbed for the bright colored balls. Jumping as high off the ground as we could we could just barely touch the gorgeous things. The big, dark shadow hovered over us and as we ran, the shadow outran us. Dad was currying the mules at the back door of the big red horse barn. He too, saw the beautiful balloon float over, or else no one would have believed Bud and me. We never knew what the beautiful thing was, where it was going or why. A few others saw it. We spoke of it often and the delicious moment of running to catch the beautiful colored balls still dazzles my "memory eyes." The joyous sunshine of childhood with airplanes, Model T Fords and balloons fill my old eyes with tears "for the good times ain't here no more."

The first time we had seen an airplane was in 1924. James and Ida Phelps along with their son Albert and his bride Anna were visiting us. They were just leaving. We were all in the side yard by the south bedroom window. A whirling noise was heard like a big beetle up above. We looked up. There was the first plane we had ever seen fly over our farm. Such a thrill. An airplane. It was moving. We stared at it. I ran to get Mama and Mrs. Phelps so they could see too. All of us shaded our eyes and watched until the little speck disappeared out of sight. Now airplanes became something to watch. When we heard the motor in the distance, we ran to the phone and called Homfelds or Leaches or Langes and yelled hurriedly - "Go outside. There's an airplane going over. Good-bye." Sometimes there was no response on the other end of the line. We ran out and watched and watched. If we were eating dinner and the warning sound was heard, everyone jumped up at once and ran outside. Planes traveled more slowly then. It took several minutes to pass over our hills and even then we traced the speck as far as our eyes could see.

That same summer, 1927, July 4th was a red letter day for me. Nothing spectacular; it seemed Dad had been so busy. We hadn't hauled any wheat or hogs to town because the granary was bare. There were no money crops. Eggs, butter and cream brought in enough for a bare existence. It was always Mama's yearly goal to have chickens big enough to fry for Fourth of July dinner. That day was very special in our lives. Independence Day - our great nation celebrated in some way our freedom from tyranny and foreign powers. This year the sun beat down unmercifully, and July 4th was no exception. Dad always considered that day a holiday. All the Bacons celebrated the nation's birthday. Dad usually sat on the front porch dressed in clean clothes, clean shaven and read the Declaration of Independence - all of it. Sometimes he read it aloud along with the Preamble and the Bill of Rights. If Mama sat down with him as she sometimes did they would repeat sections of it together from memory. And at the end they would say simultaneously. "Next winter we'll work on teaching all the kids this work of our forefathers." Well, today, Bud and I took Old Watch, went out and brought in two black fryers for our dinner. Again Mama had achieved her goal. We had new potatoes and slaw from our garden. Another goal was lemonade. So today we had polished off our fried chicken, apple pie and lemonade. The sun was broiling. Dad moved from the front porch to the long, cool hall to finish his history lesson. After the dishes were done, I went to sit in the hall and enjoy a moment of coolness. Dad's hands rested on his US history book. My eyes went immediately to the little finger of his right hand. It was only a stub. The first joint had been severed when he was four years old. Grandpa sent him to bring the ax for some clearing he was doing. Dad, anxious to do the bidding ran too quickly around the corner of the house, fell and severed completely the end of his little finger. Dad followed my eyes, spread the fingers on the red covered Mace's History and I stroked the poor crippled hand. Dad kind of giggled and said, "Thresia, did I ever tell you I took the end of my finger to school the next day and traded it to Fritz Neuner for a slate pencil?" He laughed merrily. I'm sure it brought back childhood memories. That afternoon was lovely. We let the farm chores slip completely from our shoulders. We read from the Bible. We lay on the cool living room floor on the Axminster rug and napped a little. Toward evening, Mae played the piano. Dad and I sang, "In The Garden," "What a Friend We Have In Jesus," "My Old Kentucky Home," "Old Black Joe," all the hymns in our book. After the sun set we went out to milk, gather the eggs and feed Jim and Odie. And then to bed to dream of George Washington, Thomas Jefferson and blue silk knee breeches.

I was so excited, and still apprehensive. On the last Sunday afternoon in August, Mae and I packed our few little cotton dresses, our sleepwear, a change of underwear and hose. We had a sweater in case of a cool day. Mae was given a few one dollar bills and some change because we would need notebooks, pencils, pen points, a bottle of ink and I would have to buy books. Mae had purchased most of hers the spring before. That way she could get acquainted with them during the summer - or so Mama thought.

Anyhow, Irvin dropped us off at Mrs. Slinkman's big, white, well-kept house in downtown Belle. Miss Castle, Miss Sweeney and Miss Jester were sitting on the front porch. Miss Castle and Miss Sweeney had arrived by train on Saturday. Miss Jester's father had brought her in a Model T Ford roadster with trunk strapped on in rear all the way from Liberal, Missouri. Mrs. Slinkman said it was a very old, very rattley, tacky little car. There would be one more. Orpha Picker, also a senior, would arrive on Monday morning. Sometimes she came up from Summerfield on the train or her father drove her in a fine new Chevrolet sedan. We were six in number. But the two bedrooms upstairs were occupied by an engineer and his wife and two small children. His work wouldn't be finished for a month or six weeks. So it fell to Mae and me to sleep at Mrs. Bill Lindner's across the street. Mrs. Lindner was Mrs. Slinkman's sister. So for six weeks, I really had no home base. I could say I got off to a really bad start. Miss Castle, Miss Sweeney, Miss Jester and Orpha occupied the front bedroom. I didn't feel comfortable going across the street to study my lessons, so I tried the front porch. I tried the dining room table. There was no suitable setting for my study. There were a couple of study halls during the school day but one was spent working in the library. Soon after school started, superintendent Joe Curtis had come to my desk in the study hall and asked if I would like to serve as a librarian for one hour per day. From that time henceforth it was an understood fact of life. "I must read a library book during that hour." That was my own law. Reading was my life. Here was a deep well of knowledge just waiting for me to drink my fill, and such fascinating titles: *Trail of the Lonesome Pine, Little Shepherd of Kingdom Come, Tess of the Storm Country, Bob, Son of Battle, Two Years Before the Mast.* I was especially taken with *Up From Slavery.* I loved Booth Tarkington's works of which there were several. Up until Christmas, the library was not open to the student body. Mr. Curtis was cataloguing the books according to the Dewey decimal system. Since I could not check out the books, this was the only way I could read. This introduction to new classes, four different teachers, learning names and faces of all the high school students was ambrosia to me. I had heard Mae talk about the boys and girls in her class. Now I had to associate face with name. I loved moving from one classroom to another. Our building accommodated both elementary and secondary students. The main floor was given over to the four elementary divisions. Miss Opal Jester had grades 1-2, Miss Virginia Smith taught grades 3-4, Mary Sweeney grades 5-6 and Mrs. John A. Miller taught grades 7-8. Along the side of the long hallway was the study hall. Upstairs was the auditorium. I thought it was magnificent - a huge room - raised floor toward the back where the "educational reel" booth was located and what we thought was a huge stage in the front. Along the front was an office and two classrooms for social studies and teacher's training and English combined. In the basement, science and math were taught. And since we had only four teachers and one of them had to supervise the study hall we had no need for more space. Physical education was not considered a required course so we had this physical education only in warm weather. And therefore it was in this square red brick building in four rooms that I, along with all my fellow students, received our high school education. That first year Hazel Castle was the math teacher, Frank Branson the science and world geography teacher, Logan Steen taught teacher training and American history and Joe Curtis taught all the English. There was no choice for anyone the first two years. In the third year one could choose teacher's training or vocational agriculture if you were a male. John A. Miller was the vocational agriculture teacher.

These classes were held at the old high school across town. The boys walked the distance. The exchange was made at noon. Freshmen and sophomores attended the vocational agriculture in the morning; in the afternoon they came to the high school and the junior and senior boys went to the vocational agriculture building. We had an open noon hour (one whole hour). Nearly everyone went home for lunch. Country students carried their lunch and placed it on a long shelf above the coat rack. After their lunches were eaten they usually walked downtown unless there was a difficult study assignment. If that were the case, or if a test was being given that afternoon, the study hall might be well populated with serious students, heads buried in their books.

After spending my first night at the Lindner house, Mae and I jumped out of bed just as the sun rolled in over the prairie. We raced across the street and started breakfast. Mrs. Slinkman made biscuits, such wonderful biscuits. She put the same ingredients into her pan as Mama did and where Mom's were fluffy and flaky and browned to perfection, Mrs. Slinkman's were tiny, white, flaky and looked like yeast rolls. It took quite awhile for me to accustom myself to this new kind of biscuit. There was bacon and eggs. Eggs were always placed on a small serving plate and served at each individual place setting. There was a choice of corn flakes, bran, raisin bran or rice cereal with bananas. There was a large footed compote with prunes, apricots or fresh fruit. And always preserves of some kind. This first morning, Mae and I set the table carefully, carried plates of bacon and eggs, carried trays of dishes back to the kitchen, stacked the dishes in the sink, washed and dried them, swept the dining room and kitchen, reset the table for noon and ran any errand Mrs. Slinkman asked of us. Then it was off to my first day of high school. Miss Jester wanted a large stack of magazines carried to the first grade room. I volunteered for the job. She was very grateful. So I entered upon an exciting adventure. Finding one's way certainly wasn't difficult. English, math and study hall in the morning, hurry home to eat lunch, help with dishes, back to school, citizenship and science in the afternoon and either a study hall or if one chose a softball game on the playground in fair weather. Then home again. For a few days I was spared much study because I had to locate some books to buy. Mae had kept her algebra and citizenship but the science and English texts had changed so I had to have new ones. Our teachers were very good, but they had only one tool, a book. We were told to study, study hard, work hard and success would be ours. All these subjects were almost foreign to me. In English I had had no training - no parts of speech or phrases and clauses. Verbs were just words to help me state a fact. Active or inactive, what difference did it make? Mama had told me I'd never learn algebra because I couldn't learn arithmetic. She was right. I didn't. I'm sure of one thing. I was so full of fear all that first year. So afraid I'd look and feel countrified in dress and speech. So afraid someone would tease me. So afraid I'd not give the right answer when asked to recite. I never volunteered. My heart pounded. I was miserable. To add to the misery, I had no home base, nowhere to study.

After four o'clock Mae usually had an hour to work on lessons so we went to our room at Lindner's. Her schedule was heavy: teacher's training, world geography, English and literature. This required lots of writing. About five o'clock, we went across the street to help with supper. Because we always had a heavy meal at noon, consisting of a good meat dish - fried chicken or beef or pork chops - mashed potatoes, gravy, slaw, green or yellow vegetable and a cream pie such as lemon, banana, coconut, chocolate, our evening meal was somewhat lighter. It was nearly always cold cuts, corn and dinner leftovers. Dessert was frequently tapioca over a vanilla wafer or fruit and cookies. Many times the fruit was apricots. Since Mr. Slinkman was the railroad station master at Belle, I think they had much of the cereals and fruits shipped by rail in large quantities. The Slinkman's had three children: Atwell in 5th grade, Virginia in 1st grade, and Georgia at home, so there was indeed a house full of people to care for.

Something I missed most of all that first fall away from home was my baby brother Charles Howard. He had started to school at Post Oak. He was getting orientated too. Mama was having to fry chicken for the boys' lunches every day. Charles refused to eat anything else!

One day Bud and Pete came home simply starved. They told Mama they thought someone was stealing and eating their lunch. Mama was just getting her accusations in high gear but first she wanted absolute proof, so Bud was to hide and watch the lunch bucket the next morning during recess. He did, and the sweet little thief turned out to be Charles Howard.

I was so happy to come home on Friday and see Charles and Bud and Pete. I'd been away from home for a week or more lots of times but not under such stress. Charles was just as glad to see me. We sat on the smokehouse steps and compared our school situations. His dealt mostly with fried chicken; mine looked like the Rocky Mountains.

This was the beginning of a pattern in my life for the next fifty years. Come home on Friday evening. Get up early Saturday morning, put on the wash boiler, carry water to fill it, bring in tubs, boil, scrub, rinse, hang outside on line, dry, sprinkle, get up Sunday morning, go to church and Sunday School, come home, cook dinner, put on irons, get out damp clothes and iron, put in suitcase and get back to school. Usually I did the laundry for the whole family because Mama said it was a waste of water and time to wash twice in one week, but there was little time for rest. Mama also thought Mae was working to help defray my expenses. The least I could do was to attend to the laundry and since Mae could sew, there was nearly always something to cut and sew or make over.

There was one concern I need not have ever bothered about - friends. Everyone was kindness itself. Edrie Strain (Keeney) was my seatmate in study hall. She loved to read as much as I so we read and laughed. Mildred Harris Strain I already knew, since our mothers were cousins. Our friends included Opal Smith (Branson), Fern Monebock, (her sisters Irene and Lorene were twins), Lillian Litton, Mabel Branson, Sylvia Picker. There were older friends too, especially those in Mae's class. She talked so much about them I felt I knew them better - Beryl Johnson, Sadie Sauders, Golden Spurgeon, Eva Ridenhour. I also knew Alvin Kraenow, Roy Branson and Tolas Lehnhoff. It was such a small school. In a few days I knew everyone. What I needed was a special full time tutor. Everything was French to me. In English classes we began to diagram sentences. The whole class seemed to understand what subjects and predicates were. Prepositional phrases, infinitives, lines drawn here and there: their diagrams looked so pretty on the black board. To me they were an absolute "puzzlement." One day during study hall, I asked Mabel Branson to explain what diagrams were for. What did they teach? Mabel told me to hurry back to school at noon. She brought her lunch and she would help me understand. I hurried. Mabel and Opal became good teachers. So for about a week our study hall sessions continued. I found out some of the others didn't know as much as I thought they did. As soon as I got diagrams sort of straightened out in my mind we went on to more things I didn't understand. That one hour in the library cage was my happy hour - English, science, math - who cares. I had to spend my hour reading. That hour was absolutely heaven!

The weather was very warm that fall. Until the scorching sun rolled back across the prairie and sank into the hollow behind George Tiede's barn, nobody walked the streets and sidewalks. But as soon as the first breath of cool air was felt, people flocked to their front porches. At Mrs. Slinkman's there was a crowd: teachers, students, family and the "Mr. and Mrs. Engineer" from upstairs and their two small children. We fanned with pieces of newspapers, pieces of cardboard, anything; we carried the fans to the bedroom with us. The Lindner's were a large family too: Mr. and Mrs. William Lindner, Reba, Weldon and Bill Jr. Two of their daughters had died leaving them several grandchildren to tend to. There were Boyd, Billie and Zola Mae Underwood along with four Pierce children. At the time I thought nothing about Mrs. Lindner and Reba struggling to cook, keep house and care for seven children. Today I can't begin to fathom such a task. Surely there must be a crown for those grandmothers and sisters who have reared large families of motherless children. Reba was working at Dr. Johnson's medical office as a secretary. She was also dating Marion Welch steadily.

But the September days droned on. Mae had become quite adept at helping Mrs. Slinkman. I only helped when absolutely necessary because as Mrs. Slinkman said, I was paying for my board. I wasn't at all satisfied with my progress in education. I wanted it all - quickly. I wanted to be an excellent scholar. I wasn't. I knew I wasn't. Mama expected me to do as well as Mae. That meant being on the honor roll. I dreaded our first exam period. I simply couldn't understand why everybody else seemed to understand the grammar and math when I couldn't. But I did work hard. I knew I was trying harder than the friends I associated with.

On October 1st, Mr. Slinkman came bounding into the kitchen waving a copy of the *St. Louis Globe Democrat*. My, he was excited. "Just look, Babe Ruth Hits 60th, Pirates Lose, Giants out of Race, Home Run Record Falls." Well, we got excited even though I knew very little about baseball and home run records. We knew one fact now. Babe Ruth was "King of Swat." All afternoon at school, teachers made references to how great it was to break the record and it was especially great because George Hermann was a poor downtrodden small town boy who had "pulled himself up by his own bootstraps." That bit of eloquence came from Frank Branson our science teacher. He was my favorite teacher, kind and patient. He had taught several years in one room schools and small high schools, educating himself by summer courses and correspondence. Now he had returned to his home town to live and teach.

The weather cooled a little in October; it was too cool to sit on the front porch. I still felt strange going to the Lindner's house to sit all alone in our front bedroom. So I spent more and more time in the front bedroom at Slinkman's. It was absolutely piled full of suitcases, trunks, packing boxes, two full sized beds and two dressers. It was already occupied by three teachers and Orpha Picker. So I, as a fifth occupant, could only sit on a packing crate and enjoy the "close proximity." For all these people there was one bathroom located at the head of the stairs. Lindner's had no bath. At noon and just before bedtime, lines formed. Those who needed "time to sit" were in a bad shape. I started using the outside facility at school. I felt more at home there - with the Sears catalog.

Finally toward the end of October, Mr. Engineer moved on, so the upstairs rooms were available. Miss Castle, Miss Sweeney and Miss Jester occupied the big front room. Mae, Orpha and I shared a much smaller room on the east side. It gave me quite a boost to have a home base. I no longer felt as if I were floating. Every day after school dismissed Mae, Orpha and I sat down at our little study table and prepared tomorrow's assignments. Mae was always outlining world geography and child psychology. Orpha who did not plan to teach was perusing plane geometry. Her triangles and right angles and circles looked so pretty and her solutions were always exact. She always had "E's," so did Mae in her subjects. Opal made "E's." Edrie got some good grades. I couldn't do it. I knew Mama would simply raise cain when I got my first report card, and I was not wrong. She raised the roof. "Why didn't you ask Miss Castle to help you? She had nothing else to do from four o'clock until bedtime!" I just didn't have enough nerve to do this. She knew how I was floundering, I'm sure. Orpha tried to show me. She always had time. I liked her very much! Parents did not have the rapport with teachers we now have. I'm sure if Mama had asked, Miss Castle would have helped me!

Mr. Curtis, superintendent and English teacher was a huge man. I was intimidated by his size. His voice was a big disappointment, very small and "rattley" sounding. He cleared his throat a lot and seemed to be struggling to speak louder. Students sitting in the rear couldn't hear. I realized more clearly every day that it was my lack of a good solid background in grammar. I wonder if it was lack of time in one room schools. Any one class was lucky to have 15 - 20 minutes daily recitation time with no great emphasis on learning and testing. Now as I reflect on the matter 60 years later, I'm amazed at how well I managed to care for myself.

Miss Jester had a lovely wardrobe. She was a tiny little thing, newly graduated from Springfield State Teachers College. She was also very, very pretty - dark curly hair and brown eyes. Soon every young man in town was turning his head to catch a glimpse of her. She was always melting the gelatin for her hectograph so she could duplicate papers for her 1st and 2nd graders.

Mary Sweeney was so much fun and so talented in voice and piano. She instructed Mae and Orpha and Atwell Slinkman as well as many others in piano. Every afternoon someone was running scales and the metronome was waving its hand and ticking off 3/4 - 3/4 - 3/4 or 4/4 - 4/4 - 4/4. Sometimes Mary was asked to sing for school or town functions. Then she would practice and sing and sing. I loved that!

Miss Castle was a graduate of Tarkio College at Tarkio, Missouri. I believe it was a small Presbyterian school. She never ceased talking about Tarkio and her rich cousin with whom she had lived for four years, about her mother who built furniture at their farm home in Mayetta, Kansas, her brother Marvin and her sister Geneva who was a graduate nurse. These photographs were placed on the bureau where all could see. Opal Jester had a photo of "Speedy Collins" on her side of the bureau. I must not forget to say Orpha was engaged to Burna Keeney, who worked at Bland in the shoe factory. He came every Wednesday evening to see Orpha. Many times they did not go any place. They sat in Mrs. Slinkman's living room and visited. Sometimes two or more young ladies had a date and shared the living room. John A. Miller soon introduced Opal Jester to Oral Johns, a young teacher in one of the outlying consolidated schools. Oral had also gone to Springfield, so they had common interests. Oral had a new Chevrolet roadster. Maybe that's why he was rather in demand. Anyhow he and Opal "kept company" rather regularly that winter. There was a small side room off the east side, where the stairs came down. This was made into our emergency dating room. When two or more girls had dates the same night, Orpha and Burna often used this room. Most Wednesday nights, they went to Bland to the "picture show." We didn't have a school fair that year. Some town people thought it was too expensive and too much work and not enough profit. The towns people donated the food, drink and labor. Profit was used for something very necessary, like pouring a concrete gym floor. Everybody complained bitterly about the unfinished "gym." Evidently someone misread the blueprint for the basement in that building. It was about 6 feet lower than the rest. On the northwest side were two classrooms and a custodian's closet where the furnace tried to burn. In front, running the entire length of these classrooms, was a "concrete walk." There were no guard rails or other safety measures to keep one from falling off into the "gymnasium pit." When we played competitive games, the spectators watched from this spectator walk.

Chapter 22

Campfire Girls

In late October, all of us cleaned Mrs. Slinkman's wash house garage building in preparation for a Halloween party. Everyone had a date for the evening but me. All these young women insisted I invite Casey Picker (Hermann). He was a cute freshman boy, brother of Sylvia and cousin of Orpha. But I was far too bashful. Besides, Mama would hear about it and sooner or later I'd have to explain. So it wasn't worth it! Several young couples from around town were invited. All dressed in costume. We had fun. I was included in all the games. We had peanut butter sandwiches and punch for refreshments and the first great social affair of my high school life had become ancient history. But there was Camp Fire Girls. My, my, my, Mae had joined this organization a couple of years before. She now had boxes of pretty beads earned by making her bed every morning for six weeks or for keeping her dresser drawer neat. She had a manual, a beaded head band made on a cigar box loom and finally and greatest of all she had her "gown" to wear for "council meetings." This gown was made of heavy "brownish duck," cut straight and loose to give the appearance of an Indian squaw's dress. It had coarse fringe sewed into the side seams. One wore it with moccasins and the beaded head band. I was so enamored with all this I had propositioned Mama on how to earn $1.00 for the initial fee. She said she would think of something. Well, in a few days she came up with it. "You could weed the strawberry patch." I could take a small area each day she said. Well, that summer the rain fell in stingy little showers. The ground became hard as a brickbat. The strawberry bed was full of pepper grass. The long prickly stems had a way of slipping through the hands and blistering the palms. I found I couldn't pull straight up. I had to grasp the weed down near the ground firmly, close the fist around it (like you were milking a cow) and pull sideways on it. But I worked and I slaved at it. Every morning, I worked at it and every evening too. Mama said I had to keep it clean. Not just go over it once and demand the $1.00. So every day I had to pull both big tall weeds and some of the smaller ones that grew without water. Finally I announced to Mama that I had been invited to join Camp Fire Girls. She rattled the cigar box on the cabinet shelf and said, "Well, I don't think there's that much in here." Of course there wasn't. No one in our whole community had $1.00 in money. But there was 50 cents so I took that and paid it with my word I would pay the remainder when Mama got some egg money ahead. Then on the night of the "council meeting," Mae and Orpha and Miss Castle the "head squaw" got all dressed up in their "gowns" with beaded head bands and strings of wooden beads around their necks and moccasins on their feet. They looked pretty funny. All the ceremonies were supposed to take place in the open around a camp fire. But we did well to get to the schoolhouse where I paid my 50 cents and sat around awhile on the floor. (Concrete floor in Miss Castle's math room.) I sat and admired Mae, Orpha, Sadie Sauders, Eva Ridenhour, Golden Spurgeon and Beryl Johnson. I couldn't wait to get my gown and make a headband. Somehow Campfire Girls never did materialize for me. I can't remember ever having another meeting. So Mama didn't have to keep her bargain or pay me the other 50 cents. Mama said I must ask for the 50 cents back I had paid in. But I never could do that! So much for strawberries and Indian squaw gowns and expensive organizations!

But Mama was disappointed too. She thought it quite a nice thing for young ladies. The year before she had become so interested in the thing she had cleaned the house, cooked a big dinner and invited the Camp Fire Girls to our house for Saturday dinner. My, how exciting that was! Two big cars loaded with high school girls came out to the farm. We had fires in the two front rooms. They had Camp Fire manuals to study, head bands to work on, and certainly Mama had errands for everyone not already occupied. She assigned Beryl the pie filling to stir. I made all the usual trips to spring, smokehouse, cellar, hen house and barn. She supervised the oven where chicken and dressing were sending out nose-tingling aromas. Mae and Golden put all the extenders in our dining room table making room for everyone. When the day was done we were so happy. We had got to see all these wonderful "Camp Fire Girls." They weren't just Beryl Johnson and Lillie Swanson and Sadie Sauders. They were "Camp Fire Girls." They wore "brown duck gowns"! (And beaded head bands.) This episode gave impetus to studying the Sears & Roebuck Catalog. They advertised a series of "Camp Fire Girl Mysteries." Audrey and I made a deal. I'd give her a "Camp Fire Girl Mystery" and she would give me one in return for our birthdays. That way we could each read two. We had done that with our Mary Jane Holmes books too. I gave her *Lena Rivers* and she gave me *Tempest and Sunshine*. (They cost 17 cents each or 7 for $1.00.) How we read and reread those books. I hardly ever saw Audrey now. She was in high school at Bland trying to do four years in three by taking a correspondence course. She seemed to be excelling in everything. I had difficulty understanding that too. Audrey and I had always read the same books, studied together and played all the same games. I knew I was just plain stupid!

I went home every weekend. Mae didn't. Sometimes she stayed in town for some school or town activity, play practice, school outings or something at one of the churches. But I always took the soiled clothing and went home. If Eugene Kraenow came after Alvin, I rode home with them. Mr. Kraenow and Alvin rode in the back seat so I could sit up front with Eugene. I loved getting home for the weekend. While Mrs. Slinkman's cooking was the best I'd ever tasted, I liked Mama's better - because it was home. Mrs. Slinkman cooked all the time like we did when we had company.

When Christmas came we had a small party and exchanged inexpensive gifts. Miss Jester had my name. She gave me a pretty bath towel. Mostly we exchanged scarves, table cloths, pillow cases all stamped for embroidery. The teachers had purchased many, many items and embroidery floss from Mrs. Branson and Kate. That was how they spent their evenings. But Christmas came in with a blast. It was down to zero on the evening of the elementary school program. Mrs. Slinkman had sewed nearly all night to finish light flannel dresses for Georgia and Virginia. She cooked extra and made fancy sugar cookies. Irvin came after Mae and me on Friday and it was cold! We put up a tree in the living room. We had plenty of pretty bright balls and tinsel. We now called the pretty shredded aluminum "icicles." We made chocolate fudge and divinity. We butchered and had Mama's delicious pork sausage for breakfast with biscuits and milk gravy. We had "speeches" in the Cooper Hill Sunday School program. So on Sunday afternoon everyone loaded into the farm wagon to go to the church. We huddled together on the short benches behind the curtains. We said our speeches. We sang our carols. We read the Bible story from Luke. Then came the bags of candy, oranges and peanuts. They were all sticky on the outside because Buckshot Leach had bagged it all several days early and put it in a washtub in the basement where condensation had brought about the stickiness. Selma Steinbeck and Ida Baker passed out the sticky treats as our name was called. Then each adult was given a stick of candy. Visiting friends and relatives, along with children too small to take part, also received a portion.

Sometime during the latter days of vacation, Charles Bacon came to visit. He was working in St. Louis but he had a Ford roadster. Mae was Charlie's favorite cousin. He always tried to spend part of every vacation with us. We had fun playing dominoes and rook. We made molasses taffy and put walnut pieces in it. We listened to Charlie's stories. He had worked for a short time in the lumber business in California. He had also attended a business college in Springfield, Missouri. So to us, Charlie was positively wonderful. But as I have said the weather was "so-o-o-o-o cold." When Sunday came, Charlie said he would return Mae and me to Belle since he was going on to St. Louis anyhow. He put on his new leather jacket. We had just finished supper. We climbed into the Model T - no side curtains, no heater, no really warm clothes. My astrakhan trimmed coat felt good. Mae was wearing her black plush coat, but Mama did not approve of our low cut shoes and silk hose. She gave us a parting bit of advice. "Just go on out bare footed and bare legged. You'll live and learn." We did not exactly breeze into Belle. The roads were snow covered and slick. Mae and I jumped out and pushed on all the hills. When we came to the Branson hill, the Ford stopped. We backed down the hill to a good warm fire and a hearty warm welcome from the Dolph Shockley family. Dolph and Charlie thawed the radiator out. We got in and up the hill we went and into Belle. Charlie went on to St. Louis. This past summer when Charlie visited here we recalled (he is 83) this New Year's Day of 1929. He said his roommate had to pry him out of the car when he got home. His new leather jacket had frozen to the leather car upholstery.

After having had a week at home, I was so homesick. I felt guilty staying at Slinkman's. Mae was working for her room and board. Mama was working so hard with chickens and eggs, butter and cream. Her hands looked so rough and red and I wasn't doing well. I had to study harder, make good grades. I just had to. But when I sat down to study my mind was at home. I wanted to feel Charlie's warm loving arms around my neck. I wanted to hang my clothes on my very own hook in the wood of the mantle shelf in the dining room. On the underneath side of that mantle, the initials H. L., for H. L. Lalk were carved. He had scratched them there while recuperating from burns he suffered during the winter of 1902-03 when Mama boarded there. She thought he had nearly died. He had deep burn scars the rest of his life. He caught his clothes on fire while starting a fire for butchering. You can still see H. L. on the underneath side of the dining room mantle.

Meanwhile at school Mr. Curtis had opened the library to the student body. So now I no longer had a full hour to read. I had to check books in and out. The weather was cold, very cold. I was also beginning to wonder if Mama might be right. I might get "galloping consumption" because my feet were always cold. I even missed my long underwear! This was another concession Mama had made when I went away to high school.

Earlier in the year, I was so enamored with the actual situation of being a high school student, I had been walking on air and breathing ambrosia. I was trying so hard to be like Mae, and I wasn't the least bit like Mae, in looks or brains. Where Mae was tall and slender with dark eyes and beautiful dark brown wavy hair, beautiful skin and modest mannerisms, I was so little and scrawny. My hair was a mass of curls that stood out like corkscrews. I was so inhibited I couldn't talk to people. I blushed. I stammered. I stuttered when I attempted to answer questions! Frank Branson was my most patient, supportive teacher. He waited until I composed my answer into a complete sentence. In those days a one word answer was not acceptable. We were required to write and speak in complete sentences. Since I had two classes with this kind, patient man (both general science and citizenship), I believe that he, more than any other, gave me the impetus to try harder. I kept doing things over and over hoping to overcome my fear of speaking and my embarrassment. When I blushed all the class turned and looked at me to see me blush. Then they giggled! By spring I was doing better in everything but algebra.

Something else happened early that year. It also interfered with my school work and gave all our hearts a heavy load. Small towns have such traumatic times. Everyone knows everyone else. Families have intermarried until everyone is related to everyone else, by friendship and mutual bonds as well as blood. There were those who sometimes needed material blessings: food, clothing, and fuel for warmth. The Sikes family lived across the railroad tracks on the south side of town. Lizzie (the baby Uncle Harry had delivered) was now in first grade. She was a strong, sturdy intelligent child, but so poorly dressed. Cast-offs were all she had, rough high shoes laced with cloth rag ties, and a man's coat which almost dragged the ground. Her face peeped out merrily from a heavy knitted fascinator. Miss Jester felt so sorry for her. She wanted to go right out and buy nice things for Lizzie. Mrs. Slinkman and Mrs. Travis explained that it would be money wasted. Her father would discard fancy store-bought clothes. He wanted to provide for "his Lizzie." They had tried clothing Lizzie. What she lacked in outside appearance she made up for in "scholastic achievement." She was somewhat a "loner." It could have been from lack of soap and water. She walked fast on the way home in the evening. People would say, "Oh my, oh my, watch Lizzie go. Poor little Lizzie." I can't believe Lizzie ever thought of herself as being "poor little Lizzie."

Mrs. Slinkman had two kitchen helpers who came in whenever needed. Mrs. Catherine Terrill, known to everyone in Belle as "Aunt Catherine," helped with cleaning and dish washing and sometimes babysitting. Mrs. Lone Decker helped with the heavy work, laundry and deep-down cleaning. She did any kind of work ranging from "kitchen to parlor" and she went wherever she was needed, especially where there was illness or a new baby.

Up the street from Slinkman's and on the same side as the school was a very pretty big, white, frame house occupied by Mr. and Mrs. Merritt Decker and their two children - Iva who was 21 years old at this time and Bobby in first grade. The Deckers were considered rather well-to-do. He was a grocery salesman. Iva was considered the "town beauty," and in my book, rightly so. She had beautiful golden hair with red lights shining from large natural waves. She had beautiful skin and eyes with a medium body build. In the fall Iva had come home from St. Louis where she had been working. She came home on the train in the early, early morning. I remember distinctly the clip, clip of her high heels as she walked past the Slinkman home and on toward the Decker house. I must have been worrying about algebra to have been awake at that hour of the morning. At breakfast someone asked, "Who in the world went clipping up the street at that ungodly hour in the morning?" Mrs. Slinkman was ready. "I don't know for sure and certain, but I'd be willing to bet it was Iva Decker just by the way her high heels clinked." Sure enough by mid-morning everyone in town knew "Iva came home this morning." Everyone doted on Iva's comings and goings and her dates, principally with Charlie Miller who lived across the street. He was just as handsome a man as Iva was attractive. Charlie had a Model T coupe. Iva drove it anyplace she wanted to go if her father's new Chevrolet wasn't available. Iva gave parties. Iva visited everyone; she was a frequent addition to our sewing circle in the evening. Iva "knew how" to play bridge; so did Opal Jester and Mary Sweeney. But they were afraid to admit they knew a heart from a spade in Belle at that time! Card playing, dancing and any serious dating were "absolute no-no's."

For a few weeks Iva's presence brought a "halo" around our humdrum existence. I stared at Iva whenever we were in the same room. Whatever gave this beautiful goddess such a magnetic personality made me want to grow up just like her.

Again, I was awake early in the morning. I heard Dr. Johnson's automobile go up the street. (There were so few autos in Belle we soon recognized each of them by sound.) Again at breakfast someone asked, "Where did Doc go last night?" Again Mrs. Slinkman had the answer. "Not far. Sounded as if he stopped on this side of the street. I figured about Decker's." As we walked to school, sure enough there was Dr. Johnson's car parked in front. Soon we knew. Iva was very ill - pneumonia. Everyone in town had a reason for the illness. "She had taken cold from exposure. Those foolish high heeled shoes and silk hose. She only wore a sweater to protect her from the cold when she taught school the year before," - etc., etc." But no matter what the cause Iva, was lying in that big beautiful house seriously ill - pneumonia!

All the neighbor women helped out. Mrs. Decker was so tired. Yet she couldn't rest. Lone was the main worker. She could do it all, lift, bathe, change bedding and do the laundry, cook, carry in wood and water. Iva was her love too, her niece. Everyone was simply paralyzed. All conversation dealt with Iva's state of health. It wasn't good! Dr. Johnson sent to St. Louis for new special medicines. He had consultations with other doctors. He spent all his spare time at the Decker home.

One morning just at dawn we heard Dr. Johnson's car go past Slinkman's. It was sounding slow and sad. All of us felt we knew what had happened. All of us were hoping it wasn't true. Strangely at breakfast no one asked. Mrs. Slinkman's eyes were red. Her tears fell on my hand as she served the beautiful eggs and biscuits. At school there seemed to be a hush over everything. Everybody spoke quietly and more gently than usual.

The next day as Orpha and I walked back to school at noon, Mrs. Decker and Ella Miller were out on the sidewalk talking. As we approached and spoke to them Mrs. Decker put her arms around us and said, "Come on in and see Iva. You were good friends." Ella (Dad's cousin) went with us. There lay Iva in the bedroom on a low flat table wearing a clean frilly night gown and her bare feet were tied together in a crossed position with a cloth strip. She was so pretty. Just lying there asleep. Awaiting someone to come awaken her! My mind floated all afternoon.

Those of us who knew Iva were excused to go to the funeral. She was now in a beautiful gray casket surrounded by floral pieces of every description. Her mother was distraught. She wept uncontrollably, as did her father. Lone tried her best to take care of everyone. This was actually my first brush with the death of a young person, someone dearly beloved by everyone who knew her. For weeks I wondered though, if I ought to return to heavy hose and shoes. I wasn't going to wear high heels for awhile.

We were settling into a very comfortable pattern. I was not quite so "up tight" all the time. I had gotten used to having men around the house. I had accustomed myself to having Mr. Slinkman come upstairs to the bathroom. Sharing my room with Orpha was helping me to grow up. Mr. Curtis was eating meals with us too. Mrs. Curtis had taken Joe Dick and gone home to Springfield. She never returned. Mr. Curtis had fallen in love with Verna Owens, a senior student.

As I said, we were settled. We would get up, eat our bacon, egg, cereal and toast breakfast, help with dishes, get to school, classes, at noon, rush home, eat a fine big dinner, meat, vegetables, salad and dessert, back to classes, home again, study, eat, and do a little embroidery or mending. Everybody mended rips and tears and darned their hose. Evenings were beautiful things, helping Opal or Orpha get dressed. Opal Jester had bought the most beautiful blue velvet velour coat. It was black-fur-trimmed with white specks in the fur. She had fancy high-heeled shoes and filmy silk hose and cute hats. Orpha also had pretty dress-up clothes. She always brought one nice dress in her suitcase for her Wednesday night date with Burna.

Perhaps we were too well settled. One evening in early March while Mrs. Slinkman was preparing supper, she suffered a nervous chill. She sat on a kitchen chair crying and shaking. Mae and Mr. Slinkman put supper on the table. Mrs. Slinkman went to bed. I helped Mae with the supper dishes. We fixed Mrs. Slinkman a bowl of soup and sat a little while with her. She was still shaking and her eyes were red. She kept saying "I just may have to give up my girls. I just may have to give up my girls. Oh dear. Oh dear." I believe all of us knew what we had to do. Mrs. Slinkman wasn't able to do all this work anymore. Consequently we were not at all surprised when Mr. Slinkman announced while we were crunching "All Bran" the next morning that we would have to find another rooming place, and do it fast, over the weekend. Somehow word travels on wings of wind in all small towns. Mrs. Oliver Travis sent word she would take Mae, Orpha and me. Just bring our things over that afternoon. There was an upstairs apartment ready at Mrs. John Mannieke's - the teachers moved there.

For the third time that year I had to adjust to a new and different living situation. It was with regret we left Slinkman's. They were a fine family with home comforts we would not find anywhere else in Belle. But "there's no such great loss without some small gain." Mae would not be working in the kitchen. That made me feel real good! The Travis' home was farther from the school. We had to hurry to get there and back plus eat at noon and, since there was no bathroom, everyone had to wait his turn for the outhouse. Mae, Orpha and I shared the front bedroom. Their two daughters Ruth and Ruby were away from home. Ruby was teaching at Bland and Ruth was in school at Columbia getting a degree.

Soon after we moved there the Travis' built-on a small bedroom at the rear of our bedroom and to the side of the dining room. It had space for two beds and a bureau. Mrs. Travis was so pleased with it. I think that's why she took us to board. The money she earned would pay for it. She cooked more like Mama, just plain country cookin'. There wasn't much store-bought food. I remember good home-made bread and stuffed sausage with lots of canned fruit.

After we moved to the Travis' home the seniors were preparing for graduation. Those in teachers training were applying for teaching jobs. They were also doing their practice teaching. Mae was assigned to do her "stint" at Dingley - a small rural school on Highway 28 toward Bland. She dressed especially nice for those two weeks and went off to teach. She had her application in for the Cooper Hill school. We made a special effort to go to church and Sunday School every Sunday. Dad was Sunday School superintendent. Mae played the piano and I sang. I taught a Sunday School class. We worked hard at getting Mae a job. And one evening, Hazel Castle, Mary Sweeney, and Opal Jester invited Mae, Orpha and me to have dinner with them at their apartment. Their rooms were upstairs, bare and cold. They had a big bedroom and a small, very cold kitchen. Their dinner was not elaborate. Someone had managed to bake a chicken. Together all of us made a stuffing. We mashed potatoes but our bread was all gone. Hazel went to get a loaf of bread and a tube of "chocolite," this was chocolate in a tube for hot chocolate, etc.

She forgot the "chocolite" the first time so I was sent to remind her on the second trip to not forget the "chocolite." We had lots of fun and we did have hot chocolate for dessert with a marshmallow floating on top.

One of our big events in the spring was a Negro minstrel show. We practiced our songs and our lines and our deep south speaking patterns. We had costumes and on the big night we burned cork and "made up" our faces. All our parents came out to see us along with all the townspeople. Of course it was a huge success. I finished my part in the show and was sent to the rear of the auditorium to find a seat. I hadn't been there long until a big boy, Hurst John, came along and sat by me. We exchanged smiles and a few words. My heart was going a mile a minute. I was astonished when he stuck by my side at the end of the minstrel show, followed me down the steps and out to the street. We walked to the Travis' home together, most of it in silence but words just didn't seem necessary. I couldn't believe anyone cared about me enough to hold my hand and walk me home. I arrived there before Mae, Orpha or the Travis'. They were bewildered, puzzled, astonished. Why hadn't I waited for them or why hadn't I informed them? Then it dawned on Orpha what had transpired. She had spotted Hurst coming back toward town as she came home. The cat was out of the bag. Hurst was a relative of the Travis family. They thought our friendship was just great. Orpha had fun teasing me and watching me blush. I felt so absolutely frustrated. I stayed home from classes that afternoon. I didn't want to see anyone, especially not Hurst. I stayed in bed all afternoon. I was trying to map out a course for my future. I had not pleased Mama or myself this freshman year. I had done fair in everything but algebra and that was the subject Mama doted on.

The juniors were entertaining the seniors at a banquet. The banquet was to be held at the Masonic Lodge Hall. The mothers of the junior and senior girls did the cooking and carried it down to the Hall. Their food consisted of creamed chicken, mashed potatoes, peas, hot rolls, a fruit cup and pie with coffee for dessert. Someone asked me to help serve the plates. I was in seventh heaven. Only one fly in my happy ointment, Hurst would be there. Could I avoid him? Finally I faced the situation head on. Go right on with the serving. If he tried to walk home with me, I'd run fast. I was sure I could outrun him. Mae and Orpha looked so pretty in their voile dresses. Mae's was made with a flowered strip followed by a plain pink row of fully gathered voile, row after row of it. She was feeling rather good about her situation. She had a contract to teach at the Cooper Hill school. Although Dad had to borrow $100 from the Belle Bank to take care of our room and board. Mae was considering going to Rolla summer session because an additional 10 hours college would give her a first grade certificate. Mama thought that was just the ultimate in education. So before school closed Mae borrowed $100 from Mrs. Jennie Sauders and arrangements were made for her to share an apartment in Rolla with Sadie Sauders, Ruby Travis, Ina, Emma and Eunice Pointer, and Zelma Drestlekamp.

Then it was done. The seniors had walked down the center aisle and received their diplomas. Uncle John and Aunt Ida came to our house early in the afternoon. We had an early supper. All of us walked up the hill. I rode with Uncle John and Aunt Ida in their Model T. Dad had hired Otto Wildebrandt to take the rest of the family. Mae had stayed in town for one last fling with her good friends. Baccalaureate was on Sunday evening. Commencement was on Thursday. Mae was stunning in her graduation finery. Her high heels were really high and her silk hose were so filmy.

Chapter 23

Visiting Summerfield

Where had the past nine months gone? It had only been a second since Mae and I were packing our suitcase to go to stay at Slinkman's. Now everyone was helping her get ready to go to Rolla for summer session. We had about two weeks. But it was spring on the farm: setting hens, little chickens, gardens, sewing and, since the young ladies would be doing their own cooking and housekeeping, we had to think about what Mama could contribute to the food department. Mama said we must hoe the potatoes and cabbage good. I must get the weeds out of the onions and carrots. We had to make soap too. Mama had me bring three cans of Merry War lye when I carried the eggs to the store. Mama brought out all the stale grease and meat scraps, put them in Grandma Mee's big black iron kettle under which a good hot fire had been built. With the grease we putin a big bucket of soft water and the lye. After this mixture boiled, at least three more buckets of water were added. Again the liquid boiled until it formed a jell when put out in an old saucer. Sometimes the liquid would spin a thread when the paddle was lifted. We were sure then of a fine product. When this stage was reached we doused the fire, covered the kettle and let the soap cool for at least 24 hours. After that, the blocks were cut and put on a clean board to dry. This was the only household soap we had for dishes, laundry, scrubbing floors, etc. We only bought Ivory for our daily toilet chores. So when Mae got ready to go to summer session she had a fair share of fresh groceries, a nice wardrobe of simple clean clothes and some good home-made soap! The soap had a rather peculiar smell and Mae didn't want to take it but we wrapped it in several layers of *Globe Democrat* and the smell wasn't quite so bad!

And so Mae went off to Rolla with potatoes, cabbage, onions, carrots, home-made bread, a slab of home cured bacon, some jelly, preserves and whatever else Mama thought of. I missed Mae. I had an awful lot of chores to do - chickens to feed, eggs to gather, laundry, cleaning and all the time I thought of Mae "going to summer school at Rolla." That must be Heaven.

I've said very little about how often Dr. and Mrs. Leach visited. At the end of each episode I could have climaxed the day with the same sentence. "Dr. and Mrs. Leach visited tonight." But it was true we couldn't get our supper over with until Dr. and Lena would be spotted walking down the path past the cemetery. In summer both wore rubber boots as a safeguard against snakes. In winter they wore them as a safeguard against deep snow drifts. These visits were just friendly neighborhood affairs. Sometimes others were there too, but mostly and more frequently it was just Dr. and Lena. Whenever we visited at Leach's it was an occasion. We ate supper early, put on clean clothes and walked up the hill anticipating a delightful evening of watching the toy monkey climb a string, seeing a Negro boy jig on a box and most wondrous of all was a US map puzzle to put together. And all these years Irvin and Basil had helped Dad with hay. Irvin was a strong young man. He pitched big forkfuls of Dad's favorite cattle feed; sweet, pungent, freshly cut alfalfa. Irvin rarely ate a whole meal with us but he never, never refused a piece or even two of Mama's pie. It was never important what kind, and sometimes if we had fried chicken and biscuits it wasn't hard to persuade him to the table! When Dr. and Lena didn't come to visit in the evening, Irvin and Basil did. During Mae's Senior year in high school, Irvin taught a term of high school in Hope, Missouri. In the autumn he came home every evening. He had a Model T and could drive from home each day. Later, in the cold winter he boarded. There were entertaining people in Hope - Otto Jacobia and his wife May. Ted Langenberg operated the general store. Ted's wife was Farida Baker from Cooper Hill, Olga's sister. Irvin knew both of them and he spent his loafing time at the store listening to Ted's stories about the Texas border, Mexico and the Spanish-speaking people. There was also another very interesting family in Hope. W. S. (Bill) Miller operated the blacksmith shop and had the post office. The high school classes were held in a one-room building. Since it was a one year stand, I suppose all his pupils were freshmen. I can remember a few of them - Louise Nolting and Naomi Ziegler, Anastasia Lynott, John Findlay, Noel Baker, Arthur Holland and Roscoe Matthews.

On the farm we had what we had learned to speak of as a wet spring complicated by chinch bugs. By raising extra chickens and selling a couple of loads of alfalfa hay to Dr. Tellman, we paid off the $100 borrowed earlier in the spring. But now we thought money matters might be a little easier. Mae would be "independently wealthy" with her teacher's salary. Mom and Dad had only one in high school, but Mae had to repay the $100 she had borrowed for summer session. Mae seemed to do well in her studies. Her professors were Dr. Barley and Dr. Johnson. She learned to swim. She took her turn cooking, washing dishes and cleaning. I'm sure they had fun too, but six girls crammed into a teensy, weensy apartment for eight weeks in the warm summertime can be disastrous.

Irvin had gone away to Warrensburg for summer session. He was close to getting a degree. In August, Mae and I managed to make a couple of very simple cotton print dresses. Mine was a heavy printed broadcloth - red flowers on a beige background sprinkled here and there with black lines resembling a trellis. Mama said since the material was so stout it needed to have long sleeves. I rolled them up neatly on warm days. That dress was my uniform for a couple of years. It laundered well!

September came as it always does. I was hauled off to Belle very early. Dad took a load of wheat. We had to pay tuition. I had plenty of time to walk to Mrs. Jennie Sauders home across the railroad tracks because it was just getting daylight. Mrs. Sauders was Sadie's mother. Sadie would be home for a couple of weeks until business school started in St. Louis. Mrs. Sauders was just getting up when I knocked on the front porch door! I'm sure she was a little surprised to see me so early. I went to the kitchen and watched the biscuit making process. I also ate my share. After all I had been up since before 4 AM. We had good thick sliced bacon and fried apples. Mrs. Sauders inquired if I drank coffee. Rather hesitantly I replied, "No, Mama says coffee isn't good for children." Mrs. Sauders' eyes twinkled, and as she poured a large teacup of beautiful brown fluid for me she said, "Well dearie, you're away from Mama right now, just try some." I rather liked it. When I put rich cream and sugar in it, it was still better. It was still too early to go to school. I had time to wash my face, comb my hair, put on my new broadcloth dress and sit in the living room. I was anxious to see all my friends. I hadn't seen them all summer.

There was another aspect to this year, Mae and Orpha wouldn't be around to guide and council me. I was on my own. And I was the only student from "down north." How would I get home over the weekend? I felt reasonably sure Dad couldn't come for me every Friday evening and bring me back on Monday. Jim and Odie were dear old work mules but they didn't travel very fast, even though we now had a spring wagon. This was two seats minus the top, such as our surrey had. Dad could make the trip more quickly if we had no wheat or hay to deliver. We were selling our eggs, chickens, turkeys, geese, etc. at the poultry house in Belle now. We had no store at Feuersville. The Gerloff family had gone their separate ways. Mrs. Gerloff had died, Anna married George Crider, Amanda married Charles Vincent, and Martin married Barbara Crider. For a time they lived in the little two-room house south of the store building. Mr. Gerloff could no longer manage the business alone. He and Orilla, the youngest child, drove from home to home around the countryside selling Watkins products. They were a pitiful picture. He had been a very prosperous farmer and stockman. This position had brought less prosperous farmers to his door seeking loans. There was no insurance for such business. Often the "signer of the note" had to pay off the bank. It took very little of this to break the back of any farmer, no matter now prosperous. Even though "Silent Cal" (Coolidge) was governing our country and prosperity of the roaring twenties was evident in cities and large businesses, farmers everywhere were "feeling the pinch."

When I finally arrived at school, I found most of my classmates had returned. We did not greet each other boisterously. We said "Hi" or "Hello" and went on from there. I was so afraid some boy would speak to me and perhaps pause a moment to converse. I saw immediately "Casey" had not returned! Sad! However his sister, Sylvia, had. She was one of my favorites: quiet, friendly, soft of voice, but when she laughed, as she often did, it was like music. Edrie Strain hadn't returned. She had married Boyd Keeney. How I missed her, especially when I needed someone to "talk books" to.

Only two teachers had been retained from the previous year. Frank Branson was superintendent and Logan Steen was again teaching teacher's training, English and American history. Alfred Dreysee was teaching math and the Board of Education had not found an English professor. Mrs. Clema Branson, Frank's wife, was substituting in that position. And so it was that I finally had someone who recognized that a few of us did not understand the meaning of noun, verb, adverb, adjective, etc. We had a new grammar book that year - *Tanner's Composition and Rhetoric*. It had examples of diagrammed sentences. Clema further dissected these sentences by placing them on the blackboard. There with a pointer she carefully and thoroughly asked us to "tear each one apart" word for word and put it back together. She explained what the diagram lines meant, what a modifier was, etc. After a few days in her class the light shone through. It was as if my blindness had suddenly become sunshine. English became a class to be enjoyed instead of dreaded. But the light never dawned in geometry. Alfred Dreysee was said to be positively brilliant. He rarely put any theorems on the board. He sat mostly at his desk and told us how to do the process. I never understood the book or the process or the angles. I couldn't even get my compass to make a circle! I was absolutely scared to death of anything having figures to add, subtract or mark with alphabetical letters. I sat and trembled. And to make matters worse, Alfred Dreysee was a <u>man</u>, I couldn't ask <u>him</u> to help me. I always remembered him as he had appeared at Post Oak School to walk home with Earl LeFevre.

Agriculture was my science course. Frank Branson taught that. I liked it. We kept a notebook and did lots of outlining. Mrs. Branson taught world history as well as English. That was my favorite. She had the very necessary quality of teaching by repetition. We were drilled every day in dates, historical events, titles and in English we went over and over proper nouns, common nouns, weak verbs, strong verbs, participles, gerunds. Clema had seen our need - our lack of understanding. She had grasped the solutions firmly in her little freckled hands and "hit it square in the eye." I never knew whether anyone else saw the light as I did in these classes. Maybe we were ashamed to admit our weaknesses. At last I could actually see some progress.

It was a long, long walk from the high school to Mrs. Sauders' home. All the way down School House Street, past Decker's, past Slinkman's, past Dr. Tellman's dental office to the bank corner, right turn past Uly Duncan's studio, past Charles Keeney's restaurant, Jess Birdsong's drugstore, across the Rock Island tracks, down another long row of vacant lots and few houses, up a street to the left where Chris Roehl lived and past Mrs. White Johnson's. Finally, when I thought I'd never make it, I arrived at Mrs. Sauders' for my lunch. We always had the breakfast biscuits sprinkled with water and warmed over. Fried potatoes were served often with a bite of bacon or chicken. Mrs. Sauders had a garden, so our vegetables were the well-known Missouri varieties - tomatoes, cabbage, carrots, onions, and all the common fruits. Nothing exotic or exciting. I always seemed possessed to swallow my noon meal whole. That walk back to school required all my time. I grabbed my books for my afternoon classes and ran. We had no lockers, no assigned desk or home room for books, notebooks or supplies. We carried them with us from class to class and home at night.

I practically ran back to school. Sometimes when I reached Jess Birdsong's drugstore, I would meet others who had rushed home to eat and were now rushing back. It made me feel good to know I wouldn't be the only one entering the building late. I had an absolute phobia about all eyes falling on me alone. This is where I often met Opal Smith who lived in Stringtown, a street leading off to the southeast of town. Opal had become my very best friend. She not only liked to read but she had the best knowledge of math and English of anybody in our whole class. From there we "ran" together up the street to school.

I missed my friend Orpha. She and I had grown to be very special friends in spite of the age difference and the senior-freshman status. Orpha always treated me as an equal. We had favorite little teasing phrases such as - I had dated a library due card January 32nd and she had seen a "bunch of smoke" rising in the distance - such easy teasing fun. Soon after we moved to the Travis home, Orpha invited me to spend a weekend at her parents' home in Summerfield. She planned for her father Emil Picker to come for us one warm sun-shiny Friday in April. Emil was driving a brand new Chevrolet Landau sedan - dark green. I was in seventh heaven. I had tried hard all year to imagine what being an only child would be like. Orpha had everything: beautiful clothes, new cars, cosmetics. The latter had fascinated me all school year. She applied Armand's cold cream generously before going to bed. She cleaned the powder and rouge she had applied in the morning and repaired at noon. She had clean white cloths to use for this purpose. Her father Emil operated the Summerfield Bank while her mother ran a general store.

It was only a drive of six miles through the countryside to the west until we arrived at the Picker home. Emil was a very quiet man. He said almost nothing except to ask Orpha how she was and if school had gone all right. If those things were in order then what else was there? Nothing worth talking about. He deposited Orpha and me at the front door and walked down the street to the store. Mrs. Picker was busy waiting on a customer - Mrs. Krenning. Orpha knew who it was by the team of mares and the flat-topped surrey. The mares were wearing fly nets as they stood quietly hitched to the posts outside the store.

The Picker store was very interesting. There was something of everything: groceries, dry goods, shoes, some china, (mostly plain white - the kind country people used), hardware, nails, bolts, harness, enamelware, pots and pans. Orpha put an apron on over her school dress and started dusting the shelves. She and her mother exchanged bits of news - what had gone on in Summerfield or in Belle that was exciting enough to retell. They spent a good deal of time examining some samples of dress material Mrs. Picker was considering ordering. And there was a large heavy sample book lying on the counter. In it were pictures of men's suits and large swatches of woolen materials to select from. This was a common practice in all rural communities. We had been given an "outdated catalog" by Lydia Drewel. We used it for a scrapbook. (It's still upstairs in the storeroom.)

Just at dark, Mrs. Picker closed the store, locked the doors and we walked back up the street to the house. The house was so clean and so neat. Everything was in place. We had a good supper: well cooked country ham, fried potatoes, pickles and canned corn, fruit salad and cookies for dessert. After the dishes were done, Orpha and I played a game of dominoes. Emil read his daily paper and Mrs. Picker busied herself with mending. It was still rather early when Orpha looked out and announced that Burna had arrived. His parents, Mr. and Mrs. Lee Keeney, lived almost directly across the street in a large house designated as the hotel. A few minutes later Burna was knocking on the front door. He suggested a walk down the street. It was about time for the evening Rock Island pssenger train. There just might be someone getting off. Summerfield had a station and a station master - Dee Henley. So we tripped merrily down to the station, sat a few minutes on the long bench outside, visited with Dee and his wife. Soon the train whistled as it crossed the river at Gascondy. The long Who-oo-oo-oo-oo-oo came puffing into town. It did stop. A few people got off and into buggies and cars and were whisked away. Burna, Orpha and I hiked back up the incline. We left Burna at the hotel and trotted across the street and to bed. Mrs. Picker was still in the kitchen but she had our bed cover turned down and a bright fire burning in the heater. "Just to take off the evening chill," she said, "and if you girls need any laundry done just lay it out. It will be done when you get up in the morning." My, my, what a work-free life Orpha lived. No big tubs of laundry to do. No floors to scrub. Such were my thoughts as I drifted off to sleep.

It was not yet daylight when Orpha's mother came in with dry kindling to build a "fire to dress by." She had a quick deft hand with her work and a quick intriguing speech pattern. "You kids can sleep awhile if you'd like. I'm going to the store early. There's breakfast on the stove." We did rest a little while. We ate our oatmeal and biscuits, washed the dishes, and went out to spend the day on the town. First to the store to see Orpha's Mom and help her carry in wood for the day. We had been invited to eat lunch with Mr. and Mrs. Lee Keeney at the hotel. About the middle of the morning Mrs. Picker sent us to the bank with the receipts of the week and we were to help Grace (Mrs. Keeney) with the lunch. Mrs. Keeney had also washed. She had Burna's shirts and other freshly laundered clothing hanging neatly on the clothes line. Burna and his father were sawing and splitting wood. Orpha and I helped prepare the vegetables. Mrs. Keeney was making rhubarb pie because there was a "traveling man" or "drummer" awaiting dinner in the parlor. Just before we set the table, Mrs. Keeney advised us to put down four plates for Faye's family too. Faye was married to Phillip Wiegers. They had two little boys - Edward and Weldon.

After dinner the "drummer" went on his way. Mrs. Keeney, Faye, Orpha and I sat on the wide front porch. The little boys played and tumbled. They were handsome, healthy-looking children. We walked about the yard inspecting trees and flowering bushes. People were always doing this to see if anything had been "winter killed."

Sunday morning I attended church at Pilot Knob with Orpha and Burna. This was a great pleasure. Everybody there knew Mom and Dad. My beloved Grandmother and Grandfather LeFevre were buried there. Uncle Ed and Aunt Lou were there. So was Uncle Tom and Aunt Kate. They hugged and kissed me. I had a lovely feeling - such a wonderful weekend. The afternoon passed quickly. We both had some studying to do. Orpha was always a diligent student. Any assignment was something to do right now. I always had to do my studying in between other chores. So it was a treat to sit at Mrs. Picker's big clean kitchen table and try to get that awful geometry straightened out.

Late in the evening we walked to the railroad station, boarded the Rock Island train and rode all the way to Belle! I felt as if I had spent a weekend in heaven!

Chapter 24

Sparkie vs the Model T

My clothes were so few. My broadcloth dress and my peach-checked tissue gingham held up well. At this time there was a great fad for "Bertha collars" - wide pieces of voile or lace cut in a circular fashion. We sent our collar material to Miss Minnie Gove at Linn because she had a machine with which to stitch (hem stitch really). She stitched and returned the collar. Every girl in high school had a "picoted collar." As I remember, mine was put on backwards but at the time I don't remember it bothered me. I laundered it and loved it! The broadcloth dress material was a piece from a remnant. You had no choice. You sent your money to Sears & Roebuck and they sent you a piece of material. We looked forward to arrival of the package. "I just wonder what the material will be like. Mae also had a tissue gingham, blue checked but very soft and thin. Mine wasn't - it was a heavy coarse version of tissue!

This second year of high school I was again serving as librarian. I had progressed to the sophomore required reading. *Lorna Doone* had come alive for me as we dashed madly over the Moors "in the dark of night." I thought Moby Dick and Old Ahab were hard to characterize. I was a child of the Ozarks. Seagoing people and vessels though were fascinating. *Tess of the Storm Country* and *Selections From Thoreau* were just required reading. Later I learned to love Thoreau. My evenings at Mrs. Sauders were spent well. We had so few social activities I could read and read and read.

Sometime that fall, I again decided to renew my music education. It was probably an excuse to see Opal Jester. I missed Mary Sweeney and Miss Castle so I made arrangements to take lessons from Opal. She was again living at the Mannike apartment on Main Street. And since Mrs. Sauders had no piano I went across the street from the high school to the home of Weldon and Queen Tynes to practice my lessons. Queen was Dad's first cousin (Uncle Jim and Aunt Betty Bacon's oldest daughter) and Weldon was Mrs. Slinkman's brother - old friends. So it happened twice a week I went to Queen's to practice. One evening, I went for my lesson - I didn't improve my music knowledge very much, but how I did love going to Queen's. She seemed to "dote" on my visits. She was always anxious to hear from Grandpa and Dad and all our family and in exchange she told me about her family: Earl and Rex (James Jr.), her brothers, and Peg and Cricket (Mary Overton and Sarah Jane, her sisters) who lived in Cherry Valley, Arkansas. Queen and Weldon had one son, Ralph, who was one year ahead of me in high school. This wonderful cousin had such a wide range of knowledge. She had an eternal variety of subjects for discussions and one of her finest qualities was a rare one - the ability to make a shy, homesick child feel right at home. I spent several nights in her home eating fried chicken and mashed potatoes, slaw, sliced tomatoes and flaky crusted apple or peach pie - sleeping in her high-posted spare bed - on top of monstrous feather beds. In that spare room she had the most beautiful "Gone With the Wind" lamp on a small stand by my bed.

Queen's speech pattern was smooth. It ran together but it contained numerous Ozarkian "colloquialisms." One which I've never heard anyone else use was when she wanted to tell you a certain female was pregnant she would say something like this in great surprise: "Oh - do you know something? Mrs. S_ is on her way to Boston!" Queen could also play the piano by "shape notes." So when I had trouble with a note, Queen would take her hymnal and say, "Show me where it is on the line." She could then pick it out on the keyboard for me.

Dad and Doc had been discussing the Smith - Hoover possibilities. Hoover both of them knew. He had been around in the *Globe Democrat* news since World War I, so it really was no big surprise to see the huge black headline - "Hoover Defeats Smith, Good Times Ahead." I felt I hadn't worn my Hoover pin in vain all that fall.

Now that the days were cooler in November, I was wearing my "Astrakhan" trimmed winter coat and walking the long distance to Mrs. Sauders' house twice a day was giving me a bad time. I almost had to run at noon to make it. I began to wonder if I could find a place nearer school. I asked Mama about it and explained how fast I had to travel. She said she would study about it. I'm sure she knew it really was too far from school. So when I came home the next weekend I announced I had found room and board with Mrs. Sam Travis for the same amount of money. Mama didn't scold so I felt I had made a "brilliant move." Now this was much, much better. I didn't have to spend my noon hour running a collision course since the Travis home was on School House Street directly across the street south from Slinkman's. Mrs. Travis was more talkative than Mrs. Sauders. We became firm friends. There were also some other major changes in the wind. I went home, of course, for the Thanksgiving weekend. Irvin was a brand new graduate of Warrensburg. He had accepted a teaching position at Cameron, Missouri, and would leave Sunday by train to be there Monday morning. Mae's teaching seemed to be coming along nicely. She was riding Spark Plug to and from home and school each day. (Spark Plug was Old Peg's last colt) We were going to Church and Sunday School regularly at Cooper Hill.

When I returned to Belle after Thanksgiving I found major changes. Alfred Dreysee was no longer our geometry professor. He had been replaced with Miss Hazel Castle and my beloved Clema had been replaced by Professor A. R. Diltz, a new graduate of Kirksville State Teachers College. At the Travis', Harry, their son, had come home from Springfield to be an employee in the Belle bank. Last of all these unbelievable changes, Hazel was to board at the Travis home and be my roommate. So things were working out. I was sure I would do much better in math now. I did somewhat, but in English I reverted to my former status. We started studying *Macbeth* and *Othello*. Both of these marvelous artistic works were published in tiny, blue-back paper editions. We learned a great deal about "The Moor of Venice" and "Desdemona" and "Lady Macbeth" and "Duncan" and dear old England. I was surprised years later to recall facts learned much earlier when I studied Shakespeare in more depth. Sorry to say we did not delve deeply into grammar but Clema Branson had "done her duty." She had shown us the light.

Since I was the only one in my family in high school, Dad gave me a dollar occasionally for my music lesson and school supplies. I had an idea. If I could save some of that, I'd have enough to buy each member of the family a Christmas present. That idea came about and resulted in saving about $10. I remember getting Dad a badly needed pair of suspenders, Bud and Pete a knitted tie and muffler set and Mama a crinkled crepe bedspread. I remember the price distinctly - 98 cents in Montgomery Ward special sale catalog. I even got a big package of wrapping paper and a roll of red ribbon. I was so proud. Mama kept asking where I got all that stuff. I told her I saved it out of what she and Dad had allowed me. She acted as if she didn't believe me. "Better take all of it back and get the money. Pete hasn't got a 'dud' to his name. What are we going to do. He has to go to that program tonight and he has to say that speech.

We'll have to go to Belle and get him a suit." And on and on. The blue bird of happiness had gone out of my sails. Mom fussed all morning. I wrapped my precious gifts. These were all we had. (We never had numerous gifts at Christmas time. It was always tax time.) I remember how the leaky buckets spat and sputtered on the cookstove. Mama always warmed a big bucket of wheat or oats together with the potato peelings, turnip peelings and whatever else chickens would eat. We always had a bucket of this on the "Old Bridge Beach." Sometimes it smelled good enough to eat ourselves. Mama stewed along with the bucket of wheat. "Pete has nothing to wear. We'll just have to catch some old 'good-for-nothings' and go to Belle." I was dispatched to the mailbox. We needed to know the price of fat hens. When I came to the gate at the top of the hill my heart gave a leap. There was a large brown cardboard box from Aunt May. Now this was truly a big surprise. I grabbed the *Globe Democrat* out of the box and even though the box weighed a ton, it felt light. A box always contained hand-me-down clothing, magazines and numerous treats. I ran down the hill. I really should have stopped to rest but I couldn't. I arrived at the kitchen door. Breathlessly, I almost shouted. "Look. Mama. Look. A box from Aunt May." She turned as if struck by lightning from stirring the contents of the bucket. "Oh my. Oh my. Do you suppose there might be a suit Pete could wear?" Together we cut the cord (Mom always used the butcher knife.), pulled up the flaps, first some magazines, some dresses and dress shirts. There of all things, was a boy's dress suit, brown and beige tweed, long pants, two pair of them and an almost new jacket. Mama grabbed Pete, stripped his overalls off in one fell swoop, pulled the suit pants on, threw the jacket on and pronounced it a perfect fit. Oh how wonderful. You would have thought Santa had just dropped a bag of jewels down our chimney. Such were our joys and our worries in 1928.

As we ate our fresh sausage, fried potatoes and Mom's flaky buttermilk biscuits, Mama's face wore an expression I saw few times - a relieved thankfulness. It gave her beauty, a serenity I seldom witnessed. She kept saying, "Well I never. I just never. Will wonders never cease? I must write May." In the same box was another pure treasure for me. A wool flannel coat dress, a beautiful garment, green and gold check wrap-around, thus called a coat dress. Jennie Hancks had worn it quite a lot because it had a hole in one elbow. But Aunt May had remembered to include a large piece of new material to mend the elbow. I was so pleased. I couldn't wait to cut a patch from the material, match the checks carefully and fold down the rough edges. That dress was a life saver. I lived in it when the wind blew cold. I knew it would keep me warm in snow and ice storms. I wore it for years. So Pete and I each got the very thing we needed. We felt as if we had ermine robes when we spoke our pieces and sang our carols at the program that night!

During the Christmas holidays we made popcorn balls, chocolate fudge, and molasses taffy with black walnut meats. These Mae and I could manage. If we wanted divinity or penuche we had to inveigle Mama into helping. She always countered the favor. "Yes, I'll make the candy if you work good all afternoon." Irvin came every evening. Sometimes some of the Homfelds or Kraenows came. We had a new game called Hearts and we had a new town, Cameron, and Irvin was boarding with the superintendent of schools whose name was Crosswhite. Almost every morning Mama and I made several pies. Mama's mincemeat was the epitome of perfection. After we butchered, there would be scraps of lean meat. These she boiled slowly on the back of Old Bridge Beach being careful to add water if needed. When the scrappy meat was "beyond tender" we picked off the meat and chopped it in a big bowl. We chopped fresh apple, grated some fresh lemon zest or orange zest (if we had it) threw in lots of raisins, a pinch of nutmeg, clove, etc., and sugar to make the pie real sweet. When we ladled this dark rich mixture into the shell Mama placed big lumps of butter here and there before the top crust was put into place. We never had any pie left over. Sometimes we made as many as six at a time. Some mornings we made pumpkin pies. I despised peeling the strips of pumpkin. It was always so cold and slick. But when the pies were cut and given a big dollop of sweet whipped cream, I forgot all about cold, slick pumpkin strips.

For a special treat, if the "old hens were laying good," Mama would write, "raisins 25 cents worth" on the grocery list. We always kept a list on the reverse side of a used envelope or some other bit of scrap paper such as reverse sides of calendar pages. When Mama sent for raisins, our mouths watered all the way home. Raisins meant raisin pie. Again the raisins were simmered slowly on the back of the stove, sweetened, thickened with a flour mixture, a slosh of vinegar to take away the bland taste, big blobs of butter and a cup of sweet cream. These were double crust pies. Raisins also meant "rice and raisins," a very plain dish but such a treat to us. Mama just cooked the rice and raisins separately. When we were ready to eat, she stirred the raisins into the rice, large, dark, plump and juicy. We had a large bowl of this with real cream and sugar. Brown sugar is a special treat on rice with a drop of vanilla. If anybody ever reads this, I'm sure you'll picture all of us eating biscuits every meal. It is true we ate them often but we always had what we called light bread and our fair share of cornbread. Mama had a master hand with biscuits. She could take any kind of ingredients, bacon fryings, chicken fryings, lard, butter, sweet milk, sour milk, baking powder or soda, and a pinch of salt. She judged the leavening by the degree of sweetness or sourness of the milk and the biscuits were always perfection. The so called "light bread" wasn't always so light. Our flour was made from our own wheat hauled to the mill and ground into what we called "mill flour" or "soft wheat flour."

This bread was wonderful the minute it came out of the oven but it dried out quickly. It was hard to get it to rise. Sometimes it fell flat when you set it in the oven or if you closed the oven door roughly. Everybody compared recipes that worked best for them. Some people kept the sponge in a warm place overnight. Back then everyone set the sponge late in the evening. This was made by stirring a quart of warm milk, salt, sugar, yeast and flour into a medium but not thick spongy mixture. This was covered and left in a warm place overnight. The next morning this mixture was thickened with flour, kneaded, let rise three times and baked. People of today have no idea what blessings are theirs - good white bleached flour, premeasured yeast, regulated heat for their ovens. Sometimes Mom would forget to "set the sponge" until we would all be in bed. Suddenly she would remember. She would groan and say "Oh, my - oh my, I plumb forgot that bread sponge." Up she would jump - down stairs she would thump - set the sponge - perhaps sing a verse or two of "When the Role is Called Up Yonder." That was to insure none of us would "drop off to sleep" while she was downstairs stirring up the sponge. She usually sang another stanza of something like "My Country 'Tis of Thee" as she climbed the stairs again and fell into bed. Then she would remark in a self-pitying voice, "Anybody else got anything I need to do. It's not midnight yet. There's lots of time. Well, speak up. I'll run your errands." If she sounded a bit frivolous, Bud would drawl, "Well, Mom, you forgot to bring me a drink of water."

"The bucket's empty" she would shoot back. "Roll over and go to sleep. It's almost ready for the dawn's early light." Bud would sing, "Oh, say can you see." In a minute Mom would come back sharply, "Have you boys said your prayers? Now let me hear you say 'Now I lay me down to sleep'. Come on now let me hear it. Nice and loud. You should get down on your knees."

Christmas was over. Irvin was back in Cameron. I went back to Belle, me and my coat dress. Mae saddled up Spark Plug and rode off into the sunrise. Sometimes she and Sparkie didn't always gee-haw. She wound up walking and leading him. He just didn't like the saddle. Mama never could see why Mae and I weren't expert horsewomen. She had been the greatest. But in Mama's youth every young woman rode a horse - side saddle. Mama lectured me at regular intervals on why Mae couldn't ride a horse! Why, she had ridden "Old Nig" every day to Buck Elk and every day to Indian Creek and everywhere else she went. Grandma and Aunt May rode him too. "You have to understand your horse," she said. Mae's misunderstandings with Sparkie continued to worsen until Dad made a deal with Dick Baker. Dick had a mare named "Pearl," gentle and a good riding animal. We would let him use Spark Plug in exchange for Pearl. So Sparkie went to live with the Bakers and "Old Pearl" came to live with us.

Mrs. Travis and I were the best of friends. In the evening we often tripped across the street to visit with Mr. and Mrs. Ed Biles. Mrs. Biles was one of those meticulous housekeepers. Her kitchen was a lovely big room at the back of the house. One end was a kitchen with wood cookstove, kitchen table and chairs as well as storage cabinets. The other end had a large heavy iron heating stove, some comfortable chairs, mostly rockers, and a glass-doored safe showing dainty pieces of china along with pretty painted plates! I loved looking at that room. Just as soon as Mrs. Travis and I came in, Mrs. Biles would get the ash shovel and carry the red hot embers from the cookstove to the heater. She always had a wicker basket full of kindling sitting by the side. In a few minutes the cheerful flames were warming us. Both women always had a big mug of coffee or tea. I always had tea. They sipped it slowly with great relish. Both of these women were so full of good. They never gossiped or told ugly things. I enjoyed these short visits a great deal. One evening I noticed Mrs. Biles didn't move about easily. Her conversation wasn't fun-loving and free-flowing as before. She didn't keep the fire glowing brightly either. Clearly she wasn't feeling well. As we tripped back across the street Mrs. Travis said, "Grace, we won't be visiting Ann many more times. She's dying of cancer." Well I was just shocked into silence. "Oh, not Mrs. Biles! No, dear God please." But in a very short time Mrs. Biles was gone. All of us felt badly for Mr. Biles and Louie his teenage son. Louie had returned to high school and was in my geometry class. He gave Miss Castle rather a bad time. He was not really a discipline problem. He loved fun and was good at seeing that some happened. His mother (bless her heart) had looked after Louie's clothes well. In order to make the blue serge trousers wear longer she had inserted a sub-seat so to speak. Then with the sewing machine she had sewn around and around in circles until the seat of Louie's pants appeared to be quilted. All of us thought that was pretty amusing.

Now that the Travis home had more occupants, Mrs. Travis had to cook more. One of Harry's favorite food combinations was mashed potatoes with stewed prunes. As I remember all of us liked mashed potatoes. A huge bowl of them appeared on our noonday table. Mr. Travis, Sam, was very fond of stewed fruit so we had every kind of fruit available - apples, applesauce, peaches, plums, cherries, pears, blackberries and, of course, prunes. Mr. Travis was always busy. He didn't have a place of business of his own but he helped Warren Wallace at the poultry house. Sam whistled all the time. As he walked up or down the street he whistled. Mostly just old familiar melodies such as those we sang from The *Golden Book of Favorite Songs* or church hymns.

All of us used the "outhouse." We had to go out the back door, through the back yard, open a gate and walk up a path through the chicken yard to arrive at this destination. If Sam happened to be in the "refuge" when Miss Castle or I approached he would start whistling a fast paced melody. One he did real often was "Listen to the Mocking Bird." The Lindner privy was just across the fence. I lived in agony thinking Weldon or Bill might be occupying the little house at the same time.

One evening while I was helping Mrs. Travis with the dinner dishes, her wide gold wedding band slipped off her finger. She fished it out, laid it on the window sill and said in her calm matter-of-fact-voice. "Well, I just may have to put that ring away. I've almost lost it several times lately." After a moment of thoughtfulness she giggled and said. "I'll have to tell you about the first time I lost it. It was the day before my wedding. (In those days the gold band was the engagement symbol.) I was putting wood in the stove when I lost it. I didn't miss it until much later in the day. We searched everywhere. Finally in desperation my mother said it must be in the ashes. So the wood, coals and ashes were carefully removed and sifted through. There in the very bottom of the ash bucket was the ring - burned very black." I was fascinated with the story. "How in the world did you remove the burnt soot from it!" Mrs. Travis replied. "Oh, I thought it was ruined and I'd have to tell Sam I had ruined the ring but my mother didn't get one bit excited. She said, 'No, dearie, don't fret. It isn't hurt one bit. I'll just take a piece of leather and polish it.' So after a time the ring was restored to its golden state." She laughed again softly as she recalled the wedding day.

There was another evening after school when I drove out to the Travis farm with Sam and Mrs. Travis. Sam's father was very ill. He was old. His two unmarried daughters, Eva and Nora, were giving him every attention. They were raising chickens, so on this particular day Nora was cleaning the chickenhouse and Eva was basting a new dress for Nora. We stayed quite a little while. Not much was said on the way home. I went home for the weekend. When I returned to Belle on Sunday evening Mr. Travis, Sr. had died. Miss Castle and I had to manage our own meals for a couple of days. It wasn't hard. Mrs. Travis had main dishes prepared ahead. All we had to do was "heat up" and "eat up." Every morning Mrs. Biles brought a beautiful pan of biscuits for our breakfast. There was a new brand of flour called "Aristos." It was highly recommended for hot quick breads. The biscuits were the melt-in-the-mouth kind. Mrs. Travis' cooking was always so tempting. Not quite the gourmet as Mrs. Slinkman, but just plain and good. (I had decided this a long time ago when I spent a week visiting Mae when she was a sophomore.)

And there was another sad funeral in Belle that same spring. Fred Underwood had married Fanny White and they had made a comfortable home for Fred's three motherless children. In a very short time, Fanny became ill. Her skin became a brownish color and in no time at all Fanny was gone and the Underwood children were back with their grandmother Lindner. The day of Fanny's funeral Mr. Biles watched the funeral cortege pass by and remarked to Mrs. Travis, "I'll be the next one." Those were sad times. Just when we thought Boyd, Billie and Zola Mae had a home and a mother the whole world fell apart again.

I wonder why all these things impressed me so much. Was it because I was so countrified? I found town life so fascinating. People to talk to. People to watch and to learn from. Mrs. Travis used a "darning egg" that was certainly different. She taught me how to use it, too. People always darned socks and cotton stockings. When she saw I liked the idea, she let me use the egg. I wasn't skillful and artful with it as was she, but I tried. One evening she saw me struggling with a hole in the heel of my stocking. She went to her sewing basket and fished out a beautiful sterling silver thimble. She told me to try it on. I did with great pleasure. She smiled when she saw how pleased I was and said, "Honey, you can just have that thimble. I don't know where it came from." Nothing I ever possessed has helped me through rough mending chores, or given me more pleasure when I was piecing quilt blocks as much as that thimble. The Travis family kept a cow in their chicken yard. Sam also whistled as he milked "Old Daisy." He always brought in a bucket of clean, foamy milk for Mrs. Travis to strain into crocks and set in the bottom of the safe. The strainer was a clean white cloth. This she laid in the dish pan and scalded thoroughly. Then she rinsed the strainer until the water showed no milk and took it to the clothes line in the back yard to dry. I always helped her with the dishes. This was something I set up for myself.

But this was the only year I had the Belle High School all to myself, without a sibling. The year previous I had Mae. The next two years I would have Bud, so I guess I was determined to make the most of it!

At school I continued to read every book furnished in the library. I was now ahead of the sophomore list and could sneak a volume off the junior or senior shelf. It was a pitifully small library. Not much had been added since Joe Curtis had rejuvenated it the year before. There was one book I was dying to read. The title was *The Green Hat.* I only caught a glimpse of it when Miss Castle and I were cataloging new books one evening after four o'clock. She quickly laid it aside with a remark. "I'll have to review this one." The cover was intriguing. It showed a high crowned ladies hat trimmed with flowers and ribbon with the title printed over it. Miss Castle carried it home with us wrapped in a sheet of newspaper. She immediately went upstairs and began her "review." She had read quite a lot of it by early evening when she announced there was a meeting she had to attend that evening. However, she had already decided it was "in no way fit for high school youngsters to read." Glory Hallelujah! As soon as she left for her meeting I grabbed that book and read as fast as I could. If there was something of great moment in it, I was too naive to find it and believe me I hunted. I read until I heard Miss Castle's key in the latch. I quickly closed the book and rolled over to pretend I was sound asleep. Miss Castle spent lots of time working on her scrapbooks. She saved newspaper clippings, pictures, school news, place cards and napkins from all banquets, parties and social events.

Also at school the big boys continued to tease Professor Diltz. Because he was rather small they nicknamed him "Percy." But as I remember "Percy" didn't pay much attention to them. He taught his beloved Shakespeare and history and ignored the razzing. Mr. Frank Branson was a quiet superintendent and he was also dealing with hometown friends and relatives. Logan Steen stayed in his home room at the head of the stairway and taught teacher training.

I wanted to go to visit Queen, but there was a change in the situation there. Queen's youngest brother Rex Bacon had been killed on his way to visit his wife and newborn son in a Denver hospital. He was killed instantly. His body was returned to Belle to Queen's house. Here, all of us gathered for the funeral on a warm sunny autumn day. It seemed so strange to me. I had been used to having Queen all to myself. Here was a house crowded with Bacons and Lusters (Mayme's family) and Tynes and Lindners and Slinkmans, Uncle John and Aunt Ida, Mom and Dad, Uncle Al and Aunt Vi, Grandpa, Uncle Jim (Rex's father) his brother and sister, Peg Pitts and Earl Bacon. They looked so sad. Queen cried and leaned on Weldon when they said good-bye to Rex. The minister had a very short eulogy. We went on to Liberty Cemetery for burial. There were numerous beautiful floral arrangements.

The family did not know that Rex and Mayme were expecting a child. They had been married so long they had regarded it a great secret to surprise the family when the baby arrived. It was several weeks before Mayme arrived in Belle with baby James. She divided her time between her parent's home and Queen's house. When I started visiting there again, Queen and Mayme were always busy with the baby. In spite of all the activity, Queen tried so hard to sit down and give me some special attention. I wanted so badly to have her help me with "shape notes" and tell me "who was on her way to Boston."

Every weekend at home, Dad would inquire if I had gone to see Queen last week? What had she heard from Mayme and the baby? And after Mayme and Jimmie arrived in Belle he would ask about all of them. When he came to get me on Friday he never failed to go visit with them.

As Jimmie grew from a tiny baby to infant size, I was asked to stay with him for an hour or two. This I liked a great deal. I loved to sit still and hold him in my arms. Not long afterwards, Eddie Luster, Mayme's brother was killed on his way to work. They lived next door to Queen and Weldon. Two more little girls were without a father.

That year came to an end. I loved the English and Shakespeare. I loved the one and only wiener roast we had at the Gasconade River Bridge. We called that event an outing! I did manage to memorize the Pythagorean theorem and get through geometry. I even got a few "E's" on tests by memorizing and Bud graduated from the 8th grade.

We had a good corn crop in the summer of 1929 and good hay but we hadn't been able to put in many acres. Hoover hadn't gone fishing for nothing. His "ice cream" hat and his round jolly face appeared in the *Globe Democrat* daily. We read about Coolidge in retirement as he wrote stories using a bread board on his lap. We read the *Pathfinder*, more news about "King Tut's Tomb" and the "Trunk Murders." Since Mae was teaching she subscribed to some good magazines: *The American - Woman's Home Companion - Cosmopolitan* and *Ladies Home Journal*. We tried to have some of our work done ahead so we could read when the new issue arrived. We burned the kerosene lamp late as we caught up on the serials and digested the short stories. We didn't stop until we had read every word: the recipes, descriptions of the latest patterns, home making pages, even the advertisements. Some of them were for Swans Down cake flour, Jell-O, Naptha bar soap and "Bon Ami - It hasn't scratched yet." Mama fussed because I read so much. "You come on now and get to work. You're going to put your eyes out. Do you want to go blind?" But just as soon as I could, I'd be back reading.

We were still raising chickens, but we weren't carrying them to the store in baskets and buckets. We were putting them in 30 dozen cases and hauling them to the Poultry House in Belle. We had cream cans for the cream and when we had extra butter we could always sell it at Tom Lloyd's store.

Our potatoes did well too. I spent a couple of days debugging and putting Paris Green on them. Charles Howard was big enough to help now. We worked together picking those fat striped beetles off and dropping them in a can of kerosene. And of course no farmer can forget his garden plot - hoeing, weeding, harvesting and canning - canning in tin cans sealed with smelly sealing wax.

All summer we thought and talked about a car. If Bud and I were to commute to Belle, we had to have a car. Everything we heard about cost too much. Summer was passing by quickly. We had to do something soon. Late in July, Dad wrote Mr. Fred Weissenborn in St. Louis asking him if his sons might know of a car we could afford and I'm sure Dad specified a sum of money not more than $75. We had known the Weissenborns for a time. They came to Mrs. Elsner's as summer boarders.

So it was no big surprise when we looked out and saw two cars rounding the turn at the foot of the hill. One was a long, low, Buick sedan. We recognized this as Fred's car. The one following was a Model T Ford Sedan, two door, square top. Such joy it brought to us! We had a car. Now Mama could go places again. She had been refusing to go anyplace if we had to drive Jim and Odie. Luckily there wasn't much to master about driving. Bud got in, started the motor, stopped the motor, drove to the cow barn, turned around and came to a stop in front of the granary and his driving lesson was finished. We were thrilled with our purchase. We couldn't wait to go - anyplace. We piled in, Bud in the driver's seat sitting over the gas tank. Mom, Mae, Pete, Charles and I arranged ourselves somehow in the back. Dad had the jump seat up front. It had to be folded up and turned over so we could get out of the back. We didn't bother that the car was already old and outdated (it was a 1924). The thing we wanted it to do was travel, and it did! And we did, whenever the hens laid enough eggs so we could afford a few gallons of gas (the tank only held five gallons). Having a car put new "pep in our step." We worked harder than ever. Mama's favorite slogan was used often. "Now, you'd better hunt those old hens and feed those little chickens. I guess you know what buys the gas." We ran our legs off looking after chickens, geese, ducks and turkeys. But the prices we were paid for our produce was ridiculous. Our farm crops couldn't possibly pay the interest and taxes. There would be nothing to pay on the principal. Bud and I were getting geared up for our drive to Belle High School every day. We had to have tuition money besides gas, oil and tires.

At breakfast Mama and Dad would discuss the possibility of weaning the big calves. There would be more cream to sell. Nothing anybody did brought in more money - always less and less. We read and heard about enormous corn crops in Iowa and Nebraska, but no market. That was so puzzling to me. It seemed to me somebody would want it. We read also about those poor starving people in China and India.

At the last possible moment we ordered two pairs of blue denim pants and two blue chambray shirts for Bud. Another one of Aunt May's boxes had furnished me with school clothes. On the first Monday morning we were up scurrying before daylight, milking, feeding pigs, mules and horses, straining milk, bringing milk, butter, cream and buttermilk from the spring for breakfast. Mama was frying chicken and slicing home-baked bread for our school lunches. All of us were in school now. We saved wax paper from the corn flake boxes to wrap our sandwiches. We had small glass jars for cool milk and on Monday we usually had a piece of cake or pie left from Sunday. Mae's lunch had to be ready first so she could be on her way first. Dad or Bud saddled "Pearl" and hitched her to the ring in front of the granary.

It was still very early when Bud and I picked up our lunches wrapped in newspaper and hurried out to the Model T. The morning was cool, just a bit of dew, but we knew the day would be warm and long. We drove into Belle, not at a very fast pace, there were creeks and branches to be crossed, no bridges over them. There was one concrete slab at the Boyce place. There were short steep hills and one long, long steep hill (Bumpass) both of us soon learned to know well and fear much! When we got up on the prairie we sailed into town, down main street to Schoolhouse Street, made a right past Slinkman's, Travis', Biles', Tellman's and Decker's to the school. There were no students yet - no signs of life. We wondered why. We parked our car in the tiny lot to the south of the study hall and waited. After an hour or more Mr. Frank Branson walked down the street from his home and up the broad front walk. He was soon followed by Logan Steen wearing his usual blue serge suit. Now we were sure there would be school and we realized, too, it was only 7:30 AM. Vocational agriculture classes for Bud were held at the old building across town so he went to classes there. I was certainly early once!

I loved my classes that year. I began to feel grown up. At long last I was taking teacher training. We spent two hours per day with Mr. Steen studying "Rural School Management" and "Teaching in the Public School." We also had American history and American literature. I studied every available minute because I knew how it would be at home. We would go back to the original plan in the evening - all the usual chores, peel potatoes, gather eggs, sweep the floors, make the beds, wash the kerosene lamp globes, fill them with kerosene, carry in wood, build a fire in the cookstove, help Mama with supper, wash the dishes and then we could study. So long as the weather was warm, I could carry my books upstairs and work where it was somewhat more quiet. Mornings were hectic and hurried. Sometimes we took Mae to Cooper Hill first and then on to Belle. We picked up Sophia Lehnoff along the creek road and a little first grader Dorthalene Jackson who lived with her grandmother, Mrs. Frank Bumpass, on the east side of the Bumpass Hill. This was a windfall. Each passenger paid us 50 cents per day. That would just about buy the gas.

Every weekend we did the laundry. On Saturday the big boiler was filled with buckets and buckets of soft water pumped by hand out of the cistern. Most of the day was spent bending over a wash board, rinsing, wringing each garment by hand, hanging it on the line. After they dried we gathered them in, sprinkled them down in a big peach basket ready to be ironed on Sunday.

But on Sunday morning we had to go to church first and fix a good Sunday dinner - lots of times for company. Uncle John and Aunt Ida still came frequently. Sometimes they went to church at Cooper Hill and came home with us. Uncle Will and Aunt Stell and Grandpa came often and we went there. But no matter what Sunday brought, we managed to get enough ironing done to go to school on Monday. I was very particular with Bud's blue shirts. I wanted him to look as nice as the other boys. Sometimes the ironing had to be finished on Monday evening after school.

It soon became apparent our Model T wasn't going to pull the first long steep slope of our hill. So before cold weather, Dad and the boys built a garage on a flat area about half way up the hill. Now Bud and I had to walk and carry eggs, butter, cream and books, notebooks and lunches up to the garage. Bud often carried a 30-dozen case of eggs. I sometimes made two trips or Pete and Charles helped with the rest of the produce. The problem was when Mama sent "old good-for-nuthin's" - hens that weren't laying. I'd have to help her and Old Watch catch them. She would inspect each of them thoroughly. Look them in the eye. Talk to them. Ask questions. "Now, I wonder, are you laying down on the job. I'll just bet you never have laid an egg. I'll fix you. Put this old hussy in the coop." Then she'd nab another and talk to her. "I don't know about you. You may just be a good old setter. I think I remember you. You lay such uniform, well shaped eggs. Yes, yes, yes, that's what I want - uniform eggs. I'll just keep you awhile." And when we were finished she would have culled out six or eight old good-for-nuthin's and two or three beautiful brown leghorn roosters. In the mornings I had to help tie their legs and carry them up to the garage. It was real hard to smell good and look fresh when you had to handle chickens, eggs, butter and cream every morning. And be sure to take home an empty egg case to fill.

Chapter 25

One Calf for "Three and a Half"

More and more often, we left home earlier and earlier to take Mae to Cooper Hill. This was much simpler than saddling Old Pearl and opening gates and fording Third Creek! Mae's salary was considered very good - $80 or $85 per month. She was able to purchase a nice cloth winter coat, some fancy shoes, silk hose, and a few nice dresses. In addition she got Mom some very nice silver plated tablespoons and teaspoons. We used silver only on special occasions and our company teaspoons were so thin and delicate they showed signs of breaking. For every day we had a set of bone handled cutlery. The blades were steel but not stainless. Sometimes certain foods left dark blotches on the blade. It was then Mama would say, "Now, Thresia take the knives and forks outside the fence and clean them." That meant jabbing each piece up and down in the soil until the blade became bright and shiny. I rather enjoyed seeing them change in appearance. For a while our table took on a cleaner, shinier look. Mama liked tablecloths. This was one nicety she insisted upon having. We usually got two lengths of cotton damask in what was described as chrysanthemum pattern in buff from Sears & Roebuck.

Our kitchen table was a home-made piece of furniture. It was stout beyond description, made of boards one inch thick and planed down smooth. The legs were made of four 1 X 4 boards, nailed together to form a four sided box. We always kept it covered with an oil cloth and Mama's "buff damask" on top. One summer Mae bought blue and gray paint and redid the kitchen wall and ceiling. How pretty it looked. Our linoleum was a blue and cream patterned inlaid linoleum. We had a hutch type cabinet, Old Bridge Beach, and the big table with a broad bench next to the outside wall. This bench was quite versatile. All three boys and the hired hand always ate while seated on the big old bench. On wash day it was pulled down the llength of the table so that two, sometimes three big wash tubs could be set on it. But most generally I associate that big strong table with such things as our staple foods - Mom's delectable biscuits, fried bacon, potatoes, stewed tomatoes, cured ham, fried chicken and pies of every variety as well as freshly baked "light bread."

And so it was. That autumn we had a sense of false security. Even though Mae was teaching, prices were not dependable for our farm products. Dad shipped a fine, fat, steer to Long, Wooten Commission Company in East St. Louis. In a few days the return envelope containing the check arrived. We needed the money so badly! Now we could pay some long overdue bills. We hovered around. When Dad opened the envelope his eyes bugged. His tired face fell and tears came to his eyes. The check called for $3.50. Yes, three dollars and fifty cents! That was ten cents less than we got for a case of eggs! We couldn't believe it. Dad sat down and wrote a letter explaining how much work, feed and time went into a calf. We never received a reply to Dad's letter. A few days later he sent a second letter telling the Commission Company they could take their "Christmas present" from him once but he would not do business with them anymore! We soon found this was only the first of years and years of heartbreaking prices. We had so little to sell and every little chicken, every egg, every pig and calf was so precious. We began to plan our meals very carefully, just enough, or almost enough. We had to stretch and stretch some more. Then in October we began to hear about Wall Street and market prices slumping. As teenagers, Bud and I understood very little about what the *Globe Democrat* headline meant - "Stock Prices Slump, 14,000,000 in Nationwide Stampede to Unload - Bankers To Support Market Today." In smaller headlines relating to bankers we read - "Financiers at Meeting Agree Prices are Attractive and Money is Plentiful." Well, why in the world were we getting $3.50 for a calf if money was so plentiful? This didn't make sense to me! All we could really count on was the "egg money" and Mae's salary. That year Dad had to borrow our interest and tax money from Mae. That really did something to Dad's ego. Why should anybody work, slave and deprive himself of actual necessities if you received no profit from your labor? Dad's face reflected his disappointment. His sagging shoulders looked so hurt and tired when he came in to supper after a long day's work.

The next day at school in American history class, Logan Steen lectured on "Wall Street unloading. AT&T and steel among heaviest losers - investment trusts." Most of it was definitely above my head. I only understood that our farm produce was at an all time low. Even our precious eggs were not bringing in $3.50 per case now. Mama started skimming more cream off the big crocks and churning it into butter. We carried the finished products to Belle. Sometimes we had special orders to fill. Numerous "good cooks" in Belle wanted "Mrs. Bacon's good country butter." Mrs. Lenhoff also made good butter. Sophia would trot off down one street with her wicker basket full of Lenhoff butter. I'd take my basket of Bacon butter and trot off in another direction. Sometime later we would meet at Tom Lloyd's store, drop off our empty baskets, pick up our books and school paraphernalia. We usually had to hurry on these mornings, so we walked very fast up School House Street and climbed the squeaky wooded stairs to the teacher's training room. If we were even a minute late, L. L. Steen would glare at us. He wouldn't speak a word until everyone was seated and so quiet one could hear a pin drop. No one interrupted him or asked him a question or contradicted him. His word was law and gospel!

We listened, we took notes. We prepared our assignments carefully. Each of us was supposed to be able to give a resume of every topic assigned for that day's lesson. Most of us did our lessons the best we could. Again I lived in mortal fear that I would "go blank" in the middle of our assigned subject. So every chance I had I read, I studied, I wrote and rewrote such things as the "Bill of Rights" - "The Missouri Compromise." This same pattern was also true of American literature and teacher's training subjects. My powers of memorizing were being tested. It was hard work. It was the first time in my life I realized a true satisfaction from school book learning as a high school student! My best friend was Opal Smith. She was by far a better student than I. She was a little older and engaged to Roy Branson. She was my idol. When we sat together in study hall we always compared notes, pronounced spelling lists to each other because Mr. Steen was so adamant about correct spellings in our essay question answers. He started a spelling class. If we did not spell every word correctly on our written test we had to stay after four o'clock and redo our spelling. This meant Bud had to wait for me. And it meant getting home late. Mama didn't like that one bit. It meant late chores, late supper, late everything. Naturally she fussed. Bud threatened to leave Sophia and me, so I worked and studied and wrote the 100 demons - over and over. I also studied while Bud herded the Model T through the creeks and mud holes and ground the brake down the Bumpass Hill. I didn't have to stay many evenings. I soon mastered the demons so the pressure at home diminished!

In November of 1929, we did have a pleasant headline in our daily *Globe* - "Byrd Safely Flies to South Pole and Back - Looking Over Almost Limitless Plateau - Drops Food, Lightens Ship on Perilous Trip - Crosses Glacier Pass at 11,500 feet - Flying Time For the Whole Circuit About 18 Hours." We kept a geography book open on the dining room table and studied that flat dull area at the bottom of a world map. Such a small space on that map. How could it take 18 hours to fly over it? Our world was so small. Only Mom and Dad had been out of Osage County. (Well, that's not quite true, Belle is directly on Osage-Maries County line. Belle High School was and is located in Maries County). Our big problem was how to get a Model T to Belle and back home each day. We had already learned to do battle with flat tires and high water levels in creeks and branches. It was always a toss-up when the creeks were high. Shall we hit the water slow and risk stopping in midstream or hit the water hard and fast and risk drowning out the motor? Neither seemed to work very well. What we always referred to as the Charles Lange Branch was the worst to cross. It was at the foot of two hills. It was deep and swift. Bud and I were always filled with anxiety until we were safely across that branch. Numerous times we slipped off the rocks and into the gravel and deep water. That meant taking off our shoes and stockings and scooping the gravel away from the tires. Then Bud would get in bare-footed. I'd push with all my might and main. Usually we would get out under our own power, put on our shoes and hose, start up the slope when "bang" there would go one of our tires - such trials. We always carried a tin can of "Never-Fail Tire Patch." We had to work with a water soaked tire and wheel. Jack it up, remove the tire, remove the innertube, find the hole. Usually it was big enough to be seen easily. Scrape the wounded tube to rough it up, apply some cement, put on a patch, wait for it to dry, stuff it back in the tire, replace it on the wheel and finally, pump it up. Gingerly we let the jack down and prayed it would hold until we got to school. As I look back on these daily treks to town I wonder how we did anything in school. Sometimes we had more that one flat tire per day or more than one stuck-in-the-creek affair. Hurdling the obstacle course was a full time job!

When classes resumed in January 1930, we found ourselves enveloped in a long and cold snow storm. Now it wasn't the water and gravel in the Charles Lange Branch. It was fear the ice would break through and leave the car sitting down on the creek bottom with the two back wheels up on the ice, or perhaps vice versa. We carried an axe with us to chop our way out. Of course this meant Bud had to remove his shoes and socks and climb out barefooted into the icy water and chop the ice. These vintage Fords also had to have the radiators drained mornings when we got to school and evenings when we came home. Every morning we carried a teakettle of boiling water up the hill to pour in the radiator. But this winter the snow drifted on the Bumpass Hill. We had to concern ourselves with chains and pushing. We knew we couldn't get up the hill without chains, so at the foot of the hill we stopped, laid out our chains in the snowy track, drove up on them, hooked them in place, and inch by inch went up the Bumpass Hill. At the top we removed the chains and came puffing and steaming into town. After a few weeks of this Mama and Dad had a conference and decided there had to be a better way. Mrs. Merritt Decker (Iva's mother) had some rooms upstairs she wasn't using. She sent word to Mr. and Mrs. Tom Lloyd at the store that we could stay there if we liked. So we packed some food in a box: eggs, milk, cream, butter, meat and potatoes. Mama admonished me as to what few things I could buy at Tom Lloyd's store. You will have to buy a loaf of bread and perhaps a can of corn. Sophia was to stay there too. So when we slid to an icy stop at Lenhoff's mailbox, Sophia also had a well-filled box. We decided we could do better by combining our victuals. Sophia had a few jars of canned peaches in her box and a nice loaf of home baked bread as well as the usual staples. So we set up light housekeeping in three upstairs rooms - one large sleeping room, a smaller kitchen and a smaller bedroom.

Wade and Mildred Harris had been having the same trials with their Model T as Bud and I. They came from the Summerfield end of the road. Mildred, Sophia and I were very good friends so it was only natural for Wade and Mildred to join us in our apartment at Decker's. Bud and Wade shared the small bedroom. We pooled our food. Bud and Wade carried the wood and water upstairs. Dad had promised to bring Mrs. Decker "heating stove wood" and a "big load of alfalfa hay" to pay for our living quarters. But Mrs. Decker was an angel. She looked after us as if we were her own. She showed us how to manage the kerosene stove for cooking and she kept the heater in our big living-bedroom combination going so it would be warm at noon and in the evening. She nearly always had a warm nourishing dish for us: navy bean soup, potato soup, rice cooked with sugar, milk and cinnamon. I'm sure she recognized how lacking we were in cooking expertise. But as I remember we did pretty well. Granted we were not striving for gourmet perfection for our breakfast was cured bacon, bread and milk gravy, some toast with home made jelly or preserves. At noon we had whatever was left from breakfast or some of Mrs. Decker's soup. But in the evening we cooked potatoes, meat, vegetables, etc. So we always had something to fix quick at noon. We did this several weeks always going home on Friday evening to "clean ourselves up." It was the same routine. Do the laundry, do the cleaning, go to church, come home, iron, pack up the food, do our lessons, clean the kerosene lamps, study some more, get the eggs cased, get the butter packed in the egg basket, put some clean clothes in a box, have a teakettle full of boiling water to carry up the hill to pour in the "T" radiator. Sometimes the whole family had to help carry the items up the hill.

I think Mrs. Decker rather enjoyed our company. Mr. Decker was a grocery salesman so he was on the road all week This left Mrs. Decker and her son Bobby all alone. Since Iva's death she had buried herself in work, all kinds of work. She had one of the finest gardens in town. Her potatoes were large and smooth. Her corn and beans were the best. She had a cellar full of beautiful jars, corn, beans, tomatoes, pickles, even beef and sausage. She shared many a jar with us saying always. "I've got so much we'll never use it. You've got to help me use it." Well, we were glad to oblige. One day in February the sun came out, warmed up all the old dirty snow. It ran away down the hill behind the school in muddy rivers. All the icicles melted from under the eaves of the Decker house and fell crashing to the ground. As we walked back to school for afternoon classes, Bud announced matter of factly. "I'm going home tonight." I don't remember saying anything. I just thought it would be rather nice. So as soon as the four o'clock bell rang we dashed out and headed for home. (The bell was quite a loud one attached to a wire above the auditorium door. It was a battery affair to be activated by someone in the office pushing a button.)

Mama was considerably surprised to see us walking down the hill. But she always saw some advantage in a wrong turn. So she began cleaning and casing eggs. We would take them into town in the morning. I remember it was so extremely warm Bud and I hadn't bothered to bring our warm winter coats home with us. In the night the winds shifted. The snow came down in swirls. Very early Mama came to the dining room door and gave Bud and me orders to "get downstairs right this minute - fix yourselves a sandwich, grab those eggs and that teakettle and get started. I don't want to see you anymore until the ground thaws." That was one morning she didn't tell me "coffee drinking will make you black." That was a common almost every day admonishment. "If you drink coffee, you'll turn black." We usually had a big pot of hot chocolate. Only Mom and Dad drank coffee with lots of cream and sugar in it.

We thought we just about had a year behind us. The deep snows and the icy blasts had given way to bright sunshine and warm spring days. One Saturday morning Bud's first job was to split a big pile of wood for our Saturday cooking and baking. Mom and I were just getting the big wash tubs and boilers filled for our weekly bout with dirt and grime when Bud appeared at the kitchen door. He looked pale and scared. He sank down in a chair as he explained in a rather apologetic tone of voice. "Mom have you got a little clean rag? I've cut my foot." Well, it was plain to see he had. The blood was pouring out on the floor through a good sized gash in his boot. We got his boot off, saw a deep cut just about the length of the axe blade laid wide open and bleeding profusely. Mom began to give orders. "Grace find a bandage quick. Wrap it around the cut and hold it tight while I call Doc." In a few minutes Doc came huffing and puffing into the kitchen and then he began giving orders. "I'll have to put some stitches in it, that's for D__ sure. What in H__ were you doing to fix up your foot like that?" Huff - huff -puff - puff. "G__ D__. Such a morning. Such a morning."

Mom didn't want all this going on in the kitchen so she suggested we move Bud to the front bedroom. By this time Dad had been summoned. So Dad and Doc carried Bud to the bedroom while I held the bandages tightly around the foot. We got him in a position sitting in a rocker with his foot up on a chair. Doc's hands were far from steady as he opened his black bag and began to lay out his bandage and bottles. First came the brown bottle labeled "Chloroform." Then came the needles and strong "cat gut" for stitches. I looked at Bud's face. It was very solemn and getting whiter. Bud's skin was quite brown normally. Finally Doc was ready. He gave me orders to remove my bloody bandage and hold a pan under the foot to catch the chloroform. As I did so I began to feel a creepy feeling in my brain. Doc had already opened the brown bottle. Now he began dabbing the anesthetic around the wound. Then in a minute he began stitching. That and the chloroform was more than I could take. I was bending right over the wound so I got as much or more of the wicked stuff than Bud. I had to hold on. I couldn't let go. But I could feel myself slipping, slipping. Just as Doc fastened his stitches I made it to the door, stepped out on the front porch where the cool fresh air washed the poisonous fumes from my brain. In a minute I was OK. I came back and helped Doc bandage Bud's foot and put him to bed. The wound would require several days to heal. He wouldn't be able to drive the car. It was the right foot. So now I had a new dilemma. How was I going to get to school? And there was Sophia too. What would she do? On Sunday evening Mama and Dad decided to ask Eugene Kraenow to drive me into town. They felt sure Mrs. Decker would let me "sleep upstairs" for a week or perhaps longer. So I took my box of staples, a few clean clothes and met Eugene at the top of the hill. We picked up Sophia and made our way into Belle. Yes, we could sleep upstairs. She would be glad to have us. In a couple of weeks, Bud was able to return to school and, of course, he had to have a new pair of shoes. He still looked pale and tired, but we were back in our normal world of flat tires, egg cases, butter and books.

We continued to stay with Mrs. Decker until it was "safe to go home." We didn't risk any more "one night runs." But there were other reasons to stay in town overnight. We were obligated to present a play to the public. This would furnish funds for our junior/senior banquet at the end of school activities. We chose *The Eighteen Carat Boob* as the play. I was given a character to play. I thought it was the epitome of the high school social set to be offered a part in the play. We didn't practice every night but on the nights when we did I stayed with either Opal Smith or Fern Morelock. She was Opal's cousin. Both places were such fun to stay. Opal lived with her grandparents, Mr. and Mrs. Silas Birdsong. They were always so gracious and hospitable when I stayed there. Fern was the youngest one of four daughters of Mr. and Mrs. Harrison

Morelock. When I stayed there, there were four or five high school girls in one house. But practicing for the play was exciting. I had suddenly discovered the opposite sex. I found it surprising that a "boy" would want to walk home with me. Mama had told me if I didn't go out with boys while I was in high school she would give me a wrist watch for graduation. That was something I wanted more than anything in the world. So I was hard put to make a decision. "Boys" or a watch - I had to choose. There was really no big opportunity to date, since we lived nine miles from town and only one boy had access to a car. Raymond Garver and his mother owned a car. He drove it to school sometimes and once he took me home after a wiener roast. But while we were preparing this play, Andy Lindner (Weldon) was my heart throb. We played the leading parts. He was always fun to be with when we walked home. He was class president. I was secretary and treasurer so any business dealings had to be a joint decision. We found ourselves making purchases, paying bills and planning business for our senior year. After our play, the junior/senior banquet was next on our social calendar.

There was no place to serve a banquet except the gymnasium. No way to have food prepared but to cook it. Mr. E. D. Muhleman was our junior class sponsor so it fell to Mrs. Muhleman to manage the banquet. The menu was simple creamed chicken in a pastry cup, creamed peas and carrots in a mashed potato cup, pickles, mints and pie. We donated the chickens. So Bud and I hauled them to town. "Old good-for-nuthins" - cackling and squawking all the way. Mrs. Minnie Bledsoe dressed them for us. Mrs. Muhleman cooked and creamed them. We had an old kerosene stove in the custodial quarters where we reheated all this food. I was assigned "to stir the chicken." "Don't let it stick," Mrs. Muhleman said. So I stirred and stirred. It got thick. Then it got thicker. Then it started to roll into a ball. When Mrs. Muhleman saw it she was horrified. "What happened to the chicken?" she almost shouted. Well all I knew was that I had stirred and stirred. I'd never had any experience with creamed chicken! These events were so exciting in our lives. I needed something resembling a "dressy dress" for this banquet. I knew there was no possible chance of buying anything new, after the $3.50 calf and falling egg prices. Things on the farm were getting steadily worse! There was a thought in the back of my mind. Jennie Hancks had sent a black georgette, sleeveless, long evening gown some time before. Could we make something suitable out of it? It looked hopeless to me. I did get it out of the box and bring it downstairs. Mama knew I really needed a dress. Everything I owned had been worn to school. So Mama and Mae studied it over. If the long skirt could be ripped off the waist and cut into two equal lengths the cut length could be "picoted" as the hem edge was already. Then the skirt would be two full flounces, both stitched onto an underskirt. With a black satin jacket made from new material it was really quite presentable. The only thing I disliked about it was the color. None of the other girls wore black! My hair was dark and shiny with red lights in it. I wore it in long curls hanging over my neck. (I had let my hair grow again after the horrible experience my freshman year.)

School closed the first week in May. We had all taken our final exams. I felt really good with all my knowledge. I had thoroughly enjoyed American literature. We had studied Longfellow, Whittier, Hawthorne and Poe so much we had committed long passages to memory. We had studied American history and listened to lectures and taken notes. I could quote from the Declaration Of Independence and the Constitution to please Dad and Uncle John. My grades were far from perfect but pleasing to me. I had acquired a feeling of confidence. I found I could do anything I set my mind to do. I missed seeing my school friends because when school closed we only made trips to town to sell our cream, butter and eggs.

It was a little easier now to take care of our baby chickens. We had built a brooder house out by the hen house. We had a small wood heater in it to keep our chickens warm. Chickens were such a necessary part of our farm operation we were now getting 350 baby chickens from a hatchery. But keeping the chicks warm meant jumping out of bed several times at night and going out to the brooder house to put wood in the stove. I soon took my turn at this chore. Anyone who got up in the night knew better than to return to bed without "chunking up the fire" in the brooder house.

The chickens were the only bright spot in our life so far as a livelihood was concerned. Mae wasn't going to teach the next year. She was looking around for some money making projects. So was I. Money was a commodity we rarely saw. We had gotten through a year with the Model T. Tires, gas, and inner tubes were so terribly expensive. Bud and I were so careful with notebook paper, pencils, and ink. Yes, I had to carry a bottle of ink so I could fill my fountain pen. We had to draft our essays in pencil outline, then copy in ink on unlined linen paper. Mama thought we used an awful lot of supplies. "I never saw the like." But there were also Pete and Charlie Howard to buy tablets and pencils for. Sometimes we were forced to buy "penny pencils" which I despised. The lead was so soft it smudged and the tiny little eraser was soon "used up." Mama always told me to think before I wrote, then I wouldn't need the eraser. I could never do that.

The summer brought more disappointments. It was very hot and so dry it was near to being a drought. When our sows farrowed we had no good water in "Teenies' Holler" so we moved sows and pigs to a pen by the spring. We tried to keep them shaded. Some pigs were white, so they sunburned easily. One sow had so many piglets we had to try to feed some of them with a spoon, only a few drops at a time. Some we were successful with. Others we weren't. One of our successes developed a hernia. He was everybody's pet. We named him "Rup." He followed all of us like a dog. It was one of my jobs to give him an "oil treatment" at least twice a day. I'd take any scrap of grease I found in the kitchen, catch "Rup" asleep somewhere and try to quietly administer the oil. At first he didn't like it. He would run away squealing and grunting. After a few days he seemed to realize something was causing him to feel better. He learned to accept his "oil treatment" gracefully. It was a sad, sad day when "Rup" was sent off to market. But farm animals were grown only for food or for marketing.

"Old Flora" our brood mare had foaled in the spring. The summer sun blistered us as we hoed in the garden, Dad discovered a swelling in Flora's shoulder region. She stood in the shade of the trees. Her head drooped, her withers twitched, she looked sick, she ate sparingly. Dad feared fistula, but that's what it was. The swelling opened, the infectious drainage poured down her shoulder. Dad would talk to Dr. Leach about what medicines to use. Whatever Doc recommended as a remedy we tried to get. We washed the wound with clean warm water. We tried to keep it dry with Dr. LeGears Stock Powder. Sometimes Doc came down and he and Dad held a consultation. Then they would clean it, dry it, shake their heads and walk away. Roy Nixon kept telling Dad something about "throwing an axe over their shoulder in the light of the moon." It was a sure cure. Dad didn't think so. He and Doc continued to keep the infection draining by lancing the wound. After a long, long time Flora began to improve and slowly, slowly she recovered completely. During the years she had: Bill (a twin), Jude, Lucy, Lou and Lassie. All made fine, patient work animals. Flora just gave us a colt every other year but how we loved them. They were always so sturdy and gentle. We made great pets out of them. Something that set Mom's temper off like a firecracker was for the colt to get into her egg bucket when we were gathering eggs. The colt was always following us. We would have to climb to the loft in the horse barn so we would set our bucket in the manger downstairs for safety. While we were in the loft Bill would come along, find the egg bucket, put his nose in the eggs and break half a dozen or more. He considered this quite a prank. How he would run away nickering and kicking up his heels.

As the summer wore on and almost no rain fell we started carrying water to the garden. That was real hard work. We waited until dusk. Then armed with buckets, dippers and containers we dipped and carried water for our precious tomatoes. It didn't help. The sun was too hot. We ate potatoes and cabbage, carrots and onions. We canned very little. Mama kept saying, "I hear there's a good apple crop in Illinois. We'll make lots of apple butter, and can lots of apples." She would add wistfully, "Maybe we can find some peaches - cheap." All this was after we saw our tomato plants shriveled and died.

Uncle John and Aunt Ida visited quite a lot that summer and Mae and I often walked across the hill to spend the day helping Aunt Stell. Sometimes Mae sewed all day. I helped cook and sweep and wash dishes. In the evening when it was cooler we walked home. Mae and I took turns staying a week with Aunt Ida and Uncle John. I was going to stay several days and help clean house - and actually get paid! I didn't feel good. Had I been at home I would have stayed in bed. I had such a pain in my side all the time. But Aunt Ida's house had to be cleaned. So I rolled out of bed early, tried to work. Although Aunt Ida knew there was something wrong. She would ask if I felt bad. I'd deny that I did and try to go on. Finally she sent me in the big front bedroom and told me to stay there until supper was ready. How good that big bed felt, cool and smooth. I slept, my pain was relieved and things went better. When Aunt Ida paid me she couldn't resist mentioning "my time off for a spell of bellyache." And with a rather meaningful twinkle she remarked, "I should have docked your wages." She never failed to mention that every niece or nephew who graduated from high school would receive $10 from her and "Johnnie."

Before school began in the fall, Aunt May's box arrived. In it were several good dresses. Two of them were black satin. But they were youthful styles and I wore them until there was nothing left of them. But the true lifesaver for the year was a two-piece navy blue silk suit dress. The skirt and jacket trim were a beautiful small print. The skirt was tiny accordion pleats. That dress was like a uniform. I always felt comfortable in it.

In the early fall there was a tent show at Cooper Hill. I think tent shows are a forerunner of hard times. But anyhow, Dr. Stuart moved his family into our quiet little burg, set up his tent and spread the word. He would give his audience their full money's worth, cure their rheumatism, tell their fortune and lead them to prosperity. All for 10 cents each. We went several evenings. Dr. Stuart plucked his guitar and sang. His voice did have a pleasing quality. He could tell a story with great regional accents. Eliza Leach, Buckshot's wife, took over the Stuart family, especially the baby boy. The Stuarts hadn't been in Cooper Hill long when this child became very ill. Eliza called Doc Leach. Doc recommended only liquids and such things as cereals and custards. Eliza cooked and sterilized everything for the child but he almost refused such strange food. He would wrinkle up his little nose and with such pleading in his eyes say to Eliza. "Ask man if can't have tater." For a time Doc said "No, only liquids." Finally one day Eliza gave in and baked the baby a potato. He was a well boy in no time. Over and over he pleaded, "Ask man if can't have 'taters."

There was also the Sheeter Kell tent show in Owensville. That was different from Doc Stuart's tent show only in that it was a company of actors - most of them comics. They did such skits as fireman from "Podunk" who got to the farm "only in time to save the organ and the cistern." When Sheeter kissed a young woman she fell flat on the stage. Sheeter looking quite satisfied remarked, "When I kiss 'em they stay kissed." We worked so hard to get to go to these shows. The work was nothing because there was a delightful evening ahead. The comedy was "corny" but quite understandable by children and adults alike. We carried the stories home with us. We repeated them; we laughed about them. They gave us a staple subject for years. We quoted Sheeter Kell. This was another pleasure Mom's egg money furnished. There are few people who can continue day after day and week after week with no pleasant diversion. So the tent shows, church picnics, and visiting relatives had to serve as an inexpensive way of relieving stress. Uncle John and Aunt Ida had lost money in the bank failures. They wished they had assumed the mortgage on our farm. When the Bland Bank failed we were worried sick. We didn't know where the papers were concerning our loan on the farm. Mom and Dad went to see the August Frederick family. They had shown an interest in loaning us the necessary money. This seemed like a good deal. At least we would know who held the papers. After several months the mortgage was discovered at a bank in southeast Illinois. It was returned to the Fredericks. They in turn took over the loan on our farm. But while all this was transpiring the atmosphere around our house was right out of the North Pole. Mama was sure the papers would never be found. We had just as well get ready to move. We'll have to go to town, "Where some of us can work in the shoe factory." She always avoided saying just who was going to go to work in the shoe factory. This worrisome detail of the paper put the whole family in a state of stress. The subject was never laid to rest until the day we got a letter saying the thing we were looking for had been located. I can still see Mama's face and hear the long relieved sigh as Dad read the letter. They lost no time getting it all straightened out. It was such a small sum of money as compared to today's big money deals. But at the time of the Great Depression it was a life-and-death matter.

Chapter 26

Hard Times are a Comin'

As August approached our lives took on a more hurried appearance. School was right around the corner. When Mom and Dad went to Fredericks to pay interest they spied a large orchard, both apple and peach trees growing in it. Well Mama's earlier dream of "apples – cheap, and maybe a few peaches" was about to come true. The Fredericks had had these fruits for so many years they had so much already canned they weren't planning to use many. When Mom and Dad came home they had a wagon load. How Mom's face shone. "Now I guess we'll have something to eat this winter. Nothing better to eat than an apple. And nothing better for you!" Well we certainly did have apples. We fried them, stewed them, made pies, canned them and later on made apple butter in great quantities. We made jelly and apple preserves and we cut them into slices and dried them. There's nothing better than fried apples with fresh biscuits and a bite of cured bacon for supper. A glass of cold milk makes this a feast.

The peaches were a Godsend. Some were small, soft early peaches. A big bowl of these peeled, sliced and sugared became a frequent dessert - or baked into a pie. The big firm yellow peaches were cooked and canned. The damaged ones were cooked into peach butter and sealed in stone jars for winter use.

All the other things we usually did in August were accomplished. We entertained the Women's Guild on the first Wednesday. Lydia Shockley came early in the morning to put the quilt in the frame. Of course Ida Elsner came with her. Ida came mostly to visit and examine your house. Not in "a nosy way," but just to see how different all of us were in our housekeeping! This meant getting up extra early, fixing a company dinner, having everything ready for a lunch in the afternoon. It also meant cleaning the house. Perhaps papering one room, making everything neat around the yard and porches. There was no question as to the menu. We had fresh bread, butter, apple butter, peach preserves, apple pie and peach pie, and coffee.

The ladies quilted. Lydia delivered her usual program: missionary work, church programs, donations, explaining the map showing the Bible lands, and finally an agreement on the next meeting place. Then lunch was served. Afterwards no one quilted much. They wandered around the yard, talked chickens and eggs and garden. If we had a minister, he and his wife were always expected to attend. In 1930, that would have been Reverend and Mrs. Gehard Fritz.

Threshing was always exciting. From the time the huge metal wheels began to grind the gravel on the county road as it approached our gate at the top of the hill, it was rush, rush, peel potatoes, catch and dress roosters, slice cured ham, run to the garden, run to the springhouse, run to the hen house, run to the cellar, put all the leaves in the dining room table, bring the chairs from the kitchen, get out one of Mom's buff chrysanthemum damask tablecloths and lay it on the table, and fix beds for the members of the thresher crew who would stay overnight. All these things kept us busy far into the night. I was fascinated with the big steam engine. I liked to go out in the field and watch the bundles of wheat being tossed into the hopper of the separator. I loved to watch one of the big strong crewmen toss logs into the fire box of the engine. When the dampness of the evening fell, the threshing came to a stop. The neighbors rattled past the house with their wheat wagons. A few stayed for supper but most went home to do their own chores, eat supper with their families and fall into bed for a few hours of fitful sleep. Usually the nights were extremely warm and humid. Long before sunrise, a member of the crew arose and went out to "fire the engine." They always had to wait to see when the grain bundles were dry enough to separate the grain from the chaff and straw. Most grain crops could be threshed in a day or a day and a half. Everybody seemed to work in a perfect frenzy until the neighborhood was all finished. Sometimes it rained so much the engine crew would go home. That went against our grain. If the women had "cooked up lots of food" and nobody stayed to eat we were in trouble. We ate what we could but because there was absolutely no refrigeration sometimes that precious commodity went to waste. We not only fed the men but some of the neighbor women came to visit and help. For many years Mrs. Etta Hassler always came to help. She was a fine helper. She saw what had to be done and did it. She and Mama worked together on the pies. Mama made the crust and lined the pans. Etta placed the sliced apples and or peaches in the crust and added sugar, a sprinkling of flour, cinnamon, nutmeg and big lumps of butter. Then came the big black iron skillets and we began to fry chicken on the old wood-burning Bridge Beach. Slaw was cut up in a large crock. Potatoes were set to boil on the back burners. Cabbage and green beans and corn were also cooking. We nearly always had a fire in another wood stove in the wash house. Just as soon as dinner was over and we saw what was leftover for supper, Mama and Etta sat out on the north porch to "cool off." Each took a sheet of the *Globe Democrat* to fan their warm sweaty faces. Mae and I washed dishes, dried them and put them away before we joined Mom and Etta on the north porch.

A few days later Mama, Mae and I rode on the wheat wagon and went to help Etta cook for the same crew. That was such fun getting to see all the Hassler children and sometimes other old friends like Ella, Frank and Rude Nixon. Sometimes there were as many women and children as crewmen. Big crowds never seemed to bother Etta. She cooked chicken and dumplings in a big wash boiler out in the yard. Her food was the best ever. That year Mr. Hassler was hauling his wheat directly to the elevator in Belle. Roy Nixon drove the truck and hauled load after load. On the last trip of the day, Mae and Zoa went along. Such good times as all of us had. It was almost like a Cooper Hill picnic.

When school opened that fall there were no big changes in our lives. Bud and I knew our way around. We knew the choice places for a tire to "blow out." We knew there would be the same trials with snow and ice and rain. The Charles Lange branch would be a daily challenge and so would the Bumpass Hill. We faced each day as it came. We made decisions and we matured. In 1930 there were no drugs, no alcohol and no foolishness was tolerated by our parents at home or our instructors at school. Everyone of us knew full well what it was costing our parents to send us to school. In nearly all cases we were the offspring of parents who had never had the opportunity to attend high school, and we were reminded of this almost every day. Our parents were sacrificing their "all" to see that their children had better things and a better life than they did. I thought we were having a real bad time but as I spent a night now and then in town I found out "Mr. Hard Times" had spread himself around pretty generally. Our homes were furnished with necessities only. Food was scarce unless you had a garden. Prices for farm goods had fallen to an all time low. We heard of farmers who had to pay the trucker when they sold livestock. The prices received simply didn't pay the freight. It was frightening!

Since Mae wasn't teaching she was trying to hatch, grow and sell canaries. A little later she went into white Jersey Giants chickens. I don't know which were the worst to take care of. The canary cages had to be cleaned daily and the canaries fed, watered and furnished with bath facilities. In return they sang and sang and sang. When the telephone rang or when the radio was on they thought it their duty to drown out the other music. When mating season arrived, a pair of birds were separated and placed in a square cage where the nest was already waiting for the pretty little oval eggs. Mae spent her mornings working with the birds. She sold the males easily but the females had to be sold to pet shops. The profit wasn't great but a one dollar bill was small riches in those awful days of no money at all.

But the big white chickens were lots more trouble. Mom wasn't going to let anything interfere with her precious brown leghorns. So a shed and a fence had to be built along the side of the granary. Roost poles had to be erected. The fowls were huge. They laid beautiful big brown eggs. Mae ran ads in the farm papers. She sold the eggs to individual buyers and some to hatcheries. They also were lots of work. After several months of such close confinement these big birds developed cannibalism. Mae was frantic as to what to do. In desperation she and I decided to "diaper" them. On Saturday we spent most of the day tearing strips of an old sheets into squares, catching the old hens, arranging the diapers over the bleeding rear ends and pinning the ends up on the big broad backs. Each old biddy would turn her head around as far as possible, cock her eye and try to inspect her new gear. Then they would ruffle their feathers and walk off as if to say, "Well, I guess this is the new spring fashion." These two farm ventures were like everything else. They were disasters. There's no way anyone can make a dime clear on a farm!

The Conservation Department sent out pheasant eggs to people who would spend their time feeding and caring for the baby chick pheasants. That was quite a prank to play on a brown leghorn hen. Almost as bad as ducklings or goslings. We loved the baby pheasants. They were so quick to pick up food. Their walking pattern was so different from chickens. When they were turned loose in the wild, I suppose they didn't know how to protect themselves from the wild animals. We saw very little of them after they were grown.

We were back in school when teacher's training again occupied the foremost place in my mind. One course was a concentrated three-month review of arithmetic, social studies and grammar. The other course was also on rural school management and more child psychology. I had these two classes as well as English literature with Mr. Logan Steen which meant I spent three hours per day in the teachers' training room. The fourth class was American problems with superintendent W. C. Butler. In this class we talked and studied a great deal about immigration, the good and bad concerning unions, how they were formed to protect the worker from unfair practices and to eliminate child labor. We again reviewed the Constitution and the Declaration of Independence. But it was in that teachers' training room I found myself absolutely enamoured with the deep thinking of English literature writers, of studying individual differences in psychology and finding out the meaning of "synapse." I never knew there was such a thing going on in my brain. I studied every available minute. Mr. Steen demanded your best. There were several of us who enjoyed the competition.

That fall we planned a school fair. We would decorate a car, one for each class. We would use crepe paper for crepe paper flowers. All the girls who could afford the paper were to make themselves a gold and purple crepe paper dress. We would wear them all day. Miss Castle was still the only female on the faculty so this was largely her idea. We worked hard decorating Andy's father's Ford. We cut and twisted crepe paper at school. We cut and sewed our gold and purple crepe paper dresses. The day before the fair dawned - I think it did - but daylight never quite got to earth the sky was full of thunderclouds. And such hard showers of rain as did pour down! Bud and I had to wait for the Charles Lange Branch to run down. Then we had to wait for Boyce Creek to run down. We chugged into town wet and soggy. All day it poured rain. We stood around in groups staring at the sky hoping to see some small vestige of sunlight. We almost swam home. The road was a river. Bud was a little tired of our lamenting the bad weather. He said the sun would probably come out and shine all night - tomorrow would be sunny and warm. I got real provoked at his lack of understanding. But after all he wasn't going to wear a crepe paper dress all day! While we were parading down Schoolhouse Street, the rain poured. We could feel the crepe paper fall away in long strips. We barely made it back to the school before the dressed disolved completely.

The rain didn't stop. The clouds didn't lift. Everything at home looked as if it were in danger of floating away. The creek was out in the fields all night. We did our outside chores as quickly as possible. Mama and Dad had intended to attend the fair but with all that rain falling there was no way they could leave home. On the day of the fair, the rain was still falling but in intermittent showers. As I remember the fair was not very well attended. Around noon the showers ceased. The sun did come out faintly. All of us put on our crepe paper dresses and paraded around. There were exhibits set up in all the rooms. Visual education reels were shown in the auditorium. But the automobile floats looked exactly like what they were - a mess of wet crepe paper and flowers. I had a new royal blue crepe dress for the occasion. By some stroke of good luck I had earned $3. When the Sears bargain catalog came that fall there was a notice reading: "Large selection of young ladies and misses dresses - send $2.98 and we will send you a dress of our choice." Well I mailed off my $3 and in a few days my dress arrived. It was a rather pretty royal blue long sleeved, long waisted, flounced skirt with a lace inset yoke. I thought it was pretty but a little short. I also managed to get a soft blue velvet hat. It had no frame to hold it - it just fit down in folds over my curls. Because it was so rainy, I didn't want to wear my new hat. It would get wet, I explained to Mama. She threw up her hands in disgust and exclaimed. "Well, you aren't going to walk on your head are you?" She couldn't see the use of having a new hat if you weren't going to wear it.

Since Mae was staying home raising "birds," she and Mama tried a few new recipes. The magazines were full of ways to save food. As I've said many times before we ate mostly what we grew on the farm. What we bought was stretched further and further. We did buy cocoa. It must have been rather cheap because I can remember bringing home a rather large quantity of it in a brown paper bag for 10 cents. Mae found a chocolate cake recipe that used produce we always had on hand. She made numerous cakes as well as cream pies like Mrs. Slinkman had made. She and Mama also came up with a fine stew concoction. It was full of meat, onions, carrots and potatoes. These two things were often our supper menu. Mrs. Muhleman gave me a hickory nut cake recipe. I liked it so much I'd work hours cracking and picking out the meats on Saturday evening. I'd almost have to hide the kernels in order to have some left for my cake. Sunday morning I'd cream the shortening and sugar, add the milk, flour, baking powder and vanilla. Mama would supervise the wood stove oven. Most times it came out light and browned, just right. I thought this was the best thing I could have for my school lunch. How Mama coaxed that "Old Bridge Beach" into baking biscuits and light bread and cakes and pies is still a mystery to me. There was no temperature gauge on it. She just opened the door and held her hand inside to test the degree of heat. Usually she poked in some more wood and talked to it. "Now come on old slow poke, I can't wait all day" or "Dad, get me some nice dry sticks, the biscuits won't brown unless the fire is hotter."

We had a cane patch that year - anything to supplement our diet. All of us took our turn at hoeing and weeding the cane. Mama would remind us how good it would taste after it was made into molasses, on hot biscuits, made into taffy or gingersnaps. Our mouths watered even as we hoed and weeded. We hauled the cane to Millard and Etta Hassler's to have it made into the thick brown syrup. There was so much of it, Dad took a big wooden barrel and a 10-gallon jar to be filled. When he brought it home in the farm wagon, we were so proud of it. We dipped out a big bowl-full to eat on our biscuits for supper. All fall we ate molasses cakes and gingersnaps. Mama made the best I ever tasted. The snaps were made in large quantities for lunches for four in school and something to have for after-school snacks. I can't remember exactly how she made them but I do know she heated the molasses on the stove before adding the soda. I can see the foamy mixture yet. And I can still smell in my mind the spicy aroma coming from the kitchen as we baked these large brown delicacies. They would have cracks all over the top when we sprinkled them with a bit of white sugar. Before I finish this sticky, gooey story, I want to record the education that goes with getting molasses out of a barrel on a zero-degree morning. I don't know why we never did this the evening before when we would have had daylight. Somehow it was always an early morning errand. We always had to be up before daylight to do our chores so while Mama got breakfast she would give orders. "Grace, you and Bud go draw a big bowl of molasses. Grace can carry the lamp." Sometimes the wind blew the light out and we had to struggle with a hot globe to re light it. Sure enough we had to go across the north porch, across a corner of the yard, up three steps and into the old log smokehouse. There we met up with the barrel. The molasses had to be drawn through the "bung hole," a round hole in the side of the barrel with a stopper in it. So first the barrel had to be "positioned" so I could hold the dish. The stopper had to be removed carefully. The barrel had to be braced so as not to spill any. It was hard work and on a cold morning molasses, especially if it's thick, doesn't especially want to go anywhere. One morning the barrel just simply got away from us. We couldn't hold on to it. We spilled a good deal. We broke the dish and we caught the "dickens." So much for cooking with molasses. These days I'm perfectly happy to buy a bottle of "Br'er Rabbit" at the store.

After the school fair, we settled down to less exciting things. Logan Steen lectured us on proper attire for teachers. He had only one suit, a navy blue serge. As he lectured, his black and grey streaked curls fell down and danced around on his forehead. He assigned special books from his library to be read and reviewed. I can't recall the title but one book was about a young lady (Jean someone) who went out to teach her first term of school. She was so knowledgeable about everything: academics, nature study, people. She was absolutely perfect and everyone loved and adored her. Whoever the author was evidently never taught school. But as Miss Jean in the book, I was the heroine of every situation. I was simply enthralled with the little volume.

From time to time in social studies we were lectured on government. Since all of us were so pinched for money we were interested in what was the matter with the money. Bernard Baruch was a common name in the paper. He seemed to be a well-known financier and government adviser. He was quite intelligent according to Mr. Steen. They were working on the alphabetical names for all the programs later to be put into practice under F.D.R. Pete says no wonder Mr. Hoover went fishing! (Pete is a Democrat). With a Democrat Congress there was no use for H.H. to try to push any Republican legislation. Hoover's idea was to feed people but not to pay out money. None of us could fathom what Washington D.C. was like but we certainly knew what it was like on the farm. We, like all our neighbors, often carried a basket of eggs with us when we went to church on Sunday. We stopped at Pete Langenburg's Store and sold them in order to have a little change to drop in the collection plate. Each child had a penny for Sunday School. Pete's store was a new addition to the big brick building already known as Lanbenburg's Store but was operated by Charles Berger and Ed Leach. Pete had a very small stock of goods: sugar, coffee, rice, beans, a few cans of fruits, vegetables, and a few candy bars. But his drawing card was ice cream. At last we could get an ice cream cone in Cooper Hill. In the summer we thought it was wonderful. Dr. and Mrs. Leach would drive to Cooper Hill to get an ice cream cone. How lazily we licked and nibbled. So it would last a long time. Mrs. Leach could always make hers last longest of any of us, and she never seemed to drip.

Mae and Irvin were "dating in earnest" now. Every weekend, he spent Friday evening with us. We played the only games we had equipment for: pinochle, hearts, rook and dominoes. Supper was served early. A warm fire was going in the north room. We would make a pan of chocolate fudge with lots of walnuts in it or divinity. Eggs were so cheap we used lots of them. But it also took more of them to buy a tank of gas. Often Mrs. Leach came along with Irvin or both Doc and Mrs. Leach came. Doc and Dad discussed what they thought was wrong with the economy. They did a lot of prophesying. The panic of the late 1800's had left its imprint on men their ages. You could see the fear in their eyes - fear of losing everything. Doc didn't own a farm but when there's no money for food doctor bills aren't paid either! Mom and Mrs. Leach talked about ways to save money. How they could cut down, make over, turn wrong side out and re-stitch. Mrs. Leach always raised Plymouth Rock chickens. She always carried her basket of big brown eggs when she went to the store. She bought very little: a box of oatmeal, a small can of Pet milk and a Stauffer's Wash Tablet. This was the forerunner of Clorox and Purex.

That winter had one thing that was definitely different. Irvin had never entertained the measles. But that winter he contacted some child in school. He had gone to teach on Monday morning and found out he was breaking out with a red rash. Naturally he was sent home. Everyone was excited. Irvin had to be put to bed, medicated, waited on. Basil had to be warned not to come home that evening. He was to stay with Mrs. Elsner and Ida - such excitement. And of all things who else should get the same horrible disease but our dear Uncle John. Somehow he too had escaped all those years. He and Aunt Ida were married when Dad and all the others had measles at home. Anyhow Aunt Ida sent word for Doc to come see Uncle John to verify her diagnosis. She was right, Uncle John was laid up. He was so sick, Doc was worried he might have pneumonia. He went every day for quite awhile when he could leave Irvin. I really wanted to see that the shades were pulled and that the liquid medicine was properly bitter and that Irvin got his share of the awful tasting little brown pills that Doc had given us when we had measles. After the worst was over, Irvin wanted something to do. Since he had pieced a quilt once before, he decided to tackle another. He chose the spool pattern where only one shape has to be cut. He did very well and almost got it finished before he was able to go back to school. By the way Uncle John recovered too.

In late winter, Dad always went out to dig sassafras roots. He brought quite a quantity in to dry in the wash house. From then on we had sassafras tea, cups and cups of it. Mom and Dad considered it good for us. We put sugar and lots of cream in it. The tea was such a lovely shade of pink when properly brewed. Mom used a half-gallon Karo syrup bucket as a brew pot. From the time the roots were dug until we grew tired of it, the bucket was always ready and warm for a delicious mid-morning snack. Mom welcomed the tea season. She would remind Dad every morning, "Now this will help cut back on the coffee. We've been drinking way too much coffee lately." What Mom was really saying was, "This will save a few cents." Speaking of cream for the tea brings back nostalgic memories of the big plain white pitcher we always filled with skimmed cream from the milk in a crock. Our table always had a pitcher full of cream. It was a staple in coffee, on fresh or canned fruit, on bread pudding or rice and raisins. If there should be a little left when our meal was finished someone would grab the pitcher, peer in to determine how much was left, then tip it up and drink it.

No Bacon family tree would be complete unless I mentioned the dogs. In the Bacon/Vaughan genealogy there's a story about the Vaughan boys back in the hills of Virginia. There were carrying their father's remains up a steep rocky hillside to the cemetery. All of a sudden, the dogs "treed," so the Vaughan boys set the casket down and went to see what the dogs had. This is as far as the story went. I have never heard whether Grandpa ever reached his final resting place.

The Bacons and Vaughans continued their love affair with dogs after their arrival in Missouri. Dad and all his brothers grew up with hunting dogs. Much of their sustenance depended on a good "tree" dog. Squirrel, rabbit, quail, and wild turkey were valuable meat dishes. There is a wild turkey story about Grandpa, C. P. Bacon and "Cat" Vaughan. Grandpa had just been appointed a member of the newly organized "Conservation of Wildlife." He had been indoctrinated with all the do's and don'ts of protecting wildlife. "Cat" Vaughan, who was Grandma's nephew, was walking out to visit a day at the Bacon farm and came upon a nice young "Tom" and killed it. Knowing about Grandpa's new position, he didn't dare bring it to the house. So he hid it in a fence corner. He found Grandma in the garden and informed her about the hidden, out-of-season treat. He said, "Aunt Melie, what do you think Uncle Charlie is going to say about me killing a turkey out of season?" Grandma was always a quiet little woman. She didn't hesitate a moment before replying, "Well, Fayte, I doubt he'll say much of anything - he's out behind the hen house dressing a young hen turkey right now!" It would be my guess that the Bacons, the Vaughans, and the hounds ate well that night!

Now back to the family of best friends. I can't remember ever having dogs at Linn. I do remember Johnnie Williams bringing a pup one morning when he came to work. It was so tiny. Its eyes weren't open yet and it was so skinny. Johnnie had it in his jump jacket pocket. Mom put it in a shoe box and set it behind the cook stove. Dad tried to feed it but that poor little pup wasn't with us long. I've always had my own personal suspicions.

Sometime before we left the farm I remember a brown and white spotted pup. One Sunday afternoon, all of us walked to the creek and went swimming. Dad threw Spot into the swift running water. Mae and I were frantic. Dad laughed at us and Spot seemed to enjoy the plunge. I remember how he perked his ears and followed the minnows with his beautiful brown eyes. I do wish I could reach back into that wonderful world of childhood and remember what happened to "Spot."

Soon after we moved to the Buecker farm we became aware of the wonderful world of dogs. "Old Ketch" came along with Frank, Rude, and Ellie Nixon "Old Ketch" was a typical black hound with brown spots over his eyes. Audrey had two dogs, "Shep" and "Puppy." As long as the family lived there Shep and Puppy were our constant playmates. Irvin and Basil had "Shep" and "Brownie." Every family had at least one dog so it was only a matter of "looking around" to find a pup. I don't remember which arrived first - "Spitz" or "Watch."

Spitz was a small white female with slick hair and a few brown spots. She came to us by way of Charlie Bacon. He was living in St. Louis and had lots of young friends, all hunters. So it was not unusual to wake up on Saturday to the sound of dogs barking at the brush piles on the hill. I'm sure you've guessed by now that Spitz was one of Charlie's friends. On Sunday when Charlie left, Spitz was mysteriously shut in the corn crib. Now, we had a dog! All of us loved her. Well, not quite all. Mama was furious - at

Charlie, at Spitz, at the friends. "They did it on purpose. Charlie knew all the time that the dog was in the corn crib." Spitz just had to go! She was female. We weren't going into the dog business. "No, Sir-e-e!"

Somehow, Spitz managed to stay out of Mama's pathway until the climate around the kitchen door improved. She matured quite normally and in due time gave birth to sixteen pups. My, my, my now Mama really went into a tizzy. Only one was selected from the litter and the others were taken to the creek in a hurry.

Now I know Spitz wasn't our first dog - not by a long shot. It comes back to me now because Bud and I were in Belle high school when Mr. Muhlemann offered to spay Spitz for us. The operation became a vocational ag lesson and a dreadful ordeal for the poor little animal. I'm positive Mr. Muhlemann did not know much about surgery. I'm also positive he thought she wasn't going to live. Mrs. Muhlemann said, "There were two days when I wouldn't have given a nickel for her life." But Spitz fooled us for many, many years. Mama even grew somewhat fond of her.

As times became harder, staples were also harder to come by. We hauled our corn and wheat to the mill. We weren't especially fond of cornbread but Mama made it taste good and we ate it frequently with sorghum molasses. The mill flour made a dark heavy bread, and yeast wasn't what it is today. We bought a package of "yeast foam" at the store. There were 6 little hard flat cakes in one of these packages. Mama would decide real often to make her own yeast. I would be dispatched to the lower end of the bottom field to pick the hops. These would be soaked in warm water overnight. This liquid would then be strained and mixed with hot potato water and about a cup of mashed potatoes. She thickened the hops potato yeast mixture with fresh corn meal, rolled it out into a flat cake and cut it into blocks and let it dry. "Now I'll bet we'll have some decent bread," Mom would say - and we usually did. But again, so much was left to chance. If the weather was cold, the bread didn't rise. If the weather was hot it would rise too fast and often it would fall when we put it into the oven to bake. If the fire was too hot, the bread burned on top and bottom. No matter what calamity befell the bread we ate it. One whole loaf was broken into pieces to eat warm, as soon as it came from the oven. Frequently we had to postpone supper until the bread could bake. Mama would pull the pan out sufficiently to thump the top of a loaf. If it sounded hollow it was done. But Mama always shook the pan to see if the loaves were loose and shrunken away from the sides of the pan. Then she was certain it was done! Usually with fresh bread we had milk gravy or stewed fruit. But always milk and cream, cottage cheese, and fried potatoes. All were the best with fresh bread.

Something else we ate a lot of was hominy. Some of us liked it, some of us didn't. But Dad always grew white corn. Yellow corn hadn't become popular yet. (We grew our first yellow corn in 1932.) Hominy making was quite a process. Mama made a strong solution of ashes and water for lye. This lye water was strained and poured over a large jar of white shelled corn. This sat and soaked for several days until the outside of each grain had burst and separated somewhat from the inside kernel. The water was drained time after time until all the husks were removed and only the soft white inside kernel remained. Then it had to continue soaking to be sure all the lye water was out. Finally Mama would announce. "I do believe we can have some hominy for supper." Oh, how my mouth would water. We would heat a big pan of it sprinkled with salt and sugar and drizzled with butter - it was a treat! I can also remember how red and rough Mama's hands would be by the time the hominy was ready. The hominy could then be dried but usually ours was eaten so fast we didn't worry about preservation methods. Some people sweetened their hominy with molasses but we never did. As I think of it, it might have been better than sugar. Another dish we made from meal was mush. I loved that too! Something else we could eat with cream and sugar. Mush was always cooked in the three-legged iron pot. The water had to be brought to a rolling boil. So we set the pot down next to the fire. When the water came to the second boil and salt was added, Mama stirred the meal in very slowly letting it fall a little at a time from her cupped hand. After the mixture was sufficiently thick, it had to boil and be stirred at least 20 minutes "by the clock." It was then dipped out in bowls to cool before we ate it. If there was any left it was sliced and fried for breakfast. We spread it with butter and poured molasses over the top. But we stretched everything. Mama was a very careful cook, always enough but not anything to waste.

How we did work that summer of 1930! We had reasonably good corn but not many acres planted. It had threatened to be dry early in the season but as the warm days came on, so did the rain. We had a fair potato crop and some tomatoes to can. We were more and more dependent on our own resources for food because there was less and less cash income. We heard more and more about "Mortgage, Interest and Taxes." Mom was sure we were either going to the "poor farm" or "some town where there was a shoe factory." I always knew when she was more worried than usual. When she stirred the ashes in Old Bridge Beach early in the morning she did so with such gusto we would hear the noise upstairs. Then when the fire was burning, she would tune up and sing, "When the Roll is Called Up Yonder." Dad too would sing as he took the milk buckets and set off for the cow barn. He usually found satisfaction in "That Old Time Religion - If it's good for Paul and Silas - Then its good enough for me." He had another old, old melody he also used for milking time. "Oh, I want to go to Heaven whenever I die. Just to see old Jordan roll, to see old Jordan roll, to see old Jordan roll. Oh, I want to go to Heaven whenever I die. Just to see old Jordan roll." And Mae and I were still singing occasionally - "Morning on the Farm."

Mae had done very well with her piano lessons. She could give lessons to beginners if she could find some pupils. We had so few diversions - no money - no place to go. Pleasant moments were spent around the piano. Dad didn't have his violin anymore. Times had been so hard for so long. Roy Nixon had helped us for a whole month with the hay. We knew there was no money. Our old Hauptman's cigar box on the cabinet shelf was silent when we shook it. Roy's month was up. He needed his money, so dear old Dad asked him if he would like the violin in payment. He said he would. I can still see Dad. He closed his eyes as he handed the beloved instrument over to Roy. He hurried away to the back of the barn so we wouldn't see his tears! Such is farming. You sacrifice your life and your loves for the privilege of going in debt, starving, freezing in winter, burning in summer's heat and it's always the same. Never a dime to your name. Uncle Sam is always out there regulating and demanding and poking fun at the old hayseed. People don't ever seem to realize where the food comes from!

Now that I've outlined the food and farm situation we will return to school. As I said previously, it was much easier. We knew what to expect. Belle High School was so small. Everyone knew everyone else. I was interested in the freshmen, just to learn their names, where they lived, where they had gone to school. Did they have brothers and sisters in high school? I soon knew them all!

Chapter 27

Pure Romance – A Brand New Dress

I was so anxious for Bud to look right. So was Mama. She often asked me what the other boys wore. At this time a few boys were wearing white flannel trousers. Well Mama decided immediately Bud must have a pair. We hoarded our egg money greedily. These pants had to be in readiness before school began. Nothing could have been a worse choice. In the first place Bud hated them. In the second place they were scandalously warm. Most of all they soiled so easily they were so impractical as to be silly. For boys in vocational agriculture they were out of the question! When Bud saw them he begged us to send them back and get him some overall pants. It was too late. Anyhow Bud withstood the heat and the constant reminders to "Try to keep your hands out of your pants pockets. You're getting them dirty." When winter came and money was still scarcer, Mama got a package of Putnam's dye and all of a sudden Bud's white flannels became brown flannels. Mama was excellent with the dye pot. She knew exactly how to get a good even color.

As was the custom, seniors ordered their class rings and cards in the fall. We patronized the Star Engraving Company in Houston, Texas. A salesman called on us. We met in the study hall and decided on a yellow gold base, black onyx setting with a yellow gold "B" atop that. We would receive the rings sometime the following spring. Since I was secretary and treasurer, I would be responsible for collecting the money. I believe the cost was $21 per ring. There was no senior trip or constant selling items or begging donations (where seniors are out of classes almost more than they are in) such as is done nowadays in some schools.

There were inspectors who visited the schools and sat in on the classes. The high school inspector, Mr. Dillon, always visited Belle at least once per year. He always parked his car out on the street and walked slowly up the front walk. I'm sure this was to give teachers time to get up, straighten up and start trying to act like professionals. He stuck his head in every room and asked about the equipment (even through we had none). Sometimes he sat for an hour in our teachers' training room. During that hour, Mr. Steen wrote furiously on the blackboard. Often reviewing the American history or geography facts he had been drilling into our heads for several days.

There were also supervisors from the state department for teachers' training. Miss Mary Sue Hopkins came in the fall to see how many students were enrolled, how the professor was organized and to listen to our responses as we recited. I was always petrified as long as any stranger was in the room. I think possibly Mr. Steen was too.

Wade Harris was teaching at Post Oak that year. Pete and Charles Howard were having a good deal of fun. Wade was just out of high school and like all beginning teachers anxious to be a success. Wade married Sylvia Picker that year. He also had a Chevrolet coupe purchased second-hand. So he drove from Summerfield to teach at Post Oak every day. Bud and I would meet Wade every morning and evening on our way to and from Belle.

All year there was a bad feeling between Mr. Steen and Mr. Muhleman. Mr. Steen had been senior sponsor for several classes until we came along and chose Mr. Muhleman as our sponsor. It was perhaps our fault and perhaps to our disadvantage that this happened since Mr. Muhleman was across town in another building and sometimes away on a field trip when we needed his advice. Mr. Steen became more and more incensed with his "view from the outside" only. He almost considered the senior class his property.

During the winter we spent weeks at Mrs. Decker's - Bud, Sophia, Mildred and I. Mrs. Decker was as always an angel to us. She acted as if we were doing her a favor to stay with her. In the fall of that year, her son Bob had a terrible infection in the bone of his leg and when Dr. Johnson could not seem to get it to heal, Bob was taken to Barnes Hospital. Everyone was greatly concerned. Would Bob get well? After Iva, could we see Mr. and Mrs. Decker lose another and only child? After weeks of treatment Bob and his mother came home on the train. How excited we were. Bob was getting well. Mr. Decker was so happy and so were we!

Sometime that fall Mrs. Decker and Bob came home with Bud and me and spent the night. We had such a good time fussing over Bob to see he was comfortable and well fed. Mama and Mrs. Decker had known each other before they were married. Another night, Mildred Harris came home to spend the night with us. Sometimes Fern Morelock or Mabel Branson visited us. Once Mildred and I spent the night with Sophia Lehnhoff. We all slept upstairs. But before we retired Sophia's mother carried a bucket of red hot coals upstairs to start a fire for us to undress by. Somehow the kindling didn't catch fire as it should and the room filled with smoke. It nearly choked us. We had to open all the doors and windows. But we had a snug warm bed with all three of us in it!

By this time, all of us were aware of "romance in the air." Miss Castle, our only female high school teacher, was dating Mr. Biles. Bud and I had known this for a long time. We were a part of a deep, dark conspiracy. In April of the preceding spring, I had stayed a few days at the Sam Travis home when we were practicing for our junior play. Thus I was again Miss Castle's roommate. She was trying to devise a way to go with Mr. Biles to the dairy show in St. Louis on Sunday. They needed to leave town separately. Teachers were still closely supervised in small towns. Dating seriously was not tolerated and married teachers soon found themselves unemployed. So by putting our heads together, it was arranged for Miss Castle to spend the weekend with us on the farm. No one thought anything about this because Miss Castle had spent several weekends with us. And so it was. Miss Castle packed all her dress-up clothes in a bag and we sailed out of Belle on Friday evening - so full of mischief and so full of our secret. Saturday was a fun day. Miss Castle knew about farms. She grew up on one near Mayetta, Kansas. She had a wealth of stories about college at Tarkio, her rich relatives, and her immediate family.

Sunday morning very early, Mr. Biles came rolling down the hill in his new dark green Chevrolet coupe. Mama had biscuits baking and ham frying, eggs of course were understandable, peach preserves were a welcome bite of sweetness with a cup of good fresh coffee diluted with big blobs of cream and, of course, plenty of sugar. Everyone was in good spirits. We had a special secret! The sky was just getting pink over Weaver Hollow when the happy twosome pulled away from the front of our house and headed for the dairy show at the Arena in St. Louis. All day we worked at trying to catch up on two days' work and cooking a company supper because Mr. Biles would bring Miss Castle back to our house in the evening. We had a fine supper: always the crisp brown baked chicken, dressing, gravy, mashed potatoes, green beans, etc., with fresh apple pie and coffee. We could see the happiness in their eyes as we sat around the table. We suspected this would materialize into something more than casual dating. Mr. Biles' favorite game was dominoes. We had just purchased a set of double twelves. Neither Mr. Biles nor Miss Castle had ever encountered this many dots. We had so much fun watching them count. Especially Miss Castle who was our Math teacher! It was properly late and dark when Mr. Biles departed for home. No one would guess where he had been all day Sunday or with whom. Monday morning Miss Castle arrived in Belle via the Bacon Golden Chariot and thus was born a romance which developed into a long and happy marriage. But for the time being Bud and I were sworn to secrecy. No one must know, or Miss Castle's job would be at risk!

While we were practicing our senior play I boarded at the Sam Travis home for a couple of weeks. So again I shared a room with Miss Castle. We had become exceptionally good friends. I knew all her family well by now by word of mouth. She could be lots of fun. The boys at school teased her unmercifully about Mr. Biles. She laughed and I think she rather enjoyed the razzing. During the two weeks of play practice, she kept me informed as to the progress of their romance. They couldn't actually date but since Mr. Biles lived directly across the street from Travis' they met frequently on the street. Mr. Biles was still making biscuits from that wonderful Aristos flour. It was almost a ritual for him to appear at the back door early in the morning with a pan of beautiful round, brown biscuits. Mrs. Travis thought this was so cute and so funny. So did I!

When I spoke of the Golden Chariot a few sentences back I might have aroused some curiosity. At Halloween that fall the Vocational Agriculture boys thought it would be a huge joke to paint our car yellow. They did. It wasn't a very good job and the black paint showed through, making it look somewhat like we had tried to camouflage it. In fact it looked awful! Mama and Dad didn't like the prank one bit. Mr. Muhleman made the boys try to clean the yellow paint off. All they did was smear it more. So we drove the Golden Chariot as it was. There was no choice! We still had numerous flat tires. We still fought the creeks and the deep mud holes where we slipped one way for awhile then another trying to stay on the higher, dryer red clay, knowing full well sooner or later we would slip in the deep rut and very likely be stuck! Sometimes we would use up all of our never-fail tire patch. At such times we drove home on the "rim." Somehow we managed to get the tube and tire repaired so we could get to school the next day. Usually Doc or Basil had some patch on hand. But when we drove "on the rim," we didn't need to announce our arrival - such grating and grinding on the dirt road you never heard!

We simply couldn't afford tires and tubes. We usually ordered such things from Sears & Roebuck because we could get them cheaper. When we saw we must invest in a tire, we knew it would take a week for the new one to arrive. Meanwhile we would pray the patches held.

There weren't many extracurricular activities that year. Times were hard - so hard no one could afford the price to attend entertainment. We presented our senior play, *Rose of the Southland,* to a crowd composed principally of our parents and school board members. There were always the people we could count on to buy tickets to all the school functions: Jess Birdsong, Sam Licklider, The Travis families, Slinkmans, Ridenhours, George Steiner, Doctor Ferrell, Oliver Lloyd, Queen and Weldon Tynes. We knew exactly how many people and who would attend our functions.

But teacher training was my pride and glory. We went out to visit rural schools and observe a rural situation. We went to Dixie where Ralph Tynes was teaching. We went to Fairview where Vernon Travis was located and to Hatchey School at Summerfield where Bryce Jett was teaching. These were fun and exciting as well as educational. There was a cold, cold, rainy day in the spring when Miss Mary Sue Hopkins came for her "official visit." All of us had been assigned a certain subject and a certain grade to teach. We had been making our lesson plans and practicing on our young pupils for several weeks. How I dreaded teaching a class. I knew my face was going to be red as a turkey gobbler's wattle. I knew I would shake all over and to know every word and every move would be under observation by Miss Mary Sue Hopkins. I lived in mortal fear for two weeks. I was to teach a sixth grade class in common fractions. I was first on the list of demonstrations. Of course, Bud and I arrived early. I arranged my seating pattern. I went downstairs and brought up my sixth graders. I was all ready to go when Mr. Steen and Miss Mary Sue arrived. The bell rang and I began my class. I felt calm and serene and in my element. In a short space of time my class was over. I returned my small charges to their home room and I could now sit and watch my fellow prospective teachers shake and search for words. I also felt so dressed up that day. Mae had let me wear a dark rusty red crepe dress she had been wearing for a dress-up. It was a little long for me but I was so happy that school was almost finished. Mr. Steen had stressed at great length the possibility that not all of us would be fortunate enough to find employment. He spent lots of time trying to warn us of disappointments. But he was a sincere believer in honoring a contract. If you should be offered a better job after you had signed a contract you forgot the second offer. You honored the first one. How times have changed! We were so young, so full of knowledge, so willing to solve the world's problems. After all we had studied child psychology in addition to arithmetic, geography, social studies and grammar. We had conjugated the verb "to be," we had written our themes (one on procrastination), we had memorized sections of the Constitution, and we had mastered facts about Missouri. When you add the "synapse" and "individual differences" to this no wonder we felt "so learned."

With money being so hard to earn, it was only natural I was going to submit an application for any rural school where there might be a ghost of a chance. Mae was doing the same. Jersey giant chickens and canaries had not proven a profitable investment. In April, Mae was chosen as the teacher for the Garfield School and since jobs were so scarce, it was not thought proper to award two jobs to the same family. Everywhere I went, the board members would ask, "Isn't your sister signed up to teach at Garfield?" When I said, "Yes," that ended the interview. I never stood a chance. Only a few from our class were chosen to teach. Every teacher who could possibly hold on to a job, worked hard to keep it. So very few schools were changing teachers.

Aunt Ida came through with the $10 she had promised. I immediately ordered a navy blue, wool spring coat - an article badly needed. The graduation dress was still a big question mark. I had one all picked out in the catalog. A navy blue chiffon with a bold floral pattern, flounced skirt, lace yoke, all stitched over a navy blue rayon lining which served as a slip. But Mama kept telling me we simply couldn't squeeze the money out of the hen-and-egg money. We were going to have caps and gowns so what I wore under it wouldn't matter. Maybe not, but I wanted a dress - a new dress. My best dress was the black chiffon Mae had made over for me the year before. I wanted to leave the hand-me-downs behind. I had gone through high school on Jennie Boies' dresses. True they were nice material and I appreciated them but now I wanted a graduation dress. All the other girls were telling what color and what kind of material their dresses were. I knew better than to beg. I knew there wasn't even one cent in the cigar box on the cabinet shelf. I knew how desperate we were for just simple necessities. I had decided to just wear the black chiffon and imagine it was new. I was deep in soapy wash water on Saturday morning thinking about the graduation exercises. The following Sunday evening would be baccalaureate and on Thursday, commencement. Uncle John and Aunt Ida would come for both occasions. I felt so proud! Suddenly like a bolt out of the blue, Mama shook the Hauptman's cigar box and said, "Now, I do believe I can squeeze out enough to get that dress you think you've got to have." I couldn't believe my ears. "Now get the catalog and make out the order or it won't get here in time." I flew through the morning chores. I could just picture myself in that lovely chiffon, even if it was covered by a heavy gown. Now I lived in true anxiety. What if the dress didn't arrive? What if it should be out of stock (as often happened)? What if - what if?

Chapter 28

"Up in the Air" and Down

High school hadn't been much fun; flat tires, getting stuck, pushing the Model T up the Bumpass Hill and through snow drifts, freezing my heels, pushing out of the Charles Lange Branch, carrying eggs, holding butter and cream on my lap along with books, notebooks, pens, ink bottle and freezing fingers. For two years, Bud and I had managed some way to drive the nine miles each way, haul our passengers, do our school work, do our homework, keep up with our regular chores at home. We were late only two mornings. I remember when we slipped into an enormously deep rut and got stuck out by George Thoms' farm. This good-hearted farmer pulled us out with no thought of pay. But his daughter Josie often rode into town with us. George Thoms and his wife Edna were such "good hard workers." They milked cows and Edna delivered the milk in glass quart bottles to people in town. Edna drove an ancient Model T as she took care of her regular customers. We would usually meet Edna coming home from town. Although she was in the driver's seat steering the old Ford it appeared she was lending her own strength to that motor. Such chugging and spitting and smoking and steaming on a cold morning. I would miss seeing Edna!

I would miss my study hall friends, especially those who ate lunch together in the study hall. We were all "country bumpkins." I would miss those close friends with whom I had spent nights: they were Ollie and Mabel Rogers, the two youngest daughters of John and Alice Rogers. They lived on the extreme north end of Belle in Osage County. They were friends of Mama and Dad. They had recently moved to town from a farm south of Belle. A sad thing had happened. Their daughter-in-law, Ernie's wife, had died, leaving several children, one a young boy baby. Mrs. Rogers (Alice) had brought the baby home with her to rear. He was a sweet blonde, very good looking. This baby required lots of attention so Mabel and Ollie did all the cooking, housekeeping, laundry, chickens, gardening, everything. I guess that's why I always felt so much at home there. Since Ollie always did the cooking I usually tried to help her. We peeled potatoes and fried ham and stewed tomatoes and, of course, Ollie made biscuits. Once she had to use soda and I suppose the milk wasn't sour enough so the biscuits didn't rise or have a nice texture. When we went to the table Mrs. Rogers broke one open in our typical Ozarkian style ready to receive the gravy. She was surprised to find the biscuits so tough. She exclaimed, "Why Ollie I didn't know you didn't know how to make soda biscuit." Anyhow, we thought it was funny. Her father thought they were good. He said he liked tough biscuits! During the night the baby was sick, he cried and cried. Ollie and her mother were up nearly all night attending to him. In the morning he was better, but Mrs. Rogers and Ollie were worn out. Ollie and I prepared breakfast: bacon, oatmeal and toast. We set off for school. It was quite a long walk.

There was one very exciting afternoon during my junior year. Just as the bell rang and the entire student body spewed out of the old brick building, a small airplane buzzed overhead. We watched intently. Planes were still a rarity. As we headed for home we could see the plane descending lower and lower in the sky. Right in front of our eyes that plane circled and landed in the ridge field on the Bill Dahms farm along the highway just outside the city limits.

As we paused to watch the landing other students caught up with us. They piled into and onto the Golden Chariot. Yelling "Bud, Bud, drive us out there. Let's see what that thing looks like." We were overpowered. We headed for the plane. Soon the road was full of cars and kids and townspeople. There was a crowd. All of us gathered around to see as much as we could. We soon found out the pilot would "take us up for 5 minutes" to view the town of Belle. That is, if we had 50 cents. Where in the world would I have gotten that kind of money? My brain ticked a little more. Find someone else who wanted to go up and perhaps take me for free. I spied Ollie Rogers a few feet away. I thought I could see a wistful look in her eye. Sure enough Ollie wanted to fly just as badly as I. She had one whole dollar tied in the corner of her handkerchief and she would like me to "go up" with her. So we marched up to the pilot, forked over our money and before you could say Jack Robinson we were taxiing across the Dahms hayfield. In another minute we were "way up there" sailing around over Belle. How pretty the little town looked in the spring sunshine. Ollie and I were fascinated. We looked down at the people on the ground. We felt so brave - something like Columbus must have felt when he set foot on San Salvador. All too soon our time was up and we were back, our feet on the good old flat earth. We were besieged with questions. "How did it feel to be away up there! Could I breathe? Wasn't I scared?" No, I certainly wasn't scared - except when we started home. It was then Bud lowered the boom. "I'll tell Mom on you." There was no use to beg him not to. I knew he really would!

And he did. He ran down the hill from the garage. He didn't even get to the house until he almost yelled. "Hey Mom, Ask Grace what she took a ride in. Ha, Ha, Ha. Just as well tell her, Gracie. You know she'll find out." I knew, too, I had to tell her. I felt I had to pay Ollie back for her generosity.

Well, after the confession Mom's face grew perfectly white. For just about one solid moment she was speechless. I was beginning to wonder if I had paralyzed her tongue. Then she came alive. The color returned to her cheeks and she began. "Such a silly, idiotic thing. Just to think a child of mine would get up in one of those airplanes. Just thinking about it gives me the creeps." And on and on. Finally, she came up short with the inevitable question, "Where in the world did you get the money?" I explained that I would work extra hard at something. I would earn it somehow. She gave me to understand I'd pay back the 50 cents the next day and, "Yes, you bet you'll work extra hard and no spending money for you until such a time as you learn to stay out of airplanes." I guess I soon learned, because I truly despise flying! And just a note about that spending money. There never was such a thing. Maybe once every two weeks she would allow Bud and me each a nickel. I always knew exactly what I was going to do with mine. Jess Birdsong had a particularly tasty chocolate marshmallow nut bar called "Big Mama." And in that day and time the candy bar was so big I could nibble on it all the way from downtown Belle to the school. Bud nearly always spent his for a Baby Ruth. He would wait until we started home to eat his. How my mouth would water. Sophia and I would just look out the window and admire the scenery.

I'd miss Lucille Rohrer and Fern Morelock with whom I had also spent nights. It was fun staying with Lucille. She and her brother Ralph were the youngest of the Henry Rohrer family. Usually Lucille's older brother, Wilbur, and his wife, Gusta, and their two children, Maxine and Boyd, spent the evening with us. The Rohrer house was always scrubbed so clean and we had a good supper. Mr. and Mrs. Rohrer always left very, very early to go milk out at the farm. Lucille, Ralph and I would find a nice pot of warm oatmeal on the back of the stove and a teakettle of hot water to wash our faces.

This must be the stuff friendships are made of. All these years (about 60 now) I've remembered the many kindnesses shown me by the residents of Belle.

I would miss walking downtown at noon after our lunches were eaten. That is, if I had my lessons in order. If not, I'd spend the extra time in the study hall and sometimes I'd be so buried in a book I simply couldn't wait to find out what happened next.

I'd miss the boys too, although no one really dated. All our parents made it very, very clear we were too young to date. We were very good friends. Since Andy Lindner and I had taken care of the rings, the cards, the caps and gowns and the business for the class, we had become special friends. There were several boys in our teacher's training classes too: Wilbur Matthews, Herbert Lease, Raymond Garver, Harold McQueen and of course, Andy. All of us had met the same Goliaths. We were children of the depression, but I can't remember any of them being so dependent on eggs and old "good-for-nuthins."

The days passed. Every evening I ran breathlessly to the house almost yelling. "Mama, Mama did my new dress come?" Well it didn't arrive in time for baccalaureate, but it was a happy evening. We donned our caps and gowns in the teacher training room, lined up and marched across the hall to the auditorium. We listened to the sermon by Reverend Carl A. Baldwin. We were very sober as the usual quartet composed of S. G. Licklider, Jess Birdsong, Esco Spurgeon and George Steiner sang the usual appropriate compositions. Uncle John thought it was just great. He even thought I looked nice in my black chiffon dress!

Now all we had to do was pass our exams. The teacher training exam was a state prepared test. It would not be administered until after school had closed. At any rate all of us supposed we had "passed."

Thursday evening came - the deadline - did the dress come? Mama said, "No, it didn't come." But she said it with her back to me. So I was suspicious. In a minute, she sent me to the cellar for potatoes. As I went through the hall, there on the hanger right where I couldn't miss it was "the dress." "Oh my, oh my, the dress." I felt the lace yoke, the pretty flounces of the skirt. I held it up to me. It was lovely. My new dress. My graduation dress. I flew as Mom and I cooked supper. Everyone got dressed. When we got to the top of the hill there was Uncle John and Aunt Ida waiting for us. We were a small procession as we wound our way into Belle. The Lehnhoff's were just ahead of us. We rode in the Golden Chariot with Uncle John's new Chevrolet second, followed by Dr. and Mrs. Leach in their Ford coupe.

Such excitement! We crowded into the teacher training room to claim our caps and gowns. First, I wanted to be sure everyone saw my new dress. I was so proud of it! We marched across to the auditorium for the last time. We were addressed by the Honorable Charles A. Lee - state superintendent of schools. Opal Smith Branson delivered the valedictory address. We sang our class song and one called "Spring Song." We marched out for the final time. I felt so grown up - so adult. Now all I needed was a school to teach!

The following week I went back to take the teacher training exams. They continued for two days. Bud took me, even though it meant taking two days work off on the farm. I was urged to hurry home as soon as I could. It was spring and we needed to get busy with chickens and eggs.

Mom had worked hard trying to get me a job. I now had a second grade teacher's certificate. But we were all very pleased that Mae had a job. In fact, she got two schools. She was chosen to teach at Drake, a tiny village where Highway 19 meets Highway 50. Then Mama and Mae decided to take Garfield instead: both of them thought I could take over the job at Drake. So I was dispatched to see the Nullmeyers and other board members. We had a wonderful day eating dinner and afternoon lunch with these fine people, but no success in the job department.

Old Man Depression had hold of all of us now. His grip was unrelenting. What we had termed bad times was now full fledged depression. And as Pete says, "Hoover went fishin." Nowadays when people my age speak of these dreadful times there's always someone in the group who says, "Oh, let's not talk about those awful times. I don't like to recall them." Someone will say, "I ate so many turnips I never want to see another turnip." Then all of us tell something we remember distinctly. I think my outstanding memory is of Bud and the Model T Golden Chariot. I can still feel the rear fender where I grabbed hold to push. I can see our patched clothes, the egg baskets and the butter mold. I feel the cold of the zero mornings when we rolled out of bed and started our long day. Things are certainly different now. We have more than we need! But our appreciation for these good things is sincere!

Since I was "unemployed," Mama found plenty to keep me busy. I have described our chicken and eggs and turkeys, geese, ducks, calves, and colts, plowing for corn, building fence, coaxing the garden and field crops to grow. On rainy days Dad and the boys mended harness and oiled it. We had a special "tack" room at the horse barn. They oiled and repaired farm equipment. There was never any time for rest.

So I was kept busy cleaning, cooking, laundry, gardening, and chicken feeding. Usually we had strawberries. How we loved the shortcake and berries with sugar and cream. This year we made preserves and jam. Aunt Ida also had strawberries, so Mae and I took turns helping her. Picking the berries usually took all morning. Hulling, cooking and canning took all afternoon. Then came the blackberries. Every morning long before sun up, we would hurry down the lane, our buckets rattling, our eyes still wishing we were sound asleep in our little bed. By the time we crossed the creek and climbed the gentle slope into the berry patch, we were wide awake. The berries were unusually nice in this old field. All our neighbors knew about it too. Sometimes we met Ella, Frank and Rude or Mrs. Homfeld in the patch ahead of us. This blackberry business went on for several weeks depending on how much rain we had or lack of it! The picking continued as late as we dared. That meant getting to the house and having dinner on the table by noon. We looked over the berries and picked out the largest sweetest ones to eat with cream and sugar. (And a pan of hot biscuits.) Then came washing jars, washing berries, firing the cookstove, scalding jars, cooking berries, filling the jars, fitting the lids and sealing. We always put back a big bowl full of nice ones for supper.

Sometimes in a case of real necessity, I was needed to drive the mules, Jim and Odie, to the hay fork. We put up loose hay in those days. First it was mowed and raked into wind rows. Then the men shocked it and turned it to dry. Then it was pitched by big forkfuls onto the hay wagon and hauled into the barn. The mules were unhitched from the wagon, taken to the back of the barn and re-hitched to a double tree. This was attached to a stout rope running through a pulley at ground level, another in the gable of the barn. The rope was attached to a pulley in the front of the barn and eventually to a hay fork which was stuck into the wagon load of hay. When the fork was stuck properly, a lever was pulled up to hold the hay. I said, "Get-up Jim. Get along there, Odie" and we pulled a big forkful of hay up, up, up, where the fork came in contact with the haytrack. Then it was easier. Jim and Odie didn't strain anymore. But I had to grab the double tree with one hand to hold it off the mules' hocks, hold the lines and turn around with the other hand. Young as they were, the boys, all three of them, were working in the loft. The haying season was hard work. We had to work fast. We couldn't let it get wet. It needed to dry sufficiently to prevent mold. It shouldn't get too dry or sunburned. We were always fighting against time. The alfalfa was Dad's pride and joy. It smelled sweet as we cut, raked, shocked and hauled it to the barn. The red clover was almost as pungently sweet. But I liked the alfalfa aroma best. By the time the hay was safely in the barn, the corn needed lots of attention. The boys were always busy plowing, cultivating, weeding and "laying by." No matter where they worked in the very lower end of the field or across the creek in the Polk field, someone had to take a bucket of cool water to the workers. It seems now that it was my turn too often. But I always saw such interesting things along the way. Wild roses, ripe berries, hickory and butternut trees - remember the best ones for fall harvest - wild flowers by the dozens. I could always count on meeting a couple of black snakes and if I had to cross the creek I'd look carefully for a water moccasin. They always swam away so gracefully. They seemed so anxious to find cover. When I reached my destination I'd sometimes have to wait for Dad to come up the long row - the sound of leather squeaking against the collar. The sound of brown earth being turned over and the quiet muffled plump, plump as Jim and Odie put their big feet down. They were careful not to step on the corn.

There were times when Mama could spare me a few days. Mrs. Elsner and Ida were "booked up" for the Fourth of July - that was a full house of summer boarders. They needed a maid, someone to run errands, wash dishes, make beds, etc. I was just tickled to death to help. I got to see the people and talk to them. They were city people, mostly adults. So I went to help Ida and Aunt Mag (she was Dr. Leach's sister, thus she was Irvin and Basil's Aunt Mag). The day before the boarders arrived, we dug potatoes and carrots, cut the cabbage, baked the bread, cake and pies, put fresh sheets and pillow cases on the beds, scrubbed and dusted. They usually arrived late in the evening. We had the chickens ready to fry, vegetables ready to cook, cabbage shredded for slaw etc., etc. After the big meal we washed the dishes, carried the leftovers to the springhouse and went to the barn to feed the pig and milk the cow. When the milk was strained and set in cool water, we could finally sit on the screened-in back porch and fan our sweaty little faces. The boarders looked so cool, calm and collected. They acted as if we were running around unnecessarily. When bedtime came, Ida, Aunt Mag and I all slept in a tiny center room - no windows - logs on all sides. Ida set the kerosene lamp on a tiny stand by our bed. She wanted to read awhile. I wanted her to put out the light and go to sleep. The heat and light attracted small insects and moths by the thousands. Morning came quickly. We had a repeat performance. And so it was until Sunday evening when the boarders all piled into their Buicks and Nashes and took off again for St. Louis. Aunt Mag waved good-bye with one hand while clutching a fist full of greenbacks in the other. We had all worked so hard. Now on Monday I'd help with the laundry, put fresh sheets on the beds, collect my pay, 50 cents per day, and go home to chickens, eggs, pigs and the best family in the whole wide world.

In the early 1930's, Cooper Hill was a favorite weekend spot for summer visitors. Of course, the depression was keeping people who ordinarily went to Colorado or Wisconsin or any cooler climate closer to home. Our location was only 100 miles from the city. We had the Brinkman Club and the Steuver Club where large groups came and a cook prepared meals for them. Some weekends Big Third Creek and the Gasconade River banks were lined with people fishing, eating picnic lunches, roasting wieners, or walking up and down the road. Mrs. Charles Wildebrandt cooked for the Brinkman Club. Mrs. Henry Englebrecht cooked for the Fred Herkert Club. Mrs. Buckshot Leach also kept boarders just as Aunt Mag and Ida did. The small sums of money which exchanged hands made the difference between having life's necessities and being absolutely destitute. I remember Aunt Mag sitting rather tired and dejected one evening. She was trying to trim the wick in the kerosene lamp to bring about a better light. She remarked, "Oh Gracie, how I wish we could get them artificial lights like they have in town." Aunt Mag's wish was far into the future.

The warm summer passed into oblivion. Mae went to her teaching job at Garfield. It was a rural school a few miles off the road as the boys went into Belle High School. Yes, Pete was a freshman, so were Arthur Englebrecht and Scott Bacon. Art rode a horse up the creek road every morning to our house. Bud drove Mae over to the school every Monday morning. During the week she stayed with Mr. and Mrs. Charles Francis. Their young granddaughter, Jewell Johnson, was a first grader and since her parents lived quite a distance from school, Mae was a welcome boarder to walk with Jewell. It was a large comfortable country home. Under Mrs. Francis' capable management and good cooking it was a wonderful place to stay.

Over Labor Day I went again to help Ida and Aunt Mag. They were expecting a crowd, so the beds were set up across the back porch and fitted with fresh linens. Again we dressed chickens, cooked vegetables, churned, milked, cleaned house, washed the kerosene lamps and filled them. The boarders arrived, they ate, slept, visited and sometimes fussed a little. There were two youngsters in this group: a teenage boy with his parents and a teenage girl with her parents. When it came time to "settle up" the young man wanted to pay for his "girlfriend." Her father was almost insulted. "No way, I pay for my family." The young man stormed out. He was so mad the tears were rolling down his cheeks. I've wondered all these years what happened to that romance!

After all the Labor Day visitors had waved good-bye, Ida set up the apple peeler late in the evening. On the previous day we had gathered bushels of beautiful apples and brought them into the yard. Now the peeling quartering and cooking down began. Everyone in Cooper Hill knew "Mag and Ida" were getting ready to "cook apple butter." Consequently the neighbors came to help. Some came to stay all day. Some could only help for an hour or two. Lis and Jess Owens helped all day. Lydia Shockley came in the afternoon. So did Mrs. Berger. Everyone gave their own recipes for good apple butter. Some preferred red apples, some preferred green. Mrs. Berger gave her recipe and preference as she spoke fast and to the point. "Apple butter has to be made out of green apples in August." The statement stood. No one disagreed! Without a doubt, Mrs. Berger did make good apple butter. Perhaps the best! After she had it in the jars, she let it cool and form a natural seal. Then the next morning she put the lid on and set it in the cellar. These people all used so much of this delectable spread it was cooked in a huge copper kettle outside.

So one full day was spent peeling, quartering, and cooking the apples into sauce. The following morning we watched the sun rise as Ida and I carried wood and chips for the fire we built just outside the yard in front of the garage. We poured the apple sauce into the copper kettle. We peeled more apples and cooked more sauce. Neighbors came by again and helped stir. In the afternoon we became weary. But the good news was it was nearing the butter stage. Aunt Mag would dip out a sample onto a saucer and cool it and taste it. Clarence Wildebrandt came across the road to relieve us at the stirrer. All of a sudden there was something rough in the bottom of the kettle. Our tired faces reflected our aching arm muscles. All of us took our turn with the stirrer. It felt peculiar and rough as we dragged the paddle over it. Finally it was up to Aunt Mag to stir and make the decision. She didn't hesitate . "Girls go get the twenty gallon jar from the cellar and some smaller ones. Scald them and we'll have to dip it all out." Well the cellar was up at the barn. Halfway up the hill Ida was on the ball. "We'll take the wheel barrow." Clarence guided the wheel and we loaded the big jar and several smaller ones. We washed and scalded them. We dipped the pretty red sauce out of the kettle. When we got to the very bottom there was no scorch but there was a very long crooked nail that had come loose from the stirrer! How relieved we were. We poured the butter back, rekindled the fire, added the red sugar and just as the last vestige of daylight disappeared we hauled the last jeweled jar of apple butter into the kitchen. Clarence and I carried water from the spring and washed the kettle. He and I sat on the kitchen steps and rested a minute. We had earned our 50 cents that day! I was well aware Clarence liked me. We had dated a couple of times before, with Mae and Irvin. We had met at all the neighborhood dances. He was a nice young man. So before he ran across the road to his home, he and I arranged to go to Owensville to the picture show the following evening. That was where all the grown up young people went for entertainment. Tired as I was, I felt so grown up - so adult. I was working. I could do almost any kind of work pertaining to the house or farm. Mama may have seemed a hard task master but she knew from experience that we must learn to take on whatever there was to do. And she had done well.

The following day we made grape preserves. That too was a tedious process. Picking the grapes, shelling them off the stem, washing, seeding, cooking, running them through the colander, adding sugar and stirring and stirring, washing more jars and filling them with the luscious purple jam. Later in the evening, I bathed, put on my dress-up clothes and went with Clarence to the show. The picture was a good one featuring George Abbott. It was fun! Afterward we went to Steuckenbroker's drugstore and had a malted milk. I wonder how many days' work in a hot hayfield that evening cost him?

Bud and Pete had the same trials with the Belle school and the Golden Chariot as I had enjoyed for two years. One Monday morning as they were on the side road toward Garfield, they ran over a huge grape vine which had fallen across the road. In some strange fashion that grapevine twisted around under the car and brought it to an abrupt halt. Bud tried to back - no luck - He tried to go forward - no better luck. The grapevine had him tied up. They all got out, pulled and tugged, pulled and tugged. It wouldn't budge. They were running late. Mae began to cry and tell the boys how she had to get to the school house. They knew that the car wouldn't move so in desperation Mae set off walking toward the destination. The boys spent a good part of the morning fighting that grapevine! Pete thinks this is a real funny memory! He says Mae really talked pretty ugly to the grapevine that morning.

In addition to helping "Aunt Mag and Ida," I earned a little money helping Aunt Ida clean house. That was always so pleasant it wasn't work. She always planned things so well that there was time to visit the neighbors and to go to Mr. Sterling to the store and there was always at least one trip to Linn to visit Uel, Pearl, Hope and Mrs. Benson, Aunt Ida's mother.

I still loved to walk across the hill and spent a day or two with Uncle Will and Aunt Stell. There was always a pleasant visit with Grandpa. He had to know what Dad was doing, how the crops were, how Mama's chickens and eggs were doing. Then there were the wonderful Sunday dinners at Aunt Stell's or Aunt Ida's. Unplanned, we would all meet and visit and laugh and all the children would play. We sometimes visited at Uncle Al's. I remember one cold, cold winter Sunday we drove there. Sis wasn't home so Uncle Al got out his Saxon Six and drove into Linn to bring Sis home. Mae, Dad and I rode with him. It was a wonderful day with a very good dinner and a fine organ in the living room for us to play.

A few times we visited Uncle Vic and Aunt Alta Pinet and their daughter Marjorie on a farm near Fairview. When I first remember visiting there, they lived in a fine old log house built in two big rooms with a dog run between. I remember thinking how nice it would be to have such a big, warm kitchen. Then they built a nice new flagstone house. Uncle Vic planned it carefully and did much of the work himself. He understood grafting of trees, electricity, fine cattle, horses and gardening. He learned everything from books and magazines.

That fall we were lucky again with "cheap fruit." The Charlie Francis orchard was running over with peaches, apples, pears and big purple plums. Every Friday when the boys went to get Mae, Mrs. Francis would load the car with a variety of these fruits. We stewed and ate, we canned and preserved, but we were glad to have it. It meant food for winter.

In the early winter there was a nice surprise in store for me. The Weissenborn's came out for the weekend. Fred and his sons, Fred Jr. and Richard, went rabbit hunting and we had a fine time. Since I was "unemployed" they thought it would be nice if I went home with them for a week. I was simply elated. I'd heard about St. Louis all my life - 17 years of it - and I'd never been there. To me it was Mama's World's Fair and Dad's trip to Pensacola, Florida. It was the epitome of all things great! Sunday afternoon I took my suitcase with a few clean clothes and climbed in the big Buick with the Wiessenborn men. My heart was pounding. I was actually going to see St. Louis.

The week that followed was the greatest of my life up to that time. The hard times had caused the big family to consolidate. Fred, the father, the two sons, Fred Jr. and Richard, two unmarried daughters, Eleanor and Elizabeth, a married daughter, Alma, her husband Adam Webb, and their son Arthur. The week I visited there, Aunt Lou was also a guest. This extended family lived in a big red brick house on Etzel Row in Wellston. Fred and the boys were bricklayers; only one had work. Eleanor worked as a stenographer. Adam had an electric shop where he and George Twenhoefel were partners in the radio sales and repair business.

I was flabbergasted by the sight of city buildings, bright lights and the theaters: the Fox, Loews and the Uptown. Inside, I was in awe of the beautiful design and color. The films we saw I don't remember. I only see light and color. We drove all over the city. We went to visit friends. Alma took me downtown shopping as I had $10 spending money. I bought a black suede belt to wear with the nice black cloth coat Eleanor had given me and a small close fitting knit hat. It was cute with a narrow rolled brim. I also bought a cake cover and a glass measuring cup topped with an egg beater. These were for Mom.

Alma stayed home and cooked for all these people. She realized well the enormous appetites of the men so the beef roasts she put in the oven were more meat than we ate in a week. She cut pockets in the meat and stuck carrots and slivers of onion in them. She peeled and cooked enormous pots of potatoes and other vegetables. Dinner in the evening was a feast. Everyone had funny depression stories to tell. Everyone pitched in to do the work. Some washed dishes, some dried, some cleaned up the kitchen floor and organized the breakfast because some left well before daylight (Fred and Eleanor). They were a wonderful family. They teased Adam about his radio shop, "How many did you sell today Adam? How many did you sell?" Adam would pull his gray vest around his plump middle, stick a funny hat on his head and say. "Look, Washington crossing the Delaware." Everyone laughed. He could imitate anything and anyone! After a wonderful week, I came home so excited, so full of vim and vigor. I was definitely going to get to St. Louis someday to work and to live!

Life at home that winter was interesting. We were up very early, getting the boys ready for school. Bud and Pete and Art and Scott left very early. Bant (Charles Howard) picked up his lunch bucket and headed for Post Oak. The lunches became largely my responsibility. Mama said my bread turned out better than hers so I made bread, white and whole wheat, also coffee cake for Dad. He picked out butternuts and hickory nut kernels to put in it and on top. We made cookies and gingersnaps, pies of all kinds and cakes. Alma Webb had instilled a new kind of interest in cooking. I was determined to learn to sew. I managed to get some printed percale for pajamas. I was real proud of the neat stitching I did on the bias tape I used around the neck. Mama brought me a scrap of green rayon print one day when she went to Belle, just enough for a blouse. I was real proud of that too!

Chapter 29

Forward, March!

When the church guild met, all the ladies quilted. I was sure I couldn't do that. It looked like hard work. One day when we met at Mrs. Joe Schneider's, I felt out of place sitting idly by. Besides Lydia said, "I'd never learn any younger." So I tried my hand at it and found I liked it. After that day, piecing and quilting became my favorite pastime. I began to cut and piece together a tiny flower garden. I didn't want two blocks alike so I traded small pieces of cotton percale with other quilt makers in order to have all different prints. I also finished the spool quilt Irvin had started when he had the measles. Mom and I quilted it and Mae added it to her hope chest. She had several quilts, a beautiful green and rose "pine tree." Aunt Ida gave her the material and chose the pattern.

That winter was one of the desperately hard ones. That is, if any one was worse than another. I missed my high school friends. I hadn't seen any of them since I graduated. Once or twice, I went to Belle and spent the night with Miss Castle, Miss Edna Meier and Miss Velma Fisher. Miss Meier taught teacher training. Miss Fisher taught English. (Mr. Steen had left Belle after his disagreement with Mr. Muhleman had resulted in a fist fight.) Miss Meier and Miss Castle often came out to our farm to spend a day or a weekend. Miss Meier drove a Willys/Knight. All three teachers did light housekeeping in the upstairs apartment at Manicke's. So some new friendships were formed. Miss Fisher was Pete's English teacher. She assigned papers to be written. Some of the boys weren't much inclined to follow the assignment. So Leonard Allen wrote a little two line poem:

I've been busy, busy, busy as a bee
And so Miss Fisher, I didn't get it, you see.

The rest of the paper was blank. This was a class composed entirely of vocational agriculture boys. They usually weren't much interested in English.

Miss Meier had a Willys automobile. She and Miss Castle and Miss Fisher came out to the farm at intervals for a Sunday dinner. We had fun. Miss Meier and Miss Castle had lived on farms so they enjoyed petting the baby calves, seeing the fat little pink pigs push each other around and squeal as they ate. They also knew about gardening, chickens, hard farm work and hard times. Jobs were precious and teachers in a small town had to be exceptionally careful in their choice of amusements. Shortly before school was out these three ladies came out for the day. One of our mama cats had a family of kittens. Miss Meier fell in love with one of the pretty gray and white spotted kittens. I had named him "Frisky." She wanted him so badly. Before the day was over we had made some plans. She would go home for a week just as soon as school closed. She would go home to give the teacher training exams one week later. I would return with her for the week and we would take "Frisky."

In the meantime Mae's term at Garfield closed. It was a cold, gray, rainy Friday when Mom, Dad and I crowded into the Golden Chariot along with Bud, Pete and Art. We had our big egg basket full of baked chicken and dressing, coconut cake and gooseberry pie. We had to leave home much earlier than usual so Bud could take us by Garfield.

So it was very early when we arrived. We sat through Mae's final practices for the afternoon program and acted as hosts for the early arrivals, who also had well-filled baskets. By noon, there were more people than the building could comfortably hold: Mr. and Mrs. Charles Francis, Mr. and Mrs. Louis Francis and their children, Mr. and Mrs. Will Fleischmann and their family, The Fleischmann brothers and their housekeeper Mary von Behrens, Mr. and Mrs. Clarence Johnson with Jewell and the twins Gene and Geneva. There were others: Mr. and Mrs. Hubert Hassler and John Schultz family. We had intended to eat our basket dinner outside but April is an unpredictable month. The shower came down hard. It threatened to pound the roof in. We put our baked chicken and fried ham, pickles and potato salad out on a makeshift table along with cakes and pies and good things of all sorts. We ate and ate. By the time Mae tapped the bell we were glad to settle down and let our food digest. We went through the welcoming speeches, the songs, the dialogues, the readings and Mae's farewell "thank you" speech. Then we sat down to wait for Bud and the Golden Chariot. Mae seemed real happy to have the teaching year behind her.

And then came that wonderful trip home with Miss Meier. Miss Fisher rode home to Warrensburg with us. We thought it would be so funny to put a green onion in Miss Fisher's trunk but she fooled us. She packed it and shipped it home before school was out. But we were determined. We wrapped the onion in wax paper and carried it with us, hoping for an opportunity to slip it into some of her belongings. I had also packed Frisky in a shoe box. I hated to take him away from his Mama but Miss Meier really wanted him and we always had lots of cats. He did real well on the trip to Bates County. When we stopped to eat, we saved a bite of food for him. When we stopped at the Fisher home in Warrensburg we had the chance we'd been waiting for to put the package of green onion in Miss Fisher's trunk. That was just a prank. Miss Fisher hated onions! We arrived rather late in the evening at the Meier home out a few miles from Passiac. It was a pretty, neat farm home, set back from the road in a tree-shaded yard. Fritz and Minnie Meier were well past middle age but they were so alert. Every morning at breakfast we discussed the news items. Then they planned their days work. All of us did our chores. I went out to the yard and garden with Miss Edna. That gave me a chance to play with Frisky. He soon adjusted to his new surroundings. Fritz fell in love with the playful kitten. He rubbed Frisky's back and belly. He had a soft rubber ball to roll toward him. Frisky loved all the attention he was getting.

One day was spent in Kansas City. Miss Meier had business. I didn't understand then what it was and I didn't ask. But we went to the office of the city superintendent of schools. Later we shopped for wallpaper. Miss Edna was going to redecorate the farm house. We were tired by the time we arrived at Passiac that evening. Frisky didn't bother to get out of his basket by the kitchen stove! Miss Edna and her mother were fine cooks. Every meal was a banquet. Some of the things I had never tasted although they were composed of just plain food products. They made a white sauce flavored with cream cheese to eat on toast at breakfast and they made "chess pie." It resembled Mama's buttermilk pie. They had a big garden out back of the chickenhouse. I helped pull weeds and set tomato plants. I also helped gather eggs. I had fun being helpful. It made me feel at home. The days passed quickly and on the following Sunday I was back home full of new stories and things to describe to Mom and Dad.

Before I made this trip to Bates County, I knew I would teach the next year. I had been given a contract to teach the Horse Shoe Bend School. I was simply elated. It was considered a real privilege to have a job. Even at the remarkably sorry salary of $40 per month. I wanted the summer to pass quickly. Our farm crops were sweltering in the heat, our pigs were not getting the proper diet combination. Too much corn caused them to have "thumps." Poor things, they had nothing else to eat. Soon we would find them lying in the burning sun, their sides heaving and thumping. There was no cure. No medicine. No nothing. None of them ever got better! We always fell back on the chickens, set more hens, try to take better care of them, keep them warm, feed them often and well....Maybe, just maybe, they'd be a better price - but that never happened either!

The only things we could ever depend on for sure were chickens and eggs. We had to be more and more careful with our few dollars to spend. All summer we would become more cheerful when I'd remind Mom and Dad that soon I'd be teaching school. After $20 was paid for room and board, the remaining $20 per month would buy a lot!

I felt very grown up the week before I began teaching. I got out my teacher's training text books and reread them: rural school management, child psychology. I reviewed my old notebooks from Mr. Steen's public school teaching. I expected to be using all these things constantly. But I also reviewed my own years in the one room school as a student. There was one big difference. I would now be a "teacher."

On Saturday afternoon I went for a long walk, out our lovely school path, climbed over the big flat rocks where Mae and I had our play houses, on past the pansy patch where Mae and I plucked the sassy-faced little lavender blossoms, still further over the fence and over the slick, mossy rocks, down into the ravine and up the rocky hill to the Pete Leach shanty field. I could look far across the creek and see the Homfeld house where all of us had such good times together. I turned and walked back toward the house. It was getting late. Dad and Bud had brought the cows into the cow barn to milk. I stayed a minute to watch the baby calves roll their eyes and butt their mother. I hurried on to the house to help Mama with supper. I had said good-bye to childhood and childish things. Tomorrow I would take my suitcase and my teacher training notebooks and enter into the real adult world, a new world of Horse Shoe Bend. Now I was truly an adult! As Mom had said to us so many times, "Pick up your feet – forward march!"